Catching up with
the Internet

Catching up with
the Internet

The over 50s' survival guide

P.K. McBride

Hairnet™

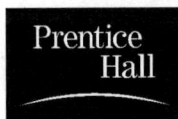

Prentice Hall

An imprint of Pearson Education

**London   New York   Toronto   Sydney   Tokyo   Singapore
Madrid   Mexico City   Munich   Paris**

PEARSON EDUCATION LIMITED

Head Office:
Edinburgh Gate
Harlow CM20 2JE
Tel: +44 (0)1279 623623
Fax: +44 (0)1279 431059

London Office:
128 Long Acre
London WC2E 9AN
Tel: +44 (0)20 7447 2000
Fax: +44 (0)20 7240 5771
Website: *www.it-minds.com*

First published in Great Britain in 2001

© Pearson Education Limited 2001

ISBN 0-130-90824-X

British Library Cataloguing-in-Publication Data
A catalogue record for this book is available from the British Library.

10 9 8 7 6 5 4 3 2 1

Typeset by Elle & P.K. McBride, Southampton
Printed in Great Britain by Biddles Ltd, Guildford.

The publishers' policy is to use paper manufactured from sustainable forests.

Contents

1

Instant Internet

IN THIS CHAPTER:

- What's it all about
- Using a browser
- Going places
- Finding stuff
- Meeting people
- Sending an e-mail

This is a chapter to be read actively, alongside your computer. By the time you have worked through to the end – an hour or two – you will have mastered enough of the basic skills to be able to make good use of the Internet.

The Net and the Web

Net = Internet

Web = World Wide Web

Let's start by clearing up a common misconception. The 'Web' and the 'Internet' are not the same thing. Some people use the terms interchangably, but they shouldn't. There is a real distinction, and if you miss that, then you are more likely to be blind to some of the possibilities of the Internet beyond the Web. So let's define the terms before we go any further.

◆ The *Internet* is the underlying framework – the computers, large and small, that store and process information for the Net; the telephone wire, network cable, microwave links and other connections between them; and the software systems that allow them all to interact.

◆ The *World Wide Web* is the most visible and the simplest way of using the Net. It consists of many hundreds of millions of Web pages, which can be viewed through *browsers* such as Internet Explorer. The pages are constructed using HTML, and this tells browsers how to display text and images, and how to manage links between pages. Clicking on a hypertext link in a page tells the browser to go to the linked page (or other file) – wherever in the world that page may be.

HTML = the markup language used to create Web pages

E-mail = electronic mail

The Web is not the only way of using the Internet. E-mail is another common use and there are others, as you will see later in this book.

Before you start...

There are a couple of concepts and a little bit of jargon that you really ought to know before you start surfing the Web.

Web pages and sites

The basic Web document is a *page* – which may just be a single screenful or may be longer so that you have to scroll down to read it all.

A Web *site* is a set of related pages, usually owned by one organisation or individual. Visitors will normally arrive at the top level page, which will act as a kind of contents list, carrying links to the other pages within the site.

Typically, a Web page will consist of several different files. The main file holds the text and the coding that tells the browser what to display and where. There will also be a separate file for each image on the page, and perhaps other files for background music or special effects.

Each of these files has to be *downloaded* from the Web before it can be displayed, and downloading can take a while. If you are connected to the Internet through an ordinary phone line, data travels relatively slowly. A page that contains only text will download in a couple of seconds, but if it has one or more big pictures or other files, it can take a minute or more.

Pages can be put together in a number of ways, and the construction affects how they download and are displayed.

◆ A simple page will display the text as soon as it downloads – so that you have something to see within a few seconds of arriving at it – then show the images one by one as they arrive (often building them on screen, a bit at a time).

◆ Some pages are built using *tables*. These give better control over layout, but browsers usually wait until all the table's data has arrived before they display any of it. Tables can be intermingled with simple text, but in the worst cases, the whole page will be one table and you will stare at a blank page for some time before the display suddenly pops into view.

◆ Some Web sites organise their pages using *frames*. These divide the screen into two or more areas, and allow part of the display to be changed while the rest remains static. Typically there will be a strip along the top, and/or a bar down the left side which will carry links and buttons for navigating around the site. Framed pages download in sections, but at least you will usually get one section quickly.

Navigate = move between pages on the Web

Traffic on the Information Superhighway

The Internet is sometimes referred to as the 'Information Superhighway', but just like ordinary highways, it suffers from traffic jams. The time it takes to download a page from a

See page 6,
Refresh

Web site can rise dramatically if too many people are trying to get online through the same service provider, or to get into the same Web site, or even to make a connection from one country to another – the highways between the UK and the USA can get very clogged.

However, the Internet is interconnected. There are always several routes between any two given points on the Internet, and if a route seems to be very congested, you can get your browser to try another one – it will do this automatically if a route fails completely.

Picking your time helps. Early evenings tend to be the busiest times; Sunday mornings are often the quietest.

The biggest library in the world?

The World Wide Web has been said to be the biggest library in the world. It's certainly enormous, and it's a wonderful source of information on just about any topic you can think of, but any book library is better organised and there will have been some quality control on its contents – sorry, folks, but there is an awful lot of junk on the Web!

Fortunately, as you will see later in this book, there are some simple techniques that allow you to find the information that you want and to return quickly to useful sites.

Hands-on time!

For the rest of this chapter, I'm assuming that you are sitting at a PC, with Internet Explorer running, and that you can get online at any time. If you do not yet have your own system set up, go to a friend or relative who has a PC and Internet access, or go to a cybercafe or a terminal at your local library.

Setting up a system and getting online is not difficult, as you will see in Chapters 2 and 3, but it takes a little time and it is not very exciting. Right now I want you to discover how easy the Internet is to use and how much it has to offer. This should prove to be a good incentive to keep you going through the setting up process!

Using a browser

To 'surf the Web' you need a browser. Almost all new PCs come with one installed, and the browser is almost always Internet Explorer, or IE for short. This was developed by Microsoft and is currently supplied as an integral part of the Windows system.

Browser = software for viewing and moving between Web pages

Internet Explorer is powerful and packed with features, yet essentially simple. For straightforward surfing, you only need to learn how to use half a dozen tools and do a couple of other things.

Back to the previous page

Forward to the next page

The Address Bar

Stop downloading

Reload a page

Links buttons

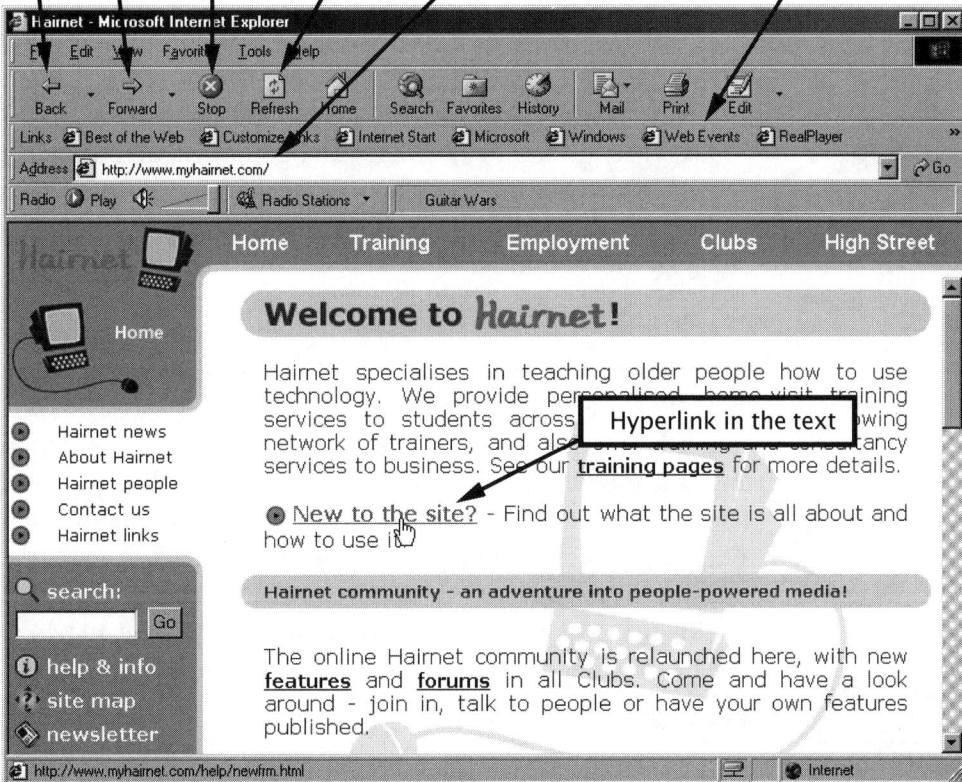

Figure 1.1   Browsing is simple with Internet Explorer.

Instant Internet Explorer

The following are the only essential tools and techniques. Learn the rest as and when you feel the need to do things more efficiently, or quicker, or smarter.

Back

Internet Explorer stores the pages that you visit. Then, if you want to go back to them you do not need to download their files again. Click **Back** to return to the page that you have just left. There is also a drop-down list of the pages visited recently – we'll look at this later (page 58).

Forward

This button only becomes active when you have used **Back** to go to the previous page. Click **Forward** to go forward again to where you were. This also has a drop-down list for more precise navigation (see page 58).

Stop

You will often follow a link to a page and then realise, once you can see it, that it isn't what you had hoped, and this may become obvious while the files are still coming in. Click **Stop** to stop the downloading. You can then go back to the previous page to try another link.

Refresh

Sometimes Web pages take ages to download, either because their files are huge or – just as likely – there is a traffic jam somewhere between you and that site. If you suspect that the problem might be a traffic jam, click **Stop** then click **Refresh**. The browser will reconnect to the site, but probably through a different – and, with any luck, faster – route.

You can also use Refresh if the display becomes corrupted for any reason, or after you have returned to a page, in which case it will check for any newer versions of the page's files.

The Address bar

We'll come back to addresses on page 42

This serves two purposes. As you navigate round the Web, the address of the current page is shown here, but you can

Figure 1.2 An address can be typed into the Address bar. As you type, ever-helpful IE will offer you matching addresses from its store of ones that you have typed previously. To use one of these, just click on it rather than retyping the whole address.

also use this bar actively. If you type an address into it, the browser will then go to that page, as you will see shortly.

Links buttons

Internet Explorer comes with some ready-made links – mainly to places within Microsoft's site, but none the worse for that. Just click on a link button to send the browser off to the linked page.

Hyperlinks

Hyperlinks are what make the Web what it is, and what make it so easy to use. Without them, you would have to know – and type in correctly – the address of every page that you wanted to visit. Surfing would be a slow, tedious business, and you would spend more time looking up addresses in reference books than visiting pages! Instead of all this hassle, you can just click on a link to go to the related page.

Hyperlink = hypertext link, a connection from a Web page to another page or other resource

Hypertext links can be attached to text and to images. The text may be a distinct item in a list, or a word or phrase within a paragraph. Wherever it appears on the page, if text is hyperlinked, it will be displayed with an underline and in a different colour (usually blue, but this can be changed).

Images can be linked in two ways. At the simplest, the whole image carries a single link. In this case, the image will normally have a blue outline. An image can also be set up as an *image map*, with different parts carrying different links.

Whether hyperlinks are in text, on a single image or in an image map, there is one simple, unfailing way of recognising them. When you place the screen pointer over a hyperlink, it changes from an arrow ➢ to a hand ⍟.

Yahoo! and we're off

Once you are into the Web, surfing between pages and sites is largely a matter of following the links. The trick to happy surfing is finding a good place to start from. Yahoo! is such a place. Yahoo! offers a wide range of services – but its main feature is a directory.

The directory holds links to several million pages, organised into a hierarchy of categories and subcategories. The organisation is clear and logical, and where a topic can fit into more than one place in the structure, it will be cross-referenced. If you are looking for software companies, for example, you can find them by starting either at *Business & Economy* or at *Computers & Internet*.

Try it: Explore Yahoo!

In this example, I'm looking for material on keyboard (musical) instruments. Follow the same links, if you like, or pick another topic.

① If Internet Explorer is not already running, start it now.

② If you are not already connected to the Internet, go online now.

③ In the Address Bar, type: **uk.yahoo.com** and press the [Enter] key (Figure 1.3).

④ The browser will connect to Yahoo! – the messages in the Status line (at the bottom) will tell you how it's getting on with downloading the files for the page. You should see the text within a minute, and the images shortly afterwards.

⑤ The top page directory shows all of the headings and the first three or four subheadings in each set. Click on the link seems most likely to lead to the material you want – e.g. *Music* in the *Entertainment* category (Figure 1.3).

⑥ A new page will load in, with links to the next level of subcategories, and some links to relevant pages. Click on a link to a subcategory (Figure 1.4).

⑦ As you go down through the level, you will see fewer links to subcategories and more links to pages. You may

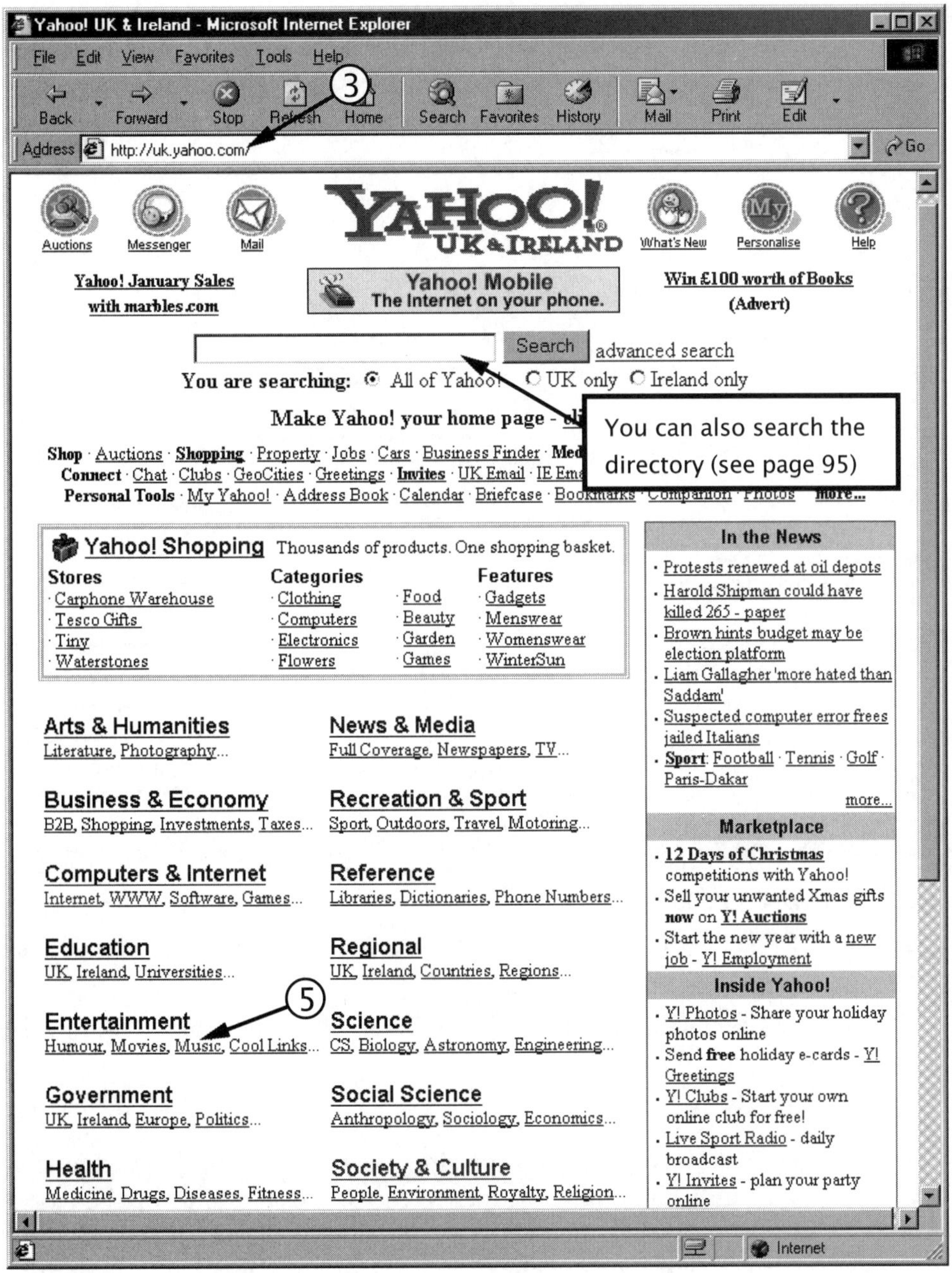

Figure 1.3 The top page at Yahoo! Come back to this another time and use the links at the top to explore some of their other services. At this point, concentrate on the directory – you may have to scroll down to see this.

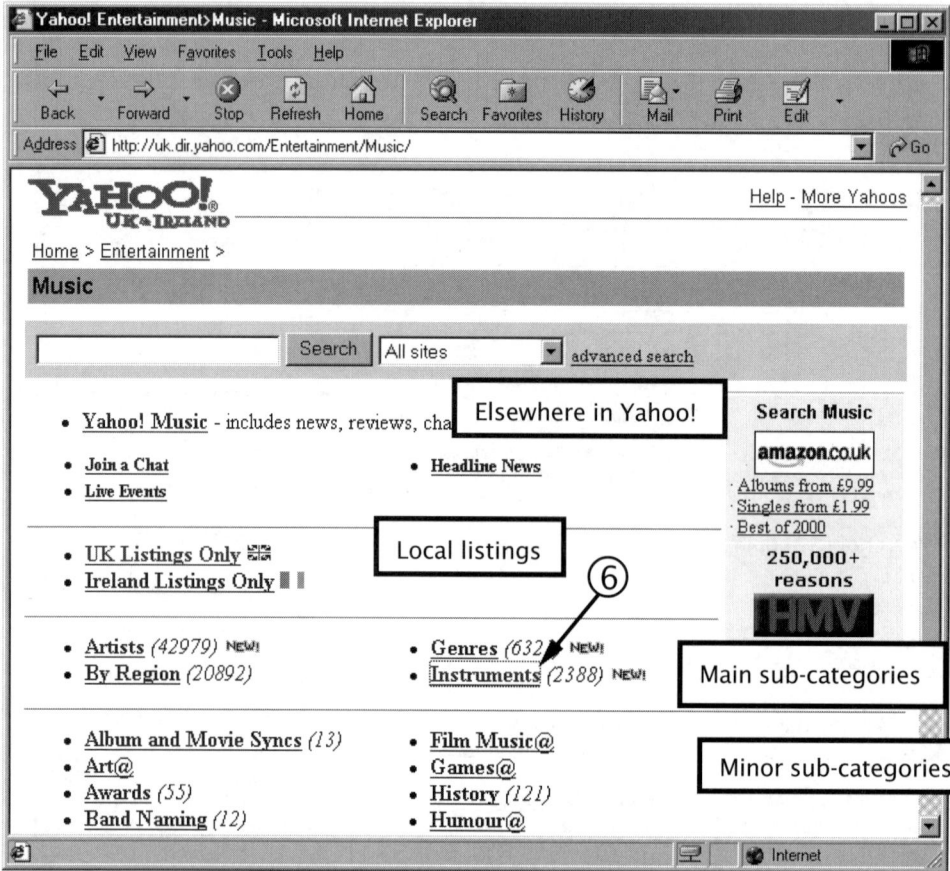

Figure 1.4 Working through the hierarchy at Yahoo!

need to go down three or four levels to find what you want (Figure 1.4).

⑧ When you find an interesting link, click on it (Figure 1.5).

Browsing

Whenever you are browsing, bear this in mind – anyone can publish anything (with very, very few exceptions) on the World Wide Web. While this is wonderful in terms of free speech, the rights of the common man, and the struggle against the control of information by governments and big business, the downside is the total lack of quality control. This is a major problem when using the search engines, as you will see shortly (page 14). It is a bit less of a problem when you start from

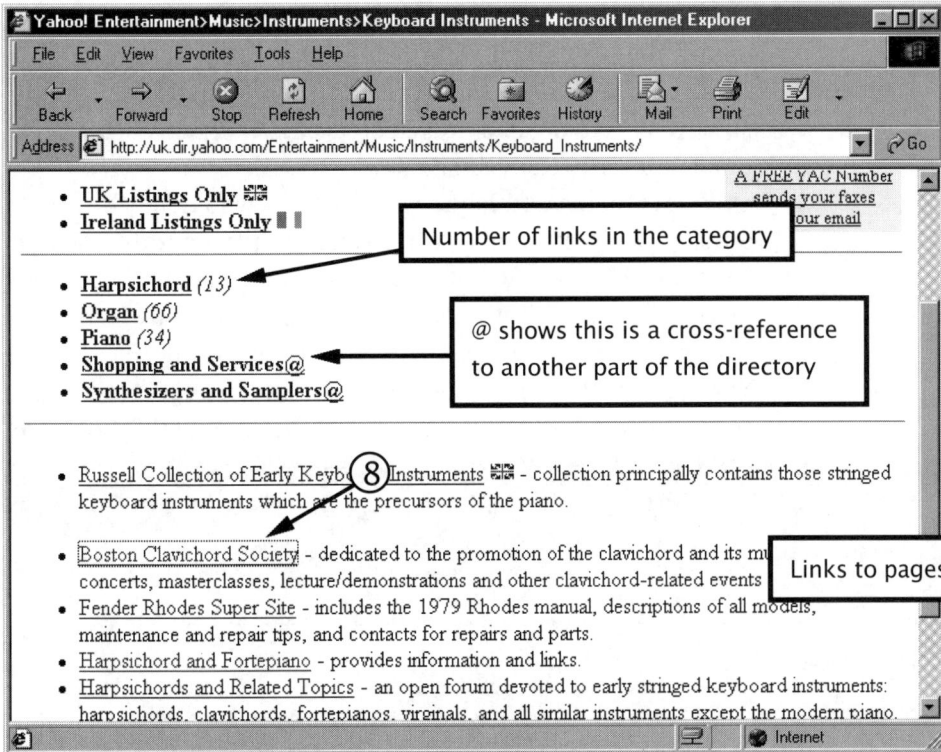

Figure 1.5 The description is normally supplied by the page's author, and though it should tell you what the page contains, it may not be a reliable guide to its quality.

Yahoo! as the pages that are linked from there have at some time been selected by somebody. Even there, however, the selection does not guarantee that the linked pages are of high quality – it's more that the directory builders have filtered out the real rubbish. You will also find that a fair number of links no longer work, as the linked page has disappeared.

But let's not get too negative. The positive fact is that the majority of pages have been created in an honest attempt to communicate a passion for a topic, or to make specialist knowledge available to a wider audience. Some pages are packed with information – and these are ends in themselves – while others will have carefully selected links to other pages on the topic, and by following these you may find what you want.

For example, one of the top links in the keyboard instruments list at Yahoo! was to the Boston Clavichord Society (Figure 1.6). This site has some very good material of its own, as well as sets of links to selected pages on events, builders, music and other aspects.

When you have finished with a page – which may be after a quick glance through, or after reading it from top to bottom – you can click on one of its links, if it has any and they look interesting, or click the browser's **Back** button to go back to where you were before. So, if you are browsing through the Yahoo! directory, you can go off to a linked page, read it, and come back to Yahoo! to pick up another link and follow that.

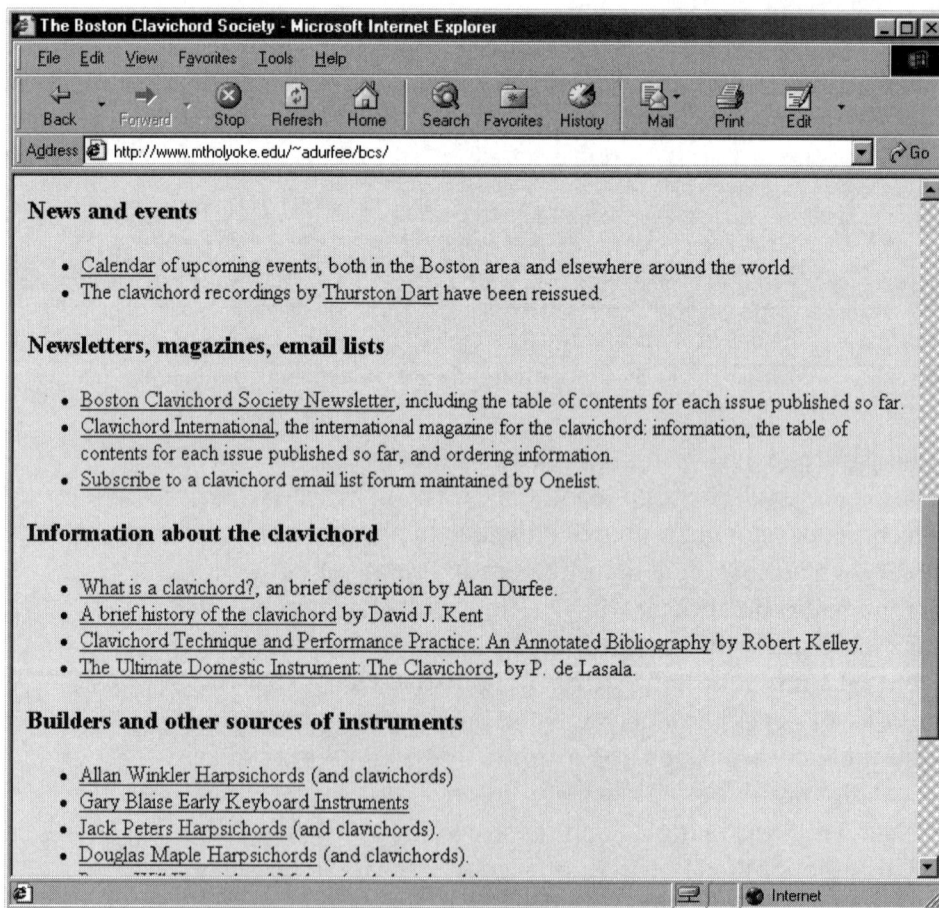

Figure 1.6 Sites run by enthusiasts can often be very good sources of information and of links to other resources.

In theory, you can click through any number of links then use the **Back** button to retrace your steps all the way back to the start. In practice, it doesn't always work this way. Sometimes the trail gets muddied. Don't worry, there are ways to solve this, as you will see later, and in any case, it's no big deal to go back to your start point and pick up the trail again from there. As Internet Explorer stores the files for the pages that you visit, if you revisit them, you will not have to wait while the files download.

Try it: Browse from Yahoo!

Think of a new topic – perhaps one of your hobbies or a special interest – and see what you can find on it, starting again at the top-level (home) page at Yahoo!

① Click the arrow by the **Back** button to drop down the list of recently-visited pages, then click **Yahoo! UK & Ireland** – this is much quicker than clicking **Back** repeatedly!

② Click on a major category heading then work down through the subcategories.

◆ Don't worry too much if you are not sure which category your topic will fit into. Yahoo! is so well cross-referenced that any reasonable start point should get you there.

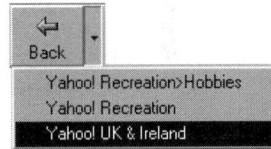

Key points about Yahoo!

All pages in the Yahoo! directory have a similar structure. Working down from the top, you have:

◆ Links to related and other major areas within Yahoo!

◆ Links to local listings. In Yahoo! UK & Ireland these are to either UK or Irish sites, but there are also Yahoo!s for many countries. The main Yahoo! is in the USA.

◆ Sets of links to major, then to minor subcategories.

◆ Links to selected pages, with a brief description of them.

As you work through the levels, you will see fewer links to subcategories and more links to pages. You may need to go down three or four levels to find what you want.

Search engines

Search engine –
Web site that has
an index to (many
of) the pages on
the World Wide
Web

Here's another way to find stuff on the Web – and this is generally the best way if you are looking for very specific information. A search engine is a site that has compiled an index to Web pages, and which lets you search through the index. There are several dozen search engines, and they compile their indices in different ways and to different levels of completeness, but some of the best know what's on 80% or more of the pages on the Web.

Ask Jeeves

This does not have the most complete coverage of the Web, but it is one of the friendliest search engines – cheerful, easy to use and quite efficient at finding things. To supplement its own databanks, it has active links to other search engines and will pass on your question so that you can search there. Ask Jeeves is also an excellent choice if you are looking to buy, rent, hire or otherwise spend money – anything from buying a book to booking a flight, Jeeves will tell you where to start looking.

Key points to note about Ask Jeeves

Keyword – a word
given in a search
to describe what
you are looking
for

◆   You can ask questions in ordinary English, but you can get much the same results – with less typing – by just giving the *keywords*. For example, 'rent house France' will work just as well as 'Where can I rent a house in France this summer'.

◆   Jeeves searches his own database then checks out other search engines, and give you the results all together.

Hit – link to a
page that
matches your
search

◆   If you want to follow up a *hit* at another search engine, you must go there first – just follow Jeeves' links to an engine.

Try it: Ask Jeeves

①   Click into the Address slot and type:
www.askjeeves.com

②   Wait for the page to load in.

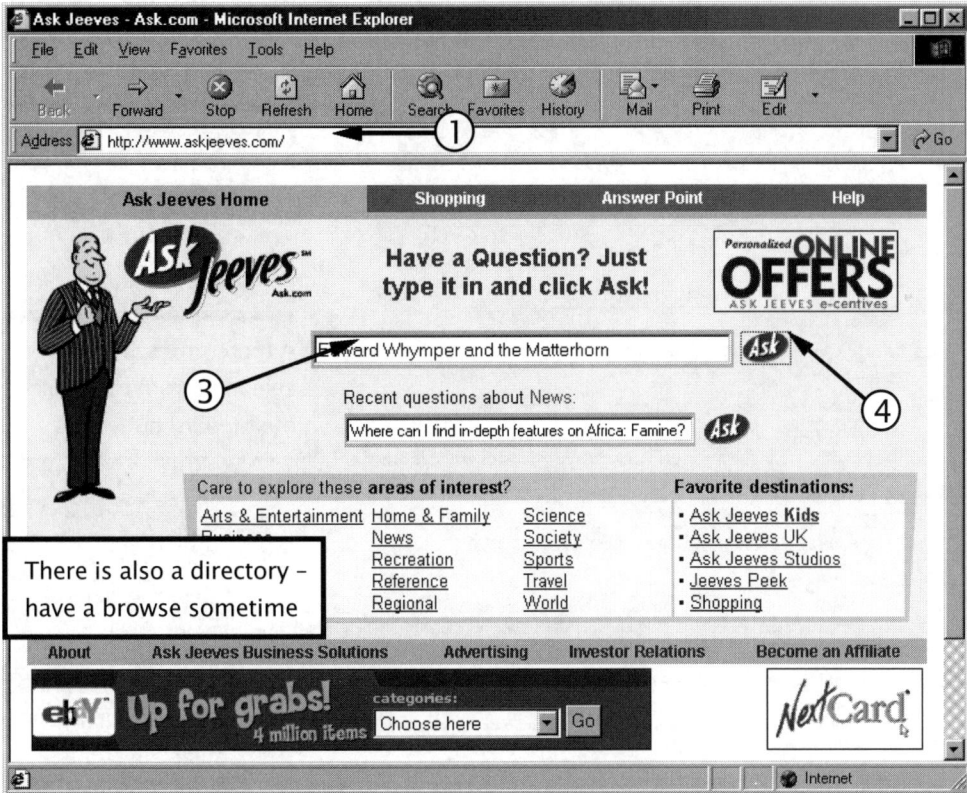

Figure 1.7 If you want to know something – anything – ask Jeeves!

③ Type your question or keyword into the top box.

④ Click **Ask!** .

Jeeves will pootle off to have a think about your question, then return with three sets of results.

◆ The first set are related questions drawn from its bank of commonly-asked questions to which it knows the answers – these often lead to entries at Britannica's encyclopaedia.

◆ The second set are links to pages that people who have asked similar questions have found relevant.

◆ The third set are links to results found at other search engines. The results are not shown – if you want to see them, you must follow the link to the search engine.

Ignore the stuff that appears in the Address bar – all search engines rewrite your questions here for their own use

Ask Jeeves Results - Microsoft Internet

File   Edit   View   Favorites   Tools

Back   Forward   Stop   Refresh   Home   Search   Favorites   History   Mail   Print   Edit

Address   Edward+Whymper+and+the+Matterhorn&origin=0&site_name=Jeeves&metasearch=yes&ads=&Ask%21.x=18&Ask%21.y=12   Go

You asked: Edward Whymper and the Matterhorn

I have found **answers** to the following questions:

Where can I find biographical resources from Britannica.com on
Edward Whymper   ?

Where can I find resources from Britannica.com on
Matterhorn   ?

A more-or-less relevant selection from the bank of standard questions

Would you like to post your question to Answer **Point**, the Ask Jeeves community site,
where other Ask Jeeves users can provide you with valuable answers?

Get your answer from an Expert at **EXP.com**

People with **similar questions** have found these sites relevant:

Edward Whymper
One of the best known names in mountaineering, and forever associated with the tragic first ascent of the Matterhorn in 1865. Whymper had ambitions of being an arctic explorer from a young age. But it was the magesty of the Alps which nurtured a passion...

Geographic Expedition's Adventure Tours, Treks to Europe
One of the pioneers of adventure travel, Geographic Expeditions operate worldwide, offer a sensationally varied roster of overland tours, walking trips, treks and expeditionary voyages to the world

Matterhorn
Matterhorn is a pyramidal peak, 4,478 m high, in the Swiss Alps on the Italian border. In 1865 a British expedition, led by by Edward Whymper, was the first to scale the jagged peak.

Swiss Guides Centennial 1899~1999 - Golden, British Columbia, Canada - History
The year 1999 will be the Centennial of the establishment in the Canadian Rockeis of the Swiss Guides by the Canadian Pacific Railway. Golden, the Swiss Guides' hometown, is proud to celebrate this historic event. The Swiss Guides Festival is our community's...

Climbing the Matterhorn photos - a 24 image series
Climb the Matterhorn (photo shows Whymper's original ice axe)

More >>

Sites found in answers to similar questions

There may be several pages of links

I can show you the response to your question on the **search engines** listed below:

What are the search results for my question on NBCi?

What are the search results for my question on GoTo.com?

What are the audio and visual results for my question on StreamSearch.com?

What are the search results for my question on Mamma.com?

Results from other search engines

Internet

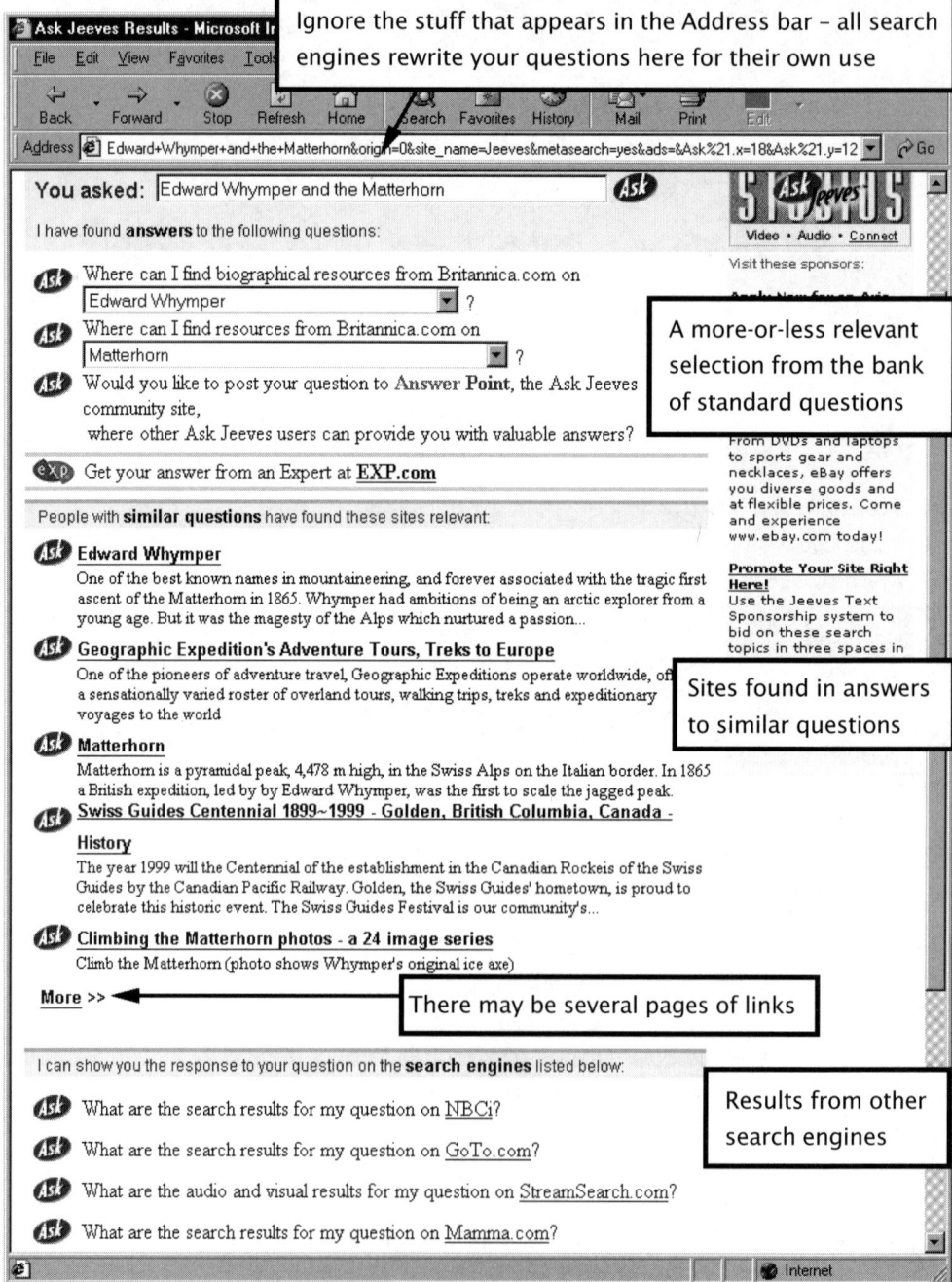

Figure 1.8   The results of a search at Ask Jeeves. Click the underlined link or the **Ask!** button to go to a page.

Unless you have asked a very vague, strange or extremely esoteric question, you should find that the top links in the **answers** and **similar questions** sections lead directly to relevant material on the subject. My search for stuff on Whymper and the Matterhorn turned up some very interesting pages on the man, the mountain and his conquest of it (a fascinating story – look it up for yourself!).

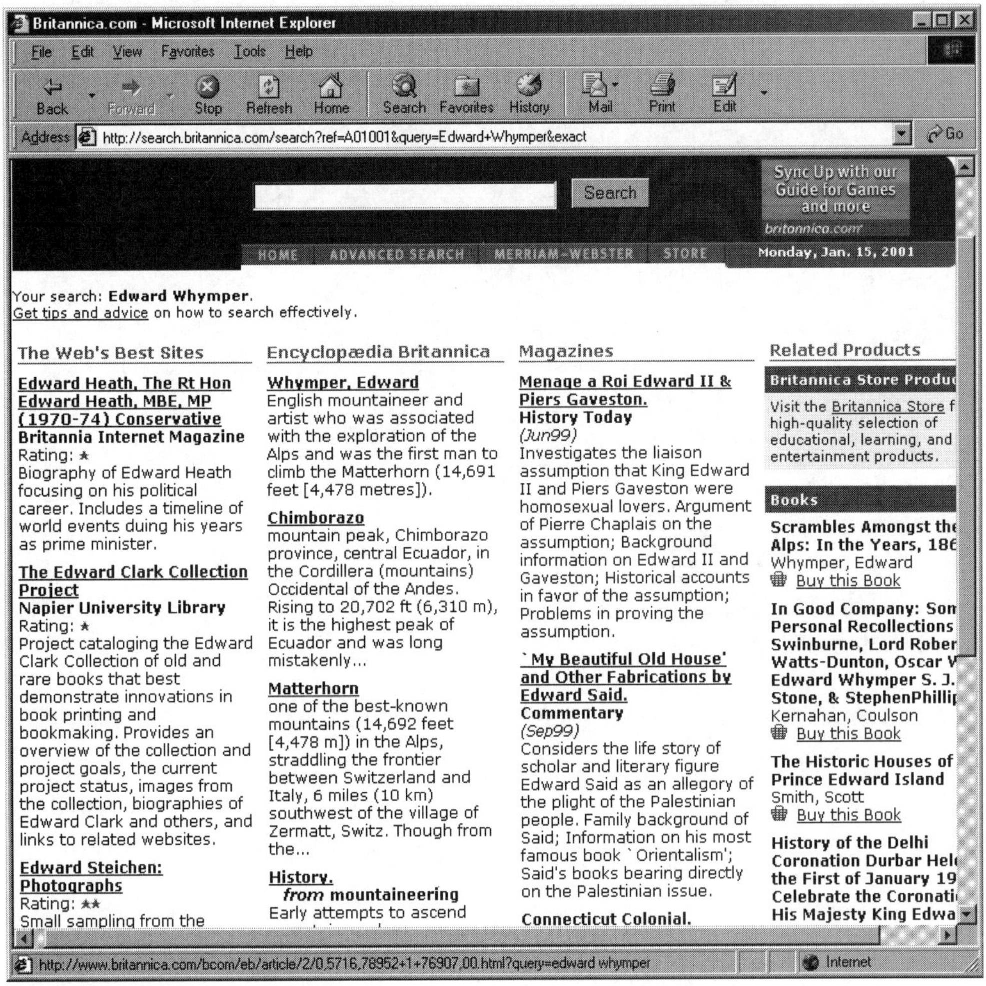

Figure 1.9 The link to Britannica.com gives you a selection of brief entries, some of which may well not be relevant – my search for Edward Whymper has turned up half a dozen other famous Edwards as well. The links from here take you through to the full Encyclopaedia Britannica entries.

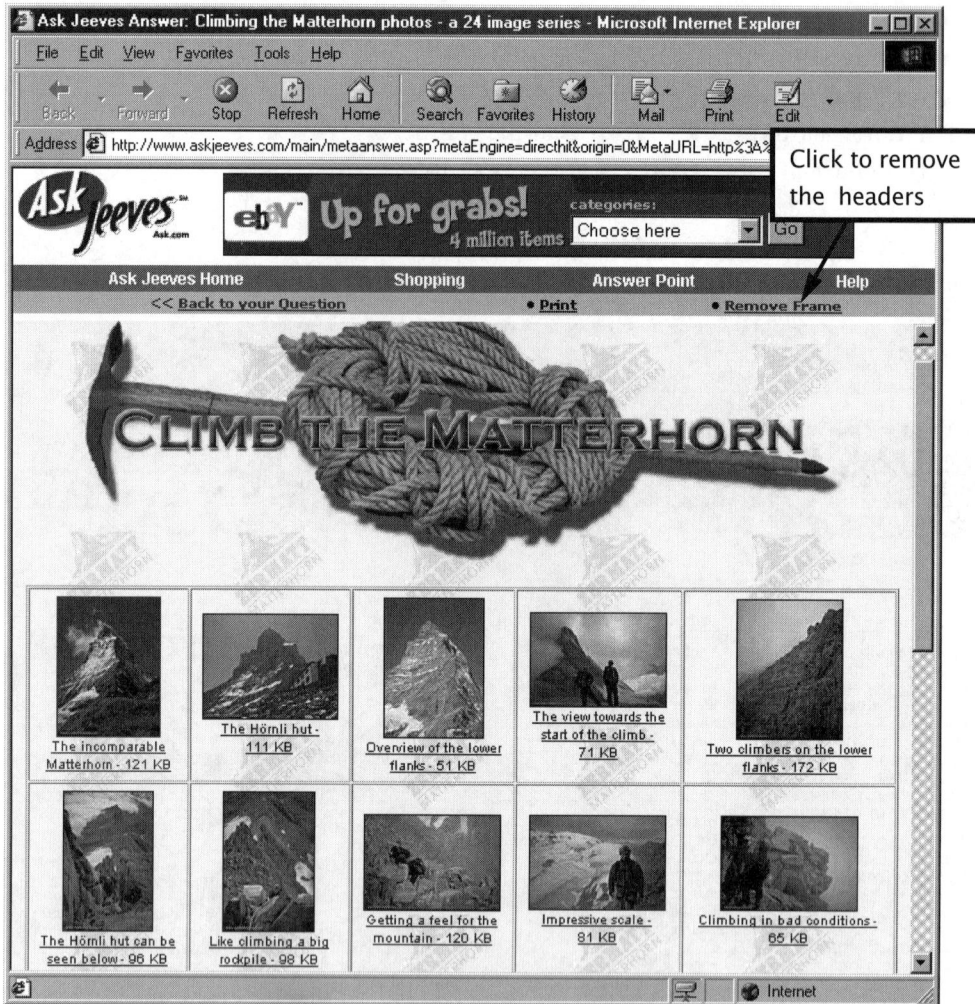

Figure 1.10 Some of the **similar questions** links take you off to new sites, but others lead to pages stored at Ask Jeeves, and displayed within the site. Notice the **Remove Frame** link. Clicking on this will get rid of the Ask Jeeves headings and – more to the point – the adverts.

Try it: Ask Jeeves...

◆ where you can buy a CD/book by your favourite artist/ writer, a car, a haggis or something equally esoteric.

◆ about your next holiday – real or fantasy!

◆ where you can find pictures of the moon or the planets.

◆ about your home town – is it on the Web?

Web communities

The Web is a great source of information, but there is more to it than simply reading other people's pages. You can publish your own pages – and that's not hard to do, as you will see later – and the Web is also a very effective medium for two-way communication.

There are many ways to interact with other people on the Internet. We'll have a quick look at just one of them now, but come back to this and look at other ways later in the book.

A *Web community* is a site – or part of a larger site – which acts as a kind of online club. It's a place where people can make new friends and meet up with old ones, exchanging ideas either directly, in a *chat room*, or indirectly through a forum or shared message board.

Chat room – site where people can talk (see page 169)

Hairnet, the over-50s computer training specialists, host a community at their site. Though this is not exclusively for the over-50s, its members are typically more mature than at most other Web communities. Communication is mainly through its clubs. There are nine of these, covering Travel & Adventure, Science & Technology, Health & Nature, Genealogy & People, Business & Consumers, Family & Society, Home & Garden, Sport & Entertainment and Art, Music & Literature. Members are encouraged to submit articles to be published as features, and to start or take part in discussions in the forums.

If a Hairnet member wants to start a discussion on a new subject, or has a question to ask, he/she can send a message to the appropriate forum. When it is published, other members can read it and send in their own comments, if they want to, or answers, if they know them. These are tacked onto the message to which they apply. Any number of people can reply to a message – or to existing replies – so that controversial or topical subjects can produce quite lengthy and lively debates. As people tend to concentrate on one or two forums, active members gradually get to know one another – which is when the site starts to become a community.

Try it: Explore Hairnet

① In the Address bar, type: **www.myhairnet.com**

② After reading the Welcome page, click the **Clubs** link at the top of the page (Figure 1.11).

③ At the Clubs page, select a club from the list in the left-hand sidebar (Figure 1.12).

④ At each club's top page you'll find links to the features, followed by a taster of a current topic in the forum, and a **Browse the forum** link – click this (Figure 1.13).

⑤ Click on a topic header to select it (Figure 1.13).

⑥ If you want to reply to a message, or start a new topic, click the appropriate link (Figure 1.14).

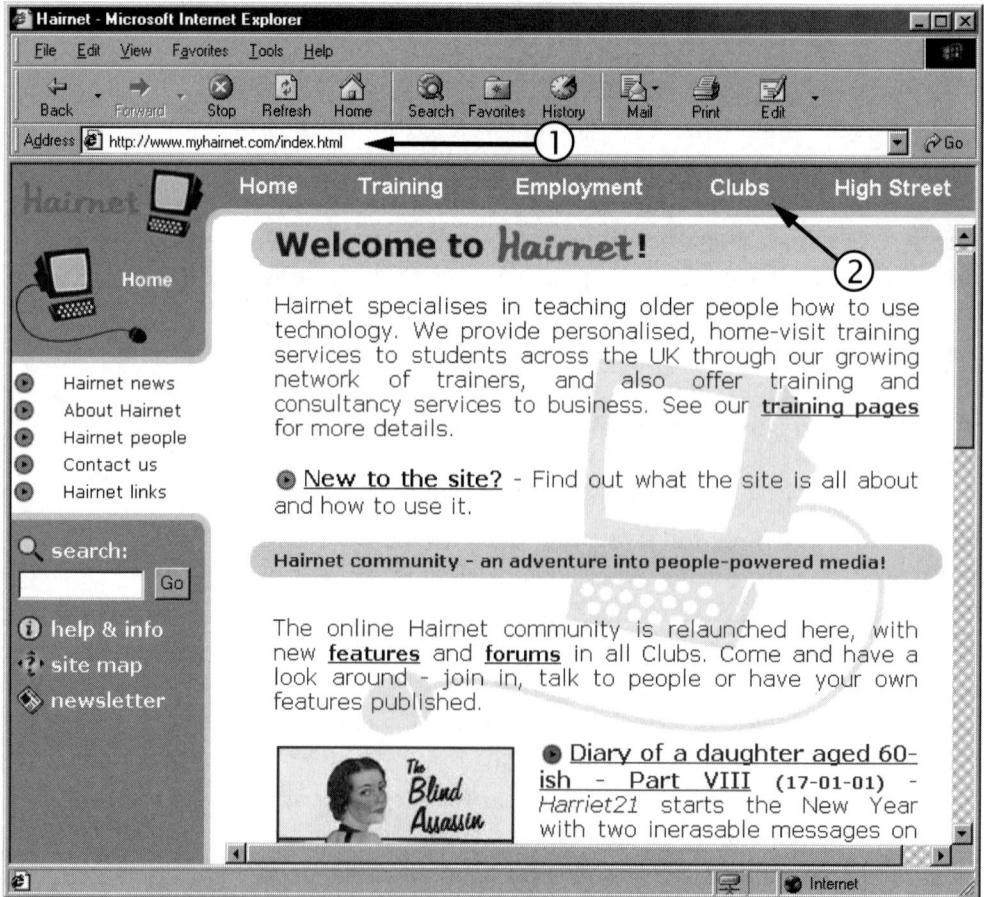

Figure 1.11 The Welcome page at Hairnet.

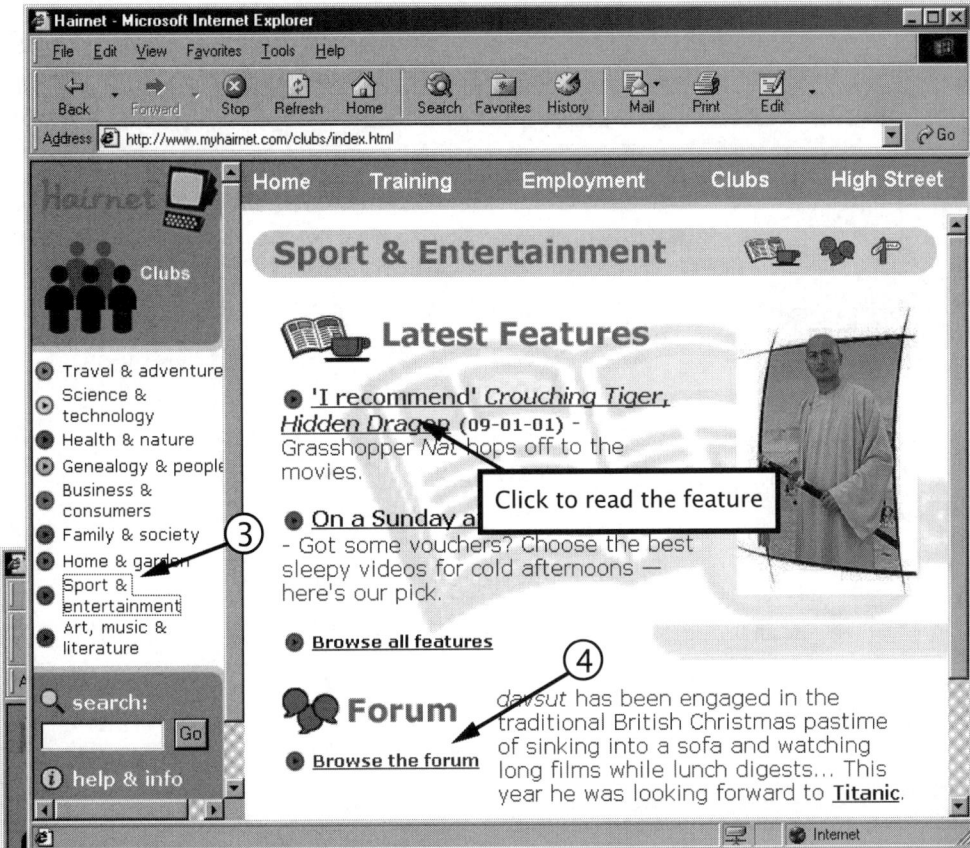

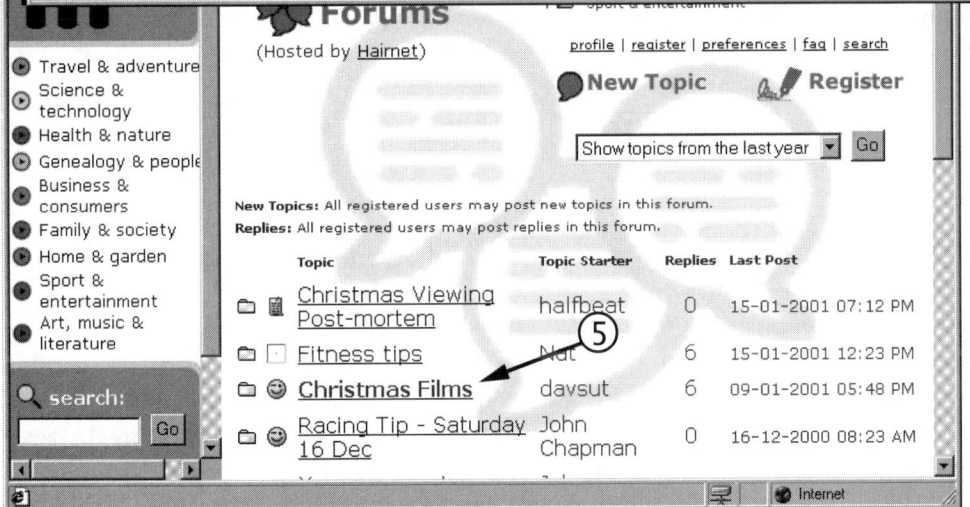

Figure 1.12 (top)   The top page of the Sports & Entertainment club.

Figure 1.13 (bottom)   The list of topics in a forum.

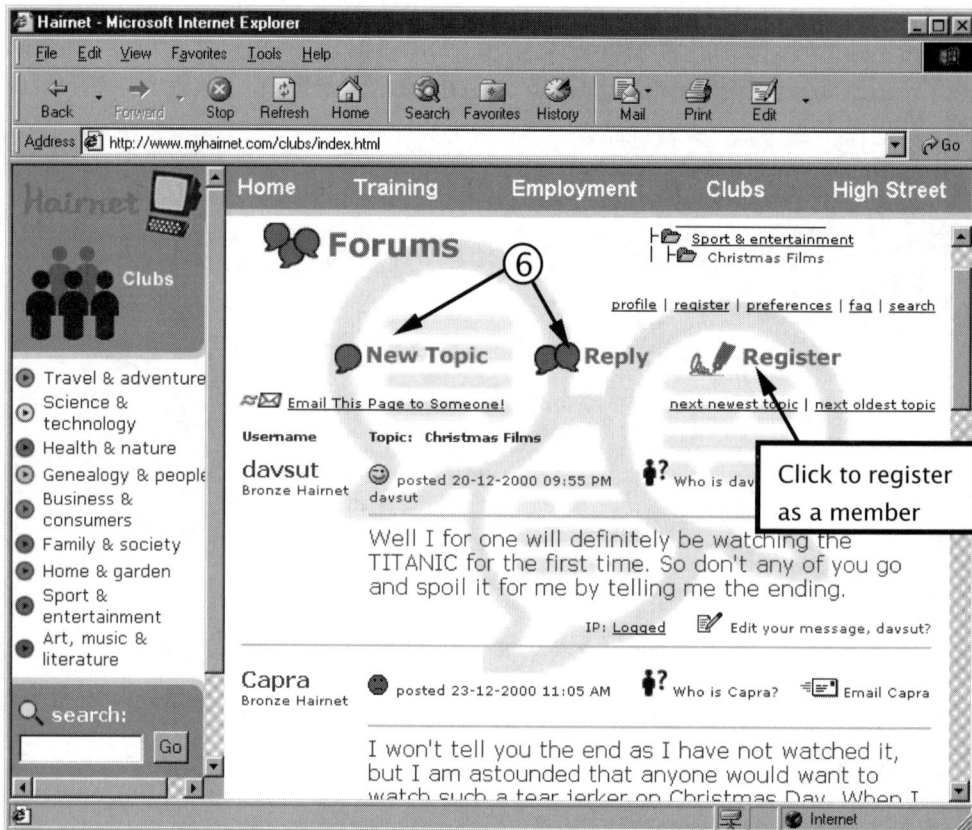

Figure 1.14 Reading a topic in a forum. If you want to join in, you must be a member – but registration is simple and free.

E-mail

Even if you only get online through Internet cafes, libraries or other public terminals, you can still have an e-mail address – read about Web mail on page 225

The World Wide Web may well be the most glamorous aspect of the Internet and the one that grabs newcomers, but e-mail is the aspect that many people find the most useful in the long run. It is quick, reliable, cheap and simple to use.

♦ E-mail is quick. When you send a message to someone, it will normally reach their mailbox within minutes – and usually within half an hour. However, it will only be read when the recipient collects the mail, and that may be anything from a few minutes later to when they get back from holiday.

◆ E-mail is reliable. As long as you have the address right, the message is almost certain to get through. And on those rare occasions when it doesn't, you will usually get it back with an 'undeliverable' note attached.

◆ E-mail is cheap. Text travels very swiftly over the Internet – you can send the equivalent of an A4 page of text in around 10 to 15 seconds. Most of us find that we can send and receive the day's messages in less than a minute – so it rarely costs more than the minimum call charge.

◆ E-mail is simple to use. You can learn the essential skills in minutes – read on and find out for yourself!

Outlook Express

Outlook Express is currently the most widely used e-mail software among private users. (People working for businesses or other organisations are more likely to use the e-mail software in its big brother, Outlook, or a Lotus-based system.)

Outlook Express is very simple to use. You can pick up your mail with one click of a button. Sending a message is almost as simple, as long as you have the person's address – and something to say!

Try it: Start using Outlook Express

① If Outlook Express is not running, start it now, either from the Start menu or from the Desktop icon.

② Identify the areas marked in Figure 1.15. If you are working on a friend's PC, check before you read any messages! If it's your own PC, and the software has been installed recently, you should have a welcome message from Microsoft. Click on it in the header pane to open the message in the Preview pane.

③ Open the **Message** menu and select **New Message**, or click the **New Mail** toolbar button.

When the **New Message** window opens, you will see that it has lots of features. You only need to deal with four of them – the rest are frills. (Actually, there are some very handy frills here, as you will see later.)

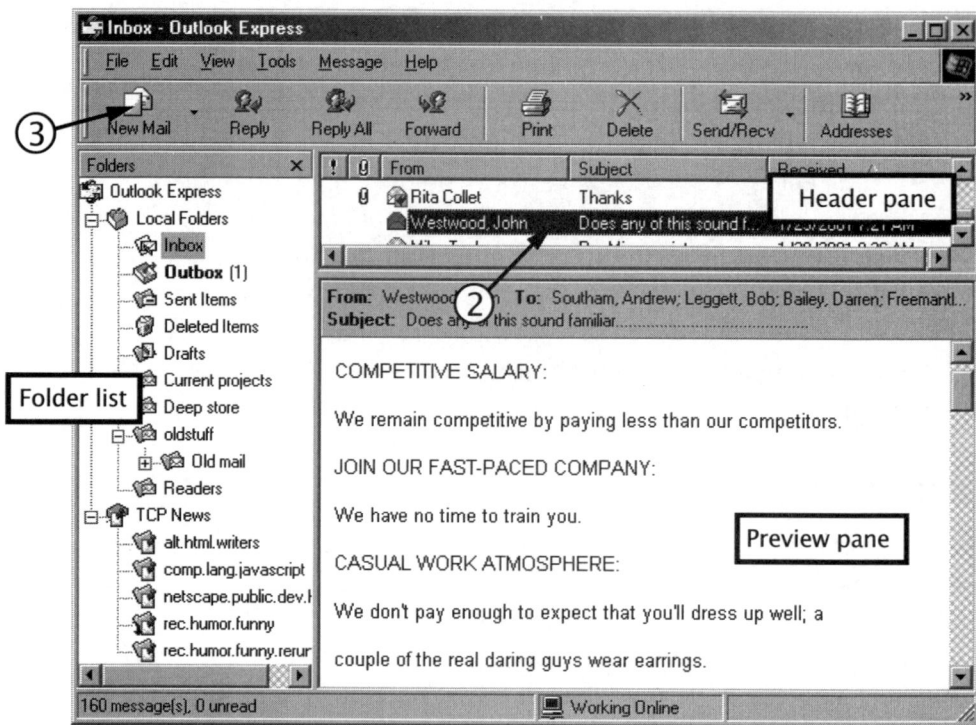

Figure 1.15 The Outlook Express window, showing the main features only. Outlook Express is covered in more detail in Chapter 7.

Try it: Write an e-mail message

① Click into the **To:** slot and type the address of the person you want to send the message to. If you do not have anyone's address at hand right now, send a message to me at: macbride@tcp.co.uk

② Click into the **Subject** slot and type a few words describing what the message is about. This is not essential, but your recipients will appreciate it, as it will help them to deal with their e-mail efficiently.

③ Click into the working space and type your message. This is not like writing a letter. You do not need to put the date or your address on the message – they will both be added automatically when the message is sent. Good spelling seems to be optional, judging by the messages I receive – even though most e-mail software now has a **Spelling** button.

④ Click the **Send** button.

If you are online, the message may be sent immediately, it depends upon the optional settings (see page 196).

If you are offline, it will be stored in the **Outbox** folder, ready for sending next time you connect to your online mailbox.

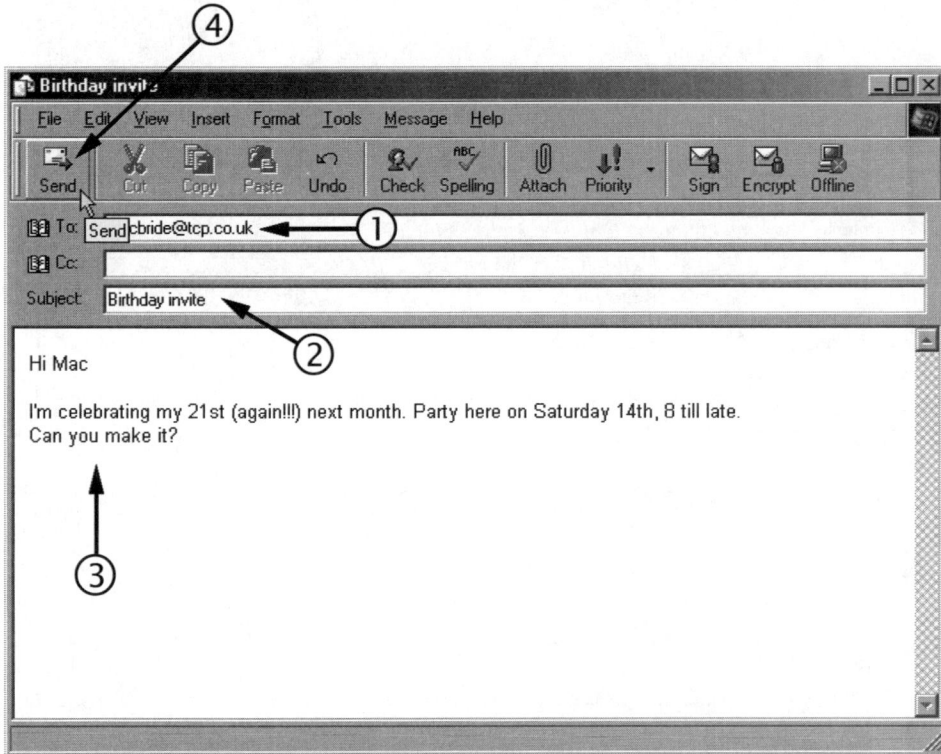

Figure 1.16 Writing a message. Most people are informal in their e-mailing, treating messages more like memos or notes than proper letters.

Try it: Send your messages

① If you are not online, go online now.

② Click the **Send/Recv** button.

◆ A progress indicator box will usually open. After a short delay you should see the indicator moving across the bar – though a short message will normally travel so quickly that you'll scarcely have time to see the indicator moving.

③ If you have had any new messages, there will be a number in brackets after the **Inbox** name. Click on the Inbox to open it, then click on a message in the Header pane to read it.

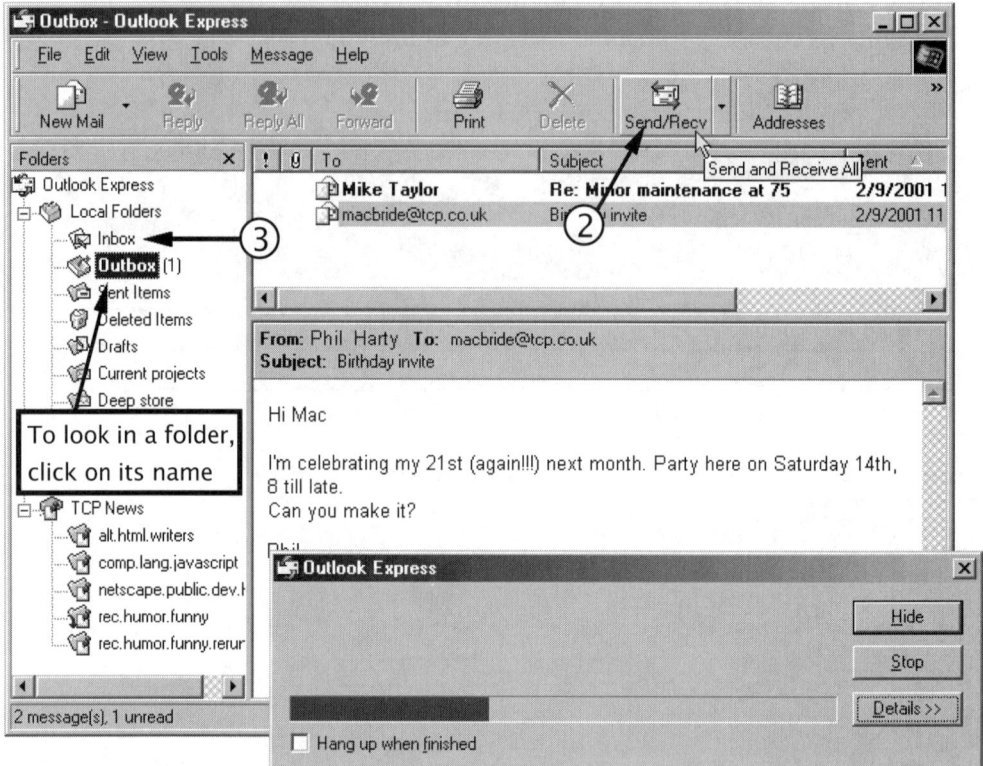

Figure 1.17 Sending a message – if the messages have been building up over a few days, you could go to the Outbox to check through them, but you wouldn't normally bother.

Going offline

When you have finished working online, close the connection properly – don't just close the browser and/or switch off the computer.

Try it: End your online session

Working on a PC, at home:

① Right-click ▣ in the Taskbar tray (next to the clock).

② Select **Disconnect** from the pop-up menu.

If you click **Status**, it will display
the **Connected to**... dialog box
(see below)

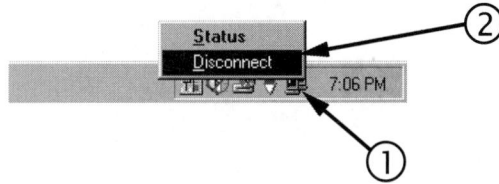

Or

① If the [Connected to ...] button is present on the Taskbar,
click it to bring the **Connected to**... dialog box into view.

② Click **Disconnect**.

TCP is my service provider

This also shows how much data
has been received/sent – bring
the box into sight any time that
you want to see how fast the
connection is working

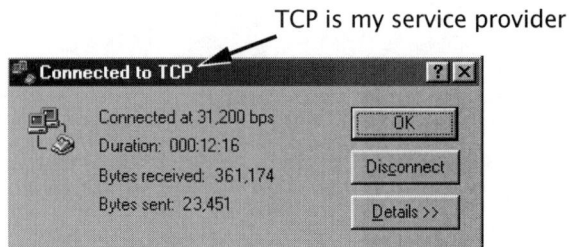

Connected to TCP

Connected at 31,200 bps
Duration: 000:12:16
Bytes received: 361,174
Bytes sent: 23,451

OK
Disconnect
Details >>

Using a public terminal in a library or classroom:

◆ Ask the instructor how to end. You probably just have to
'log off' – this ends your session, but leaves the computer connected and ready for the next person.

2

The Net and the Web

IN THIS CHAPTER:

- What's the Internet?
- Ways of working online
- Internet addresses
- Getting connected

This chapter aims to answer some of the frequently asked questions about the Internet. Go offline and take the time to read it – if you understand something of the background, it may help you to make better sense of some of the things you will meet on your later travels around the Net.

The Internet FAQs

FAQs = Frequently Asked Questions. You'll find FAQ lists at lots of places on the Internet

What is the Internet?

The Internet is a set of *inter*connected *net*works – hence the name – which links millions of computers throughout the World. The networks vary greatly in the number of computers that are connected to them, and in the way that they are organised. The networks fall into two main types:

◆ A LAN (Local Area Network) will normally be limited to a single office or one building, but may extend across a campus. At most, the computers at the far ends of the network are unlikely to be more than a mile apart.

◆ A WAN (Wide Area Network) joins distant sites. It may link a firm's offices in different cities or extend over many countries.

On a LAN, the computers are normally linked by cable; on WANs, the links may be through cable – normally public or private phone lines – or via microwave links.

Internet Service Providers are sometimes called *Internet Access Providers*

The computers on a LAN can share the printers, modems, disk drives and other resources attached to the network. On any network – including the Internet – the users can communicate with each other and share their data files with others if they want to.

All LANs and most WANs are owned by individual organisations and exist mainly to provide internal communications and other services for the organisation's own employees and users. Some WANs act as *Internet Service Providers* (ISPs). Members of the public and/or businesses can join these networks – usually for a small charge.

Domain name – used to identify an organisation on the Internet (see page 42)

The computers that are linked through these networks vary from giant supercomputers down to desktop machines – mainly PCs and Apple Macs, but also old Archimedes, Amigas and others. They are owned and run by millions of separate firms, governments, universities, charities – indeed, every size, shape and type of organisation – and by individuals.

Who's in charge?

There is no central authority or governing body, though there is the *Internet Society* which provides coordination and standardises the rules of cooperation, and InternNIC (the Network Information Center) which controls the allocation of domain names. There are also specialist and regional bodies, such as RIPE (Réseaux IP Européens) which enables administrative and technical collaboration between service providers and other active organisations in Europe.

The Internet relies on cooperation, driven by goodwill and enlightened self-interest. And it works!

How did it start?

This is a practical, how-to, book, not a history, but you should know a little about the Internet's past as it helps to explain some aspects of the present.

The Internet story starts in the late 1960s when the US government's Advanced Research Project Agency was asked to develop a long-distance communications network that would be robust enough to withstand nuclear attack. It came up with ARPAnet which linked four computers in different places in the USA.

What made the ARPAnet system robust was the fact that it was multi-connected and data travelled around it in small blocks or packets. This system is still used. Each packet is labelled with its origin, destination and position in the stream of data. The safe receipt of each packet is acknowledged, so that both ends of the connection know how the transmission is going. If a packet doesn't get through, it is re-sent. If the connection between any two nodes is broken (or bombed, in the original scenario), it will re-establish itself via an alternative route, and any packets of data that didn't reach their destination will be sent again along the new route.

The Internet has been proved to be bomb-proof. The Allies were unable to knock out Iraqi communications during the Gulf War, because they were using the Internet!

From those initial four computers, the net grew slowly over the next 10 years to connect around 200 computers and networks in military and research establishments within the USA, plus a few overseas links. It proved, beyond doubt, the practicality and benefits of inter-networking. By the mid-1980s

Usenet news-
groups are still in
use today

several academic and research inter-networks had been set
up including *Usenet* and *NFSnet*. These combined with
ARPAnet to form the basis of the Internet.

Three crucial points arise from the past:

NSFnet was the
National Science
Foundation's
internetwork. Its
high-speed cables
are the backbone
of the Internet in
the USA

◆ The Internet was initially centred around government-
funded research and academic organisations. It was not
set up as a commercial proposition, and commercial activities on the Internet are a relatively recent innovation.
There are still Appropriate Use rules that control profit-
making activities on parts of the Internet.

◆ The Net originally linked mainframe computers, most of
which ran the Unix operating system. PCs, Apple Macs
and other personal computers only began to be linked
up later. As a result, the Internet has retained a distinct
Unix flavour. This has been reinforced in the last few
years thanks to Linux, a freely available version of Unix,
which is now widely used on *Web servers*.

Web server – a
computer that
stores Web pages
and other files

◆ The multi-connection, packet-based system has stood the
test of time. Even when natural disaster or human error
knocks out part of the network, connections can normally be made through alternative routes.

The main complaint is speed, not reliability. There are
times when the Internet is so busy that 'traffic jams' build
up at key points and it takes ages for data to get through.
Sometimes you can make the multi-connectedness work
for you to overcome a jam – by breaking off a connection and trying again, you may be able to get your system to find a different, and faster route. We noted this
when looking at the Refresh button (page 6).

How big is it?

This is actually a meaningless question, so instead of giving
you a meaningless 'think of the biggest thing that you can
then double it' answer, let's break the question down into
manageable chunks.

How far does it stretch?

The Internet is everywhere. Today, wherever you are in the World, if you are within reach of a phone line – or can pick up a signal on your mobile phone – you can access the Internet. Having said that, the cost, ease and speed of access varies enormously.

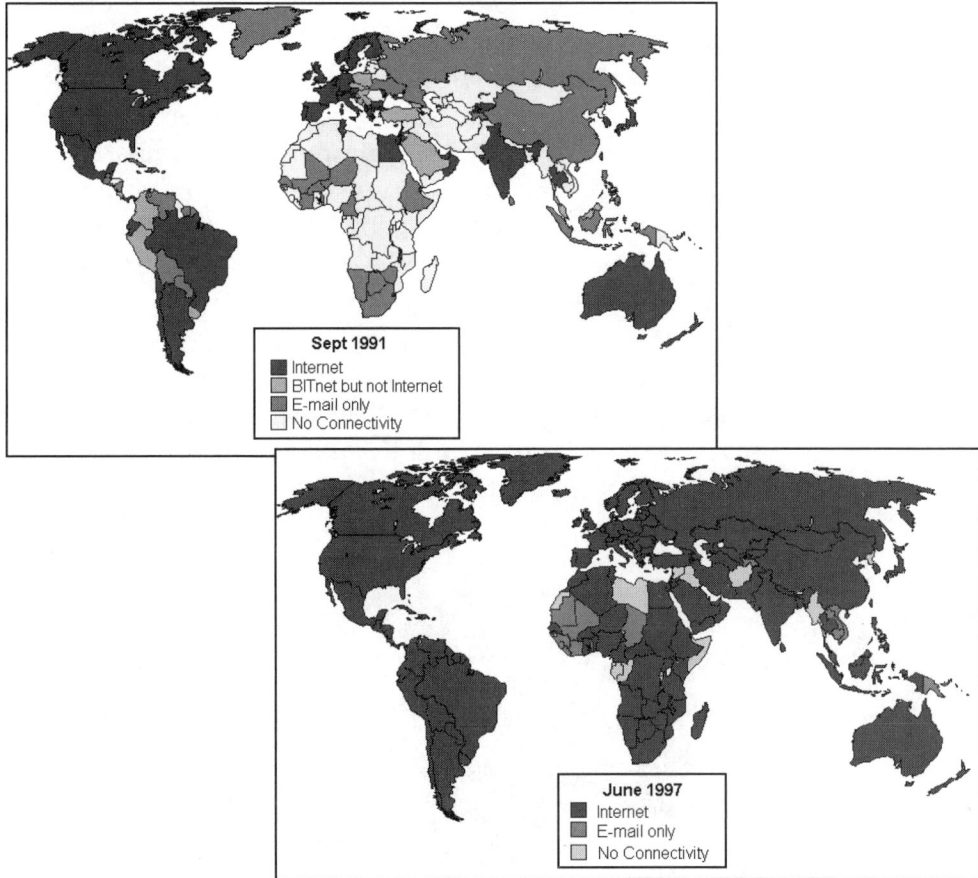

Sept 1991
■ Internet
■ BITnet but not Internet
■ E-mail only
□ No Connectivity

June 1997
■ Internet
■ E-mail only
□ No Connectivity

Figure 2.1 Who's connected? Lawrence Landweber, an American academic, tracked the spread of the Internet through the 1990s. By the time of his last map in 1997, almost every country was connected – and the remaining ones were connected shortly afterwards. What the maps don't show is the quality and cost of Internet access. In the USA and some of the more developed countries, fast, reliable and very cheap access is widely available; in the Third World access is generally expensive and harder to obtain.

The USA is way ahead of the field. The telephone network reaches into every town and village, and is highly reliable. Local calls – and most people get on to the Internet through a local call – have long been unmetered, so costs are negligible. If you want to pay a little more for a faster 'broadband' line, the option is widely available. Computers are cheap enough for the majority of the population to be able to afford, and people can get free access in any case through terminals in libraries and other public places.

The UK is behind, and falling behind further. Unmetered local calls have recently been introduced – with a flat rate fee – while broadband access is two years behind schedule. The price of computers is falling steadily, but they are still beyond the reach of many people. However, most libraries now have terminals and virtually all pupils and students can get online through their schools and colleges.

In the rest of the developed world, Internet access is generally as good as, or better, than in the UK, but there are many parts of Africa, Asia and South America where only the urban rich currently have regular, easy access.

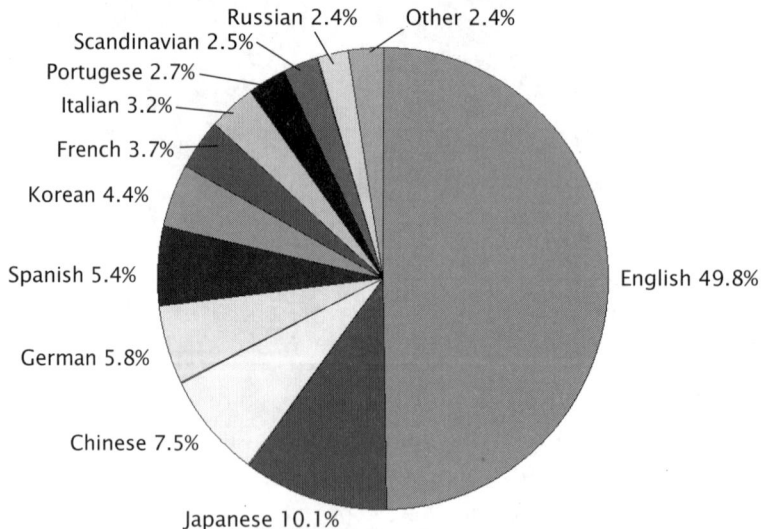

Russian 2.4% Other 2.4%
Scandinavian 2.5%
Portugese 2.7%
Italian 3.2%
French 3.7%
Korean 4.4%
Spanish 5.4%
German 5.8%
Chinese 7.5%
Japanese 10.1%
English 49.8%

Figure 2.2 The languages of the Internet at the end of 2000. Only a few years ago, English was by far the language of the majority of users. On present trends, Chinese will be the majority language in five years. (Source: Global Language Statistics at **www.glreach.com**)

How many computers are connected?

The total number of computers that can be connected to the Internet is as hard to count as the number of Internet users – see below – but it is possible to get a clearer idea of the number of computers that are acting as hosts.

Host – computer permanently connected to the Internet and offering a service to Internet users.

The trick is to set up a program to work its way through every combination of Internet address numbers and see which ones respond. (Actually, you need to set up lots of programs to do the same job from different start points, because it would take ages for one to do it alone.) It will not give you an accurate count, as there are too many things that can go wrong – a computer may fail to respond because it is off for some reason, or the phone line to it may be down or jammed with traffic; the same computer may have a number of different addresses, one for each of the various services that it hosts.

Accepting that the figures are only approximate, the host counts still tell a clear story of growth – and the Internet is growing at a phenomenal rate. In 1990 there were only around 100,000 host computers. Ten years later, there were almost 100 million! The boom must start to tail off some time, but at the moment the growth curve is still getting steeper.

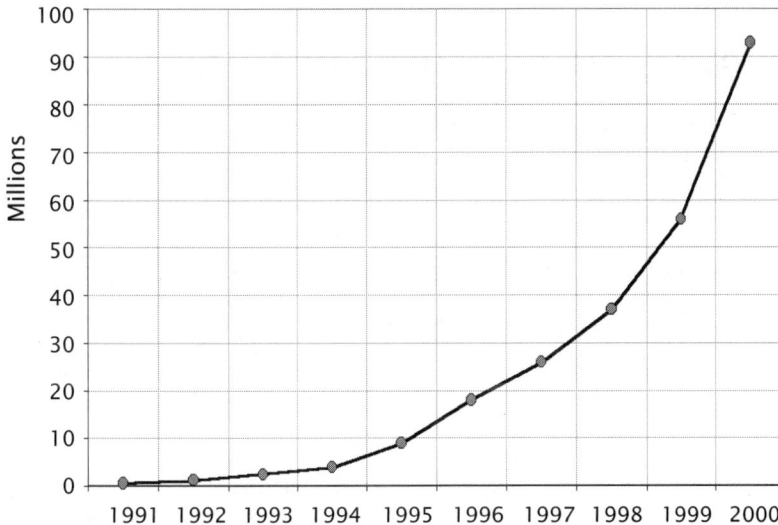

Figure 2.3 Growth of the Internet, as measured by the number of hosts. (Figures from the Internet Software Consortium at **http://www.isc.org**)

How many people are online?

Now we are really getting into guesstimates! There is no way to make an accurate count of the number of people who have access to the Internet. People get online through so many organisations – businesses, government agencies, schools and colleges, as well as Internet Service Providers – and few of these are able or willing to publish numbers of their users.

So what's the best guess? NUA Internet Surveys came up with these figures:

Internet users, November 2000

Canada & USA	167.12 million
Europe	113.14 million
Asia/Pacific	104.88 million
Latin America	16.45 million
Africa	3.11 million
Middle East	2.40 million
Total	**407.10 million**

The only way to keep up with the Net is through the Net. For the latest NUA surveys, go to **www.nua.ie**

I think that you can assume that the decimal places are wrong – in fact, at best these may be within 10% of the correct numbers at the time. Given the exponential rates of growth, they will be far higher by the time you read this book.

Ways of working online

You have already met the two most popular and widely used aspects of the Internet – the World Wide Web and e-mail – in Chapter 1. These are not the only ways that people can use the Internet to communicate and share resources. Here are five other ways. The first three, mailing lists, newsgroups and file transfer, are widely used.

Mailing lists

Mailing lists have grown directly out of e-mail. The concept is simple. In a mailing list, communication is through a newsletter circulated through the standard e-mail system. The newsletter is written by one person or organisation – usually with contributions from list members – then sent by e-mail to the members. Mass e-mailings are not hard to set up and involve no more time, trouble or cost for the sender than a single-address e-mail. (The main extra work is done at the sender's mail server, which has to go through the mailing list, picking up each address in turn and sending a copy of the newsletter off to it.)

You can easily send a message to groups of people – see Chapter 7

There are mailing lists for all kinds of topics, but with the emphasis more on the academic, professional and serious hobbyists. Some – largely those that provide specialist information – charge a fee, but most are open to anyone and free of charge. It is worth checking out the lists of lists at ListQuest (**www.listquest.com**) to see if there are any that interest you.

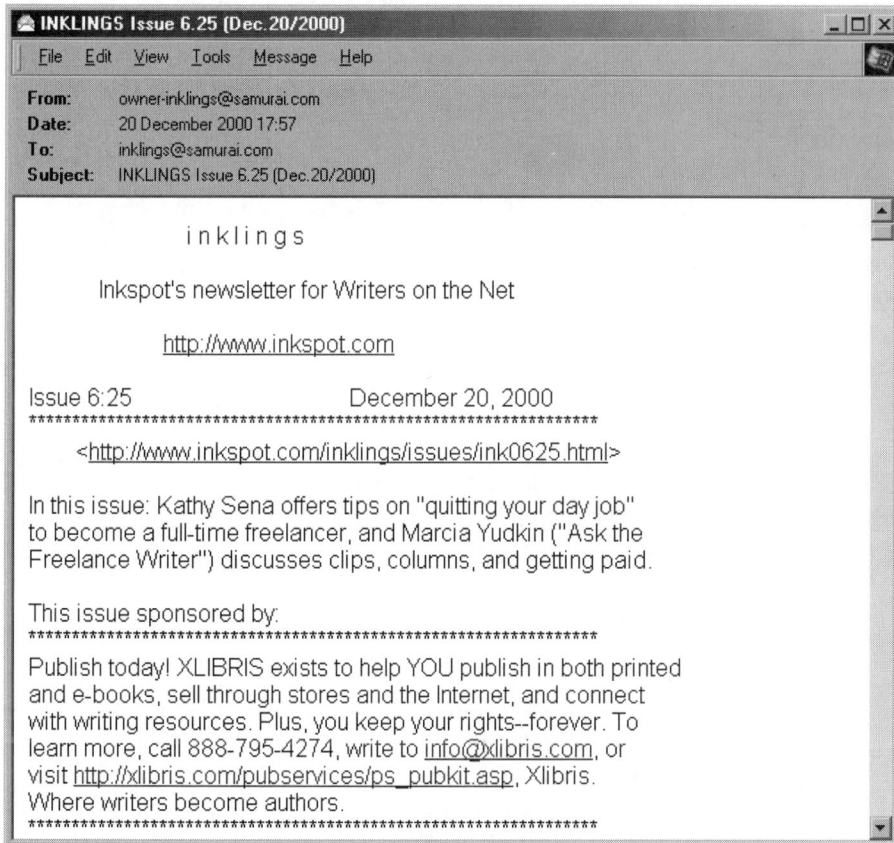

```
INKLINGS Issue 6.25 (Dec.20/2000)
File   Edit   View   Tools   Message   Help

From:     owner-inklings@samurai.com
Date:     20 December 2000 17:57
To:       inklings@samurai.com
Subject:  INKLINGS Issue 6.25 (Dec.20/2000)

                    i n k l i n g s

        Inkspot's newsletter for Writers on the Net

                http://www.inkspot.com

Issue 6:25                    December 20, 2000
*****************************************************************
     <http://www.inkspot.com/inklings/issues/ink0625.html>

In this issue: Kathy Sena offers tips on "quitting your day job"
to become a full-time freelancer, and Marcia Yudkin ("Ask the
Freelance Writer") discusses clips, columns, and getting paid.

This issue sponsored by:
*****************************************************************
Publish today! XLIBRIS exists to help YOU publish in both printed
and e-books, sell through stores and the Internet, and connect
with writing resources. Plus, you keep your rights--forever. To
learn more, call 888-795-4274, write to info@xlibris.com, or
visit http://xlibris.com/pubservices/ps_pubkit.asp, Xlibris.
Where writers become authors.
*****************************************************************
```

Figure 2.4 Inkspot was an excellent source of news and ideas for writers and one of the best (free) mailing list newsletters. Unfortunately it lost its funding and had to close down in early 2001.

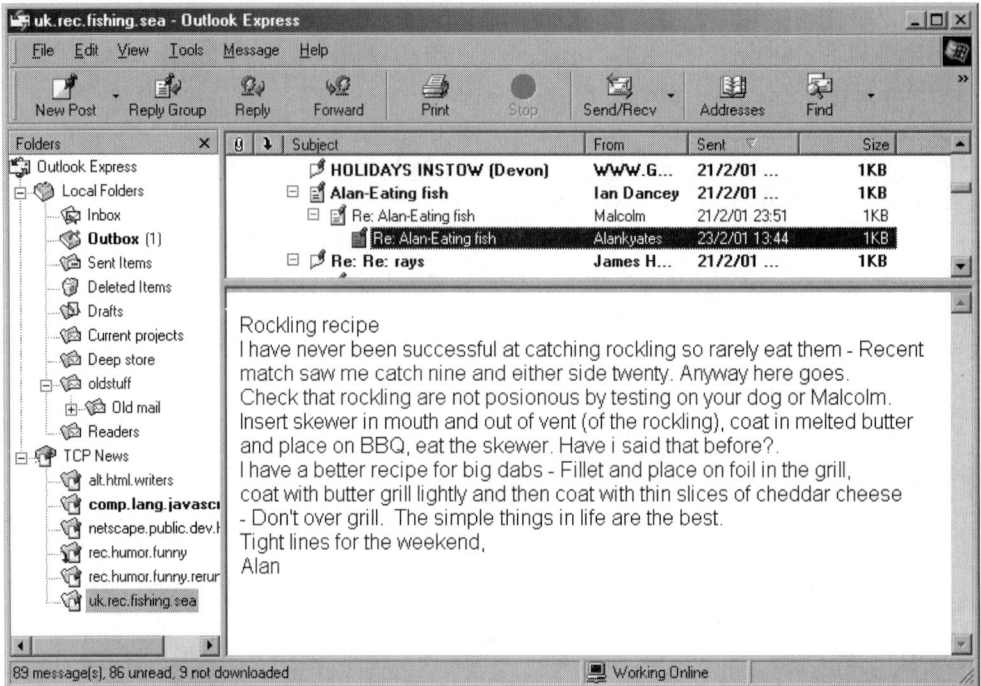

Figure 2.5 This exchange had started with a request for recipes for rockling. Malcolm's suggestion was less than helpful.

Newsgroups

At first sight, these are similar to mailing lists. Each is dedicated to a specialist topic – though the range is much wider than mailing lists, and includes far more frivolous, pointless, exotic and erotic topics than you will find in the lists. They are also text-based and are normally accessed through e-mail software. But there are some very significant differences.

Mailing lists are the electronic equivalent of newsletters sent through the post; newsgroups are the equivalent of the letters pages in newspapers. People will send in their 'articles' – perhaps thoughts on a current issue or a request for information – and others may respond to these. Controversial topics can often stimulate long exchanges of sometimes heated views. The software groups articles and their responses into 'threads', so that others can follow the exchanges.

Though newsgroups are read through e-mail software, the articles are not sent out like e-mail. When you link to a group, only the headers (containing the names of the senders, the subjects and dates) are downloaded at first. The bodies of the messages are only downloaded if you choose to read them.

You do not have to join a newsgroup to read its articles, or to send in your own contributions.

Some newsgroups are 'moderated' – they have someone who reads the articles and filters out those which are off-topic, irrelevant or otherwise not worth circulating. Most are unmoderated, and these are either a free, open and democratic exchange of views or a terrible 'waste of *bandwidth*'. It depends upon the group and on your own viewpoint.

Bandwidth – the capacity of your connection to the Internet

Newsgroups can be excellent resources. It is well worth spending a little time sifting through them to find the gems that appeal to you. You'll see how in Chapter 8.

File transfer

The Internet is the biggest software store in the world, and it's open all hours! There are millions of gigabytes worth of files out there, all ready to be downloaded. The files are mainly programs – fully-fledged applications, utilities, games and much else – but also include documents, images, sound and video clips.

You will find files at the Web sites of computer software and hardware companies, who use the Net to distribute demos of forthcoming software, updates and 'patches' to fix the bugs in the software they've already sold you.

Shareware sites are another major source of files. As well as *shareware*, there's plenty of 'freeware' and some of it is very good indeed. In fact, all of the software that you need to explore every aspect of the Internet can be obtained, for free, from the Internet.

Shareware – cheap, try-before-you-buy software

These kinds of files are normally transferred using FTP (File Transfer Protocol). This is a different technique from the one used to transfer Web page files.

Freeware – software available free of charge

We will be looking at downloading files from the Net in Chapter 5.

Gopher

It's hard now to imagine the Internet without the World Wide Web, but the Web has only been in use for the last six or seven years. In its early days, communication was mainly through e-mail and newsgroups. If you wanted to read files that were stored on a remote computer, you either had to download them – which was tricky because you had to know where they were first – or login to the computer and give commands directly to it. It all required skill and dedication, and ensured that the Internet remained the almost exclusive province of the techies.

Gopher was the first attempt to make the Internet more accessible for ordinary folks. The software was developed at the University of Minnesota, home of the Golden Gophers baseball team and its name is a reflection of this, as well as a pun on *go-for*. Gopher was a menu-driven system that linked many of the Internet's databases into a unified information service.

As a Gopher user, you would normally start by linking to one of the Gopher servers, where you would see a menu of

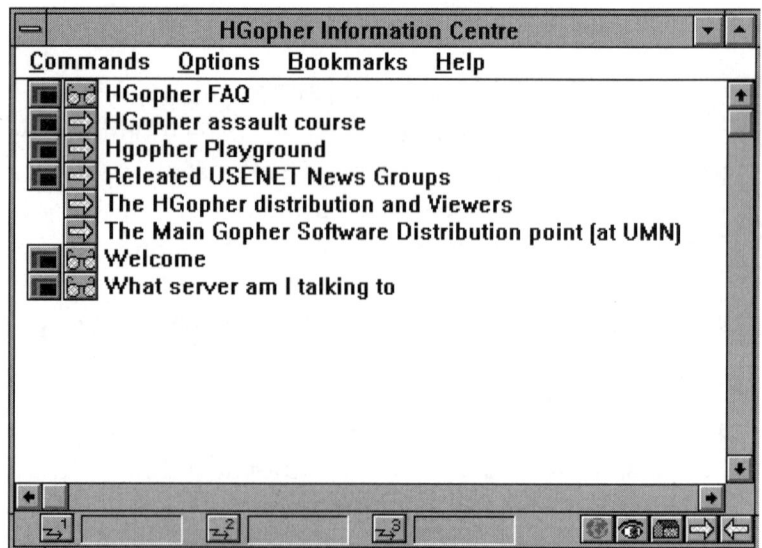

Figure 2.6 A Gopher main menu seen here in the HGopher viewer – ⇨ indicates the option leads to a menu; ⚏ marks a document that you can read online.

options. At the top few levels, most of the options led to other menus, but once you had narrowed down to a fairly specialised area, you would get links to documents. Gopher viewers – the software that you ran on your computer – could display any plain text files and well as some types of images and formatted documents.

The Gopher system made Internet resources available to the non-technical, but it had one major flaw. As material could only be reached (easily) through the menus, someone, somewhere had to update one or more menus whenever anything new was added. As the system was run almost entirely by volunteers, mainly university lecturers and students, in their spare time, there was a limit to how quickly new material could be added. Compare this with the free-wheeling Web, where people publishing new pages can get them known by cross-linking from their own existing pages, or by encouraging search engines and directories to include them.

At its height, the Gopher system encompassed several hundred thousand documents. The Web is still growing fast, but has already gone far beyond the point of accurate countability – the Google search engine currrently has an index of over 1.3 billion pages, and there are loads that it has not yet found.

Telnet

This allows you to log on to a remote computer and use it as if your machine was directly attached to it. You can read documents, run programs, send e-mail and use any other services that it offers. There are restrictions, of course. The host computers set strict limits on where you can go and what you can do within their system. They won't let you have access to people's private files; you normally cannot store files of your own; and you definitely cannot run programs that may damage the system.

Telnet is falling out of use. It was popular with computer science students and enthusiasts, as a way to get facilities that would not otherwise be available to them. Nowadays, cheap PCs offer much the same range of facilities.

Internet addresses

Every computer, every file, every person on the Internet has their own unique address. And these addresses tell you not only where something is, but also how to contact it.

Host computers

The host computers – the ones that are permanently connected to and offer services to the Internet – have numeric addresses, in this form:

194.73.82.242

Each of the four numbers is in the range of 0 to 255, which is what you can store in one byte. The whole address then takes only four bytes, the same as 'this' (or any other four-letter word), but there are enough numbers to identify over one million billion computers. That should keep us going for a few years yet.

Number addresses may be compact and efficient, but they are not at all memorable. Fortunately, you do not have to remember them. Read on...

Domain names

Every computer site that is linked to the Internet has its own unique address, also referred to as a *domain name*. This is made up of two or more names, separated by dots, e.g.:

www.virgin.co.uk

The central part of the address identifies the organisation, and this is usually derived directly from its name. That first example is, of course, for the Virgin company.

The other parts of the address follow certain conventions.

The country code

At the right-hand end there will be the country code, though this is omitted for US-based and international organisations. Examples are:

au	Australia	ca	Canada
co	Colombia	do	Dominican Republic

fr	France	fi	Finland
de	Germany	hk	Hong Kong
ie	Ireland	in	India
it	Italy	jp	Japan
tv	Tuvalu	uk	United Kingdom

The country code is usually a good guide to the location of the organisation, but people can register in another country. Why bother? Because you can get cool names that way! *buy.it* and *sell.it* have already gone, as have many other Italian names that produce English phrases. If you're in television, how about a name that ends .tv? thriller.tv has gone, but when I last looked, comedy.tv could be had – for only $100,000 a year!!

Type of organisation

The next part of the address, working from the right, identifies the nature of the organisation. (This can be omitted.)

The most common ones are:

com	commercial (USA and international)
co	commercial (outside the USA)
edu	educational (USA)
ac	academic (outside the USA)
net	network provider
gov	government department
mil	military
nhs	hospital or other NHS facility (UK)
org	non-commercial organisation

On the left-hand side there may be one or more other names to identify a computer, or part of a computer, within the site. These are more variable, as they can be set by the organisation. Some common ones are:

www	the organisation's Web site
mail	the organisation's e-mail site
search	a search facility at the site

Some typical examples are:

ftp.microsoft.com

The *FTP* server at *Microsoft*, a *com*mercial organisation, based in the USA.

micros.hensa.ac.uk

The computer on which the *micros* files are stored, at the University of Lancaster (*hensa*), an *ac*ademic site in the *UK*.

sunsite.unc.edu

This is a *site* sponsored by *Sun* computers, in the University of North Carolina, an *educ*ational organisation in the USA.

www.tcp.co.uk   *and*   mail.tcp.co.uk

The Web site and e-mail server of my ISP, *TCP* (Total Connectivity Providers), a *c*ommercial organisation in the *UK*.

Uniform Resource Locators (URLs)

URLs are not case-sensitive – i.e. it doesn't matter if you use lower-case or capital letters

With so many millions of Web pages, files, newsgroups and e-mail addresses that can be reached over the Internet, a standardised and systematic way of identifying them is essential. URLs provide this. Type a URL into a Web browser and – as long as you have typed it correctly – the browser will go to the right site and locate the item.

There are different styles of URL for each approach to the Internet, though they all follow much the same pattern:

type://hostcomputer/folder/filename

Web pages

Many of these are instantly recognisable from their *html* or *htm* endings, which shows that they are hypertext pages.

http://www.eno.org/Booking/diary.htm

This one is the event *diary* in the *Booking* area at Web site (*www*) of the English National Opera (*eno*).

http://homepages.tcp.co.uk/~macbride

Here's my home page, in case you want to drop by. Like the URLs of many personal home pages, this consists of the address of a computer at my service provider, followed by a tilde (~) and my user name.

The URL of the top page of a site may just consist of the site address, with an (optional) slash at the end. This will take you to the opening page at Microsoft's site.

http://www.microsoft.com/

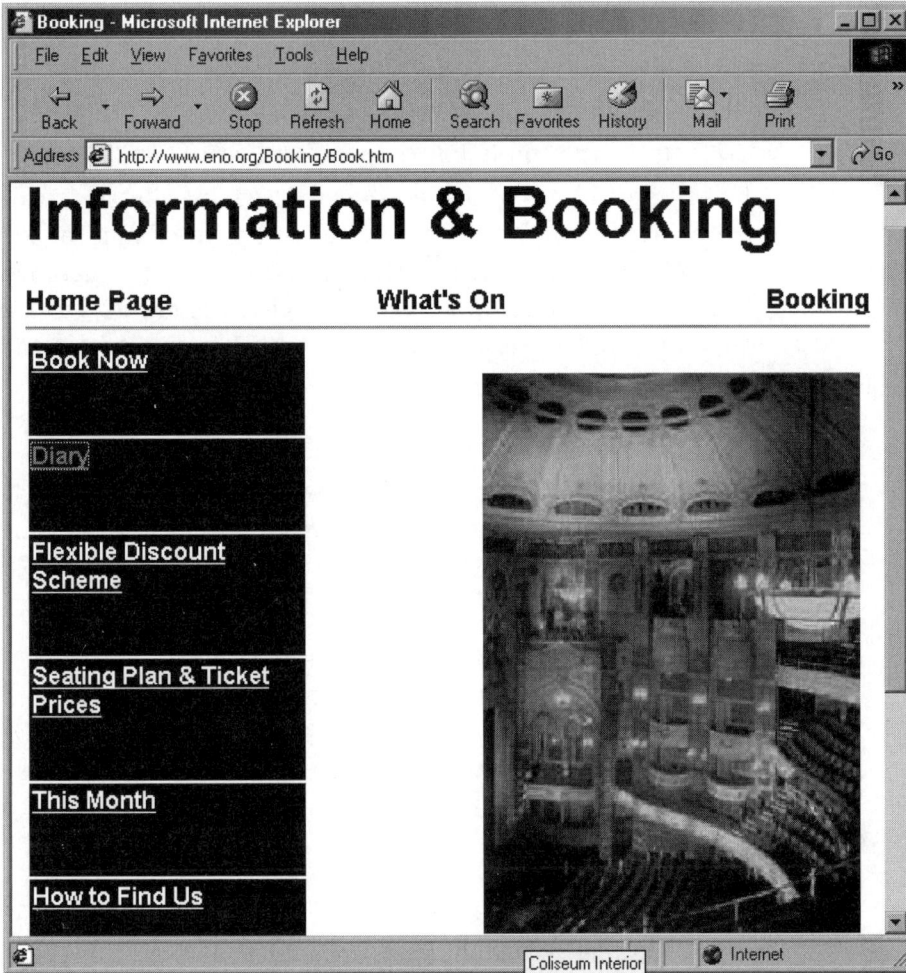

Figure 2.7 If you know the URL of a Web page, you can go directly to it, rather than having to work your way down through a site. This can make getting to places much quicker, especially where a site uses lots of graphics on their top level pages.

The URLs of Web pages can sometimes be very complex, making typing them in a real chore. Fortunately, you rarely have to do this more than once – if at all – as browsers can capture and store addresses in several ways. Look out for History (page 88), Favorites (page 79) and the AutoComplete facility (page 75).

Files for FTP

These always specify the path from the top to the directory containing the file. The filename is the last item on the list.

ftp://ftp.temple.edu/pub/info/funstuff/smiley.txt

This is the address of the file *smiley.txt*, which will tell you all you want to know – and probably a lot that you don't – about the smileys and abbreviations (page 246) that are sometimes used in e-mail and newsgroup messages. It is in the *funstuff* directory, inside the *info* directory, in the *pub* directory of the *ftp* computer at *Temple* University in the USA.

Newsgroups

You would rarely bother with a newsgroup's URL because it is simpler to locate the group through the News routines of your mail and news software. If you feel the need, the URL takes this shape.

news://news.tcp.co.uk/rec.humor.funny/

This links to my *news* server at *TCP*, and selects the newsgroup *rec.humor.funny*. Note that this only works for TCP members. If you want to reach this newsgroup, change 'tcp.co.uk' in the URL to the name of your service provider.

E-mail address

This is another URL that you would rarely type into a browser as it is simpler to use the mail software. However, it is regularly used in Web pages so that visitors can drop you a line. Come to my pages and you'll find this link to me:

mailto://macbride@tcp.co.uk

After *mailto://* the URL is a normal e-mail address (page 202).

Getting connected

Getting connected to the Internet used to be quite a technical business, but not any more. Virtually all ISPs now provide a CD which not only contains all the software that you need, but also installs it for you. All you should have to do is follow a few simple instructions and decide what name you would like to have for your e-mail. The trickiest bit is choosing an ISP, and even that is not too bad.

ISP = Internet Service Provider

ISPs fall into three groups, on the basis of their charges:

♦ Some charge a flat fee for access – typically around £10 per month; and connection will be through a low-cost or 0800 phone number. These providers vary in size from the mightly AOL, down to local firms like TCP, my ISP, but they all aim to provide a good, reliable service to keep their paying customers. Telephone support is usually good, and charged at low-cost rates.

♦ Some charge for usage. This may be metered by the provider and charged through a credit card, or the connection may be through an 0845 (or similar) number, where part of the phone charge is passed on to the provider.

♦ Some are, in theory, completely free – even to the extent of using 0800 numbers, or unmetered phone calls. Several free services were set up in the belief that they could pay for themselves by the advertising revenue from the service's home site. These largely disappeared in the first pop of the dot.com bubble. Any free services/free phone being offered now should be looked at very closely.

If a service claims to be free, check its phone charges

In the first instance, I recommend signing up for a free trial with AOL, or any other provider. You need to see how you use the Internet before you know what you want from an ISP.

If you find that you are spending an hour or more every day online, then you should be looking for a flat-fee, unmetered service – and for an unmetered phone line, such as BT's Together.

If you mainly use the Internet for e-mail, with only occasional forays into the Web for specific information, then a service that charges by usage makes far more sense.

Hardware and software

The modem converts computer data into a signal that can be sent down the phone line – and back again! 56k is the current standard for new modems

You don't need the biggest, all-singing, all-dancing computer to get online. Far from it! Any PC or Apple built within the last five years should be fine. The absolute minimum would be a Windows 95 machine with 20Mb free space on the hard drive, and a 28.8k modem. If you are buying new, all modern computers come with a far higher specification, much more disk space and an internal modem.

Your machine will almost certainly have Internet software already in place, but in any case, when you use your ISP's installation CD it will install the latest software as part of the setup.

The only other part of setting up that may cause a little head-scratching is linking to your phone line. If there is no phone socket within easy reach of the PC, you can pick up a phone extension kit from any DIY store and fit it in minutes.

3

Internet Explorer

IN THIS CHAPTER:

- The screen, the menus and the toolbar
- Internet Options
- Addresses and the Address bar
- Favorites
- History
- Searching
- Printing

We had a quick look at Internet Explorer in Chapter 1, but at that stage, I only tried to cover enough to get you working online. This chapter takes a much closer look, and will show you how to set up Internet Explorer to suit the way you work and to use it effectively.

The screen

Internet Explorer, like most modern software, can be customised in many ways, so it's always dangerous to say 'your screen should look like this...' because there's a better than even chance that it won't! So, bearing this in mind, your Internet Explorer window should look like the one below – as long as you've got all the toolbars open (and we'll see how to do that in a minute), and as long as it's set to the same size (mine is a little over 800 by 640 pixels), and, of course, as long as you are at the Danger Mouse site!

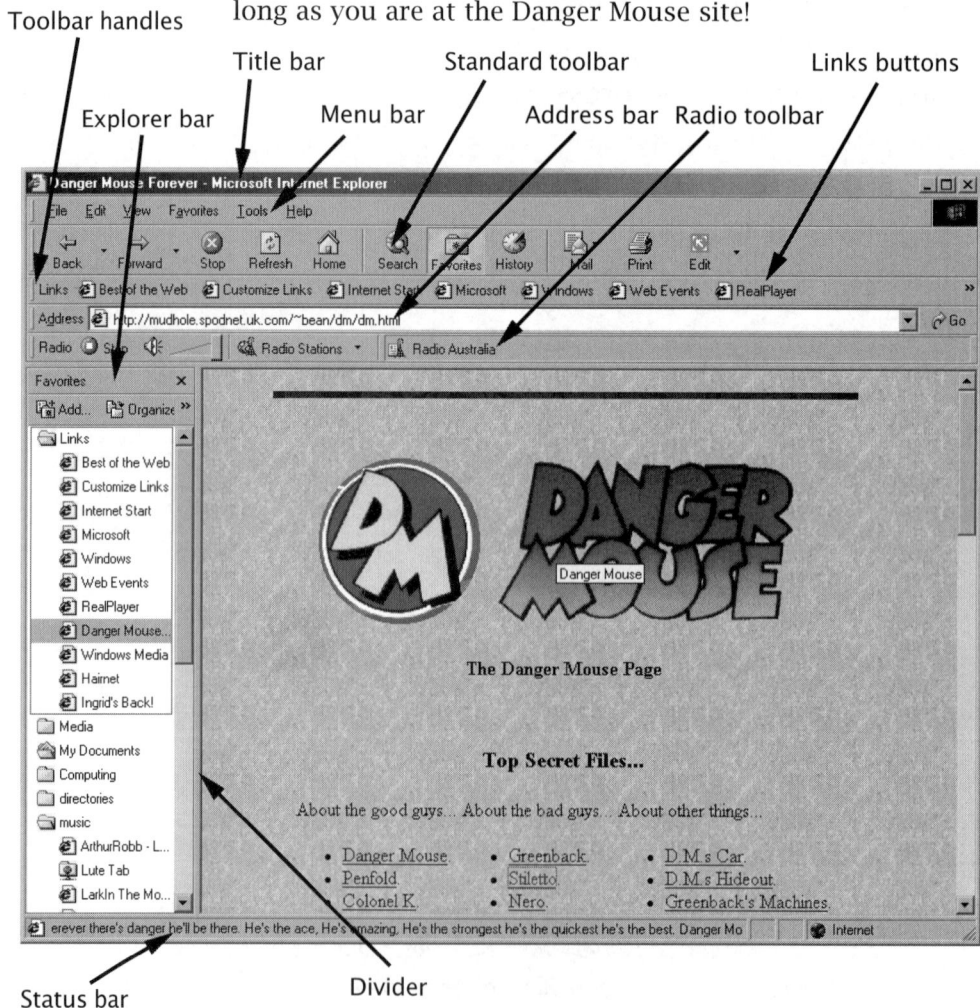

Figure 3.1   The Internet Explorer window, with all the elements displayed.

Try it: Get to know the Internet Explorer display

Try to ignore any differences between your screen and my screenshot, and identify the labelled features. Apart from the title and menu bars, these are all optional.

◆ **Title bar** – notice that this shows the *title* of the current Web page. This is not the same as its URL, which you will see in the Address bar.

◆ **Menu bar** – gives you access to the full set of commands.

◆ **Standard toolbar** – providing single-click access to the most commonly-used commands (page 58).

◆ **Address bar** – shows the URL (the Web site and filename) of the current Web page. You can type an URL here to go to a site (page 75).

◆ **Links buttons** – single-click links to selected sites. There are predefined links to various Microsoft sites. You can remove any or all of these and add your own through the Organize Favorites routine (page 81).

◆ **Radio toolbar** – the controls for tuning and listening to Internet radio (page 145).

◆ **Toolbar handles** – drag these to move the toolbars. They can be in any order down the screen, and can sit two or more on the same line.

◆ **Explorer bar** – in which you can run a Search (page 90), or display your Favorites (page 79) or History (page 88).

◆ **Divider** – click and drag on this to adjust the width of the Explorer bar. You may appreciate more space when using the Explorer bar for a search.

◆ **Status bar** – shows the progress of incoming files, telling you how many files have been loaded and how much of them have come in. When all the files for a Web page are in place, you'll see '*Done*'.

Some pages have JavaScript routines to scroll messages in the Status bar (there's one in the screenshot). These can be a bit distracting, and the bad news is that it is very easy to set them up!

JavaScript = programming language which can be used on Web pages

The menus

It is worth going through the menus to get an idea of how they are organised – and therefore, where to find commands when you need them. We will be looking at many of them later in this chapter as we explore Explorer, so at this stage, I'll skim over those very briefly.

The File menu

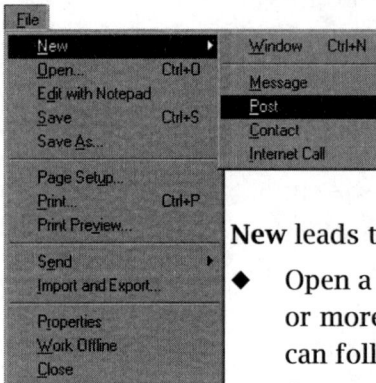

The commands on this menu are mainly those that deal with the whole page as a file, and the rest are those that control Explorer itself. If you have used Word – or any Microsoft product – you will recognise many of these.

New leads to a submenu from which you can:

◆ Open a new Window – it's sometimes useful to have two or more copies of Explorer running at once so that you can follow up links in several directions.

◆ Start to write a new e-mail **Message, Post** an article to a newsgroup, or add a **Contact** to your Address Book. In practice, you would normally do all of these through Outlook Express.

NetMeeting = Microsoft facility for keeping in touch with friends online

◆ Make an **Internet Call**, if you have NetMeeting installed – this is of limited value to ordinary users.

Open... calls up the Open dialog box where you can enter an Internet address or browse for a file on your PC.

Edit with Notepad (or your Web page editor) is intended for use with your own Web pages. It copies the HTML code that makes up the Web page into your editor, where you can correct the errors that showed up when viewed in the browser.

Save is normally 'greyed out' (unavailable). It can only be used with documents other than Web pages, where these have been opened in the browser.

Save As... allows you to save a Web page – use the *Web page complete* option to save its files at the same time.

Page Setup..., **Print**... and **Print Preview**... give you control over your printouts (page 92).

Send has three options:

◆ **Page by E-mail** copies the page, and its images, into Outlook Express ready for you to send on to a contact. You can add your own comments to the page, or delete bits before sending, if required.

◆ **Link by E-mail** also starts to create a new message in Outlook Express, but this time only the address of the page is copied in.

◆ **Shortcut to Desktop** puts an icon, with a link to the page, on your Desktop, so that you can return to it later by clicking the icon.

Import and Export... is mainly for experienced users who have switched to Internet Explorer from another browser (or who are planning to switch *from* IE to another). Its routines will convert the favorites (page 79) and cookies (page 66) files between the current Internet Explorer format and other browsers' formats.

Properties just gives you some details about the current Web page. These are rarely of any interest.

Work Offline should be turned on when you are browsing files stored on your hard disk. These include those that you have chosen to save, and those pages which you have visited recently and which are still stored in the cache (page 63). Some Web pages cannot be viewed offline (unless you save them to disk) either because they contain changing material – typically adverts! – or because of their structure. If you try to view one of these, you will be prompted to connect.

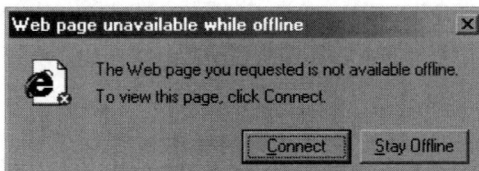

Close shuts down Internet Explorer and disconnects you from the Internet.

The Edit menu

Edit	
Cut	Ctrl+X
Copy	Ctrl+C
Paste	Ctrl+V
Select All	Ctrl+A
Find (on This Page)...	Ctrl+F

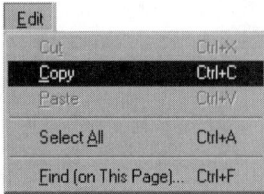

These commands are mainly for copying text from the Web page into a word-processor. Two points to note here: they can all be called up with keystroke shortcuts (some of which you may recognise); and they only work for text – you can copy images, but not from this menu.

Cut and **Paste** are usually greyed out, as you cannot normally edit a Web page in Internet Explorer.

Copy copies any selected text into the Windows Clipboard, ready for pasting into another application. You may get more than you bargained for! There is often more to a Web page than is immediately visible. For example, the address beneath a link will be copied, though you do not see it on the page.

Select All selects all the text on the page.

Find (on This Page...**)** calls up the **Find** dialog box. Type the words you are looking for, set the Match and Direction options if required, then click **Find Next** to set it going. If the words are on the page, they will be highlighted.

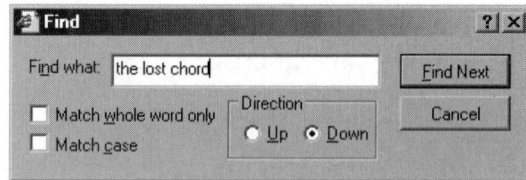

Find

Find what: the lost chord | Find Next

☐ Match whole word only | Direction ○ Up ⊙ Down | Cancel
☐ Match case

The View menu

View	
Toolbars	▶
✓ Status Bar	
Explorer Bar	▶
Go To	▶
Stop	Esc
Refresh	F5
Text Size	▶
Encoding	▶
Source	
Script Debugger	▶
Full Screen	F11

Largest
Larger
• Medium
Smaller
Smallest

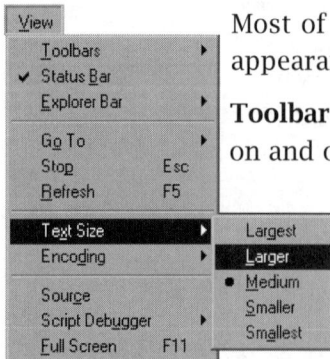

Most of the commands here are concerned with the screen appearance.

Toolbars, **Status Bar** and **Explorer Bar** turn screen elements on and off. We'll come back to these shortly (page 60).

Go To offers the navigation options, **Back**, **Forward**, **Home** and links to the last few pages that you visited. If you work with the mouse, these are all more readily accessed through the toolbar. Otherwise, as you can reach menu commands through the keyboard (page 266), these offer a useful alternative.

Stop and **Refresh** do the same jobs as the toolbar buttons (page 6).

Text Size allows you to set the size of the text. The main body text and the headings are all affected equally – if you opt for *Large* text, you get very large headings.

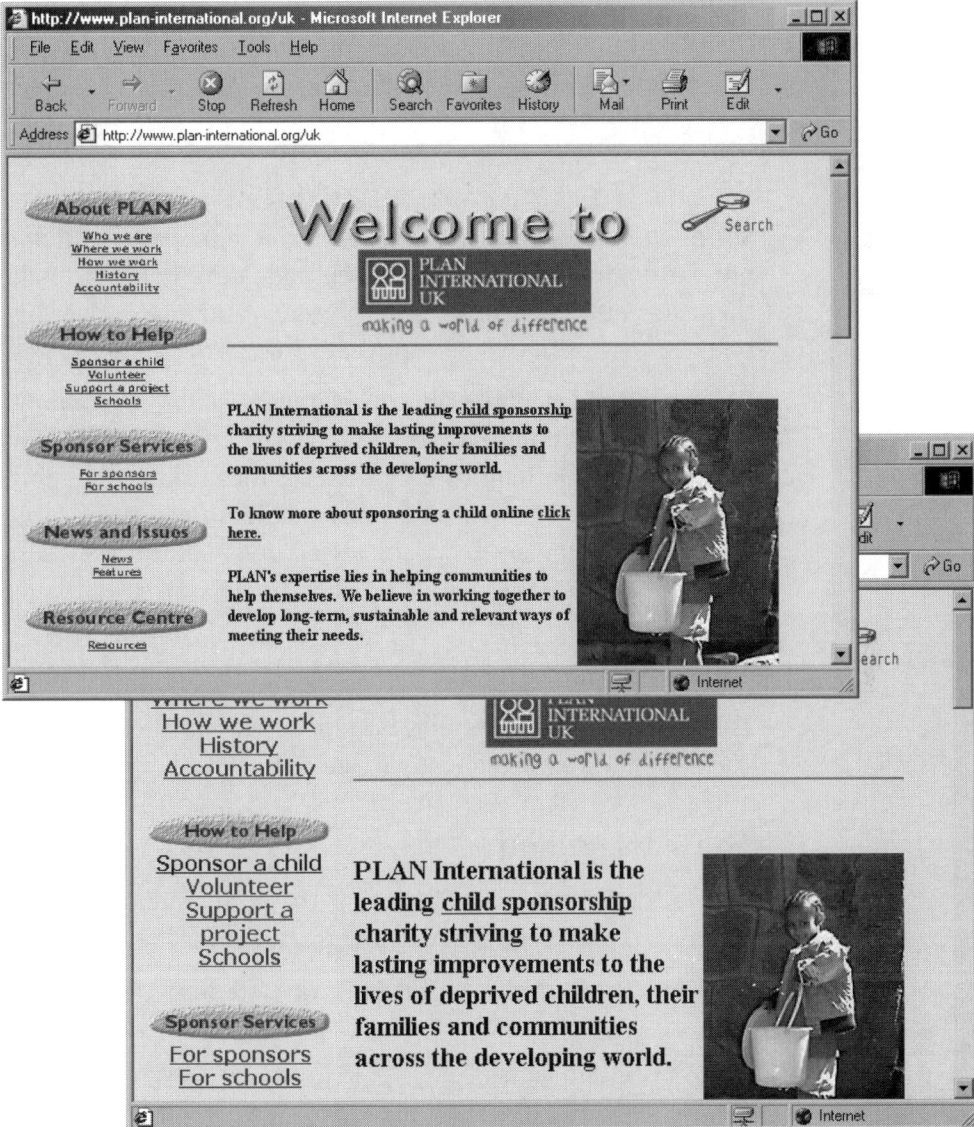

Figure 3.2   The same page, seen in the same size window, but with the Text Size set to Smallest (above) and Largest (below).

Encoding selects the character set. You should not need to change this, and if it does get changed, set it back to Western European – unless you want to read Hebrew, Arabic, Chinese or other scripts!

Source starts up Notepad and displays the HTML document that produces the Web page. Sometimes it's fairly easy to see how the HTML relates to the visible page. Sometimes it's hard, even for an expert, so see how they relate! Have a look – but try short, simple pages to begin with! When you have finished looking at the HTML, just close the Notepad window.

Script Debugger may not be present on your system, and is not for beginners. This is for Web page developers, to help them sort out any problems in the active and interactive routines in JavaScript or VBScript that can be written into pages.

Full Screen hides all the framing elements except for a skinny version of the Toolbar. If your screen resolution is 800 × 640 or less, then you may find this useful for viewing the more crowded Web pages – some page builders design for large screens, and they do not display well on smaller ones. Press [F11] or click **Restore** 🗗 to get back to normal.

The Favorites menu

This is where you store and organise links to selected sites. We'll get back to this shortly (page 79).

The Tools menu

This is a mixed bunch – about all these commands have in common is that they don't belong on any other menus!

Mail and News gives you several ways to start Outlook Express.

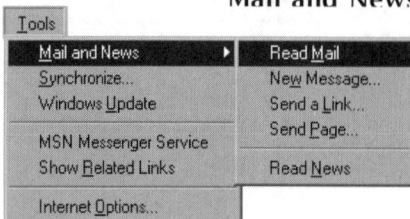

Synchronize... is used with offline working (page 84).

Windows Update is a link to the page at the

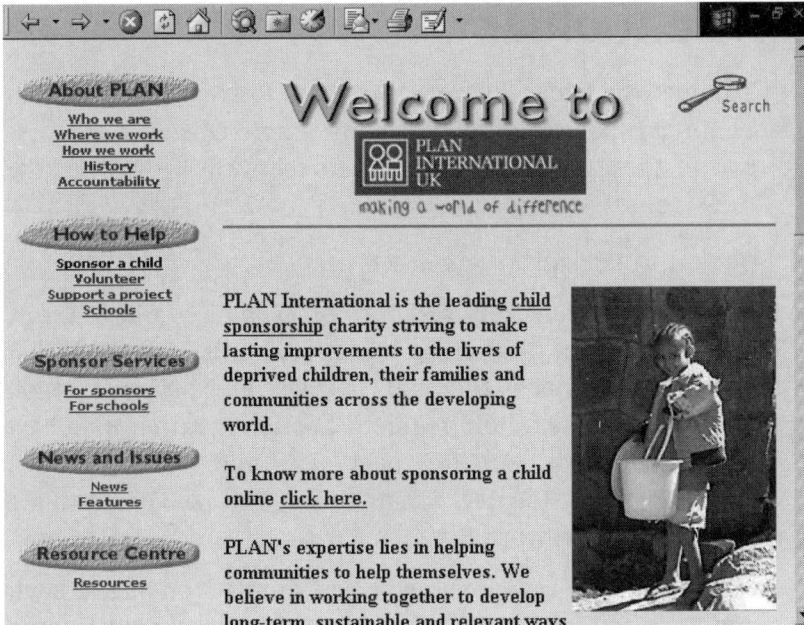

Figure 3.3   Full Screen view maximises the space for Web pages. The smaller your screen, the more you will appreciate this.

Microsoft Web site where you can get the add-ons and 'patches' (to cure bugs in the software) for your Windows system. It's a free service, and worth using regularly.

MSN Messenger Service can help you to keep in touch with people. One of its key services lets you know when your friends (at least, those who are registered with Messenger) are online. Visit MSN at **www.msn.co.uk** to find out more.

Show Related Links works if you are on a page which has implemented the 'related links' feature. It will lead you to more pages on the same topic.

Internet Options… is used to customise Internet Explorer to suit yourself (page 61).

The Help menu

This menu offers a number of routes into the Help system, which is used exactly as in other Windows applications.

The toolbar

You met the **Back, Forward, Stop** and **Refresh** tools back in Chapter 1 (page 6). Let's look a little more closely at the first two of these, before moving on to see what the rest of the tools do.

Back and Forward drop-down lists

The **Back** and **Forward** buttons each have a little arrow to the right, indicating a drop-down list. The **Back** list holds the pages that you were last at. You can click on one of these to jump directly back to it, rather than having to work back, one page at a time. Once you start going back, the pages that you have come back from are added to the **Forward** list.

As long as you are moving between simple Web pages, **Back** and **Forward**, and their lists, work well. If you visit framed pages (Figure 3.4) or sites that open new windows to display material, Internet Explorer often loses its way. If Back does not take you back to a site, use the History (page 88).

Home

This will take you back to the place you have designated as your home page – the page that Internet Explorer will connect to when you first go online. You can choose your home page in the options (page 62).

Search, Favorites and History

These open, or close if already open, their displays in the Explorer Bar.

- ◆   For the Search facility, see page 90.
- ◆   For the Favorites list, see page 79.
- ◆   For the History list, see page 88.

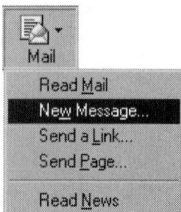

Mail

Clicking the **Mail** button opens a drop-down list with the same set of Mail and News options that you can get from the **Tools** menu.

Print

Print sends the current page to the printer, using the default settings. This won't always give the best results. Pages may print out better in *Landscape* mode (sideways), and if the page contains frames, you may well not get the part you want. For anything other than simple pages, you should work through the Print dialog box (page 92).

Edit

This is for people who are creating their own Web pages. Clicking the **Edit** button takes the page into the default editor. Clicking the arrow opens a drop-down list of the editors on your system.

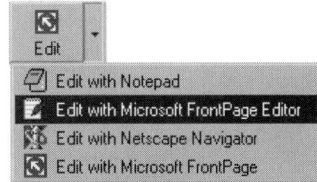

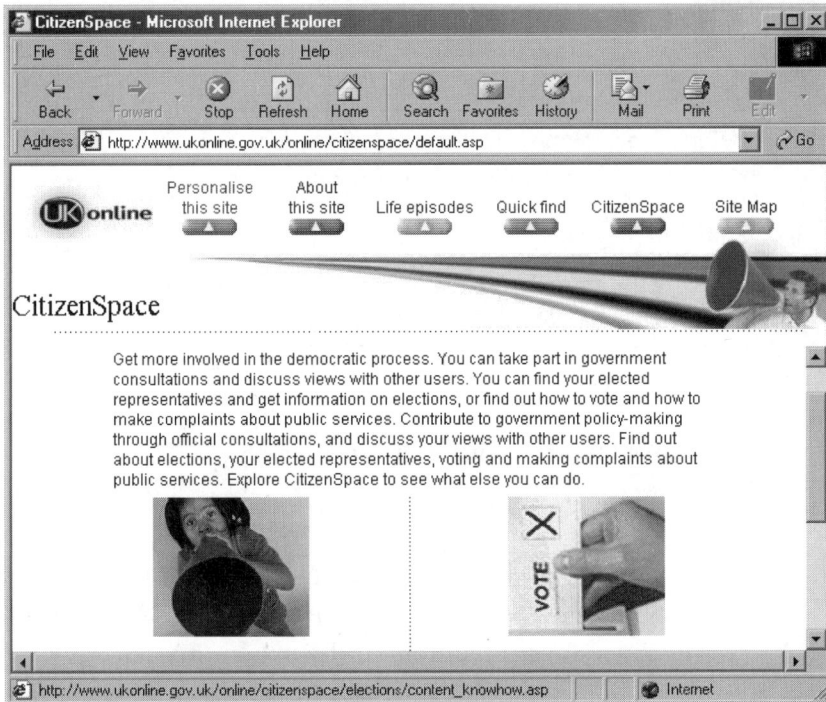

Edit with Notepad
Edit with Microsoft FrontPage Editor
Edit with Netscape Navigator
Edit with Microsoft FrontPage

Figure 3.4 An example of a Web page that uses frames. The top frame acts as a 'navigation bar' and remains visible until you move right out of the site. As you click on its buttons and links, the related material is displayed in the bottom frame. A framed page can be divided horizontally, vertically, or both. You will quite often meet pages with a thin frame at the top carrying the site's name and logo, and one down the left holding navigation links.

Customising the screen

Though Internet Explorer is very easy to use, it is also a very sophisticated piece of software with a great many optional settings. Some of these will not make much sense until you have been surfing for a while; others you may want to set at an early stage. Start by getting the screen to look the way that you want it.

Bars and toolbars

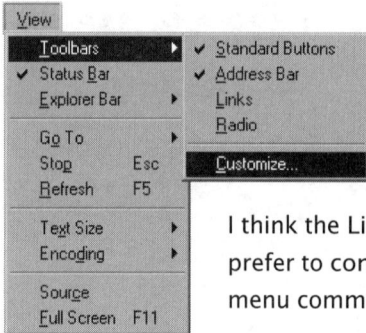

View	
Toolbars ▶	✓ Standard Buttons
✓ Status Bar	✓ Address Bar
Explorer Bar ▶	Links
	Radio
Go To ▶	
Stop Esc	Customize...
Refresh F5	
Text Size ▶	
Encoding ▶	
Source	
Full Screen F11	

Apart from the Menu bar, all of the bars can be turned off if you find you don't use them. Open the **View** menu, point to **Toolbars** and click on the bar's name to turn it on (✓) or off.

I think the Links and the Radio are both a waste of space. If you prefer to control the browser through the keyboard, using the menu commands, then the Standard Buttons can be turned off.

Customising the Toolbar

The contents and appearance of the Standard toolbar can be altered to suit yourself. You can add or remove buttons, set the size of the icons and choose whether to show text labels on all buttons, on a selected few, or on none.

Try it: Customise your toolbar

① Open the **View** menu, point to **Toolbars** and then click **Customize...**

② To add a button, select it from the left-hand pane and click Add -> . It will be added below (i.e. to the right) of the current selected item in the list on the right.

③ To change a button's position, use the Move Up (left) and Move Down (right) buttons.

④ To remove a button, select it and click <- Remove .

⑤ If you make a mess of the display – it can happen all too easily! – click Reset to restore the default selection.

⑥ Click the arrow to the right of the **Text options** slot and choose how to handle the labels.

⑦ Set the size of the icons as required in the **Icon options** drop-down list.

⑧ Click ☐ Close ☐ when you have done.

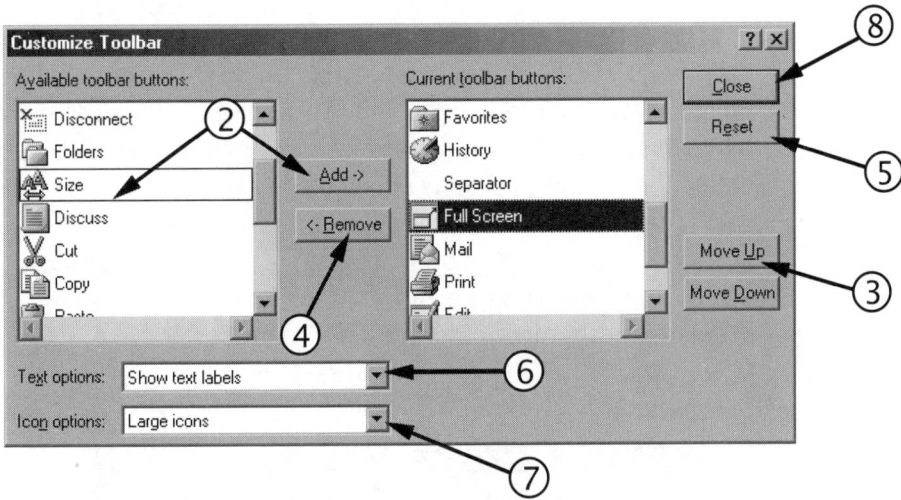

Internet Options

There are loads of these, and they should all be left at their default settings until you have spent enough time online to understand what they are about. For some of them, a couple of sessions will be enough for you to know what you want, but others should not be tackled lightly. In particular, you shouldn't touch anything that might reduce the security of your system until you are clear about the implications.

Have a look now at the scope of the options to see what you can set. They are all controlled through one multi-tab dialog box.

Try it: Explore the Internet Options

① Open the **Tools** menu.

② Select **Internet Options**...

③ Start to work through the tabs.

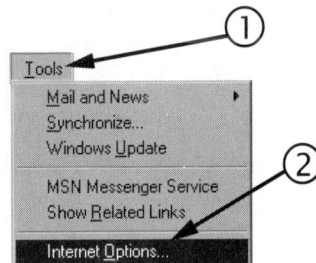

General options

The options on this tab are important, but safe to experiment with – the worst that can happen is that you might make a bit of a mess of your screen – and that is easily rectified.

Home page

The term 'home page' has two meanings. It can refer to the top page at a Web site, but in this context, it refers to the page that the browser connects to when you first go online (or when you click the **Home** button). Some people like to start their online sessions at one place – typically a site where they can get the latest news, weather or share prices, and which has a directory or search engine that they can use to track down information, or a chat room or games room where they regularly meet old (and new) friends.

◆ The default is a page at MSN (MicroSoft Network).

How long do you want to keep your History? Set the number of days here. For more on History see page 88

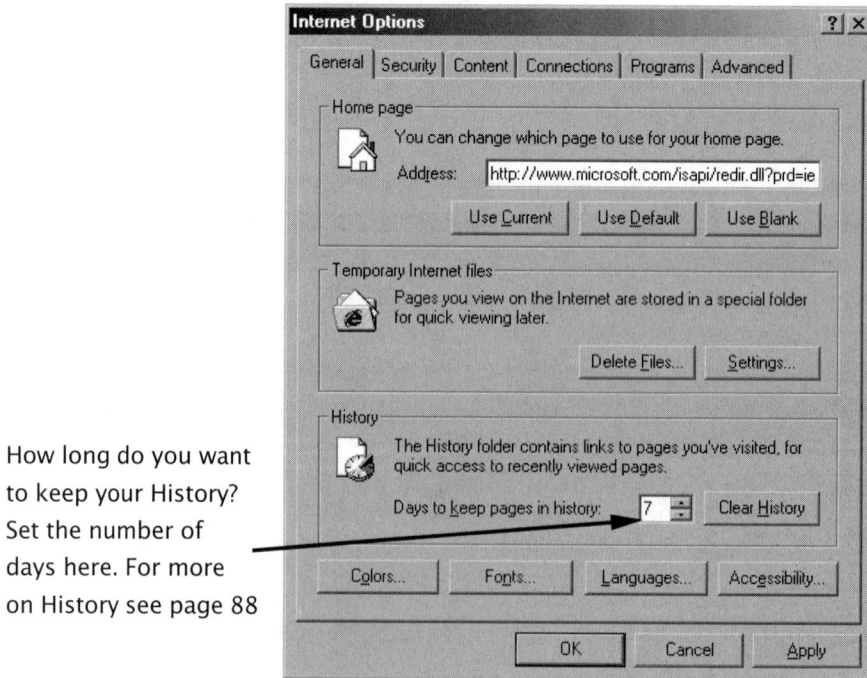

Figure 3.5 The General tab of the Internet Options dialog box. These settings can be changed at any time.

◆ If you find a site that you would prefer to use, then next time that you are there, open the Internet Options dialog box and click Use Current.

◆ If you like to start at different sites, depending upon what you want to do, then there is no point in wasting time going to a home page. Click Use Blank.

Temporary Internet files

We've noted that when you visit a page on the Web, the files that create the page must be downloaded on to your PC before they can be displayed. But what happens to those files when you move on to the next page? Rather than simply throw them away immediately, Internet Explorer stores them in a cache. If you return to that page, either during the same session or later, it will then use the files in the cache, which is much quicker than downloading them again. It also means that you can revisit pages offline, as you have their files, and read them at leisure without worrying about the telephone bill.

Cache = space for temporary storage of files

The **Settings** let you set the size of the cache to suit the way you surf and the amount of free space that you have on your hard disk. If you have plenty of space and you tend to go back to sites a lot – perhaps following up a succession of links from one start point, or perhaps because you like to revisit sites offline – then give yourself a big cache. If space is a problem, cut the cache right down.

You can also choose when Internet Explorer should return to the site to check that the cached files are still up-to-date. For home users, this is normally best set to Automatic, which tells Explorer to check on the cached files when you revisit a site that you last visited in an earlier session, but not to bother with those that you are returning to the same day. Business users, with a fast and permanently open connection to the Web, may find it more efficient to tell Explorer to revisit all cached pages at the start of each session, so that up-to-date files are there, ready and waiting, at your favourite sites.

Web page files tend to be small. A plain text page will rarely be more than 2Kb; one with a dozen smallish images might have a total of 50Kb. 10Mb of disk space should be enough to hold the files for 200 or more pages.

Tip: If you are ever short of disk space, click Delete Files...

Try it: Change the cache settings

① Click Settings....

② Choose when to check for newer versions of stored pages.

③ Drag the slider, or edit the numbers to set the amount of disk space.

④ Click OK.

Disk space is rarely a problem on newer PCs with hard disks of 10Gb or more

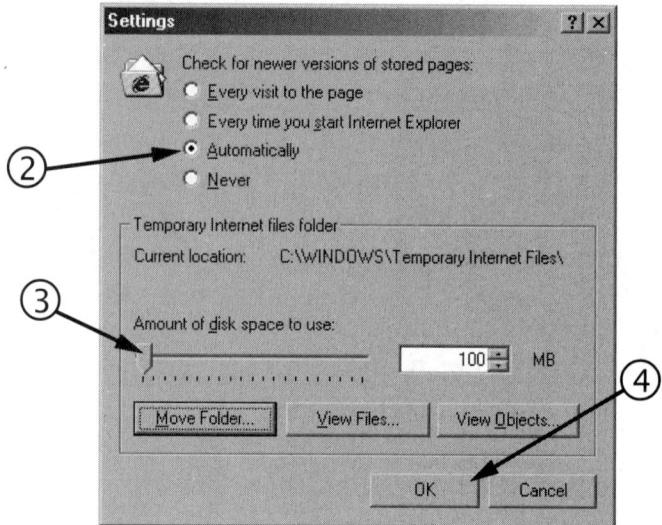

Settings ? ×

Check for newer versions of stored pages:

○ Every visit to the page

○ Every time you start Internet Explorer

● Automatically

○ Never

Temporary Internet files folder

Current location: C:\WINDOWS\Temporary Internet Files\

Amount of disk space to use:

100 ⬍ MB

Move Folder...   View Files...   View Objects...

OK   Cancel

Colours and fonts

When people are creating Web pages, they can choose what colours to use for the background, the main text, and the text that carries hyperlinks, and they can choose their fonts. They can – but they don't always bother. You can set the colours and fonts to use on those pages where they are not specified.

You can also insist that your own choices are used even where they have been set by the page builder, and you may want to do this in the interests of visibility. (Some people have very strange ideas of what makes a good-looking page!)

Getting the colours that give you a good, readable contrast is important for visibility. Changing the fonts will have less effect – the default settings are probably as clear as any.

Try it: Define colours and fonts

① Click [Colors...].

② At the **Colors** dialog box, click on a colour that you want to change.

③ Select a new colour from the palette and click [OK].

④ Click [OK] again at the **Colors** dialog box.

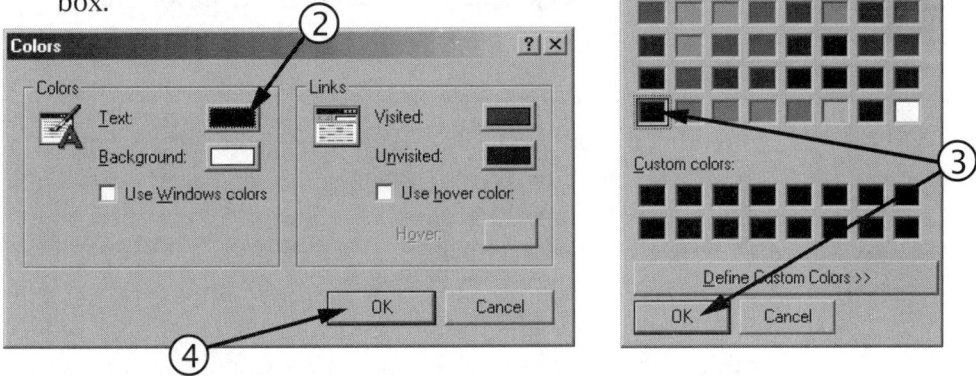

⑤ If you want to change the fonts, click [Fonts...] and pick fonts for the *Web page* and for *plain text*.

⑥ If you want to ignore the specified colours and/or fonts and use your own to display Web pages, click [Accessibility...] and turn on the **Formatting** options.

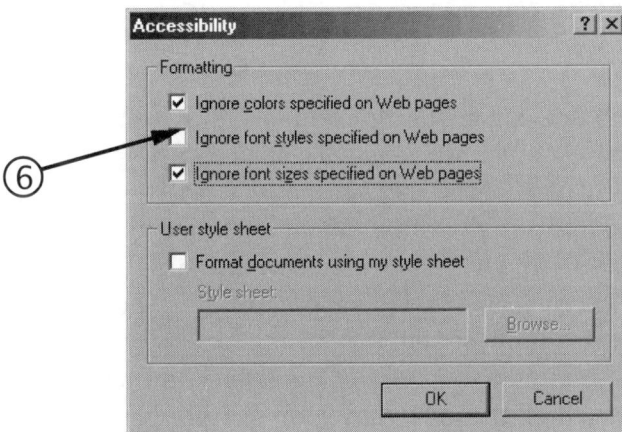

⑦ Click [OK].

Security options

The Security settings must be treated with care. If all Web pages were simply static displays of text and images, there would be no problem. But some are much more than this. They contain active and interactive elements, which on the one hand make pages more interesting and more responsive to visitors, and on the other hand offer opportunities for stupid or malicious people to make life difficult for others.

Active elements

The active and interactive elements are produced by chunks of code or small programs written in Web-enabled computer languages such as JavaScript, Java, Visual Basic or ActiveX. These may be merely decorative – adding a bit of movement – or an essential part of the page's functionality. Java is often used to create pop-up, drop-down or slide-out menus for navigating around a site. ActiveX controls are regularly used by online banks and retailers to ensure that your connection with them is secure.

The options on the Security tab let you control whether, and in what circumstances, these programs are allowed to run. If you disable them completely, you will find that you simply cannot use some very useful and perfectly safe Web sites. If you allow them to be run on any page, there is a real danger that you will one day find that a program has got into your hard disk and erased or corrupted files, or otherwise messed with your system.

Cookies

A cookie is a small file that is stored on your computer's hard disk by a Web site, and which can be read by that site. If the site offers a 'personalised page' service the cookie will hold the options and other details that you set, so that they are there for you when you return. Some sites use cookies to keep track of their visitors, recording when they visited and which pages they viewed; they may go further and try to use cookies to build a database of the habits and preferences of visitors, selling the information on to third parties.

You can choose whether or not to accept cookies. I don't like giving sites access to my hard disks, but if you don't accept cookies, it can create problems. It's not just that this stops you from having personalised pages at sites (something I can live without), there is also the fact that some sites will only let you download their pages if you accept their cookies. There is an in-between position, which is to ask for a notification before a cookie is set. This way you at least know who is writing to your hard disk, and can choose not to accept it from a site, but there are some really irritating sites that want to write, or rewrite, their cookies for every new page – sometimes for every image on a page – that you download.

Adjusting the settings

The default settings are designed to give a sensible balance between security and usability, setting different levels of restrictions depending upon whether a page is at a *Trusted site*, your *local intranet* (web running on a local area network and only open to people inside the organisation), the *Internet* in general or a *Restricted site*.

For each zone, you can set your own levels. I'd recommend that, until you are a much more experienced user, you leave things as they are except for the way that your browser handles cookies in the Internet zone. Even this is probably best left until you have had a couple of weeks online, and it is something that you may need to come back to.

Try it: Set the Security options

① Switch to the **Security** tab.

② Select the **Internet** zone and click Custom Level....

③ Scroll through the options until you reach **Cookies**.

④ If you are very security conscious and don't mind being shut out from some sites, select *Disable*. If you like to know what's happening to your PC and are prepared to respond every time a cookie wants to come in, select *Prompt*. If you think I'm just paranoid and you want easy browsing, select *Enable*.

⑤ Click OK.

Internet Options ? | X |

General | Security | Content | Connections | Programs | Advanced |

Select a Web content zone to specify its security settings.

① →

Internet   Local intranet   Trusted sites   Restricted sites

Internet
This zone contains all Web sites you haven't placed in other zones

Sites...

Click **Sites**..., and type in the site's address to add it to your Trusted or Restricted site lists

Security level for this zone

Custom
Custom settings.
- To change the settings, click Custom Level.
- To use the recommended settings, click Default Level.

② →

Custom Level...   Default Level

You can revert to the default level for a zone at any time – just select it and click this button

OK   Cancel   Apply

Security Settings ? | X |

Settings:

③ →

Cookies
   Allow cookies that are stored on your computer
     O   Disable
     O   Enable
     ⊙   Prompt
   Allow per-session cookies (not stored)
     O   Disable
     ⊙   Enable
     O   Prompt
Downloads
   File download
     O   Disable
     ⊙   Enable
   Font download

④ →

Some sites erase their cookies at the end of a session

Reset custom settings

Reset to: Medium   Reset

If you experiment with the settings and need to get back to how they were, select the level from the **Reset to** list

⑤ →

OK   Cancel

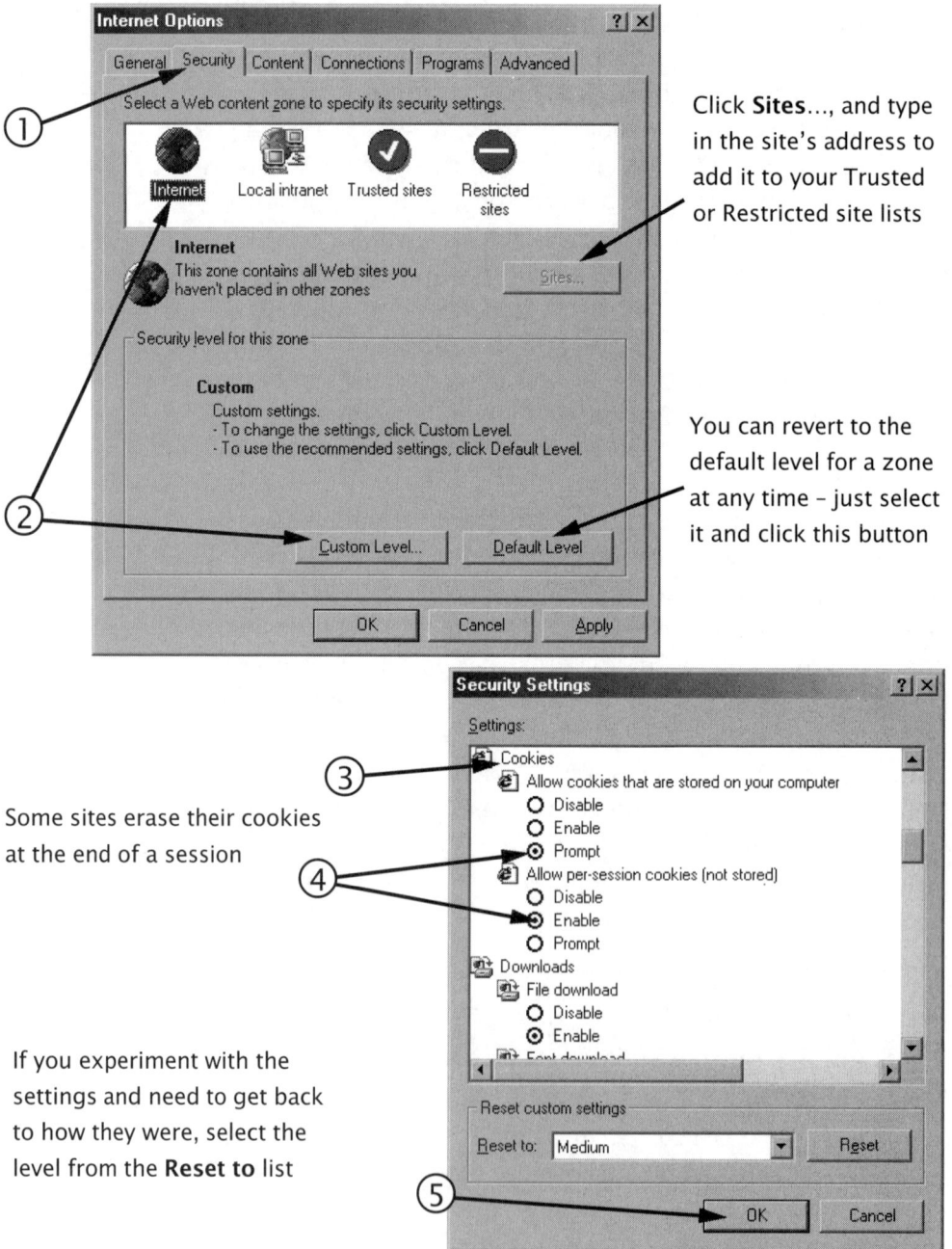

Figure 3.6 The Security settings should be tackled only when you have been surfing long enough to have a good idea of how you want to work and what problems might arise.

Content options

This tab is primarily here for those people whose children (or grandchildren) use the PC to access the Internet. It allows you to limit the sites that they can visit. This is controlled through the Content Advisor.

Content Advisor

The system is based on *rated sites*. There are a number of organisations, of which the main one is RSACi – Recreational Standards Advisory Council (Internet), which rate sites on the levels of language, nudity, sex and violence. It's then up to you to decide what level of each of these is acceptable for the kids to see.

While this makes surfing much safer, it really does limit what is accessible, for the simple fact that many sites do not have an RASC rating. This does not mean that they are porn sites, just that they don't know or care about RASC, or they haven't got round to applying for a rating, or that RASC has not yet managed to rate them. Remember that there are literally thousands of new sites and millions of new pages coming online every week. It simply is not possible to keep any rating system up to date.

Internet Explorer recognises this and has options to deal with unrated sites – you can either open them up completely or control access through a password. There's another, and more important, password and that's the one that turns the whole system on and off.

AutoComplete

I'm not quite sure why this is in the same tab as Content Advisor, as it's a very different aspect of the system. Auto-Complete tries to do your typing for you. It watches when you type a Web address or enter details into forms, and tries to complete it for you, offering up addresses or words that you have typed before and which start with the same letters. It's quite a handy feature, especially with addresses.

The rest of the options on this tab can be safely left to the system. You have to be really keen to bother with these!

Try it: Set your Content options

① Switch to the **Content** tab.

② In the **Content Advisor** area, click Enable...

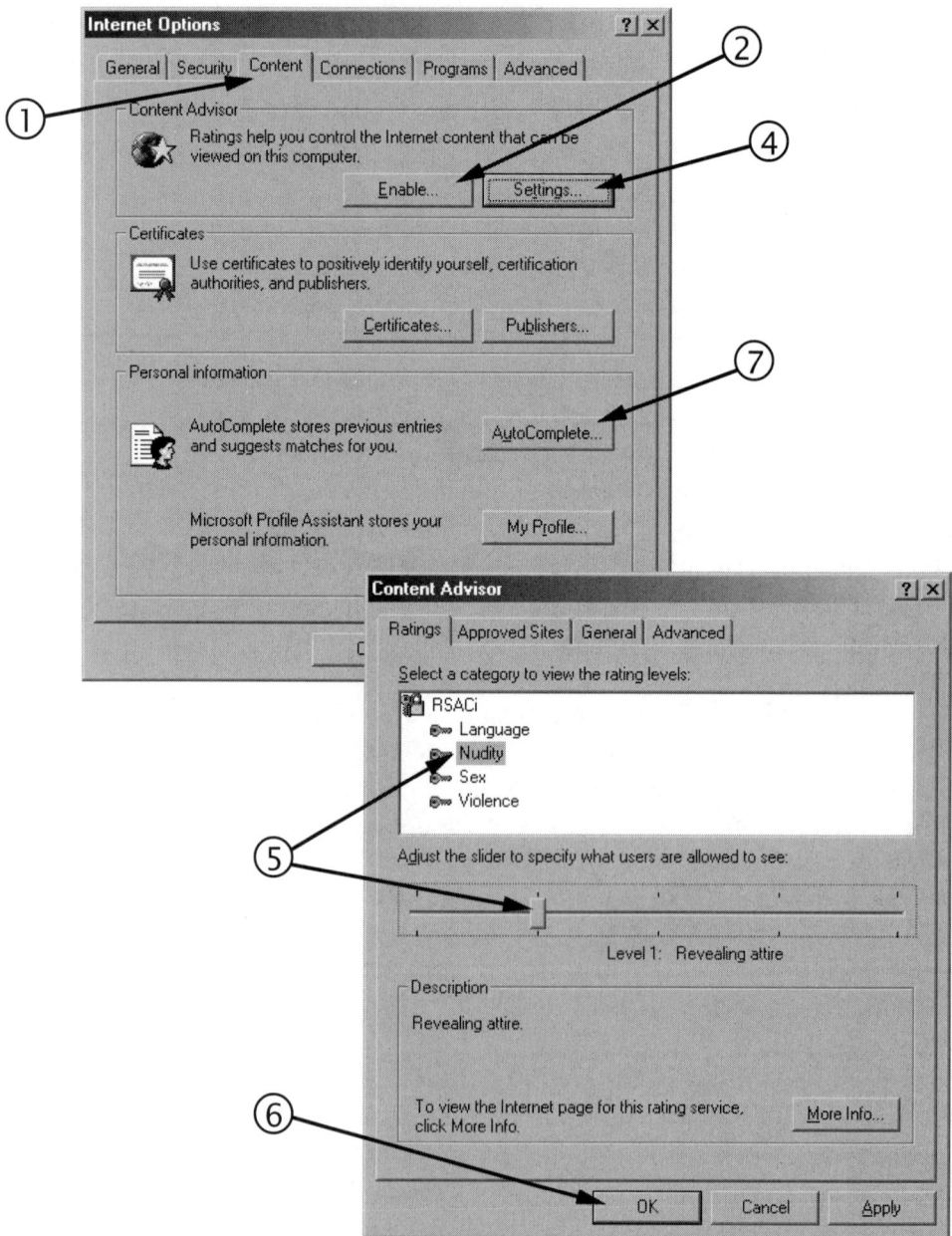

Figure 3.7   The Content Advisor lets you limit what the kids can see.

③ Enter a password. Make sure it is one that you can remember. If you forget it, you'll have to reinstall Internet Explorer if you ever want to change the Content Advisor!

④ Click [Settings...].

⑤ Select each category in turn and adjust the slider to set the limits.

⑥ Click [OK].

⑦ Back at the **Content** tab, click [AutoComplete...].

⑧ Turn on **AutoComplete** where you want it. It's certainly useful for **Web addresses** and the other options may prove to be handy.

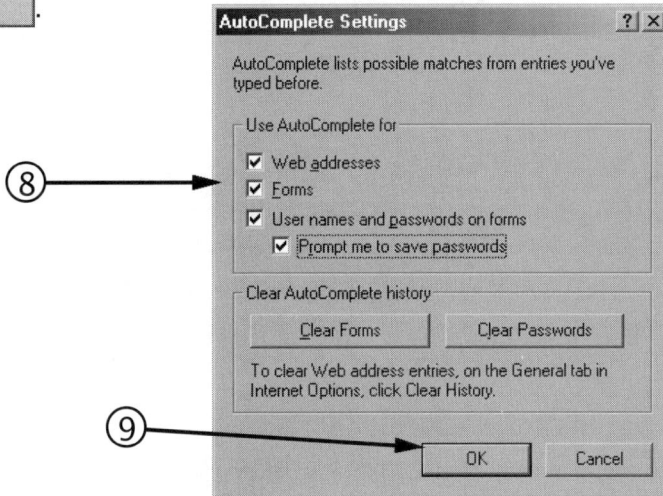

⑨ Click [OK].

AutoComplete Settings ? ×

AutoComplete lists possible matches from entries you've typed before.

Use AutoComplete for

☑ Web addresses
☑ Forms
☑ User names and passwords on forms
   ☑ Prompt me to save passwords

Clear AutoComplete history

[Clear Forms]   [Clear Passwords]

To clear Web address entries, on the General tab in Internet Options, click Clear History.

[OK]   [Cancel]

Connections options

Unless you are testing a new Internet Service Provider, you are unlikely to have more than one connection, so the only option that you need to set on the **Connections** tab is how Internet Explorer should manage the dial-up connection.

You can set it to dial-up for you whenever a connection is needed – i.e. when you type or click on the address of a Web page that is not stored in your temporary Internet files folder, or when you start to send an e-mail. There are two versions of this option: one for those working on a local area network, the other for single computer users.

The alternative is *Never dial a connection*, which leaves it up to you to start the dial-up connection when you want to go online.

Automatic dialling will normally save a bit of bother but can occasionally be a nuisance. There will be odd times that it sets off when you don't want it to, but it's simple enough to cancel.

Try it: Set the Connections options

① Switch to the **Connections** tab.

② If you have more than one connection and want to change the default, select it and click ⌊ S̲et Default ⌋.

③ Select a **dial** option.

④ Click ⌊ OK ⌋.

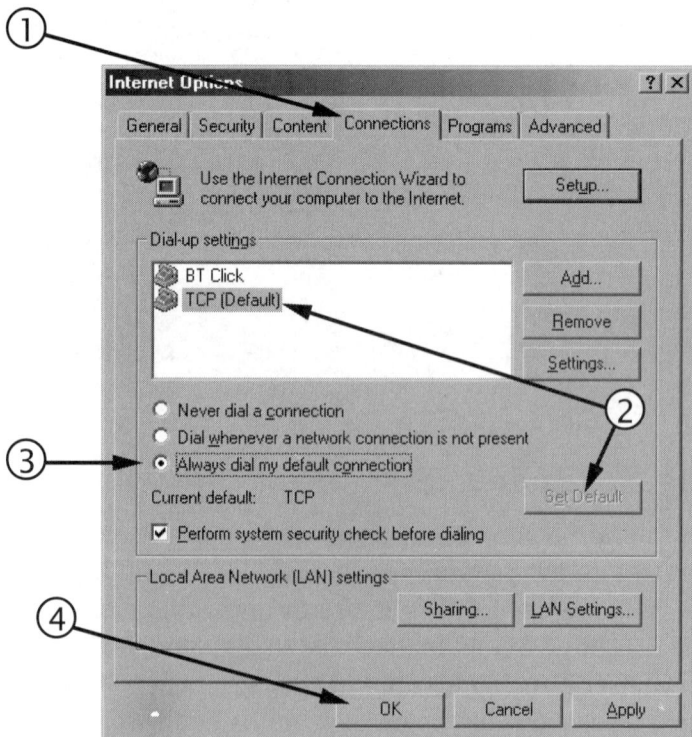

Figure 3.8 You can set up a new dial-up connection from the Connections tab – click **Setup...** to start the Wizard – but it is normally far easier to use the provider's installation disk!

Programs options

While working online in the browser, you may want to use another Internet program – the most obvious example being your e-mail software to send a message. Internet Explorer has toolbar buttons and menu commands that you can use to call up related programs, and it is on this tab that you define which applications to use. If you have more than one suitable application of each type, they will be included in the drop-down list. Check them out, and select the one you want to use as the default under each heading.

Try it: Choose your Internet programs

① Switch to the **Programs** tab.

② For each type, click the arrow to open the drop-down list and select a program.

③ Click [OK].

If you have been experimenting with different home and search pages and want to restore the default selections, click here

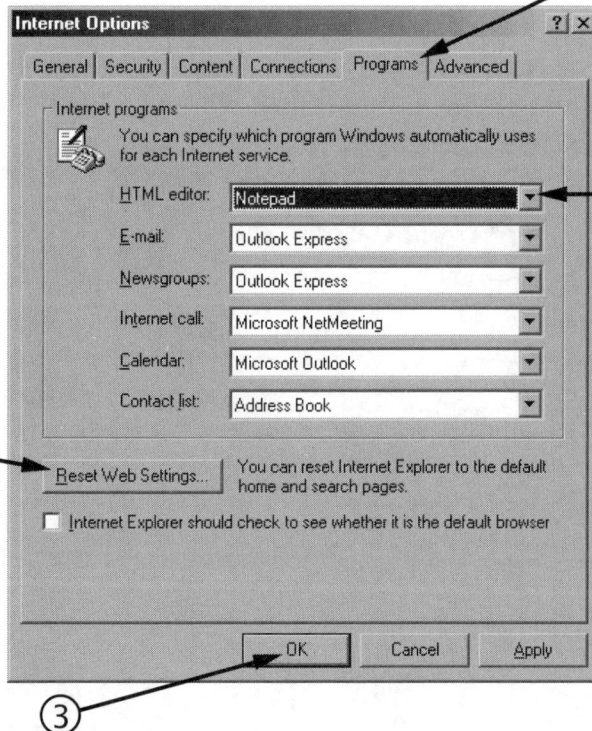

Figure 3.9   How much choice you have on the Programs tab depends upon what applications you have on your PC.

Advanced options

There are over 50 options here! They can, of course, all be left at their defaults, and I would recommend that you wait until you have been browsing for a few weeks before you touch any of them – with two exceptions. If you have your screen set to high visibility, you should turn on the Accessibility options at an early stage.

When you feel ready, there are two sets of options that you might like to adjust. The *Browsing* options will tweak the way that Internet Explorer works. Experiment with these – there is nothing that can do any harm.

The *Multimedia* options control the display of sounds and graphics. You can choose whether or not to play sounds, animations or videos – all of which are purely decorative but add notably to downloading time. Turning these off, especially video, will result in faster browsing. You can also opt not to show images, which will also speed up your browsing but will make it impossible to view those many sites that use images to hold their links.

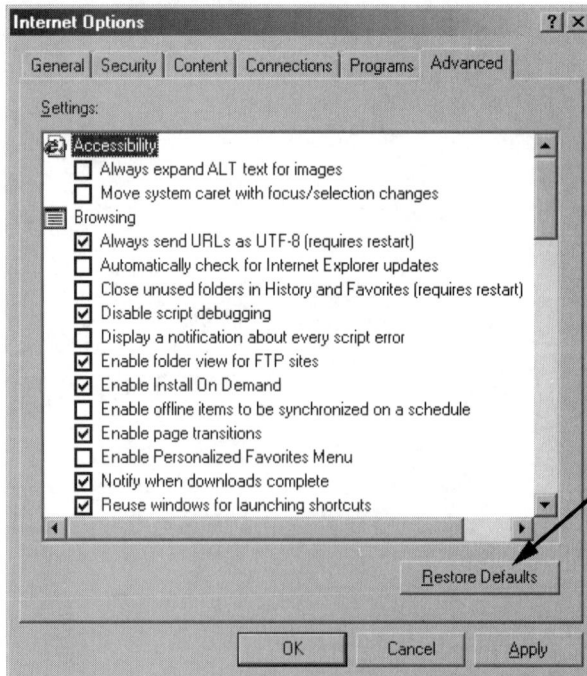

If your experiments with the settings produce undesirable results, restore the defaults

Addresses and the Address bar

You saw in Chapter 1 how you could go to a site by typing its URL in the Address bar. Let's have a closer look at this.

URL = Uniform Resource Locator, the address of a file on the Internet

The first thing to note is that you rarely need to type an address twice. Internet Explorer remembers every URL that goes into the Address bar. Obviously, this includes all those that you enter; less obviously, it also includes URLs that are generated by sites as you move around them. In practice, this means that if you want to return to any site – or to a specific page within a site – you do not need to retype the URL.

AutoComplete

The AutoComplete facility is the first effort-saver. When you start to type an URL into the Address bar, Internet Explorer will search back through past URLs and offer you those that start with the same letters. Its 'best guess' will be popped into the Address bar to complete the URL, and this may change as you type more letters.

Try it: Use AutoComplete

① Start to type an address that you have typed before.
② Accept the completed address in the Address bar or select it from the drop-down list.
③ Press [Enter] or click 🔁Go .

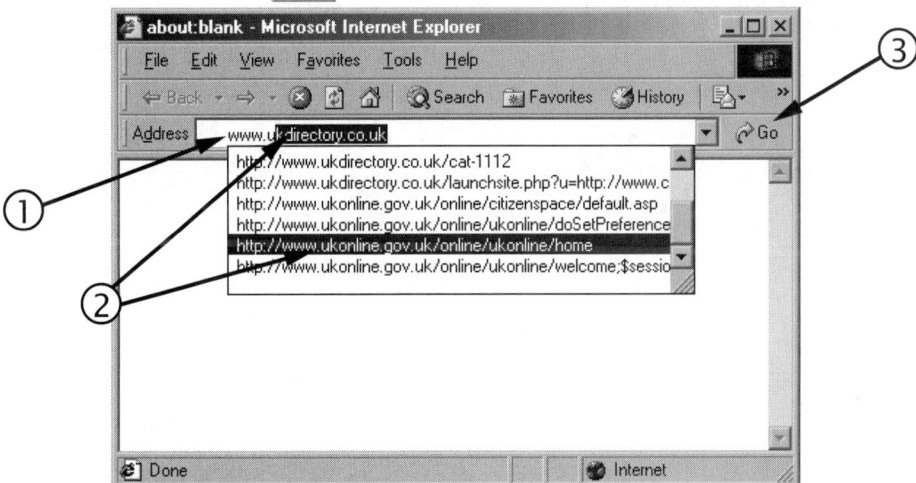

Selecting from the Address bar list

This is even easier to use, but slightly more limited than AutoComplete. The addresses that you type – but not those generated within sites – are stored close at hand in a list that drops down from the Address bar. You can select one from here by simply opening the list.

Try it: Reuse a typed address

① Click the down arrow on the right of the Address bar.

② Scroll through the list to find the address.

③ Click on the one you want.

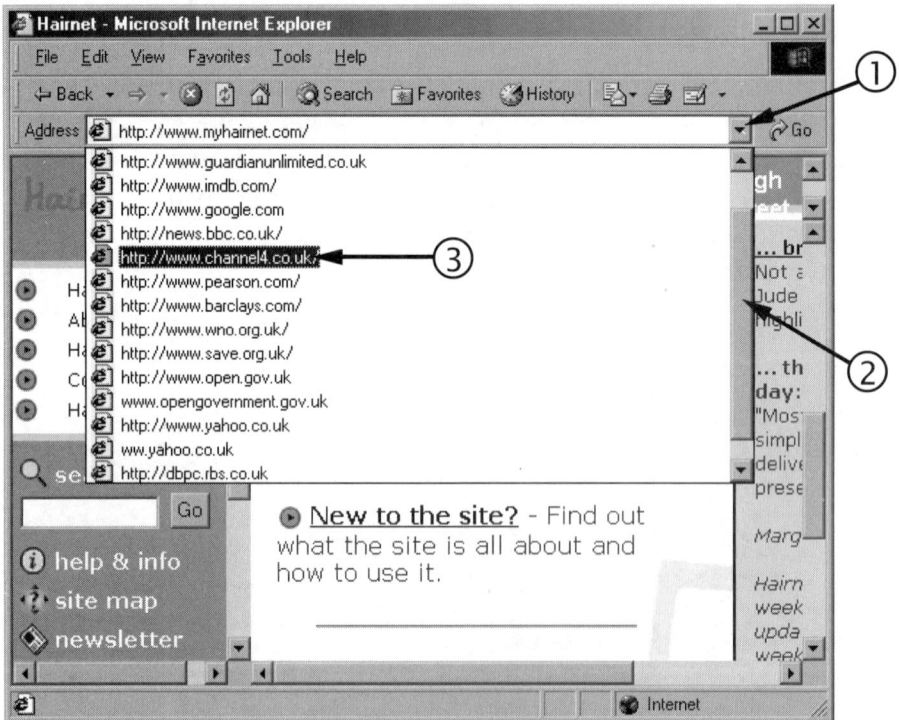

Address lists and History

The addresss that you can recall into the Address bar are part of the History facility. They are discarded when they reach their time limit or when you click Clear History on the General tab of the Internet Options dialog box.

Guessing addresses

To type an address, you have to know it, but how do you find out the address of a site?

You will see URLs all the time when you are browsing, but as these will normally be hyperlinked, you can follow them by clicking and so don't need to worry about the actual address. The addresses that you will type in are normally those that you meet offline.

You will find URLs in papers, books and magazines, on adverting hoardings, at the end of TV or radio programmes, on letterheads and brochures, and in many other places.

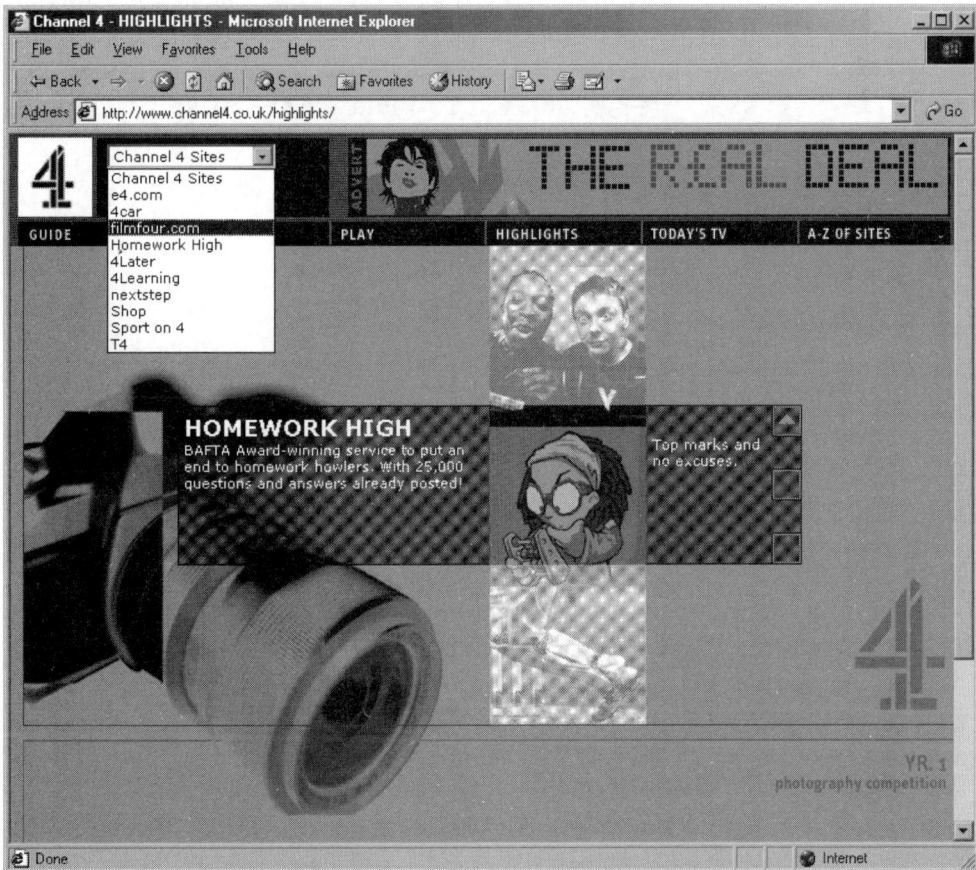

Figure 3.10 Some URLs can be guessed. The most likely URL for Channel 4 was the right one – **www.channel4.co.uk**.

If an organisation exists in the real world, as a High Street store, trading business, public service, charity or whatever, you can often guess its URL. This is especially true of larger businesses. The pattern is:

www.organisationname.type.country

www indicates that the URL is of a Web site. This is only a convention, not a necessity, but it is normally worth adding.

The *organisationname* will often be its actual name, where this is a single word or set of initials, e.g. Tesco, IBM or BBC, or a 'Web-suitable' version of it, where the name has several words. The problem is that URLs may not contain spaces, and ways around this include replacing the spaces with dots or hyphens, or simply removing them and closing up the gaps, e.g. 'The Times' becomes *thetimes*, 'Private Eye' hyphenates to *private-eye*, and even 'Fortnum and Mason' drops its spaces to become *fortnumandmason*.

For more on Internet addresses, look back to page 42

The *type* reflects the nature of the organisation:

◆   for a business, it will be *com* (if it is American or international) or otherwise *co*.

◆   for a central or local government agency, it will be *gov*.

◆   for a charity or other not-for-profit organisation, it will be *org*.

The *country* is only present if the organisation is not American or international. In the UK, *uk* is normally used – *gb* is possible, but scarely ever used.

Some examples of guessable URLs:

Channel 4	www.channel4.com *or*
	www.channel4.co.uk
BBC	www.bbc.org.uk
Daily Mail	www.dailymail.co.uk
The Guardian	www.guardian.co.uk
National Trust	www.nationaltrust.co.uk
Sainsbury's	www.sainsbury.co.uk
Welsh National Opera	www.wno.org.uk

Favorites

Addresses are a pain to type. One mistake and you either don't get there at all, or you find yourself at a totally unexpected site. (Try **www.microsfot.com** some time.) Anything which cuts down address typing is a good thing.

Favorites are one way of being able to return to a site without having to retype its address. A favorite is the address of a site, or page, captured directly off the page and stored in an easily-managed list. To return to a favorite, you simply click on it in the **Favorites** menu.

You can store your favorites in one simple list, but this can soon get unwieldy. If there are more than about twenty items, the menu takes up an inordinate amount of screen space and it can take a while to find the favorite you want. The solution is to organise your favorites into folders, which then become submenus in the **Favorites** system.

Favorites can be accessed through the Favorites menu or through the Explorer bar. We'll start with the menu approach.

Try it: Add a favorite

① Find a good site!

② Open the **Favorites** menu and click **Add to Favorites**...

③ The **Add Favorites** dialog box will open. Internet Explorer will have derived the **Name** from the page. If you are happy with the name and want to add the link to the main **Favorites** list, click [OK].

Otherwise

④ Edit the suggested name, or type a new one – you want something that will work well as a menu item, so aim for short but meaningful.

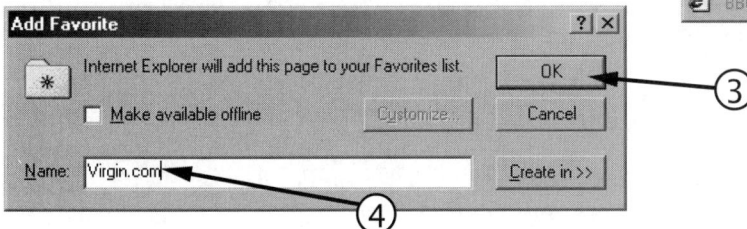

You can also add a page to your Favorites by right-clicking on it and selecting **Add to Favorites**...

⑤   To store it in a folder, click [Create in >>] to expand the dialog box.

⑥   In the enlarged dialog box, if there is a suitable folder, click on it.

⑦   If not, click [New Folder...].

⑧   Type a name for the folder and click [OK].

⑨   Back at the Add Favorite dialog box, click [OK].

We'll get back to the **Make available offline** option on page 84

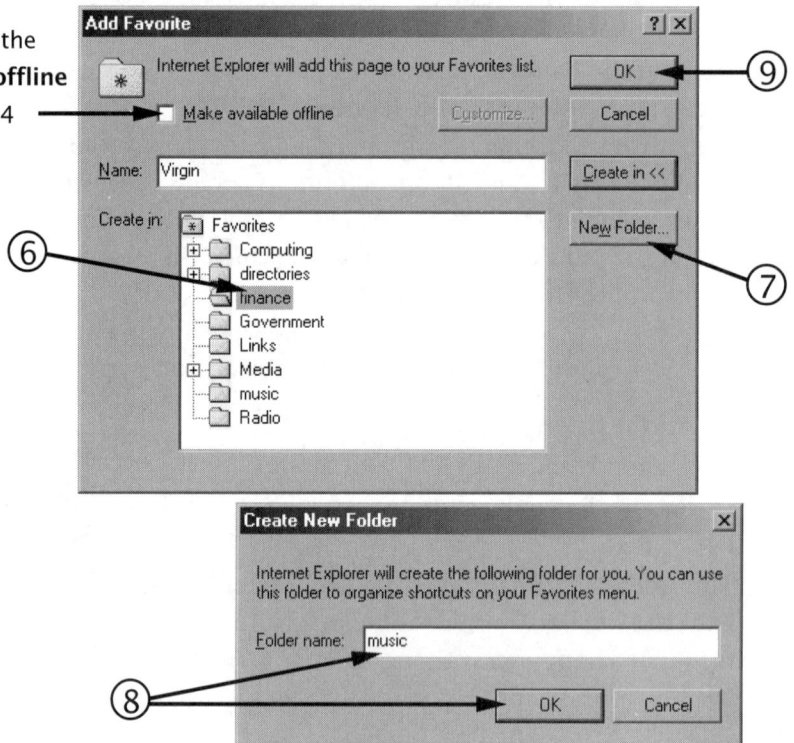

Add Favorite   ? X

Internet Explorer will add this page to your Favorites list.   [OK] ← ⑨

☐ Make available offline   [Customize...]   [Cancel]

Name: Virgin   [Create in <<]

Create in: [*] Favorites   [New Folder...]
⑥ →   ⊞ Computing
              ⊞ directories
                 finance
                 Government
                 Links
              ⊞ Media
                 music
                 Radio   ⑦

Create New Folder   X

Internet Explorer will create the following folder for you. You can use this folder to organize shortcuts on your Favorites menu.

Folder name: music

⑧ →   [OK]   [Cancel]

Returning to Favorites

Even if you haven't yet added a Favorite of your own, there will still be some – mainly to Microsoft's sites. To return to a Favorite site, just pick it from the menu.

Try it: Use the Favorites

①   Open the **Favorites** menu.

②   If the Favorite is in a folder, open its submenu.

③   Click on the one you want.

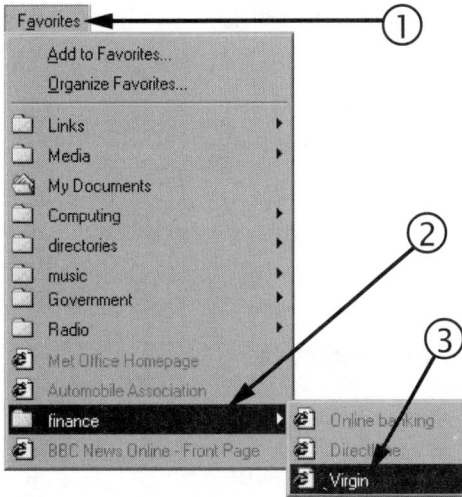

Organising Favorites

When your Favorites list gets so long that you can't find things quickly, it's time to organise it by moving related items into suitable folders. And if you don't have suitable folders, you can soon create them.

Try it: Create a new Favorites folder

① Click **Organize Favorites** on the **Favorites** menu.

② Click **Create Folder**.

③ A new folder will appear. Give it a suitable name.

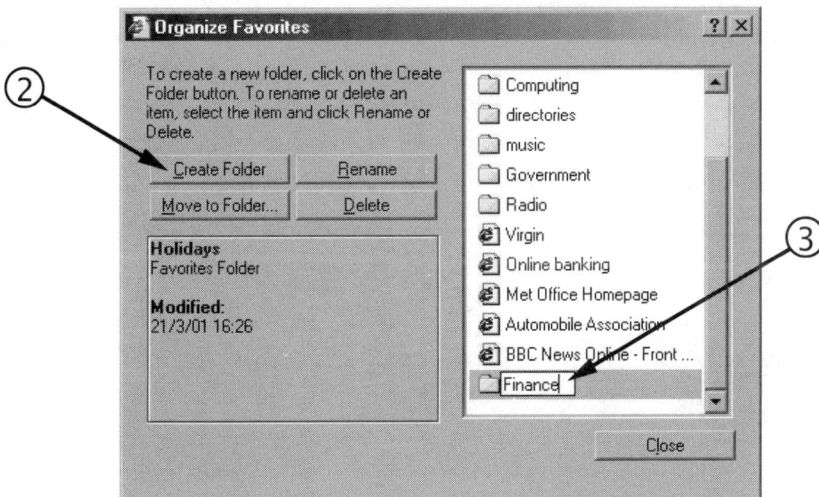

Try it: Move favorites into folders

① Drag the link on to the folder and drop it in. If you pause over the folder first, it will open and you can then place the link exactly where you want it in the list.

Or

② Select the link and click **Move to Folder**.

③ Select the folder from the list and click ⬚ OK ⬚.

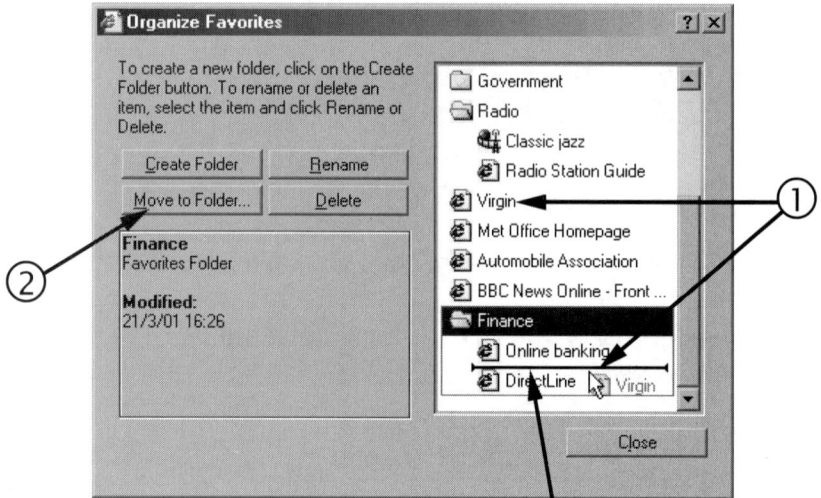

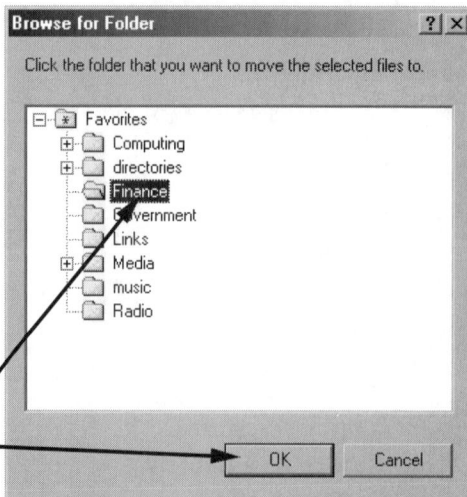

You can move favorites into a new position within the same, or a different, folder – as you drag the link up or down the screen, a thick black line will appear to show you where the link will be inserted when you release the mouse button

Favorites in the Explorer bar

If you want to visit several favorites during a session, you may find it worthwhile to open the Favorites in the Explorer bar. (It is rarely worth it for a single use, as the Explorer bar takes up useful screen space.)

Try it: Use the Favorites in the Explorer bar

① Click ⊡.

② To return to a favorite, open its folder (if necessary) and click on the link.

③ To add a new favorite, click ⊞Add... then continue as on page 79.

④ To organise your favorites, click ⊟ Organize... and drag them into their new folders (see below).

⑤ When you have finished with the Favorites, click ⊠.

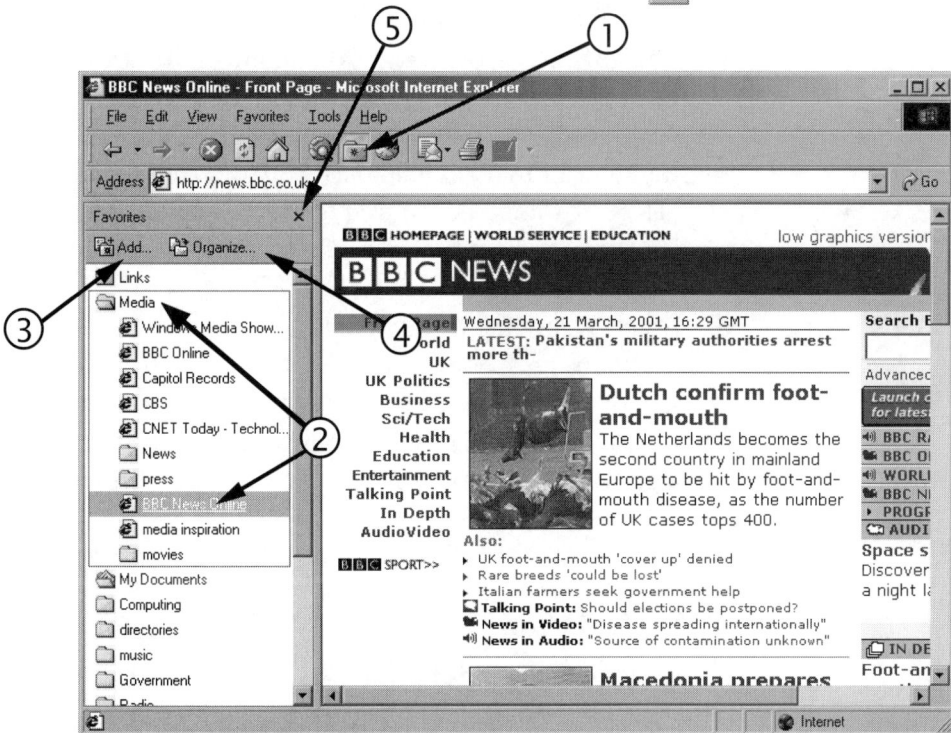

Figure 3.11 You can organise favorites in the Explorer bar – just drag them to a new place. If you need a new folder, right-click anywhere in the bar and select **New Folder**.

Offline viewing

It often takes less time to download a page – especially if it is mainly text – than it does to read it. If there are sites that you want to read regularly, you can get Explorer to download their top pages – and the ones linked to them, if you like – in one continuous operation. You can then read the pages offline, reconnecting if there are links that you want to follow up.

Offline viewing is set up through Favorites, using the **Make available offline** option. Pages are downloaded using the **Synchronize** command.

Try it: Make a site available offline

① When adding a favorite, tick the **Make available offline** checkbox, and click **Customize**... to set the options.

Or

② Right-click on a favorite (in the Explorer bar or the menu), select **Make available offline** and click on **Customize**...

◆ The Offline Favorite Wizard will guide you through the options – respond to the prompts, clicking **Next** after each stage and **Finish** at the end.

③ If you want to download pages linked from the top page, select **Yes** and set the number of levels. (You can come back and change this later if experience shows that you have asked for too many, or too few, pages.)

④ If you get online through a dial-up connection – as most home users do – then it is best to download the pages when you use the **Tools – Synchronize** command.

⑤ If you want the pages to be downloaded automatically at a set time regularly, select or create a schedule.

⑥ To create a schedule, set the time and frequency.

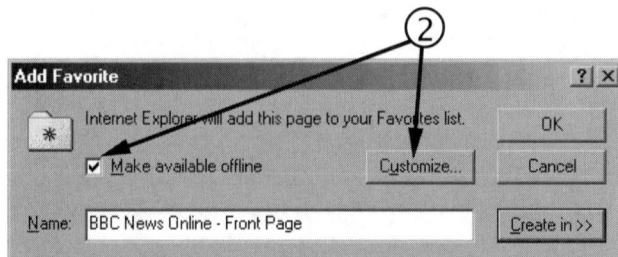

Offline Favorite Wizard

Set up the following page:

Name: BBC News Online - Front Page

URL: http://news.bbc.co.uk/

If this favorite contains links to other pages, would you like to make those pages available offline too?

○ No
● Yes

Download pages [2] links deep from this page

Note: If you have limited hard disk space or you want to reduce synchronization time, it's a good idea to limit the number of linked pages you store.

< Back   Next >   Cancel

Offline Favorite Wizard

You can synchronize this page any time you are connected by choosing Synchronize from the Tools menu. You can also set up a schedule to synchronize this page automatically.

How would you like to synchronize this page?

○ Only when I choose Synchronize from the Tools menu

● I would like to create a new schedule

○ Using this existing schedule:

Guardian Update

< Back   Next >   Cancel

When would you like to synchronize this page?

Every [1] days at [12:00]

Name: My Scheduled Update

☐ If my computer is not connected when this scheduled synchronization begins, automatically connect for me

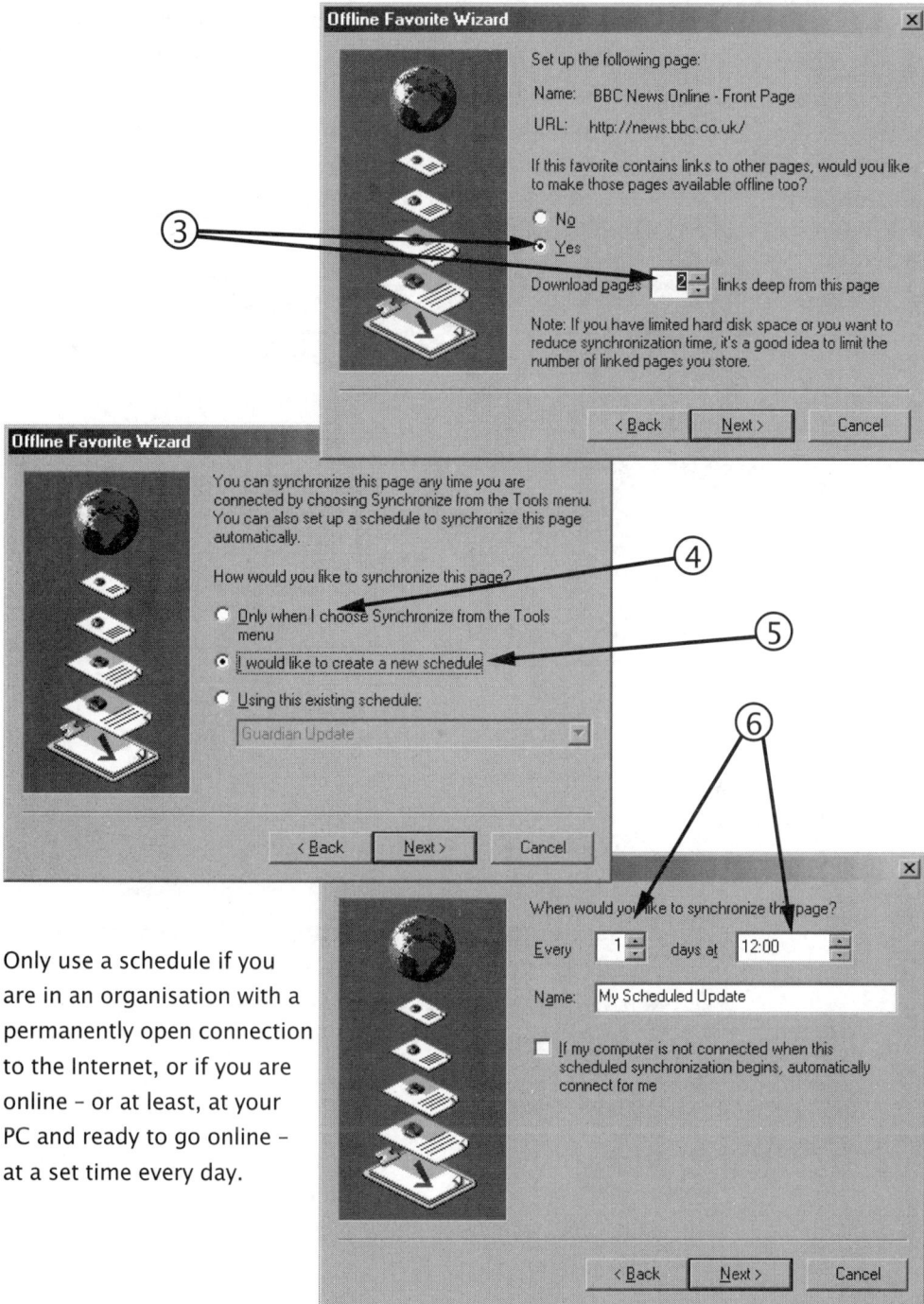

Only use a schedule if you are in an organisation with a permanently open connection to the Internet, or if you are online – or at least, at your PC and ready to go online – at a set time every day.

< Back   Next >   Cancel

Figure 3.12 Working through the Offline Favorite Wizard.

⑦ If you have to login to the site, with a user name and password, then write these into the Wizard so that they are entered for you when you synchronise.

⑧ Click **Finish** to close the Wizard, then complete the favorite as usual.

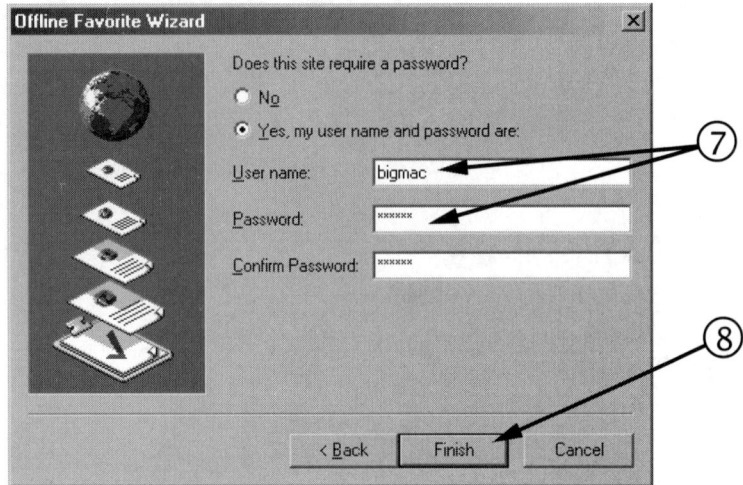

Try it: Synchronise your offline favorites

① Go online.

② Open the **Tools** menu and select **Synchronize**.

③ Tick the items that you want to synchronise.

④ If you want to adjust any settings, click Setup...

⑤ At the **Synchronization Settings** dialog box, select the schedule to change and click **Edit**.

⑥ Set the new times or frequency, or other settings as required and click OK .

⑦ Back at the **Items to Synchronize** dialog box, click Synchronize .

It can take some time for pages to download, so you might want to get on with your e-mail or other work while you wait – browsing elsewhere isn't a very good idea as it will slow the download further.

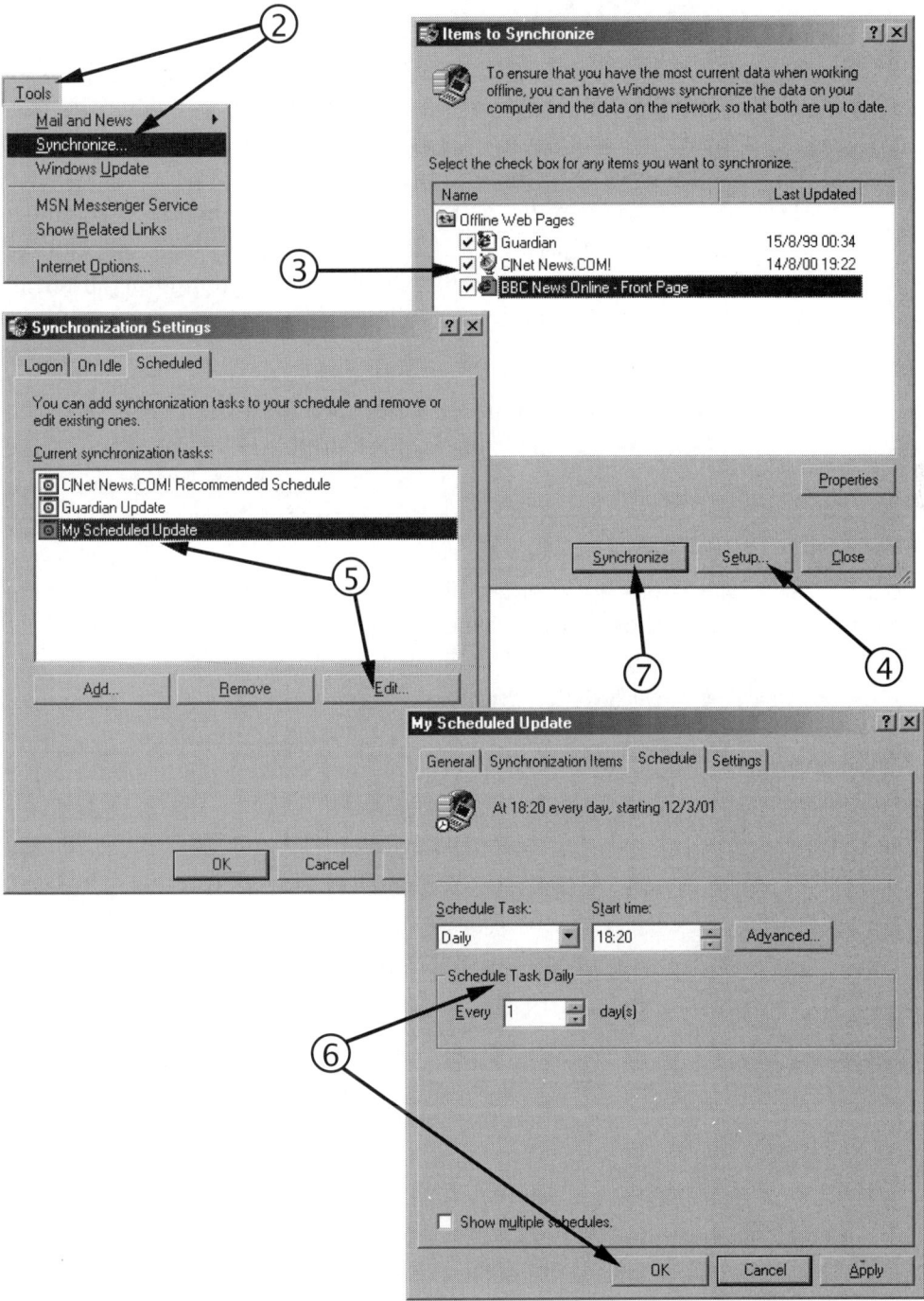

Figure 3.13 Synchronising offline favorites.

History

As you browse, each page is recorded in the History list as an Internet shortcut – i.e. a link to the page. Clicking the **History** button opens the History list in the Explorer bar. Click a link from here to go to the page.

If you are online at the time, Internet Explorer will connect to the page. If you are offline, it will display the page if all the necessary files are still available in the temporary Internet files folder, otherwise it will ask you to connect.

The list can be viewed in four ways:

♦ **By Date** groups the links into folders by date and then by site. This is useful if you don't know the name of the site – and you may well not know where a page was if you reached it through a hyperlink – but can recall when you were last there.

♦ **By Site** groups the links into folders by site, arranging these into alphabetical order. This is probably the most convenient view most of the time.

♦ **By Most Visited** lists individual page links in the order that you visit them most. If there are search engines or directories that you regularly use as start points for browsing sessions, they will be up at the top of the list.

♦ **By Order Visited Today** lists the individual pages in simple time order. Use this view to backtrack past the links that are stored in the drop-down list of the **Back** button.

The History list also tracks some of the other files on your PC. The list includes My Computer, as a 'site' folder, and files of types that can be opened from within IE or by linked applications.

Try it: Use the History list

① Click on the **History** button in the toolbar.

② In the Explorer bar, open the **View** menu and select the view required.

③ Click on the name to open the day and the site folders (if relevant in that view).

④ Click on a link.

⑤ To close a folder, click on its name.

⑥ Click ▣ to close the Explorer bar when you have done.

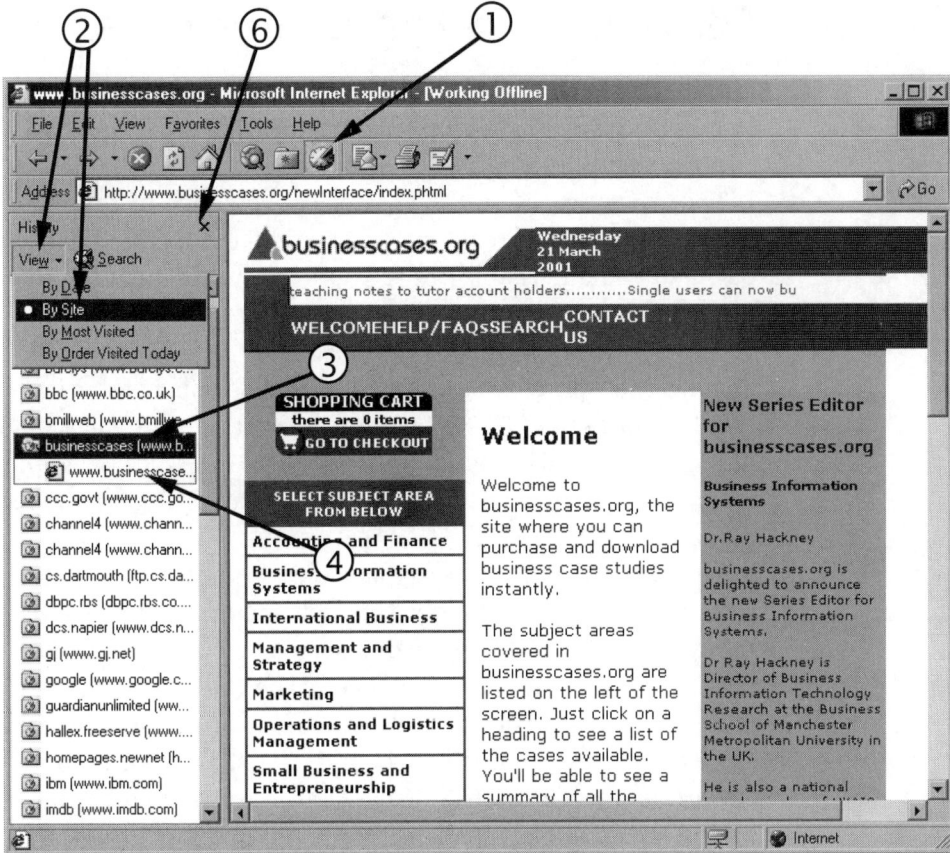

Figure 3.14 Working offline with the History list.

Swamped by History?

If you visit a lot of sites during your online sessions, and/or have set the number of days to keep the History links to a high value, then your History list could get very long. Beyond a certain point, its value as an aid to better browsing starts to diminish.

See page 76 for setting the History options

I would recommend that you set the days to no more than seven. The situations in which the History is most useful are those where you want to look back in leisurely offline time at pages that you glanced at while online, and you are most likely to do that either on the same day or within a couple of days. When you find sites that you will want to return to regularly, don't use the History - add them to your Favorites.

Searching in the Explorer bar

Rather than going direct to a search engine, you can run a search in the Explorer bar. This has one big advantage and a couple of limitations.

The advantage is in the greater convenience of browsing through the search results – these are listed in the Explorer bar, and remain visible while you view linked pages in the main display area.

The first limitation is that the Explorer bar takes up valuable screen space. This is not too bad if you have a large monitor, but on a 15", 800×640 screen it doesn't leave that much room for displaying linked pages. (In Figure 3.15, the window in the bottom image is set to the full size of an 800×640 screen.)

The second limitation is that you can only run a simple search through the Explorer bar. This is normally at Excite – though it will also try the same search at UK Plus and MSN Web Search if Excite fails to deliver. (The **Customize** link lets you change this order and other aspects of the search.) If a simple search does not deliver the goods, you can go on to run an advanced search (at Excite), but this occupies the main screen, not the Explorer bar.

Try it: Search from the Explorer bar

① Click on the **Search** button in the toolbar – if you are not online, you will have to connect now to get any further.

② In the Explorer bar, type one or more words to describe what you are looking for and click Search .

③ When the results come in, click the links in the Explorer bar to view the pages in the main window. If you like, you can follow up links in the main display – the search results will remain in the Explorer bar until you close it.

④ If a simple search does not deliver the goods, click the **Advanced Search** link – or better still, go directly to a Web directory or a search engine. And we'll do thiat in the next chapter.

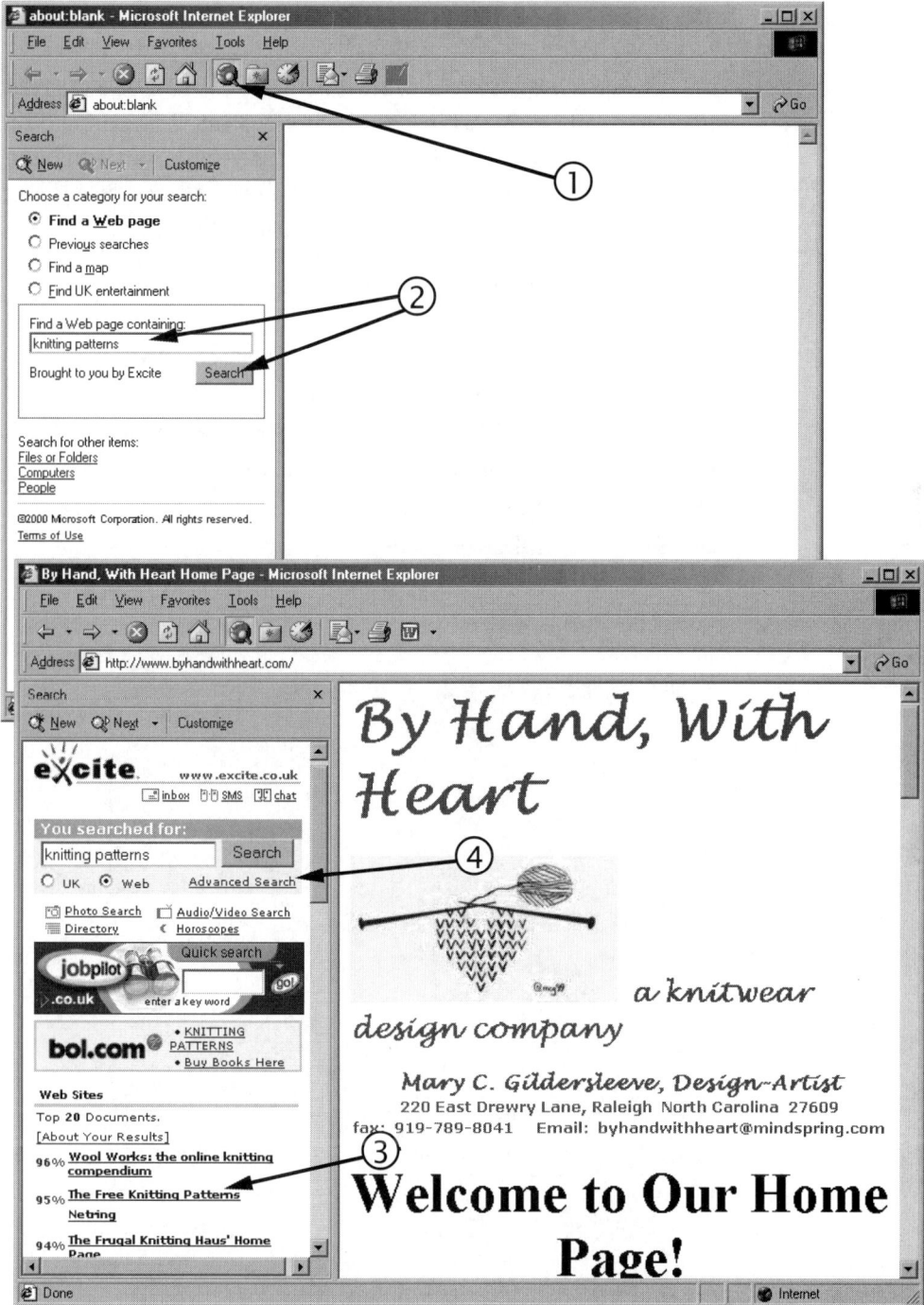

Figure 3.15 Searching from the Explorer bar.

Printing Web pages

Framed page = one divided into parts which can be changed independently

Most of the time, if you want a printed copy of the current page, it is enough to click the **Print** button. Sometimes you need to do more. This is the case with very long pages and with framed pages, when you only want to print part of them. With these, you need to go into the **Print** dialog box.

Try it: Control the printout

① If the page uses frames, and you only want to print the contents of one part, click into that part now.

② If the page is very long, open the **File** menu and select **Print Preview**, to see which printed pages you will want.

③ Open the **File** menu and select **Print**.

④ Select the pages, if relevant.

⑤ Set the number of copies.

⑥ If it is a framed page, select how you want to print it.

⑦ Click [OK].

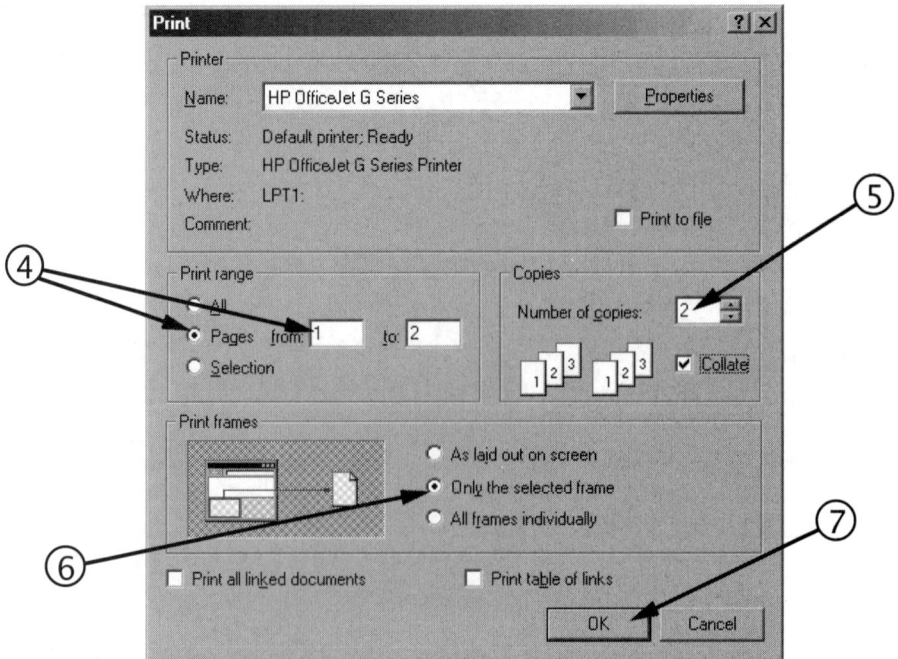

Figure 3.16 Take control of your printout using the **Print** dialog box.

4

Searching the Web

IN THIS CHAPTER:

- Web directories and portals
- Search engines
- Search techniques

There is an enormous amount of information – of greatly varying quality – published on the World Wide Web. The problem is finding stuff that's worth reading on the topics that interest you. Web directories and search engines offer different ways to track down material.

Web directories

If you can find a good start point on a topic, you can usually follow it through from page to page using the hypertext links that they so often contain. However, with so much information spread over so many pages on so many sites over the Web, the problem is where to start looking for stuff. And it's not just a matter of quantity – there is no quality control on the Web. Anyone can publish anything, and no-one checks it for accuracy, relevance or even literacy.

Stuff – Web pages, files, news stories, any kind of material that may be stored on the Internet

Directories offer promising start points. There are a number of these, some focused on specific topics, others providing a systematic overview of the Web's resources. All directories contain sets of links, organised into a hierarchy of categories and subcategories. They are always compiled by humans (as opposed to the 'spiders' used by search engines) but they work in several ways.

There are a few where every linked page has been viewed, assessed and reviewed by someone from the directory. Though these may only have a few thousand links, at least there has been quality control – you can expect that the pages linked from these are more likely to be worth visiting.

Others are largely compiled by self-submission, relying on those who created the Web pages to select the appropriate place in the directory's hierarchy. Descriptions of contents are also produced by the pages' authors. Clearly you don't have the same guarantee of quality here.

Portals

Directories which offer other services for their visitors – as most now do – are sometimes called portals. The aim is to get people to see their sites as the main gateway into the Internet – the place where they will normally start their online sessions, and to which they will return often during sessions. Why? Because the more time that people spend at their site, the greater the value of their advertising space. And that is an important consideration as people are rarely willing to pay for the services on the Internet.

Yahoo!

We dipped into Yahoo! in Chapter 1, but it's well worth a return visit for a closer look. Yahoo! was the first of the general directories and is still by far the most popular. At the end of 2000, Yahoo! UK was getting over three million visits a week – and that's just one of many Yahoo! sites world-wide! It is growing rapidly, both in size and scope. When I first came across Yahoo! six years ago it had direct links to less than 30,000 pages. Its links are now beyond counting, but are well into the millions. Despite the size, good organisation makes it simple to locate stuff – and if you don't know where to start in the menus, you can tell it what you are looking for and run a search.

Apart from the subject directory, Yahoo! has many other facilities for Net users and has a special directory and activity area for kids, called Yahooligans!

Web page authors are invited to submit their pages for inclusion, but they are not linked until they have been viewed by someone from Yahoo! (they have lots of volunteers as well as a core of permanent staff). The quality control is not that stringent, but at least they weed out some of the dross.

In Chapter 1, we saw how the directory was structured, and how to locate material through it. Sometimes, however, there is no obvious place to start looking for a topic, but this is not a problem as you can run a search.

Searching Yahoo!

Yahoo! searches give you four types of results: category headings, which point you to the right part of the directory; Web sites listed within the directory; pages in the Web at large; and news stories from Yahoo!'s news service. The category headings, sites and news stories are always listed in the search results. If you want the Web pages, click that link when the other results come in.

A search can be through the whole of Yahoo! or – once you are into the menu structure – within the current category. A restricted search is advisable if a word has more than one meaning. For example, a general search for 'tornado' turned up 2 categories, 147 sites and 45 news stories, most on the nasty weather thing, but also on RAF planes, sports cars (and an Irish sports team), music, high school magazines, and even

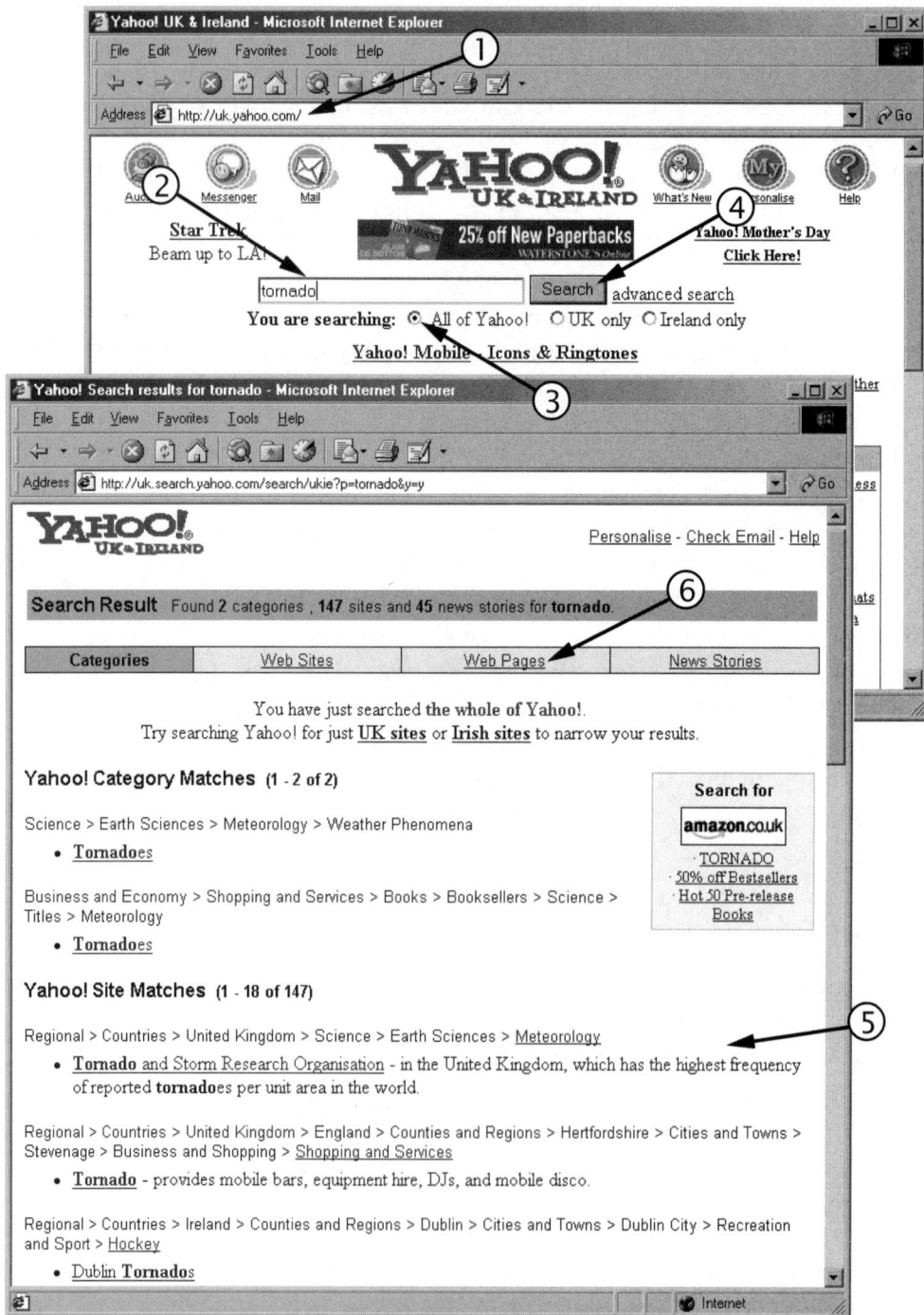

Figure 4.1   Running a search at Yahoo!

one on somebody's pet. Starting the same search within Science>Earth Sciences produced 40 matches – all relevant.

Try it: Search at Yahoo!

① Go to Yahoo! at **www.yahoo.com** or **uk.yahoo.com**

② Type into the **Search** slot one or more words to define what you are looking for.

③ Select where to search – all Yahoo! or just the UK or Irish sites. (You only have this option at Yahoo! UK & Ireland.)

④ Click Search .

⑤ Scroll through the results, or use the **Web Sites** or **News Stories** links at the top to jump down the page.

⑥ Use the **Web Pages** link to find pages beyond Yahoo! (This takes you to Google which we'll be looking at shortly.)

Advanced Searches

If a simple search produces too few – or, just as bad, too many – results, there is an advanced search routine, where you can define what you are looking for more exactly.

The words that you give to the search can be treated in one of four ways (see Figure 4.2):

♦ *Intelligent default* – looks first for those pages and other items that contain all of the search words, and then for those that contain any of them.

♦ *An exact phrase match* – should be used for people's names, titles of books, films, *et al.* It should also be used for phrases where the words may turn up separately on the same page and refer to something else, e.g. *motor boat*, when you don't want to know about sailing *boats* which may have *motors*.

If you write the search words in "quotes" Yahoo! will do an exact phrase match

♦ *Matches on all words (AND)* – will give you those items that have all of the search words somewhere on the page, though in any order, e.g. *hotel cornwall golf sailing* to find that idea holiday!

♦ *Matches on any word (OR)* – should be used where there are alternative spellings or where the same concept can be described by different words, e.g. *peking beijing*.

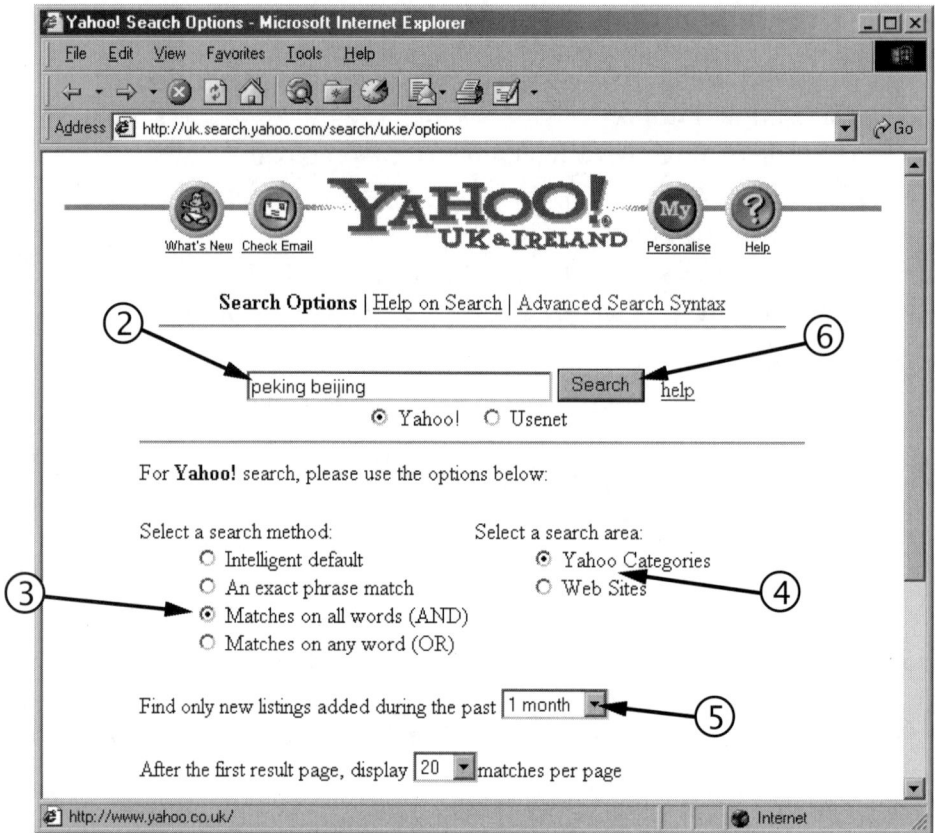

Figure 4.2 The Advanced Search page at Yahoo!

You can also choose between Yahoo! categories and Web sites, and restrict the search to items that have appeared since a certain time – anything from one day to six months.

Try it: Run an advanced search at Yahoo
① Click **Advanced search** by the Search slot.
② Enter your search words.
③ Select a search method.
④ Select the search area.
⑤ Set a time limit, if required.
⑥ Click Search .

Refining your searches

There are several special codes and structures that you can use to refine your searches. And note that these can be used in any search slot at Yahoo! – you don't have to go to the **Advanced Search** page.

+ before a word insists that the word must be present. Use this to narrow down a search, e.g. *golf* compared to *golf +volkswagen*

– before a word insists that the word not be present. Use this to cut out obvious irrelevances, e.g. *football* compared to *football –american* (You'll still get thousands, but not as many as otherwise.)

t: restricts the search to page titles, ignoring the same words in the text of pages, e.g. *paddington* compared to *t:paddington*

u: restricts the search to the URLs of pages. This is useful for locating pages at a known organisation's site, e.g. *u:apple* not *apple*. (This particular example produces a dramatic reduction in the number of results.)

" " put quotes around words to match only that exact phrase, e.g. *royal ballet* compared to *"royal ballet"*

* is a wildcard – something which can be replaced by any character(s). Attach it to the end of a word to find any words that start with the given letters, e.g. *bowl** will find *bowls, bowler, bowling* and the like.

You can combine these codes, but you must do it in the same order as they are listed above.

Note that these codes are not exclusive to Yahoo! + – "" and * will have the same effects at many search engines.

Excite

Excite is another leading portal. It offers regularly updated news, weather and share reports (and horoscopes), plus a range of other services – all of which can be accessed through a personalised home page. It also has an extensive directory, which is why we are looking at it now.

The first trick at Excite is to find the directory! It's not exactly hidden, but it is only one of the site's attractions. There are two routes into it. The quickest is through the **Web directory** link on the top page – and we'll come back to this in a moment. Before we go there, I'd like to take you on a

Figure 4.3 The directory is only one of the services offered by the Excite portal. You can personalise the top page, changing the colour, content and layout to suit yourself. Excite want you to use their home page as your home page (see page 62).

quick detour through the 'Excite Channels'. At first glance this looks like a directory, with a set of headings and sub-headings, covering a good range of topics, but it is actually more of a magazine. The pages at the top contain tasters of stories and articles (with links to the full copy), along with a Contents list that will get you deeper into the directory, plus links to sets of Web sites relating to the current heading. As you explore the site you'll find activities, picture galleries, sound and video clips and other material.

Try it: Explore Excite Channels

① Go to Excite at **www.excite.co.uk**

② Click on a heading in **Excite Channels**.

③ Click on a title to read the rest of an article.

④ Use the **Contents** list to go deeper into the channel.

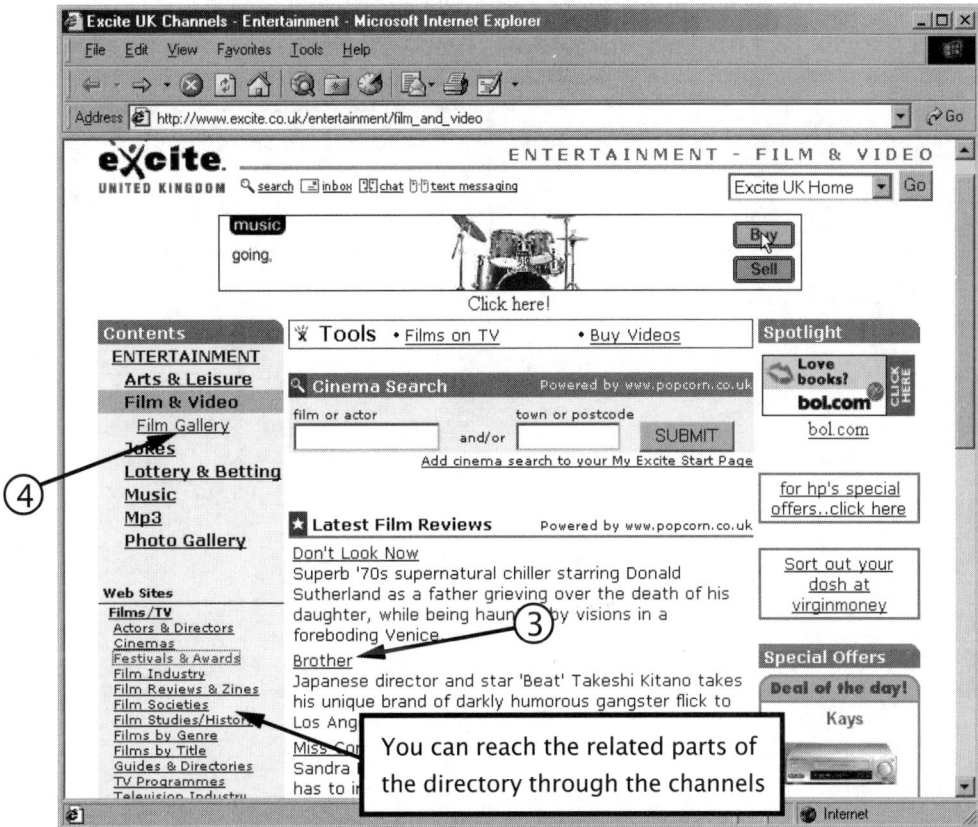

Figure 4.4 There's some interesting content in Excite channels – have a look one day.

The Web directory is organised into a hierarchy of categories, as at Yahoo! As you work down through the hierarchy, you will find – again, as at Yahoo! – that each page will have a set of related subcategories listed at the top, and links to Web sites beneath. The deeper that you go into the structure, the more of each page will be devoted to site links.

As a general rule, the Excite directory is more informative than Yahoo! Links to Web sites have descriptions so that you know what to expect – and these have been written by Excite people, not the sites' owners. All listed sites at have least been given the once-over, and some have been examined more carefully. Look out for the hand-picked (and reviewed) sites.

Try it: Use the Excite directory

① Click the **Directory** link on the top page at Excite.

② Click on a heading or subheading.

③ Work down through the hierarchy to focus on your topic.

④ Read the site descriptions and click the links.

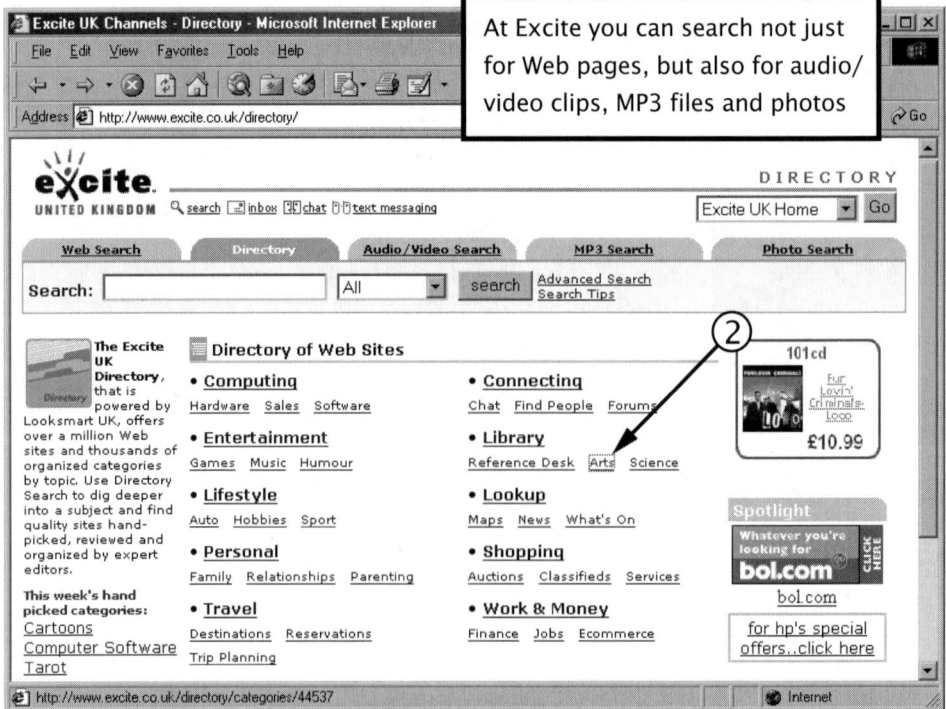

Figure 4.5   Starting to explore the Excite directory.

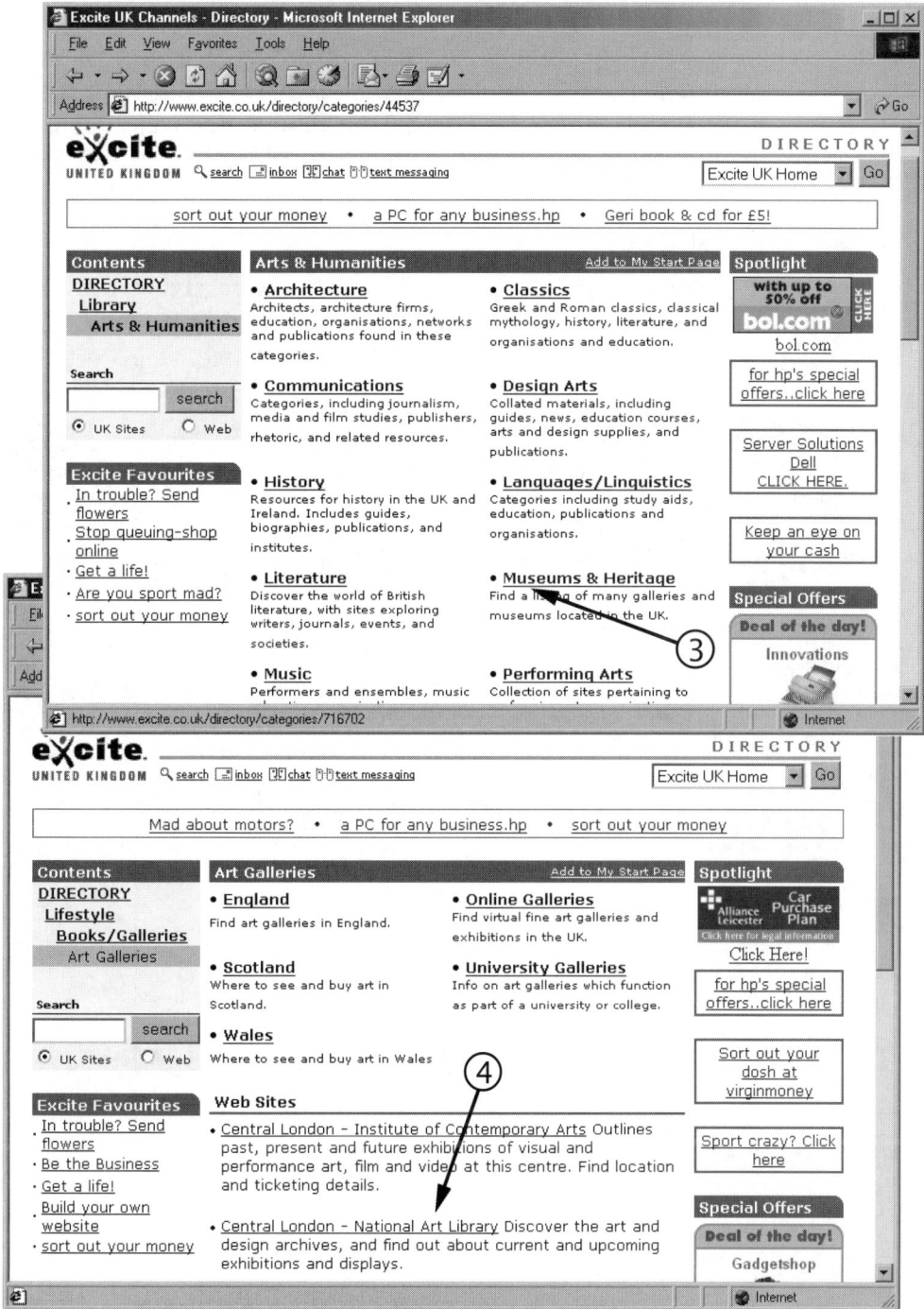

Figure 4.6 At Excite, the site descriptions are brief but informative.

At the time of writing, Excite UK claimed to have links to around one million sites in its directory. This is a sizeable number, but if you can't find what you want among these, you can get links to many, many more sites (over 50 million at the last estimate) through its search engine (see page 118).

AltaVista

AltaVista made its name as a search engine, and we'll be back to look at it in that capacity later (page 122). Its directory is nicely organised and marked by clean, simple layout. Its pages have relatively few advertisements, links to features elsewhere

Figure 4.7   The top page at AltaVista – there are lots of services on offer, on top of the core directory and search facilities.

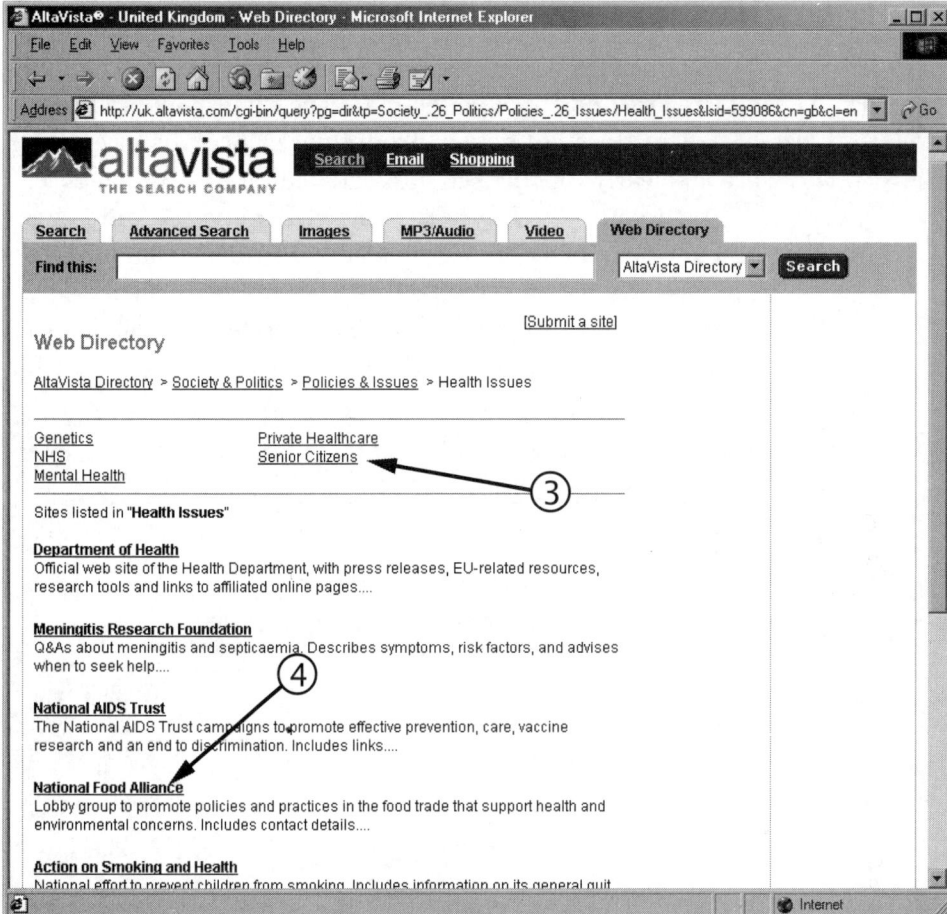

Figure 4.8 Three levels down in the AltaVista directory – pages follow the usual pattern with subcategory links at the top and site links below.

in the site or and other distractions. These don't just clutter up the pages, they also take time to download, so clean pages load faster.

As at Excite, the site links are accompanied by brief but informative descriptions.

Try it: Explore AltaVista's directory

① Go to AltaVista at **uk.altavista.com**

② Click on a heading in the Web directory area.

③ Work down through the hierarachy to the desired topic.

④ Read the site descriptions and follow the links.

UK Directory

The Yahoo!, Excite and AltaVista directories covered here are all UK versions of Web sites that have their main base in the USA. This does not detract from their value – the directories are all clearly UK-focused, but retain an international core.

UK Directory is different. It started in the UK and is specifically geared to UK Web sites, and in particular to those that provide services and facilities within the UK. This works better with those organisations that operate nationally or over a large area than it does with purely local ones. It's good for

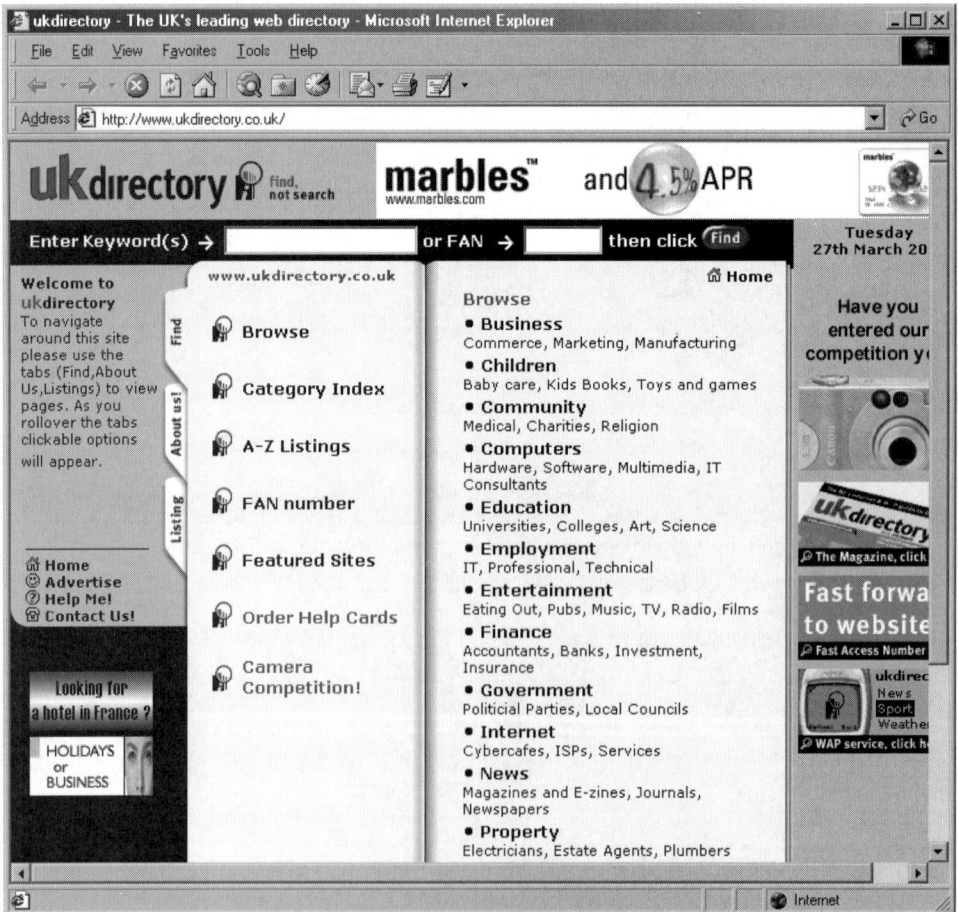

Figure 4.9 The top page at UK Directory. FANs (fast access numbers) offer quicker navigation within the directory – if you know an organisation's FAN, you can jump to its entry. But if you know its Web address, you can bypass the directory altogether!

finding national charities, magazines and newspapers, mail-order retailers and special interest events. It's not so good for finding a local tradesman or a club. Some categories are subdivided by region, but even here the areas are too large to be practical in most cases. If I'm looking for a plumber, I want one who lives in or close to Southampton – somewhere in the south of England isn't good enough. (And the keyword search won't do the trick either. Searching for 'plumber southampton' produced an interesting range of activies in the town, but no plumbers.) For this kind of information, you are better off at the electronic Yellow Pages at **uk.yell.com**.

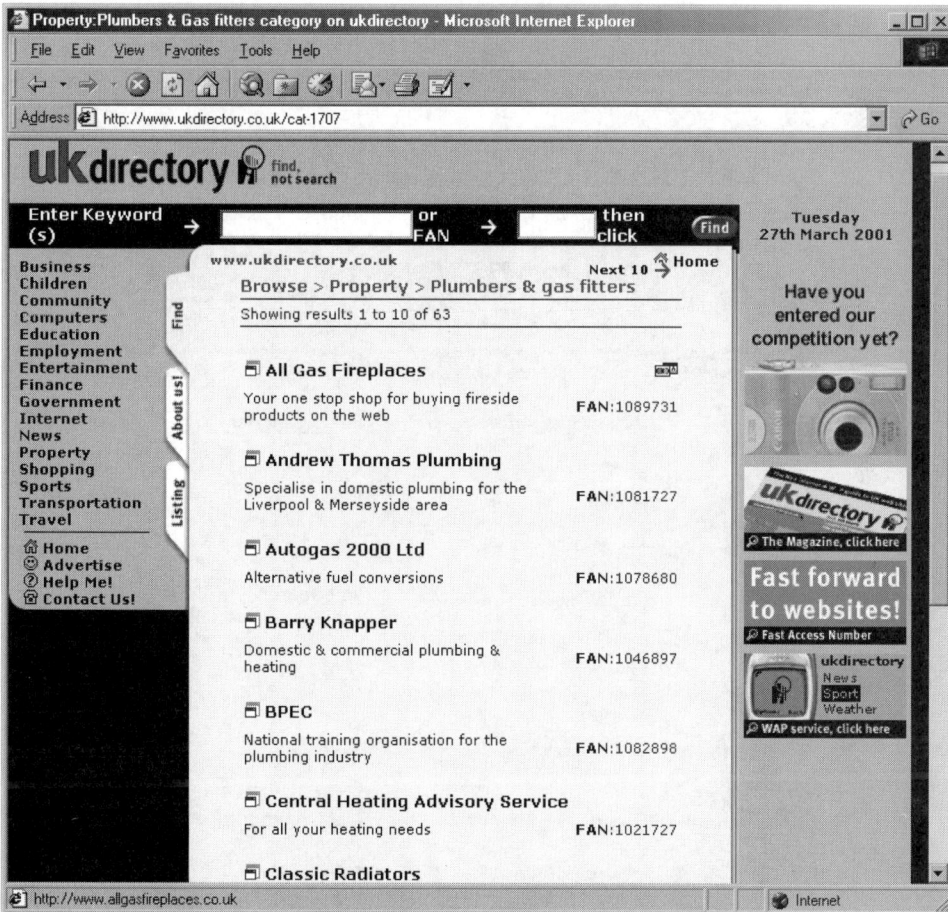

Figure 4.10 The UK Directory is good for national organisations and specialist suppliers – not so useful for finding a local plumber.

InfoSpace

When I first found InfoSpace, it was a specialist people-finder site. You can still use it for this, as you will see later (page 203), but nowadays it claims to be the 'ultimate' directory. I'm not sure that I would agree with that, but it is certainly a very good one. You can find all sorts of stuff here.

How you find stuff depends upon what you want. InfoSpace has a whole collection of directory and search facilities, each tailored to its material. Let's start with Web sites.

Try it: Find a Web site through InfoSpace

① Go to InfoSpace at **www.infospace.com/uk**

② In the **Net Search** area, click **Web Directory**.

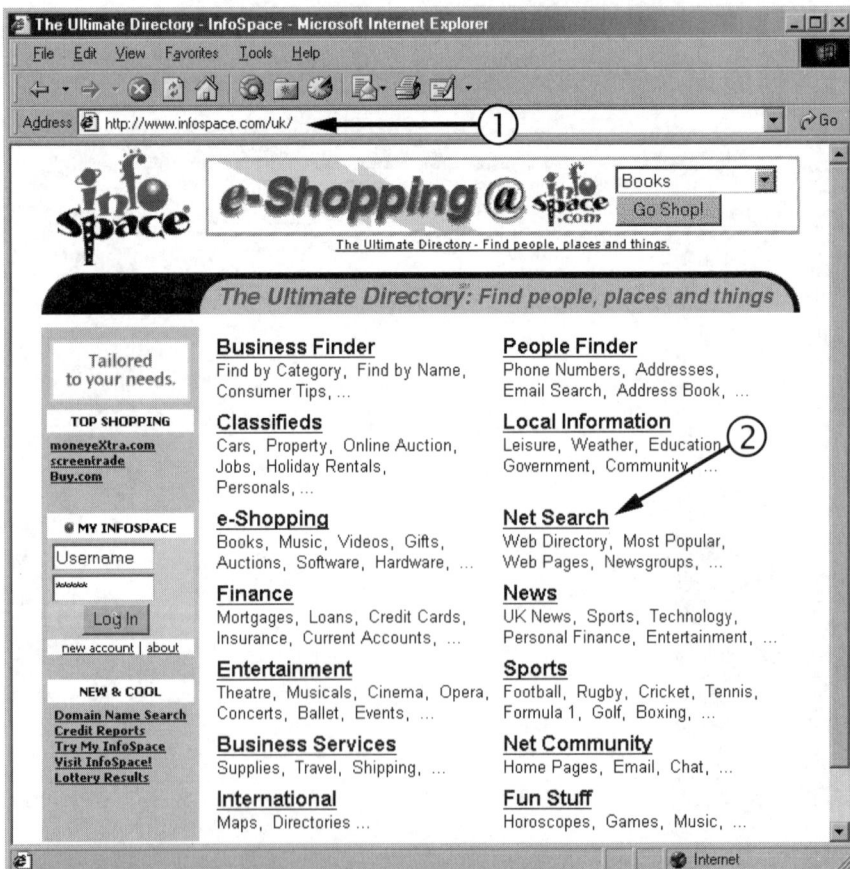

Figure 4.11 You can find all sorts of stuff through InfoSpace.

③ Click on a category heading.
④ Click on a subcategory heading, if appropriate.
⑤ Enter a keyword to define what you are looking for and click Find .

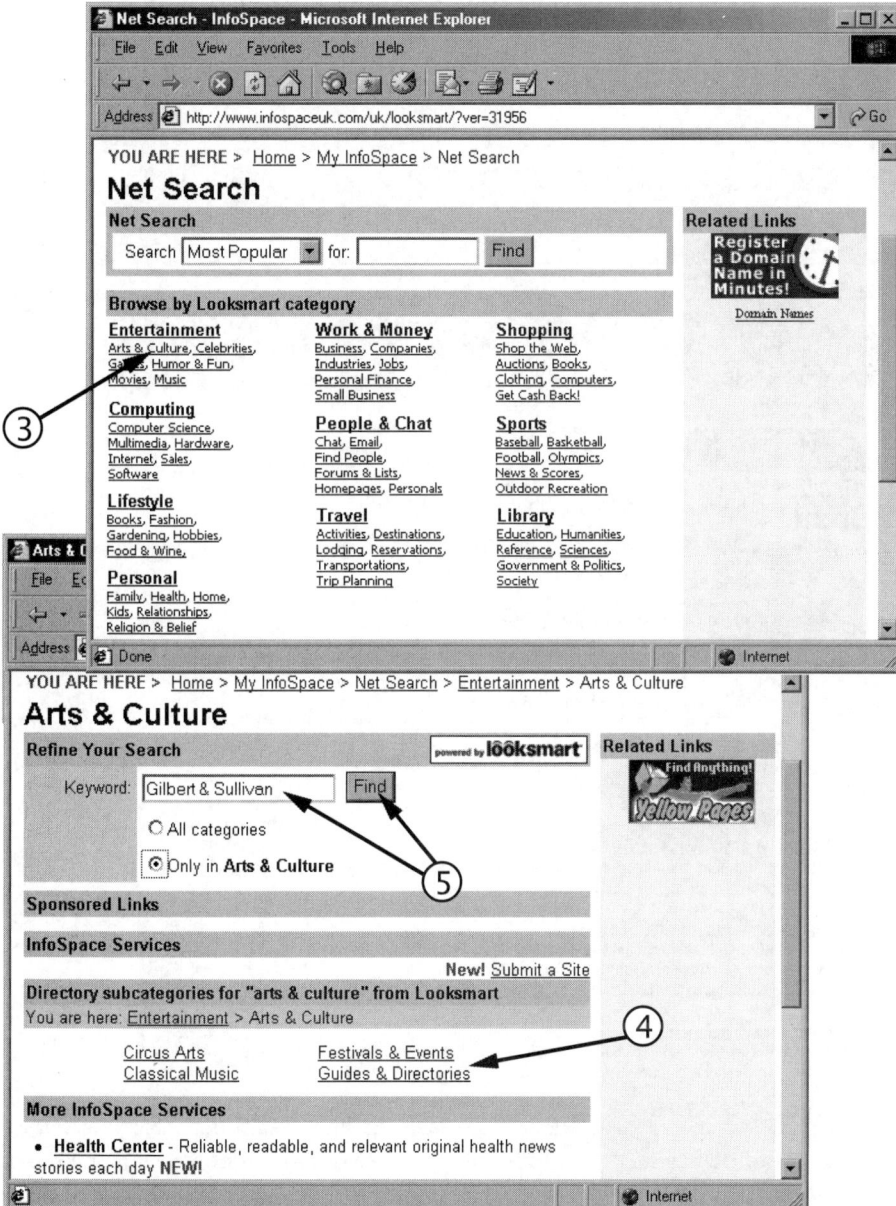

Figure 4.12 Using the Web Directory at InfoSpace.

For news, weather, sport and business and similar what's-happening-now stuff, InfoSpace uses more of a magazine format, listing digests of stories with links to the full text.

Try it: Catch up on the news at InfoSpace

① On the top page, click on a **News** or **Sports** heading.

② Skim the digests and click a title to follow a story.

Or

③ Click a **More News** link to see what else is happening.

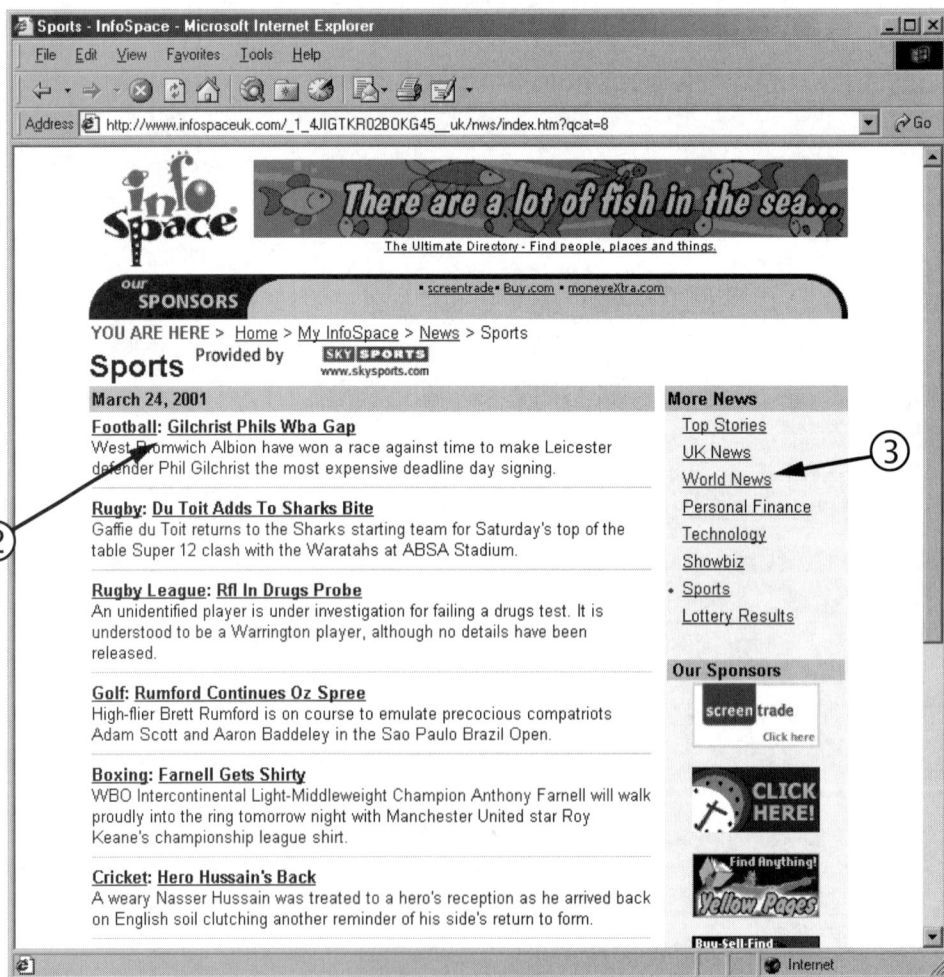

Figure 4.13 Reading the sports news at InfoSpace – you don't get the same kind of in-depth reporting on the Web that you do in a good paper, but it's a great way to grab the latest headlines.

In the Entertainment area, you are back to a search routine, but this time the search is for a real place, not a Web site.

Try it: Find out what's on at a cinema near you

① On the top page, click on **Entertainment**.

② Click on **Film** in the **What's on** area.

③ Enter your **Town** and the **Title** and click [Get Listings].

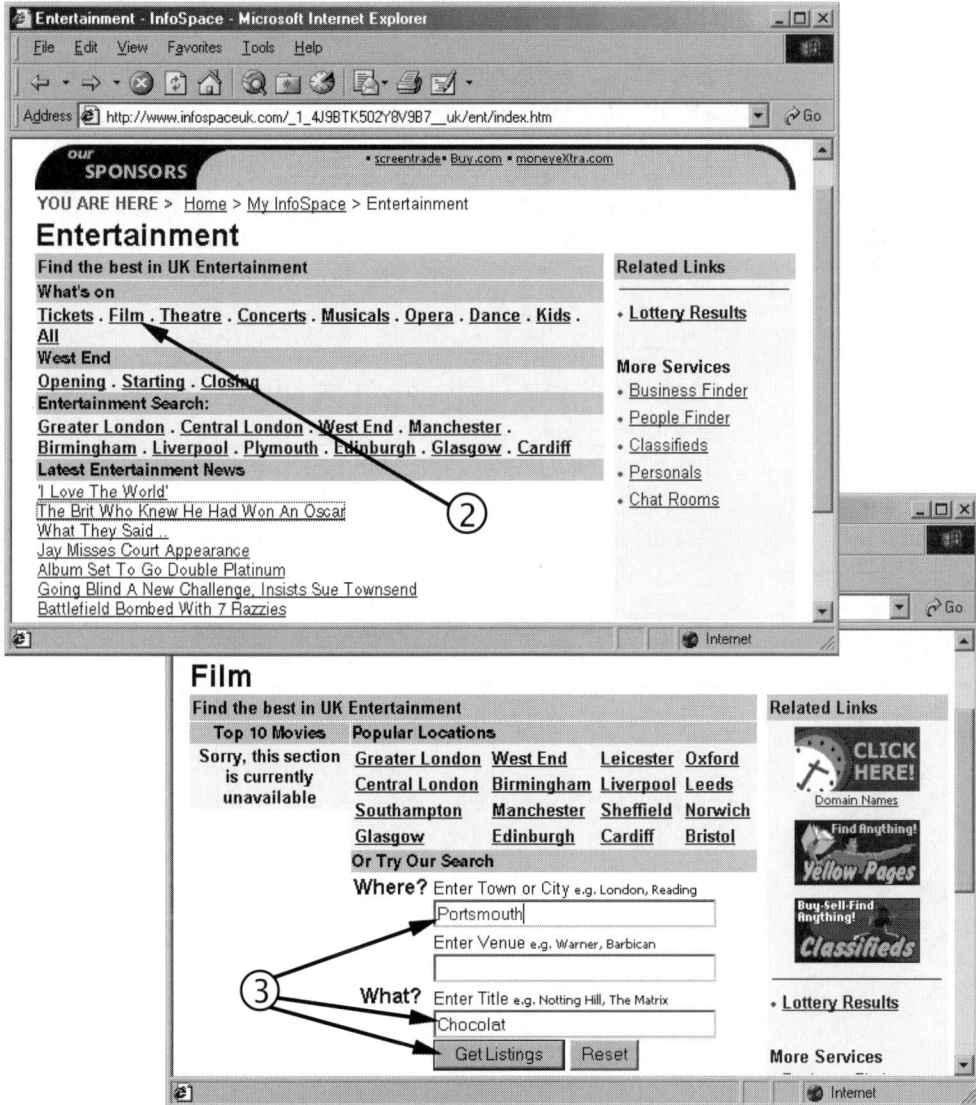

Figure 4.14 What's on at the movies? Find out at InfoSpace.

Searching the Web

You can find most things by browsing through directories, but it can take a while – especially if you are researching an esoteric topic, or if you want to track down all the pages on a topic. This is where the search engines come into play. At these sites you can search the Web to track down pages that meet your specifications. (To be exact, you can search their databases that hold key information about pages and sites on the Web – a direct search through over a billion pages would take far too long!)

Three key points to note about search engines:

♦   Search engines vary in the way they build their indexes of the Web, but they all use some kind of automated system. They have 'spider' programs that steadily work their way through the Web, testing out each route they come across and sending back information on the pages they find. Some will only pick up selected items from Web pages – typically the title, anything listed in the *keywords* and *description*, labels for images and text from the top few lines; others will scan right through the page. Some will only read the top page at any site; others delve into every page.

Web pages can contain data, not shown on the screen, marked as 'keywords' and 'description'

♦   Because these are automated systems, with no human intervention, there is no quality control. At best, a search engine may calculate how many links at other sites point to a page, which gives some indication of how useful people have found it. Search engines will give you more links than directories, but they will include a lot more rubbish in those links!

♦   Some search engines are more complete than others, but none can offer a 100% coverage of the Web, as pages are being added and changed constantly. If you don't find what you want at one, it is often worth trying another.

Search techniques

Most search engines allow you to define searches in similar ways. The techniques listed here will work at all the major (and most other) search engines.

Keywords

◆ Use the roots of words for maximum effect; *boat* will find *boat*s and *boat*ing – *boats* will probably not find variations on the word.

◆ If you give several words (in a simple list, and not using logical operators such as AND and OR, discussed on page 97), a good search engine will find and list first those pages that contain all of the words, followed by those that contain some or only one of them. Some poorly-designed ones give you results that match any of the words, and in an order of their own devising!

Logical operators

Multiple keywords can be joined by logical operators that define the relationship between them. The operators can be written in capitals or lower case.

◆ AND specifies that both words must be present; e.g. *boat AND wood* will find *wood*en *boat*s, *boat*s made of *wood*, as well as the *Boat* Inn at Fleet*wood* and other things you didn't want!

◆ OR says that either word will do; e.g. *tunny OR tuna* to find pages about fishes of the *Scombridae* family in both UK and US sites.

◆ NOT specifies that pages containing the following word are not wanted; e.g. *goldfish NOT card* when you want the things for your pond, not your wallet.

Special symbols

+ (must have this word) – (must not include this word) and "quoted phrases" have exactly the same effect as at Yahoo! (page 99).

Google

Google is one of the newer search engines, and one of the fastest and best. It has a phenomenally large database – over 1.3 billion Web pages at the time of writing – and is optimised for speed. It's not just that the searches are fast – over 21,000 results in a fraction of a second in the example – the whole site is pared down to the minimum, so you don't have to wait for flashy graphics, adverts and other irrelevancies to come in before you can start searching or following up results.

Google uses its special 'PageRank' technique to rate sites. This notes not just how many links point to a page, but also where they come from. If a high-ranking site has a link to a page, then it is worth more than a link from a less important site. The sum total of ranked links produces the rating for the page. Pages are also relevance-rated on the basis of where your search keywords appear within them. If the words are in the page's title, and/or occur several times within the text, it is highly likely to be more relevant than a page which has only a single occurrence of the words.

The relevance rating and PageRank score are combined to produce the results list. So, even though this may have many thousands of references, the chances are that the top page of results will contain some good links.

If you do not define your search tightly enough, even the best ranking system will still produce far too many results. No problem, there is a simple solution – at Google you can run a search within a set of results. In fact, narrowing your search by stages can be one of the easiest ways to find things. If you use multiple words, logical operators, etc. to define the search very closely at the start, there is a danger of being so restrictive that you miss a lot of potentially interesting stuff. And the more complicated that you make a search, the greater the chance of typing errors. Keep life simple.

In the example below, I'm trying to track down a Fats Waller recording – specifically 'Honeysuckle Rose'. Search for a special song by your favourite artiste, or for something totally different – something that you can look for in at least two stages.

Try it: Search at Google

① Go to Google at **www.google.com**

② Enter one or more words or a "phrase" to define your search generally.

③ Click [Google Search].

④ Look through the first page of results to see if this has turned up what you want.

⑤ If you have hundreds or thousands of results and they are too general, go to the bottom of the page and click the **Search within results** link.

⑥ Enter more keywords and click [Search within results].

⑦ If you are still getting too many, and you need to narrow the search further, run another search within the results.

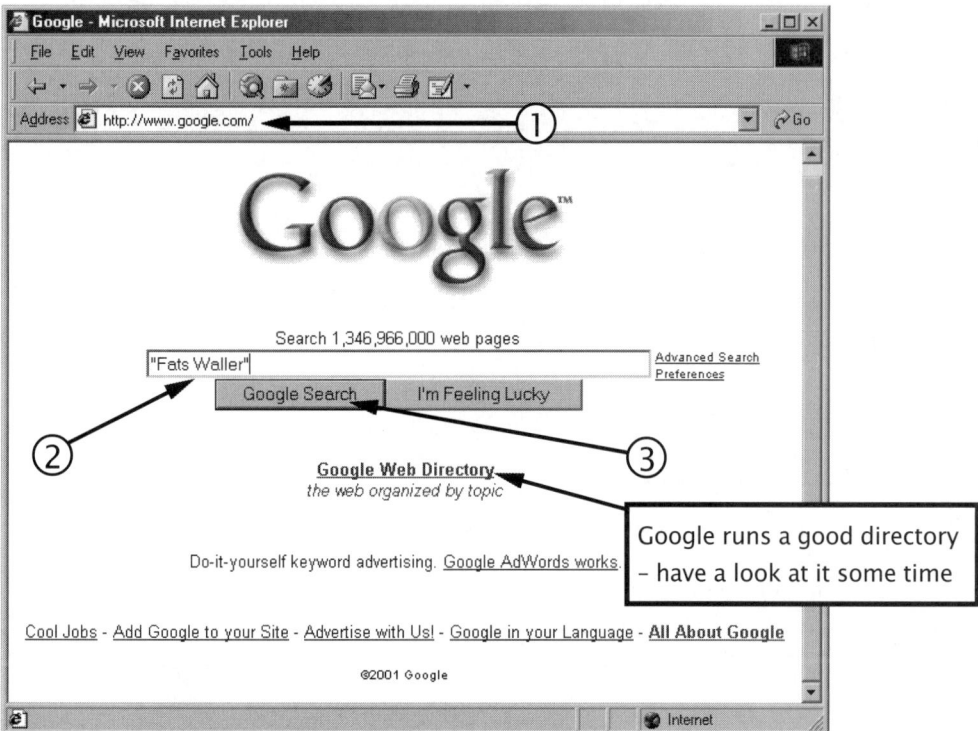

Figure 4.15 Putting quotes around the name makes sure that the search is for that great jazz pianist, and that other people named Waller, or cooking fats, diet plans, etc. are all ignored.

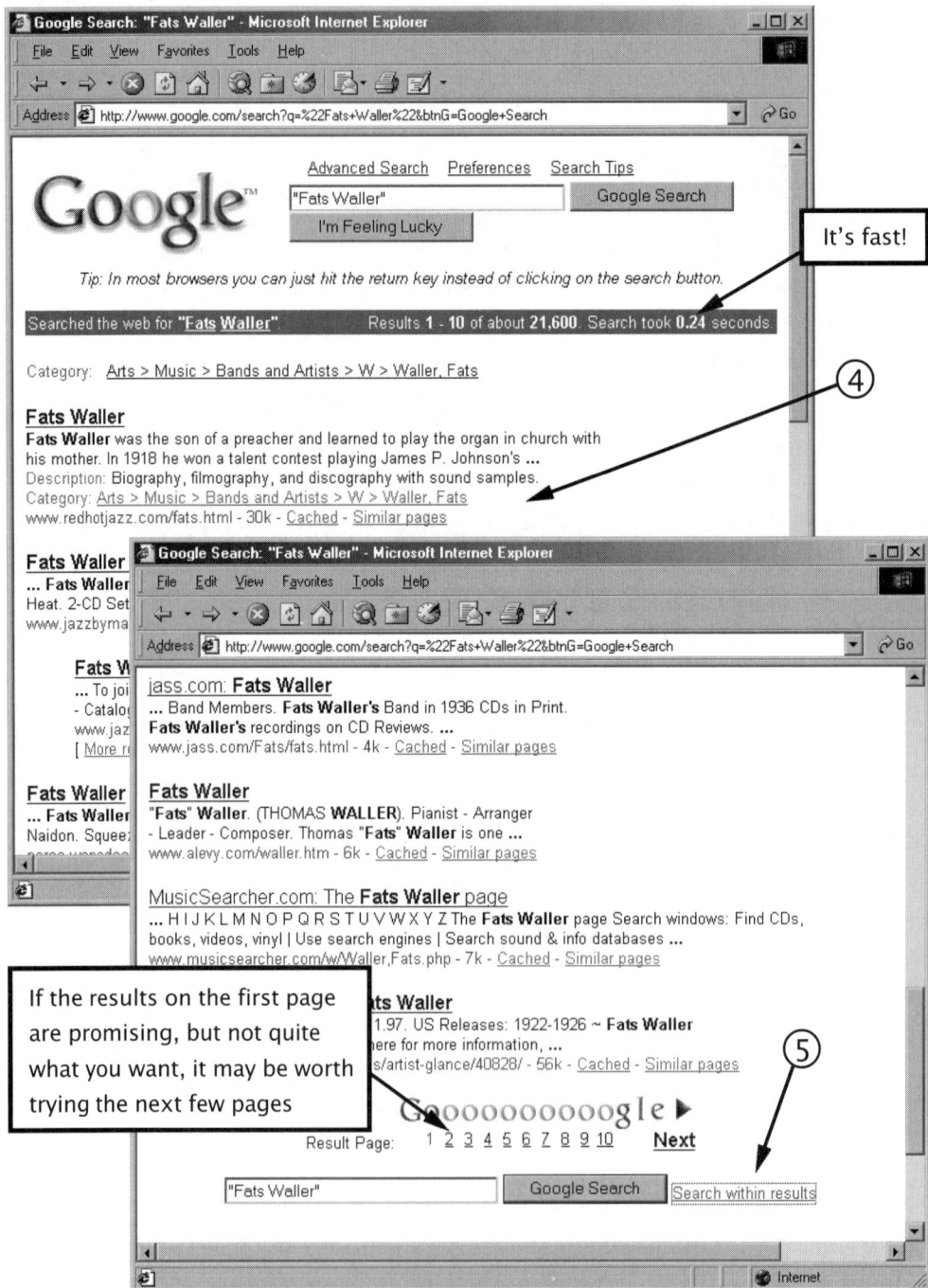

Figure 4.16 The most relevant and highest-rated results should be found on the top few pages.

Figure 4.17 Searching within the results reduced the results from over 21,000 to 1890 – and all the ones on the top page were very relevant.

Excite Search

As well as the directory, Excite provides a very good search engine. In fact, it is so good that it is used for searches in the Explorer bar (page 90), and by portal sites such as MSN – even WebCrawler, which got its name from the 'spider' that it used to send off to create its own database.

The Excite database is huge, and as at Google, the real problem is to define the search closely so that you do not get too many matches. For example, suppose you wanted to find classical – and not folk – music for the harp (or whatever you play). A simple search for *classical harp music* will give you over four million results! I would guess that most of these are pages that contain only the word 'music', but these are all well down the list. There are enough that match all three words to fill many pages of results first. Unfortunately, quite a lot of these have 'folk', which I didn't want. Before we look at how Excite's advanced Web search offers a neat solution to that problem, take a few moments to experiment with the standard Excite search.

Try it: Search at Excite
① Go online, if you are not already connected.
② Go to Excite search at **http://www.excite.com/search**
③ You can search for *News*, *Products*, *Photos*, *MP3/Audio* and *Video* as well as *Web sites* – select the type.
④ Enter two or three words to define your search.
⑤ Click Search .
⑥ Check through the summaries of the results on the top page to see how closely these match what you are looking for.
⑦ If the results look promising, follow up the links.
⑧ If the results are too far off target, click **Advanced Web Search**.

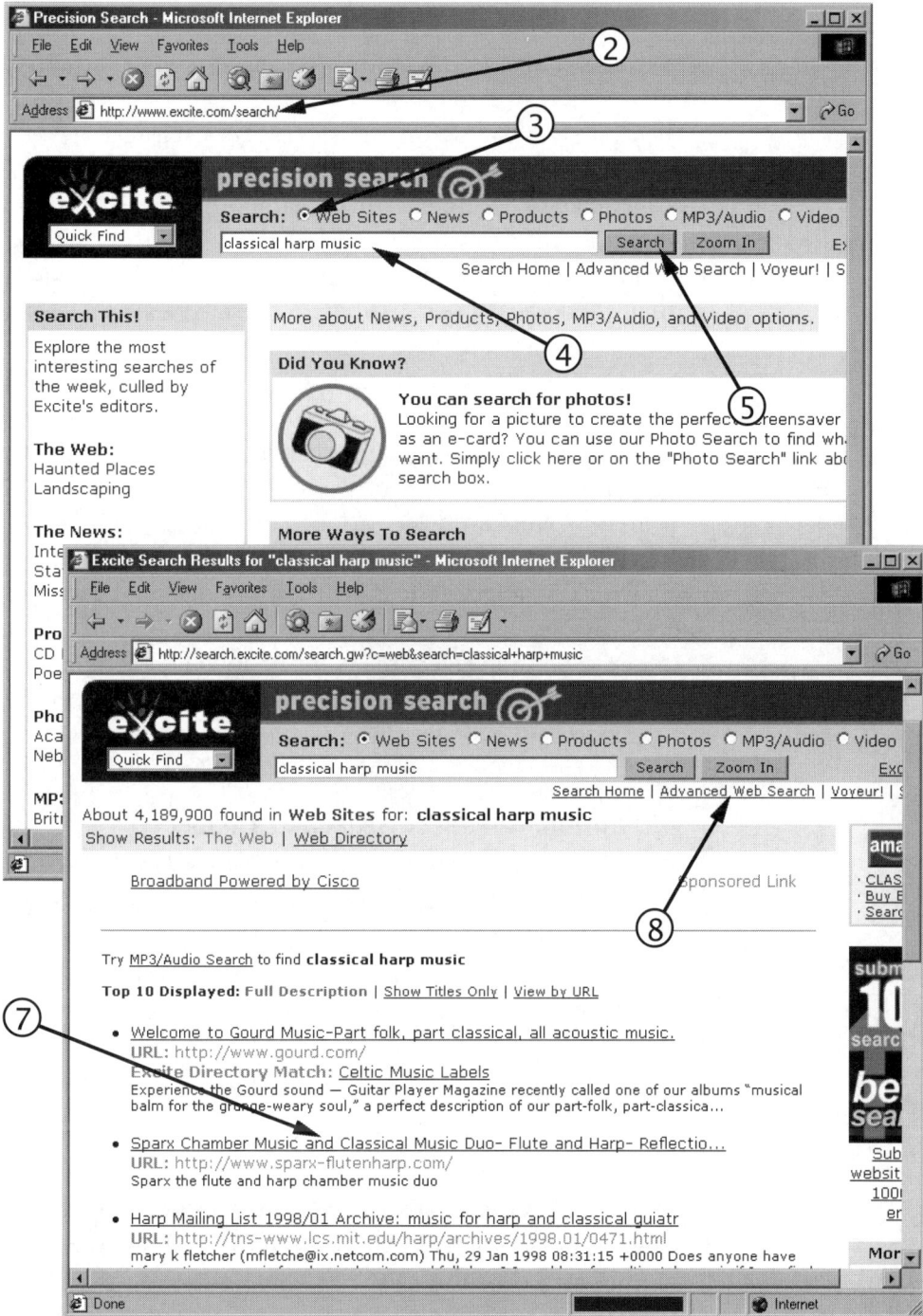

Figure 4.18   Running a simple search at Excite.

Excite's Advanced Web Search

I like Excite's Advanced Web Search – it's simple to use and it works.

The first step is to define the search. For each search word (or "quoted phrase") that you enter, you select whether it is to be included or excluded, using the options *Must Have*, *Good to Have* and *Must Not Have*. The effect is identical to using the + (include) and – (exclude) operators – in fact, the search routine will convert your settings to these codes.

By default, there are boxes for four words, but more can be added if required – and it's a rare and specific search that needs more than four.

At Step 2, you can specify the display style – how many to a page, and whether or not to show the summaries.

At Step 3, you can select a language. Increasingly, especially where it is not in English, Web site creators label their pages with the language it is written in – the search engine spiders have no way of knowing otherwise.

At Step 4, you can select the country. If you are looking for information, it rarely matters where the Web site is, but if you want to buy over the Internet, a local supplier will be cheaper.

Try it: Run an advanced search at Excite

① At the Excite search page, click **Advanced Web Search**.

② Enter the words to search for, and for each, select **Must Have**, **Good to Have** or **Must Not Have**.

③ Set the number and style of the results display.

④ Select the language, if not English.

⑤ Select the country, if relevant.

⑥ Click Search .

⑦ If you don't get the sort of results you want in the top page – where the best matches should be listed – then click **Modify Your Advanced Web Search** and try again.

◆ Switching words from **Must Have** to **Good to Have** will bring you more results – or switch the other way to specify more tightly.

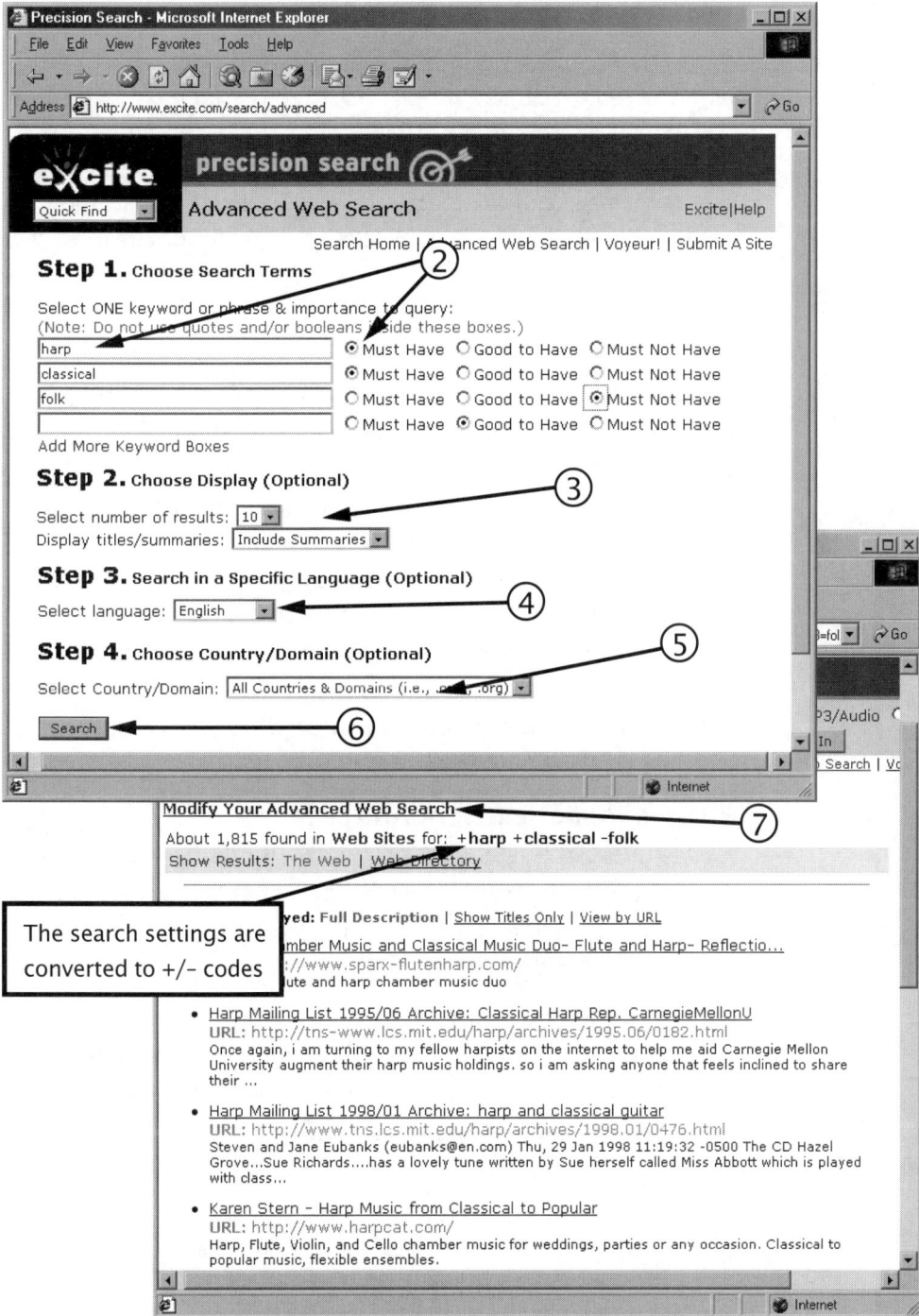

Figure 4.19 Running an advanced search at Excite.

AltaVista

AltaVista claims to be 'the most powerful and useful guide on the Net'. We had a look at its directory on page 104, but it was as a search engine that it first made its name. In this capacity it certainly turns up the results.

You can ask your questions in plain English – although it only actually looks at keywords in a question. For example, 'steam railways in Wales' will produce the same results as 'Where can I find out about steam railways in Wales' – and take half as long to type!

Some other features of AltaVista are well worth noting.

◆ You can search for images, video or audio clips, instead of Web pages.

◆ As at Google, you can run a search within the results, allowing you to narrow a search down in stages.

◆ The results are accompanied by some suggestions for questions which may help you find what you want.

◆ You can turn on a Family Filter, then leave youngsters to their own searches, without worrying.

◆ It doesn't just handle plain *English*, you can search in any major language.

Try it: Run a search at AltaVista

① Go to AltaVista at **http://www.altavista.com**
② Enter your search question or words.
③ Select the language, if not English.
④ Click **Search**.
⑤ Follow up any interesting links.
⑥ If the results are not specific enough, enter another word to define the search more tightly, turn on **Search within these results** and click **Search** again.

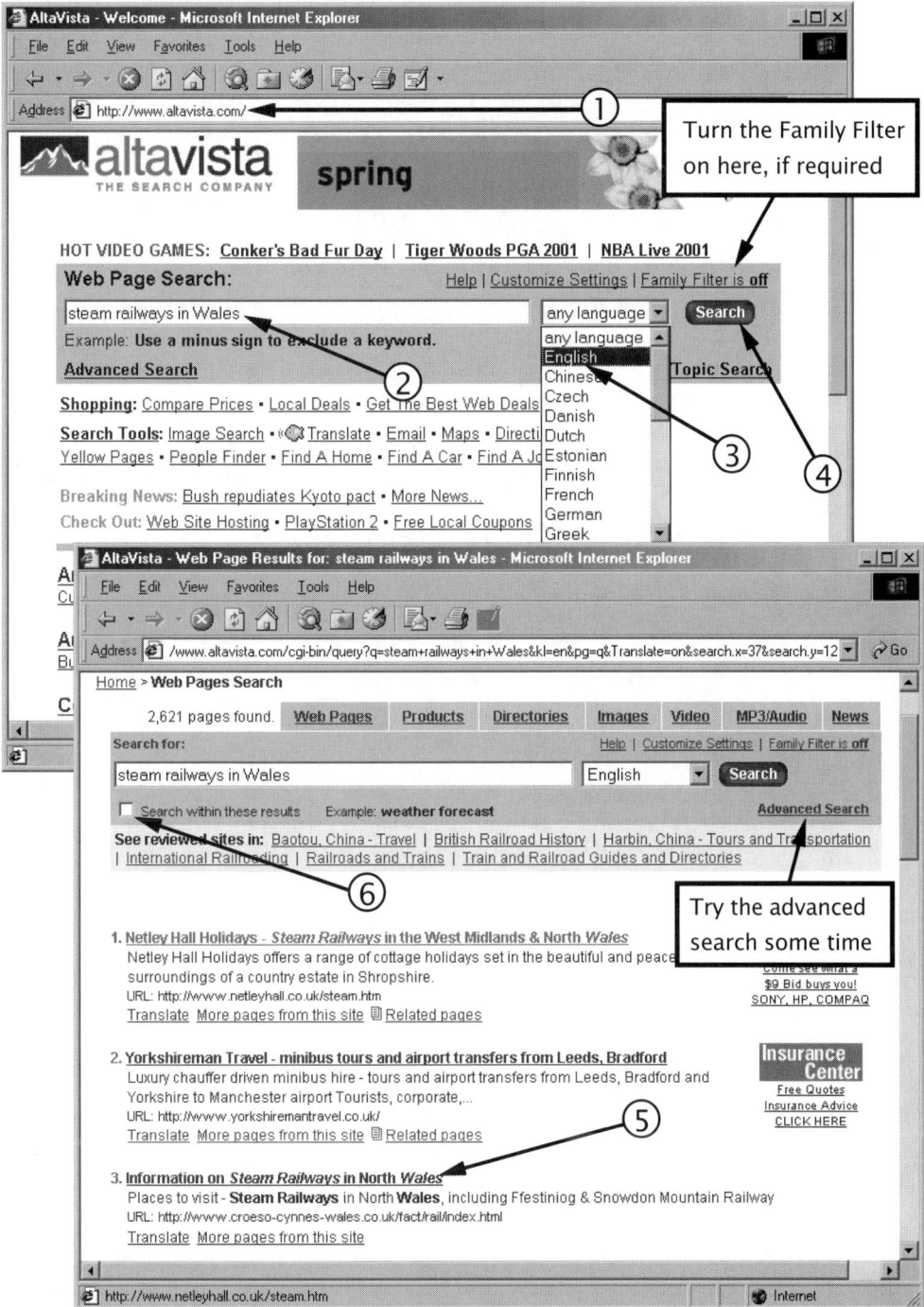

Figure 4.20 Searching is simple, but effective, at AltaVista.

5

Mining the Internet

IN THIS CHAPTER:

- Stores of knowledge
- World Wide maps
- Media on the Web
- Internet radio
- Files from the Net

There are treasures to be found on the Internet – great sources of information, images and entertainment – so get out there and get digging!

There's gold in them thar URLs!

The Internet is a tremendous source of knowledge, but it's not so much a treasure house of information, as a gold mine – there's a wealth of nuggets, but you have to dig them out for yourself!

This is not as daunting as it may sound. If you look in the right places, the gold-to-tailings ratio is high, and in any case, you get to see some good scenery while you are prospecting. So, grab your pick and let's get going before this metaphor gives out.

Stores of knowledge

Dictionaries and encyclopædias

A steadily growing number of the 'standard' reference books are being made available online. Amongst others, you'll find well-known names including Britannica, Encarta and Hutchinson's encyclopædias, Webster's dictionary (and the Oxford English Dictionary, if you are a paying subscriber) and Roget's Thesaurus.

There are also many more less-known, but equally useful names. If you want to look up the meaning of a word, Dictionary.com is an excellent place to go. A single query here gives you definitions from the American Heritage Dictionary, Webster's and WordNet (run by Princeton University), as well as relevant entries from other reference works.

Try it: Look up a word online
① Go online and head for **www.dictionary.com**
② Type the word into the **Look up** slot.
③ Select the **Dictionary** option.
④ Click OK .
⑤ Scroll down to see all the definitions and references.
⑥ Go back to the front page and look the word up again using the Thesaurus option, or click **Roget's Thesaurus**, if you want the word's synonyms and antonyms.

① ④ ③ ② ⑥ ⑤

Dictionary.com - Microsoft Internet Explorer

File Edit View Favorites Tools Help

Address http://www.dictionary.com/

≡○ **Dictionary.com**   **Look up:** picayune   **OK**

Search: ● Dictionary ● Thesaurus

Start your day with the **Word of the Day e-mail**. It's free!

Ask Doctor Dictionary
Have a question about words,
grammar or language?

Bookstore

Help
Help using Dictionary.com

Other Dictionaries
German, Greek, Latin,
Spanish; more...

Roget's Thesaurus
Find synonyms and
antonyms

Translator
Translate text and Web pages

Word of the Day
Today's word is:
abstruse
-Subscribe to the mailing list
-Browse through the archive

Writing Resources
Grammar, usage, and style
guides; writing tips; and other
resources

ADVERTISEMENT

There are also foreign language and translating dictionaries

Cool Too
Free softwa
Dictionary.
Thesaurus.

Fun & Ga
Daily cross
search puzz

Downloadin

Dictionary.com/picayune - Microsoft Internet Explorer

File Edit View Favorites Tools Help

Address http://www.dictionary.com/cgi-bin/dict.pl?term=picayune

pic·a·yune (pĭk'ə-yōon')
adj.

1. Of little value or importance; paltry. See Synonyms at trivial.
2. Petty; mean.

n.

1. A Spanish-American half-real piece formerly used in parts of the southern United States.
2. A five-cent piece.
3. Something of very little value; a trifle: *not worth a picayune.*

[Louisiana French picaillon, *small coin*, from French from Provençal picaioun, from picaio, *money*, perhaps from Old Provençal piquar, *to jingle, clink*, from Vulgar Latin *piccāre, *to pierce*; see pique.]

pic'a·yun'ish *adj.*

Pronunciation Key

Source: *The American Heritage® Dictionary of the English Language, Third Edition*
Copyright © 1996, 1992 by Houghton Mifflin Company.
Published by Houghton Mifflin Company. All rights reserved.

Internet

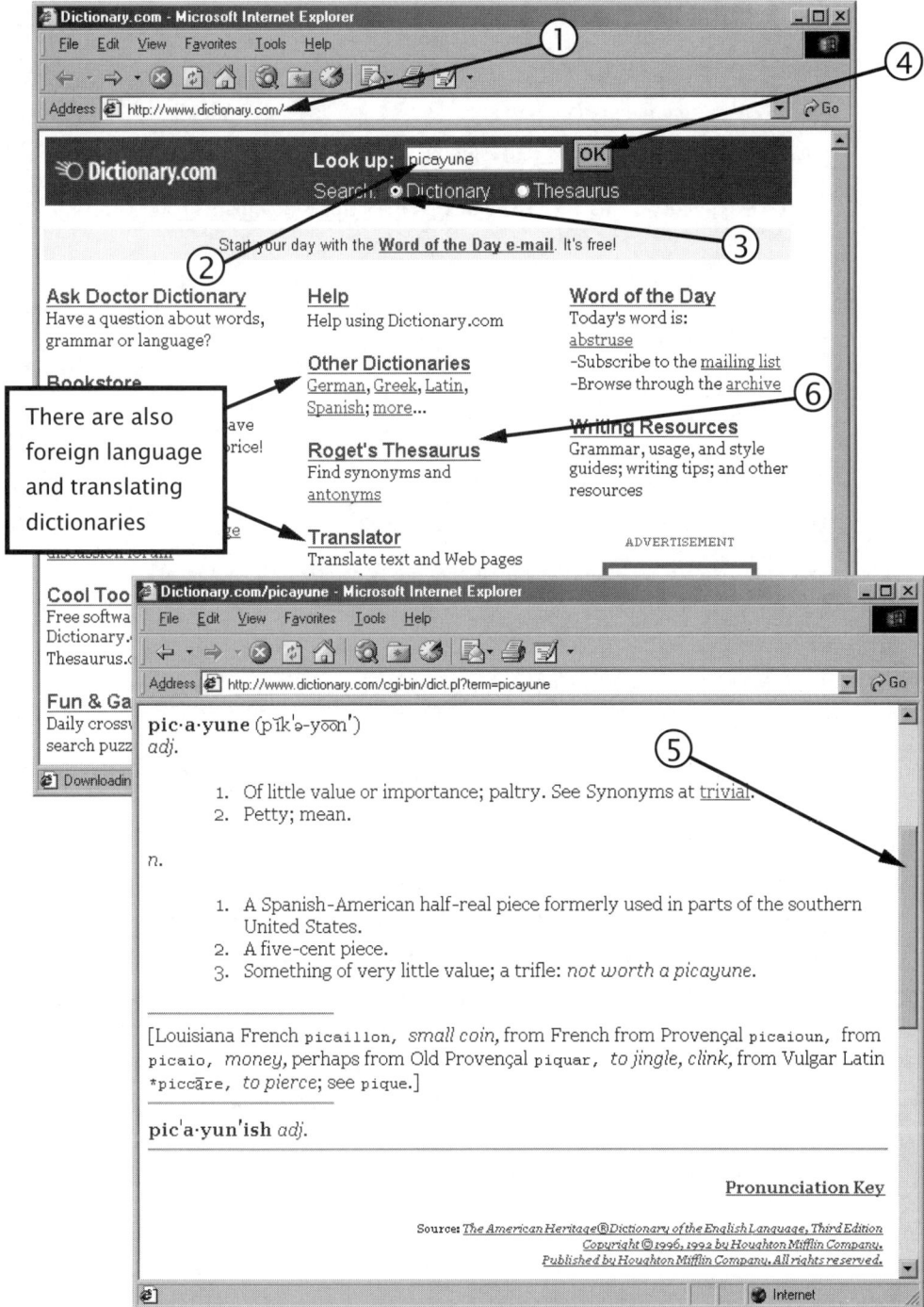

Figure 5.1 Looking up a word at Dictionary.com.

Unimportance - Microsoft Internet Explorer

File   Edit   View   Favorites   Tools   Help

Address http://www.thesaurus.com/roget/V/643.html   Go

Go: **Home** - **Headwords** - **Categories** - **Help**

V. WORDS RELATING TO THE VOLUNTARY POWERS; INDIVIDUAL VOLITION

II. Prospective Volition

2. Subservience to Ends; Degree of Subservience

Unimportance.

[Antonyms: importance.]

[**Nouns**] unimportance, insignificance, nothingness, immateriality.

triviality, levity, frivolity; paltriness; poverty; smallness [more]; vanity (uselessness) [more]; matter of indifference [more]; no object.

nothing, nothing to signify, nothing worth speaking of, nothing particular, nothing to boast of, nothing to speak of; small matter, no great matter, trifling matter; mere joke, mere nothing; hardly anything; scarcely anything; nonentity, small beer, cipher; no great shakes, peu de chose; child's play, kinderspiel.

toy, plaything, popgun, paper pellet, gimcrack, gewgaw, bauble, trinket, bagatelle, Rickshaw, knicknack, whim-wham, trifle, "trifles light as air"; yankee notions [U. S.].

trumpery, trash, rubbish, stuff, fatras, frippery; "leather or prunello"; chaff, drug, froth bubble smoke, cobweb; weed; refuse (inutility) [more]; scum (dirt) [more].

joke, jest, snap of the fingers; fudge (unmeaning) [more]; fiddlestick, fiddlestick end; pack of nonsense, mere farce.

straw, pin, fig, button, rush; bulrush, feather, halfpenny, farthing, brass farthing, doit,

Done   Internet

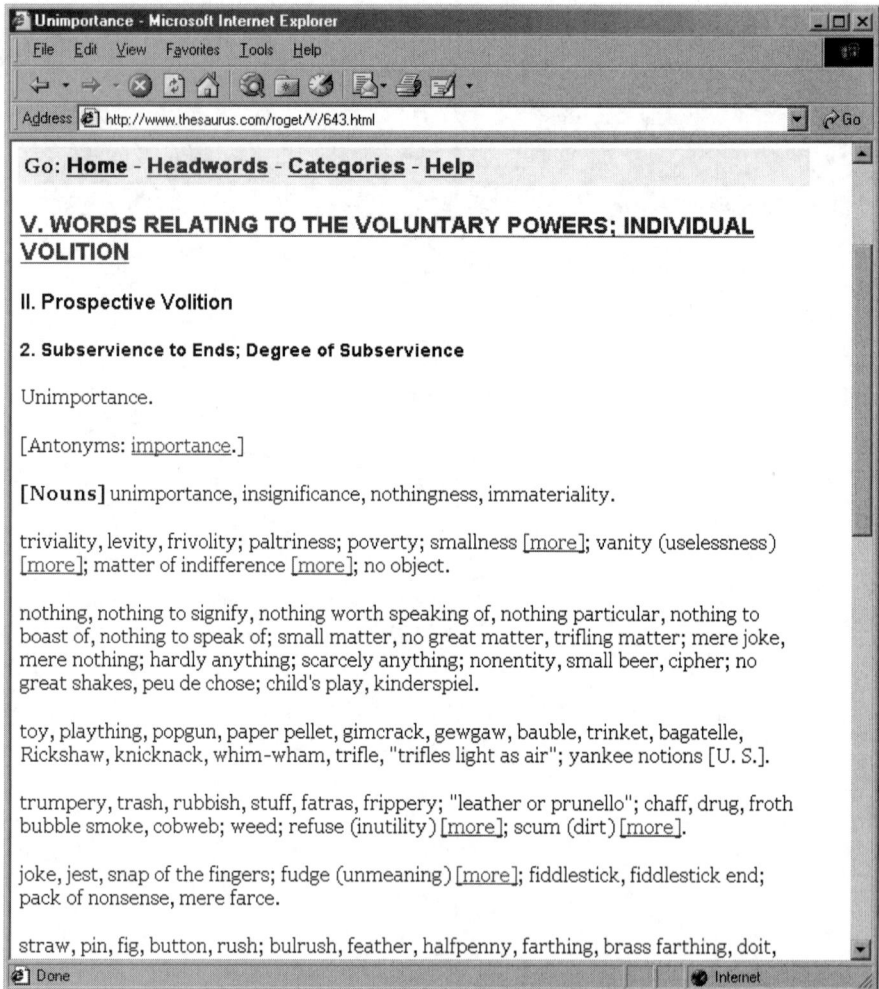

Figure 5.2 Reference works aren't just for the important things in life. Use the thesaurus to find the *mot juste* for the fatras and frippery you want to describe. And on the subject of trivia, try *Mike's English/American dictionary* at **www.effingpot.com**, a comprehensive guide to the variations in the language; or the much shorter, but far funnier, *What a load of codswallop, pet!* (**www.wmin.ac.uk/~sfgva/ukus.htm**), which focuses on the potential for embarrassment in the differences between UK and US slang.

Try it: Delve into Britannica

① Go online and head for **www.britannica.com**

② Type in the word in **The Web's best search** slot.

③ Click Search .

④ At the results page, select an entry from **Encyclopedia Britannica** (second column). You can also pick up a link from **The Web's Best Sites** (first column), or an article in the **Current Events** or **Magazines** lists (third column).

⑤ If the article has a picture, you can click on it to see a larger version of the image.

Figure 5.3 Britannica is free, online – they hope you will be inspired to buy it on CD.

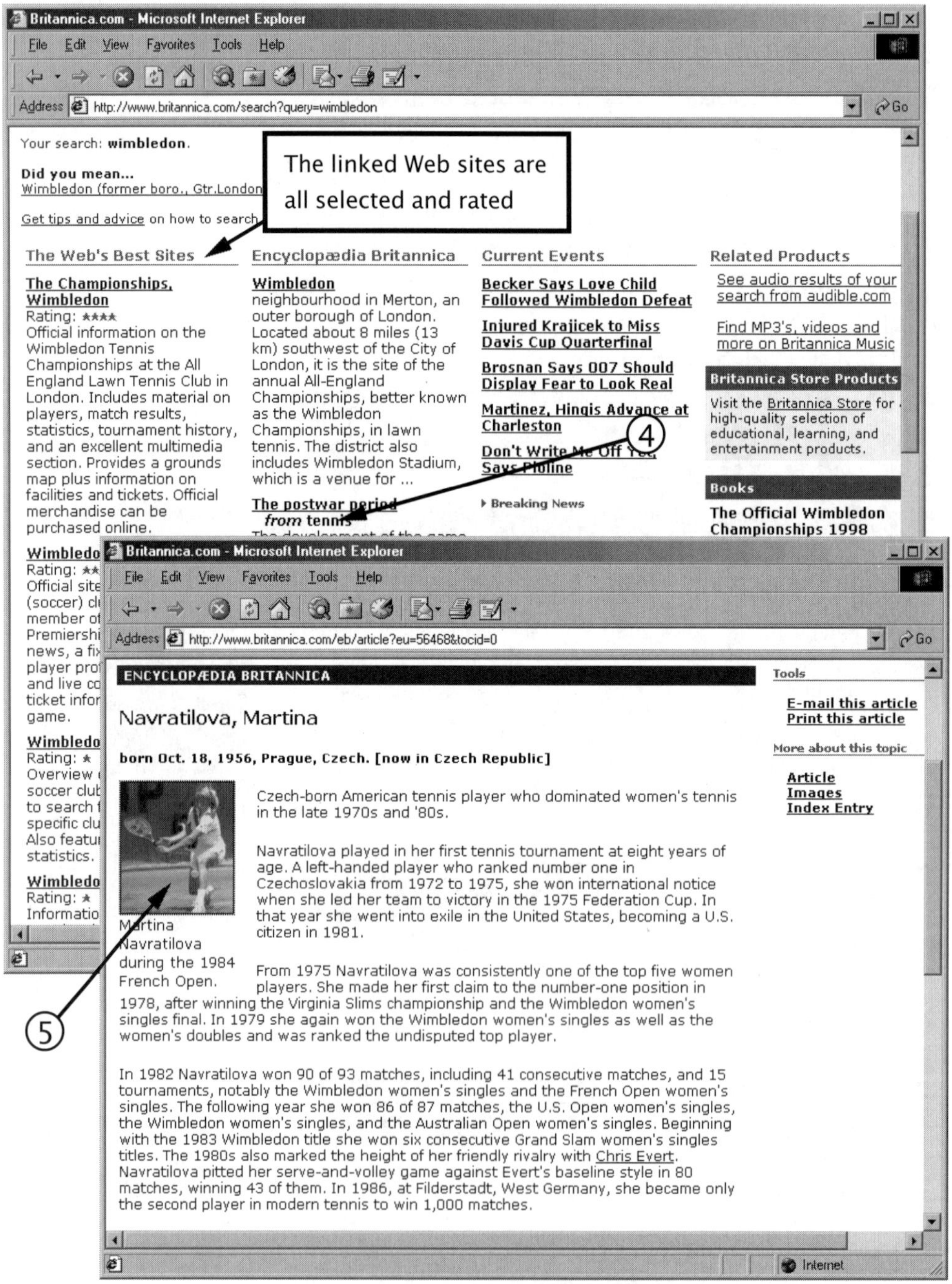

Figure 5.4 Encyclopædia articles – even the long ones – load in quickly as they are almost entirely text. Images are small (but carry links to larger versions), and there is very little advertising or other extraneous matter.

Xrefer

This is like **Dictionary.com**, only more so! Xrefer gives you
access to 50 major reference books, including dictionaries of
art, accounting, British history, business law, earth sciences,
linguistics, medicines, music, psychology and Shakespeare.

Try it: Look something up at Xrefer
① Go to **www.xrefer.com**
② Type in the word in the **search** slot.
③ Select the area to search.
④ Click **GO**.

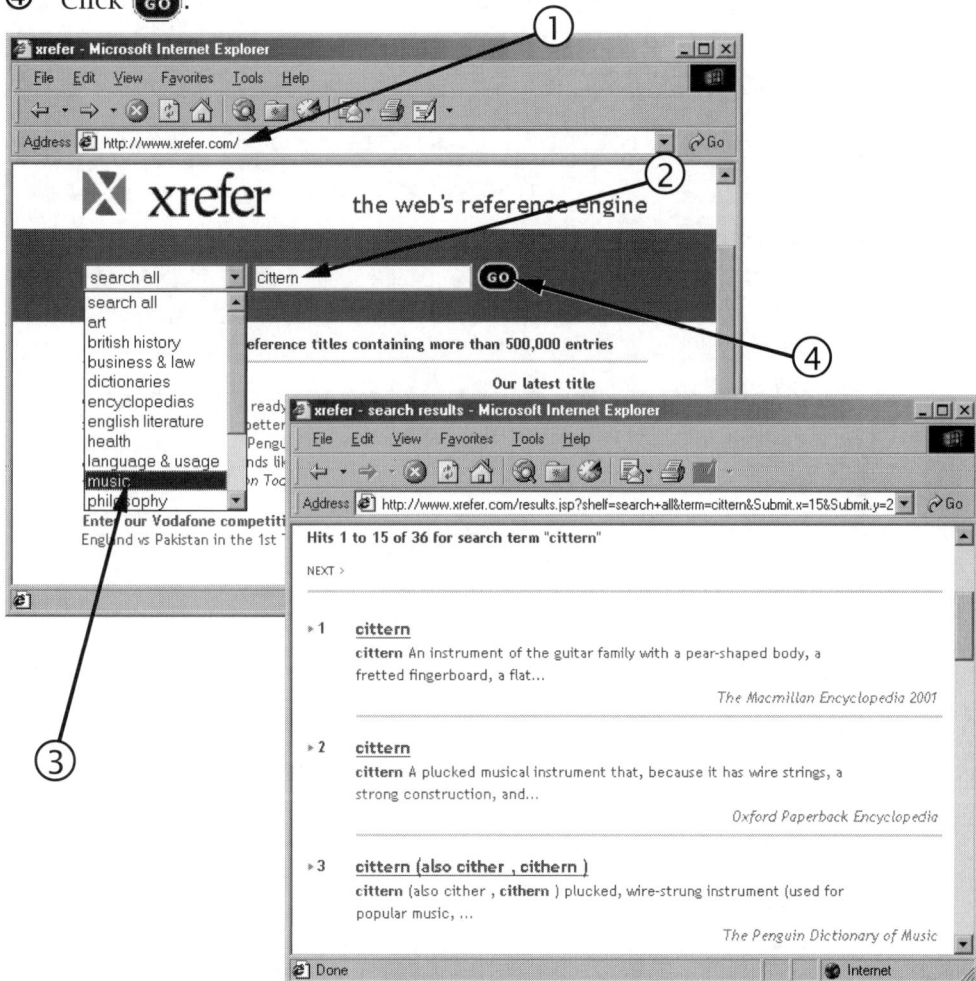

Figure 5.5 At Xrefer, you can search through 50 top reference books at a time.

Web libraries

Many paper/book libraries have a Web presence, but they normally only use this to describe their facilities and resouces – not to make their books available electronically. However, digital libraries are coming, though the format is still developing. Here are three very different types of online libraries.

The Electric Library

This is a reference library, containing more than 2000 classic books, over 200 full-text newspapers and magazines, 2000 newswires, hundreds of maps, thousands of photographs and more, all of which can be searched simultaneously with a

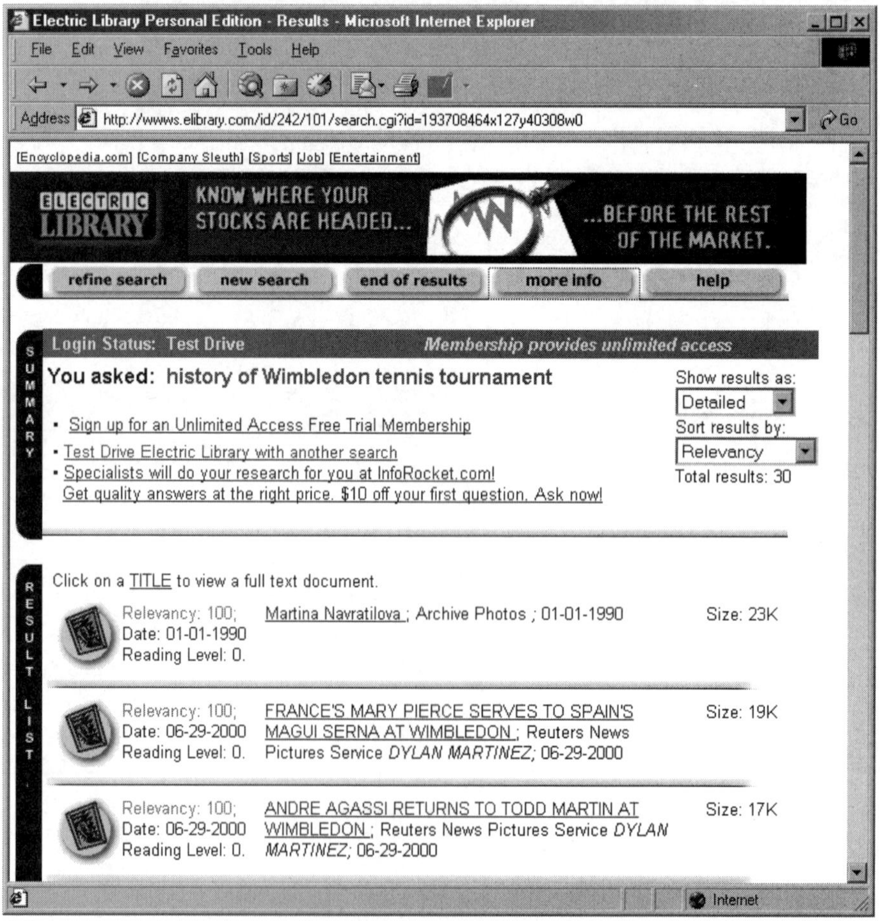

Figure 5.6 Take a test drive at the Electric Library.

single query. Compared to a Web search, this is drawing on a much smaller database of information, but it is of far higher quality – and it's all 'family-friendly'.

It's a nice idea, but unfortunately, it's not free – there's an annual fee of $59.95 (about £40). If you want to find out more about it, take a free 'test drive', at **wwws.elibrary.com**

Project Gutenberg

This is a public lending library! Project Gutenberg is an ongoing collaborative effort to put literature online. They currently have works by over 1000 authors, ranging from David Phelps Abbott to Edward Huntington Williams, with Thomas De Quincey, Herodotus and Beatrix Potter in between.

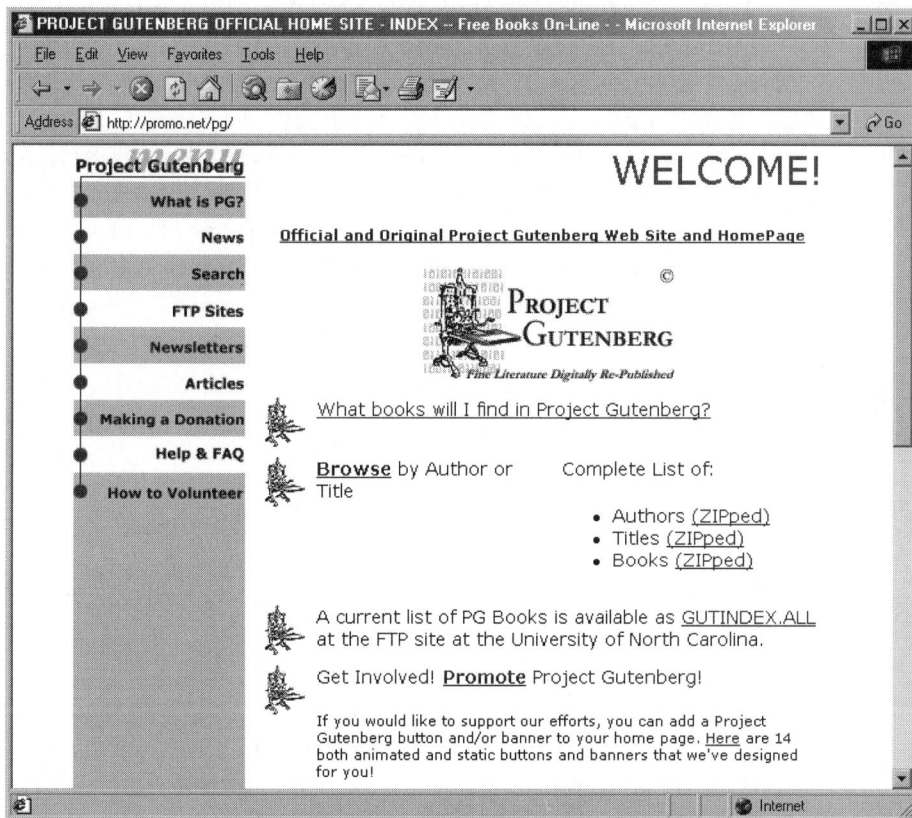

Figure 5.7 Project Gutenberg is spreading fine old literature through digital publishing – and there are books here you'd be lucky to find in your public library.

Zipped =
compressed with
WinZip (page 155)

The books are stored as plain text, Word documents or HTML, and normally in *zipped* files. Compressed text does not take much space – a full book will typically make a zip file of 200 to 300Kb, which will download in two or three minutes. When you've got the text on to your machine, you can read it on-screen or print it out. For sheer convenience, a paper copy may be worth the time and cost of printing it out.

Go over to Project Gutenberg (at **http://promo.net/pg**), and explore. As there are so many books, you must expect to spend a while browsing the shelves, but it's all nicely organised and downloading is straightforward – just follow the instructions.

The WWW Virtual Library

This is a cross between a library and a Web directory. Its links lead to Web pages and other Net resources, but these have been selected and catalogued by human 'librarians' – all experts in their own specialist fields.

The top level of subject areas can be viewed in a hierarchy, as at Yahoo!, or in a (long) alphabetical list. Within each topic, you will find a table of contents, leading on not only to sets of sites, but also to discussion groups, glossaries, and other directories and virtual libraries.

The WWW Virtual Library began life as a purely academic resource. Its range has expanded so that it now also contains a good selection of non-academic material, but it remains a high-quality resource.

Try it: Browse around the Virtual Library
① Go to the library at **vlib.org**
② Select a subject area. If you pick a main heading, you will be taken to a submenu to select a subheading, before reaching a links page.
③ Scroll down the links page, or use the **Table of Contents** to jump directly to the ones that you want to explore.
④ Click on a link.

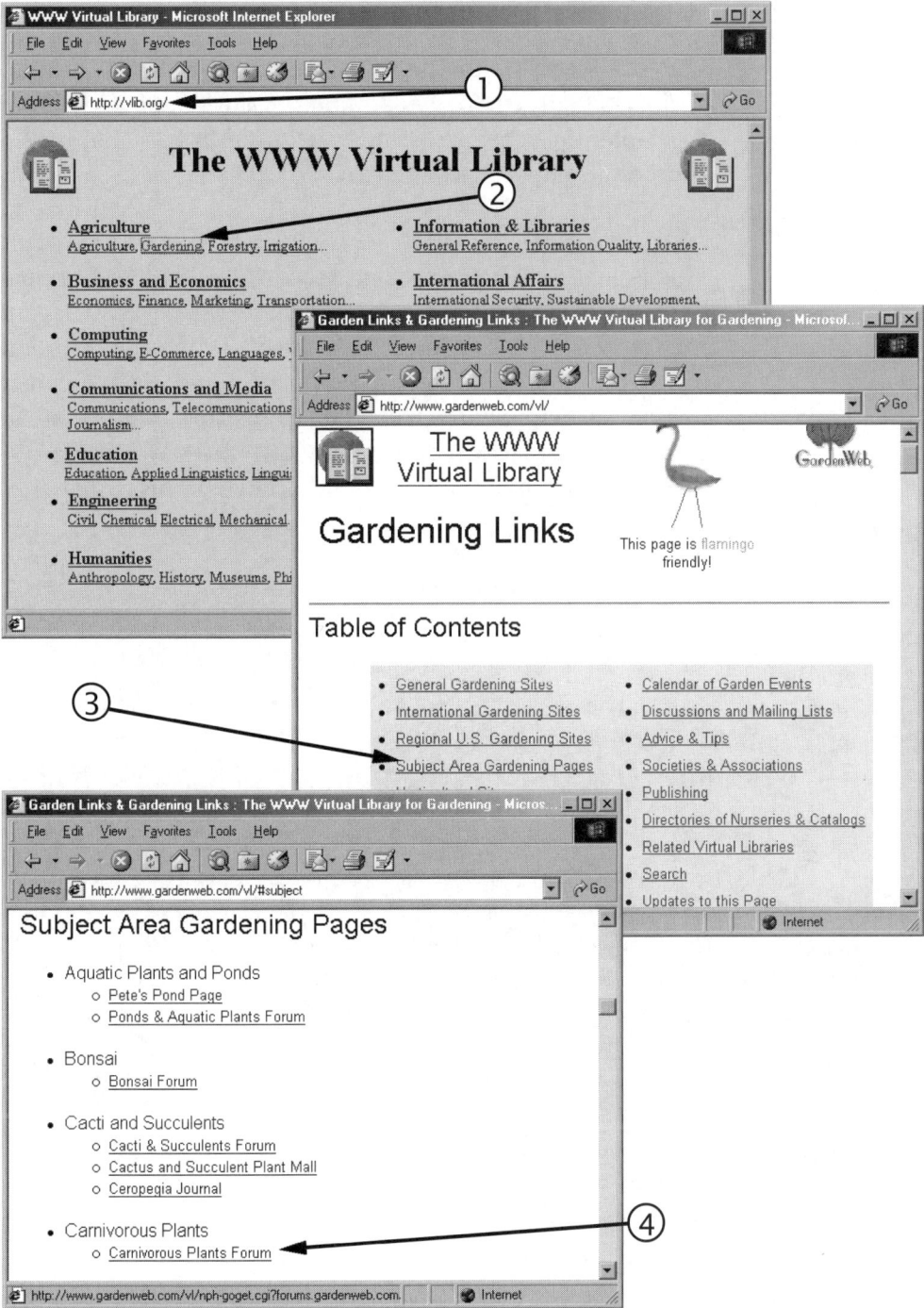

Figure 5.8 The WWW Virtual Library is an excellent source of high-quality links.

Worldwide maps

With the Web at your fingertips, you need never buy a map again. (Actually, there will still be times when buying a map is simpler and cheaper!) However, the Web has many good sources of maps – here are two.

The Map Machine

This is just one of many good reasons for visiting National Geographic's Web site. The Map Machine can generate a map for pretty well everywhere. These are atlas-style maps – good for identifying rivers, mountains and boundaries, and just the job for helping kids with their homework, but not much use for going places. You can play with the Map Machine, at **http://plasma.nationalgeographic.com/mapmachine**

Figure 5.9 You can get a map of anywhere from National Geographic's Map Machine – and they look much better in colour!

Streetmap

The Map Machine may be fun, but this site is really useful. Streetmap gives you what you might expect from its name – and more. You can get a detailed streetmap for any town in the UK, plus roadmaps – at a variety of scales – and, sometimes, aerial photographs. You can locate a place by name, post code, Ordnance Survey or Landranger reference, latitude and longitude or even telephone code! You can then use its 10km scale roadmap to plot a route to the town, and a 500m streetmap to find your way to the house.

Try it: Plan a route at Streetmap
① Go to Streetmap at **www.streetmap.co.uk**
② Enter a place name, post code or other identifier.
③ Click search .
④ Click the zoom controls to change the scale.
⑤ Click the arrows around the edge to scroll over the map.

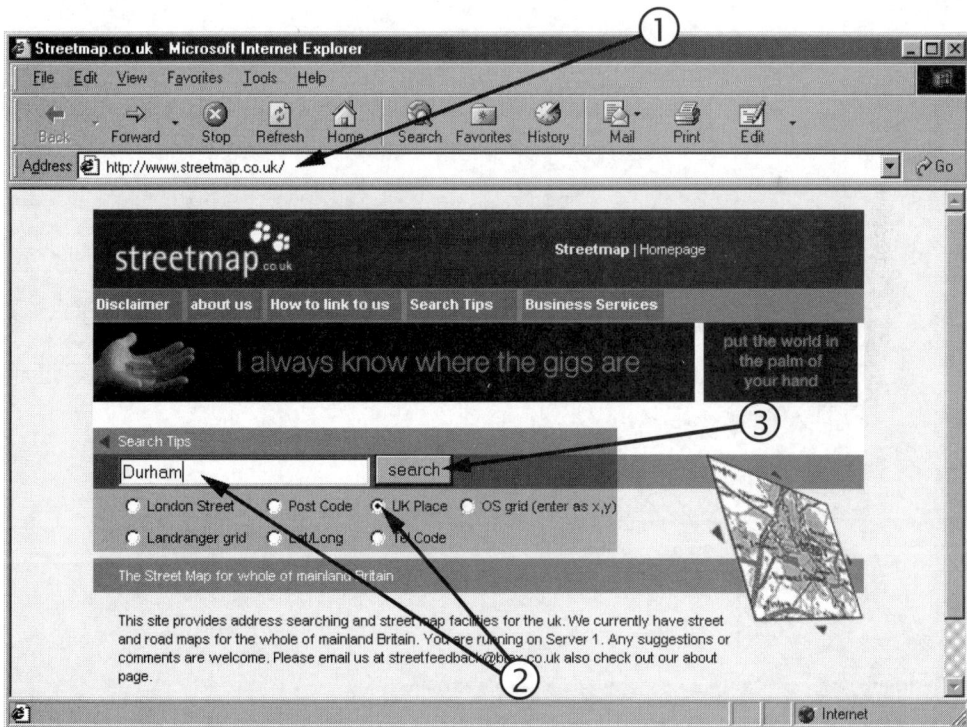

Figure 5.10 Thanks to Streetmap, you can have a street map for any town in Britain.

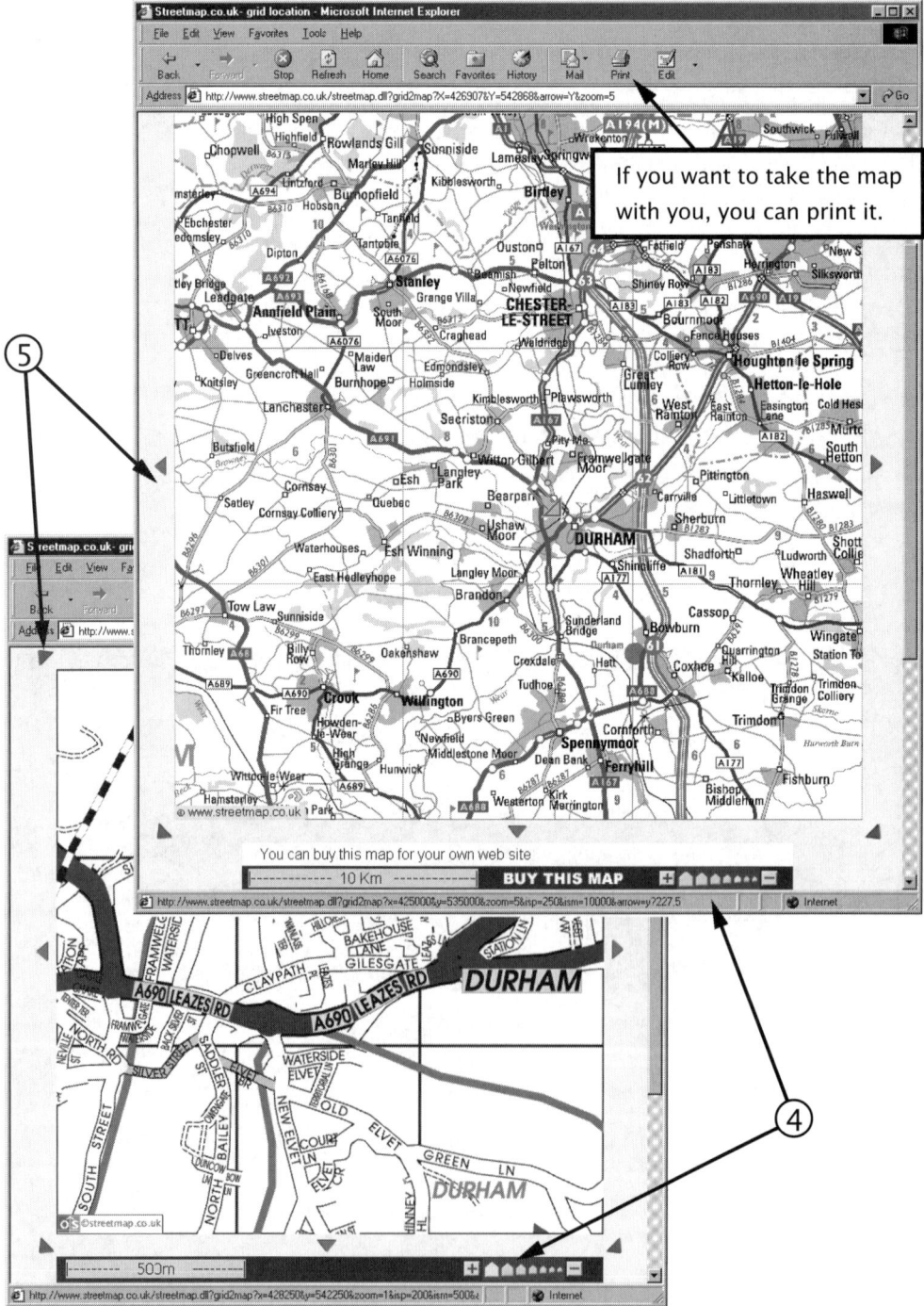

If you want to take the map with you, you can print it.

Figure 5.11 Streetmap has the maps to get you anywhere in Britain.

The media

Newspapers

Most directories and portals carry some news and sports results, but if you really want to read the news, then turn to the papers. Many of the national papers and some of the local ones now have Web sites, and these normally carry the same stories and range of features as the printed editions.

The *Telegraph* (**www.telegraph.co.uk**) was the first of the UK nationals to go online with its *Electronic Telegraph*. It has now been joined by *The Times* (**www.thetimes.co.uk**), The *Guardian* (**www.guardianunlimited.co.uk**), the *Financial Times* (**www.ft.com**), the *Daily* and *Sunday Mirror* (**www.mirror.co.uk**) and many more besides.

You may have to register before you can access a paper's site, but registration is free.

Figure 5.12 *The Times* site aims to keep the look and feel of the printed paper, except that here, as at most news sites, the front page is used for leads-ins to the main stories.

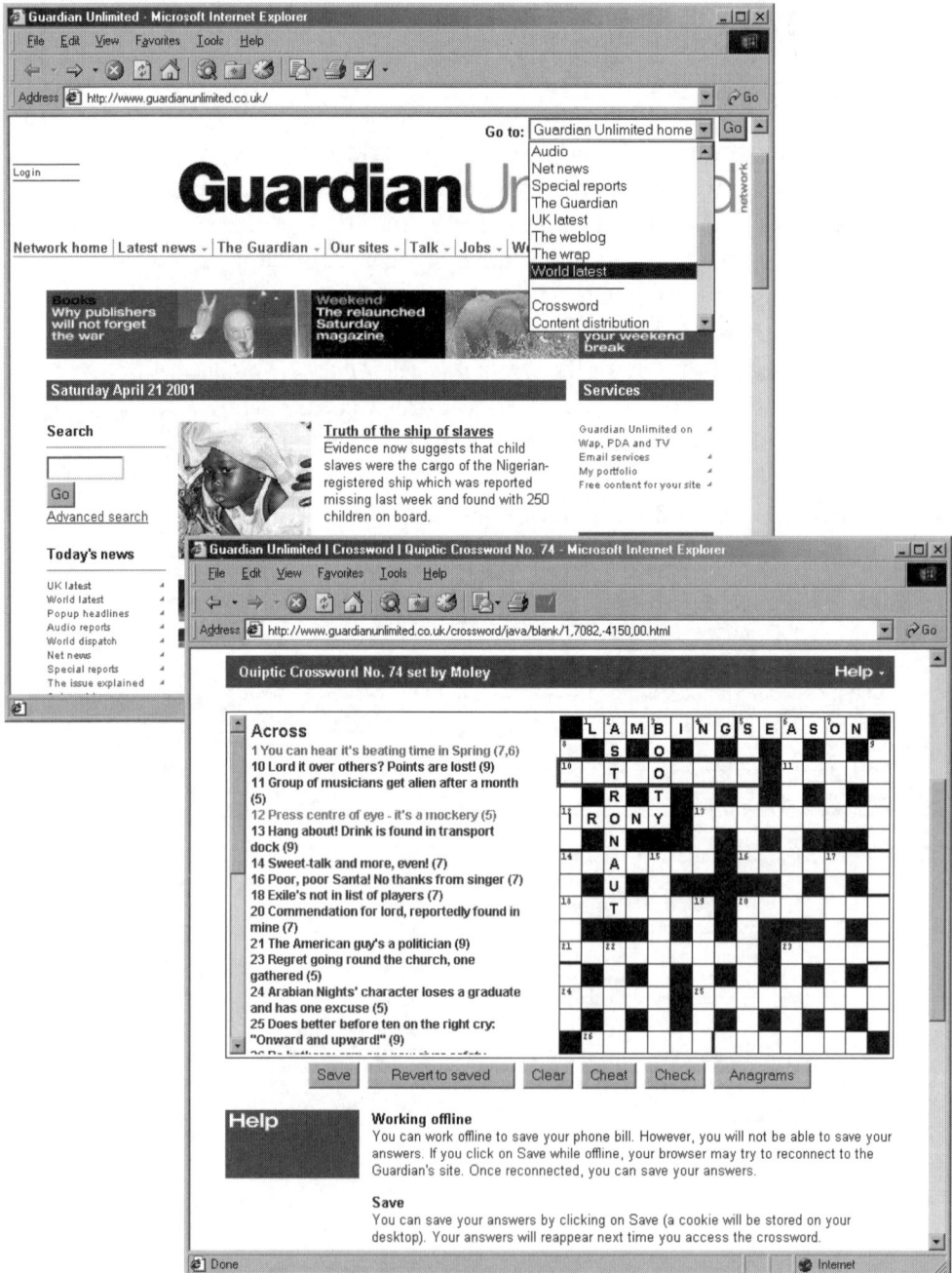

Figure 5.13 Immediate access to major stories, and simple ways to reach the different sections of the paper are key features of the *Guardian*'s site. And the crosswords are great – you can do them online (where there's a cheat mode!) or print them out.

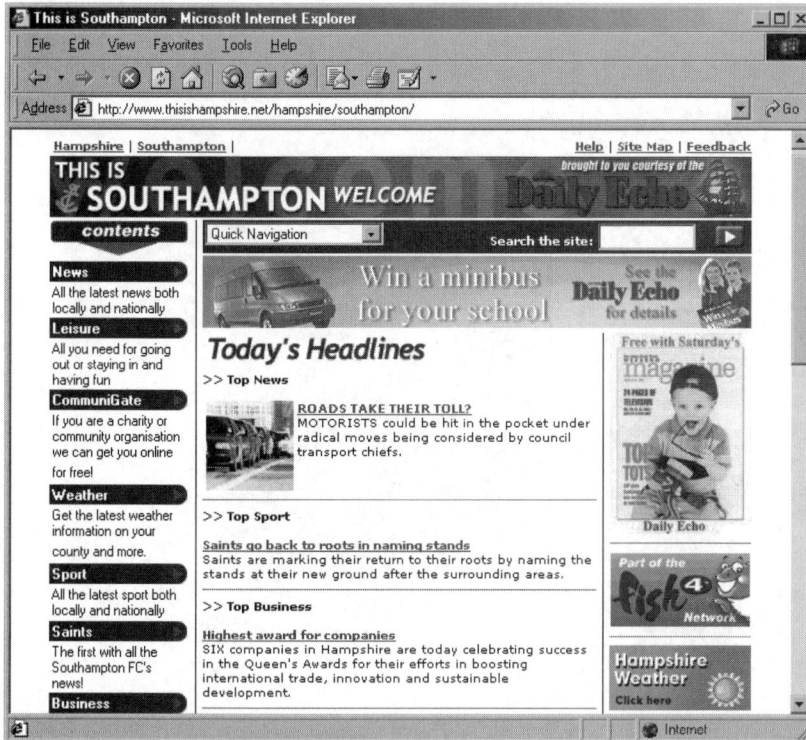

Figure 5.14 It's not just the nationals that have gone online. Local papers are discovering that the Web may be worldwide, but it works equally well for communicating within a town.

Magazines and e-zines

Many magazines are also published electronically, either in whole or part – and the choice stretches from *Private Eye*, through *Cosmopolitan* to *Scientific American*, with most computer mags in between. Some are subscription-only, but most are free and none are as convenient as their paper equivalents for reading on the train or in the bath! I suspect that making the content available online does not actually affect the printed sales that much, as it's far easier to buy a copy if you want to read more than a couple of stories – and a taster on the Web may encourage you to buy.

There are also an increasing number of e-zines – magazines which are only published electronically. These include many computer-focused ones, such as *Cool Doctor*, for new

If you want a foreign paper or magazine and can't get it locally, see if it is published online

e-zine = electronic magazine

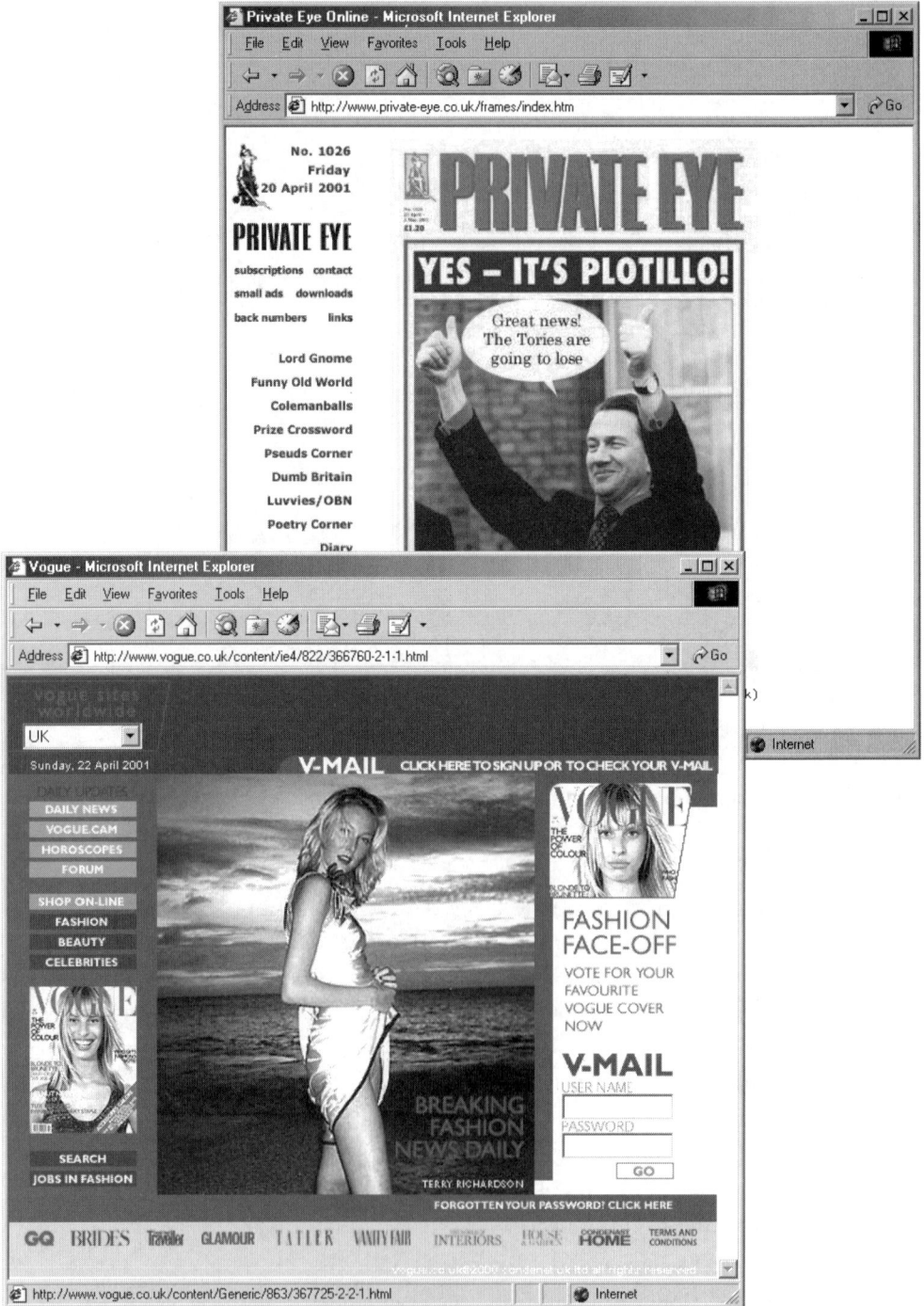

Figure 5.15 Most magazines are now also published online...

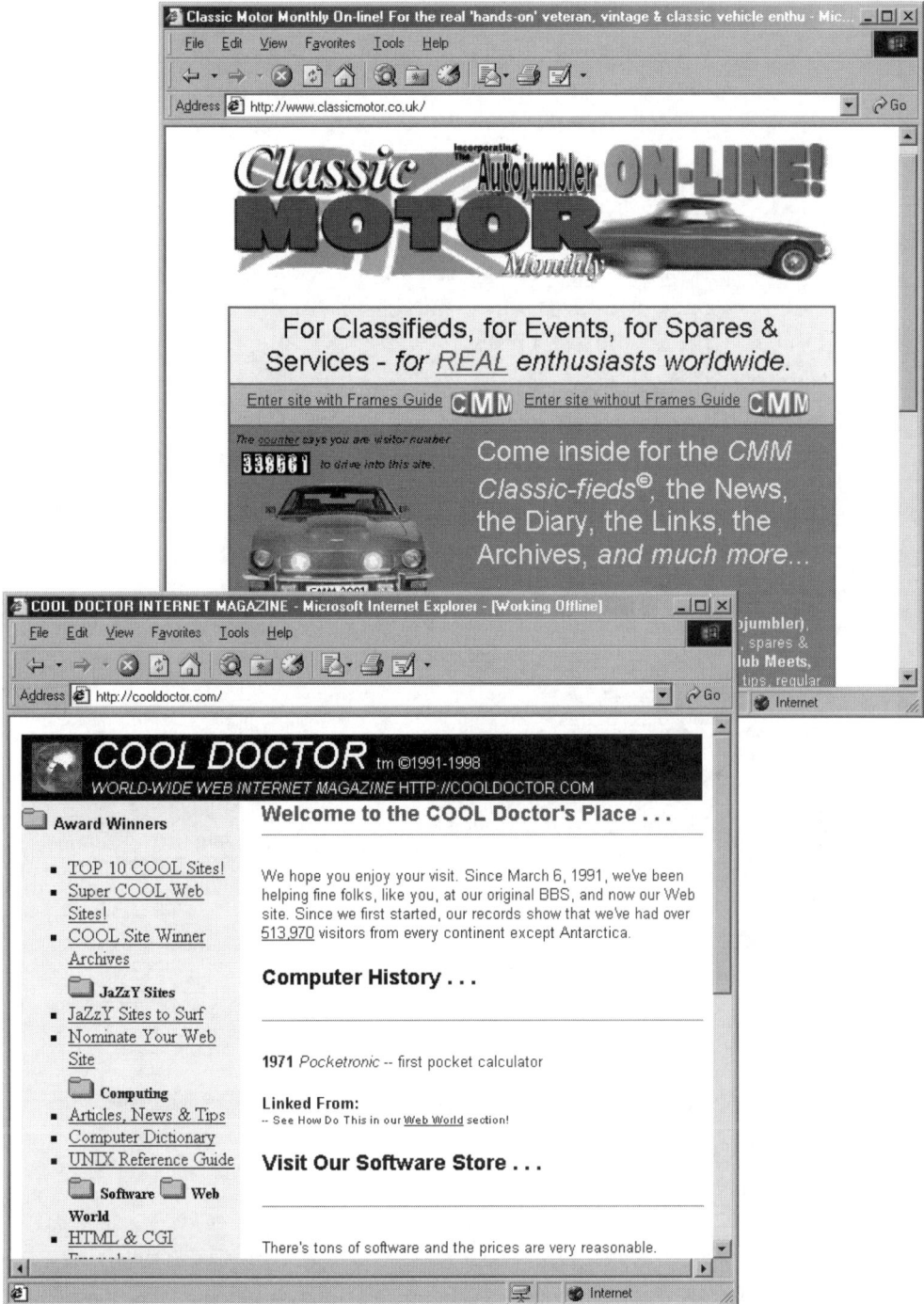

Figure 5.16 ...while some magazines are only published online.

computer and Internet users. But there are many others on a wide range of special interests, plus a whole bunch of 'alternative' magazines covering music, politics, film, sex, free speech, the occult and the weird.

TV

All the TV companies now have their own Web sites, which they typically use to tell people what's coming, to give the background or more details of current programmes. Some do far more. The BBC's Web site is one of the most popular

Figure 5.17 The BBC News site offers live audio/video reports – the picture quality is poor (as always on the Web), but you can get the latest news when you want it.

UK sites, because it is not just an extension of their standard broadcasting. This is an education, entertainment, analysis, news and sports resource of the highest quality. One of its features that I find most useful is the up-to-the-minute news. You can view the most recent news broadcast at any time, or follow up individual stories – many with live audio/video feed.

Visit the BBC's main site at **www.bbc.co.uk** or go straight to the newsroom at **news.bbc.co.uk**.

Internet Radio

Want some music while you are surfing? You can now listen to radio broadcasts from all over the world through your PC.

The radio reception is not 100% brilliant, but it's not bad. The problem isn't in the quality of the sound but rather in its continuity. New compression techniques have reduced the size of sound files, but they still take a lot of bandwidth and there's not much to spare. If you get online through an ISDN or other high-capacity line, you'll have no problem. If you link through a dial-up connection, data rarely comes in faster than 2Kb per second. That's just enough to cope with a broadcast, but if you are also surfing elsewhere, that will add to the overall quantity of data. Expect breaks in transmission of a second or so at a time, and expect other sites to download more slowly.

Try it: Listen to the radio while you surf

① Open the **View** menu, point to **Toolbars** and turn on the **Radio** toolbar.

② Click on **Radio Stations** and select **Radio Station Guide**. This will take you to **WindowsMedia.com**, where they have links to radio stations all over the world.

③ Stations can be listed by format, language, country or other features. Pick a feature from the first drop-down list, then the required format, language or whatever from the second.

④ Select a station and click Play > .

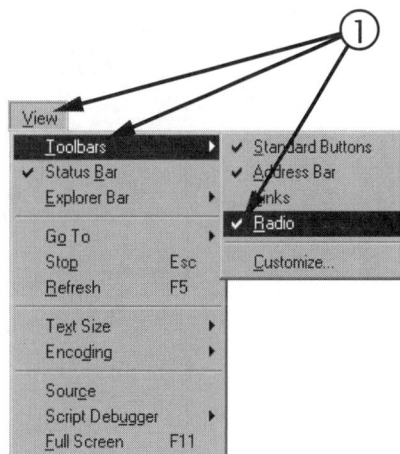

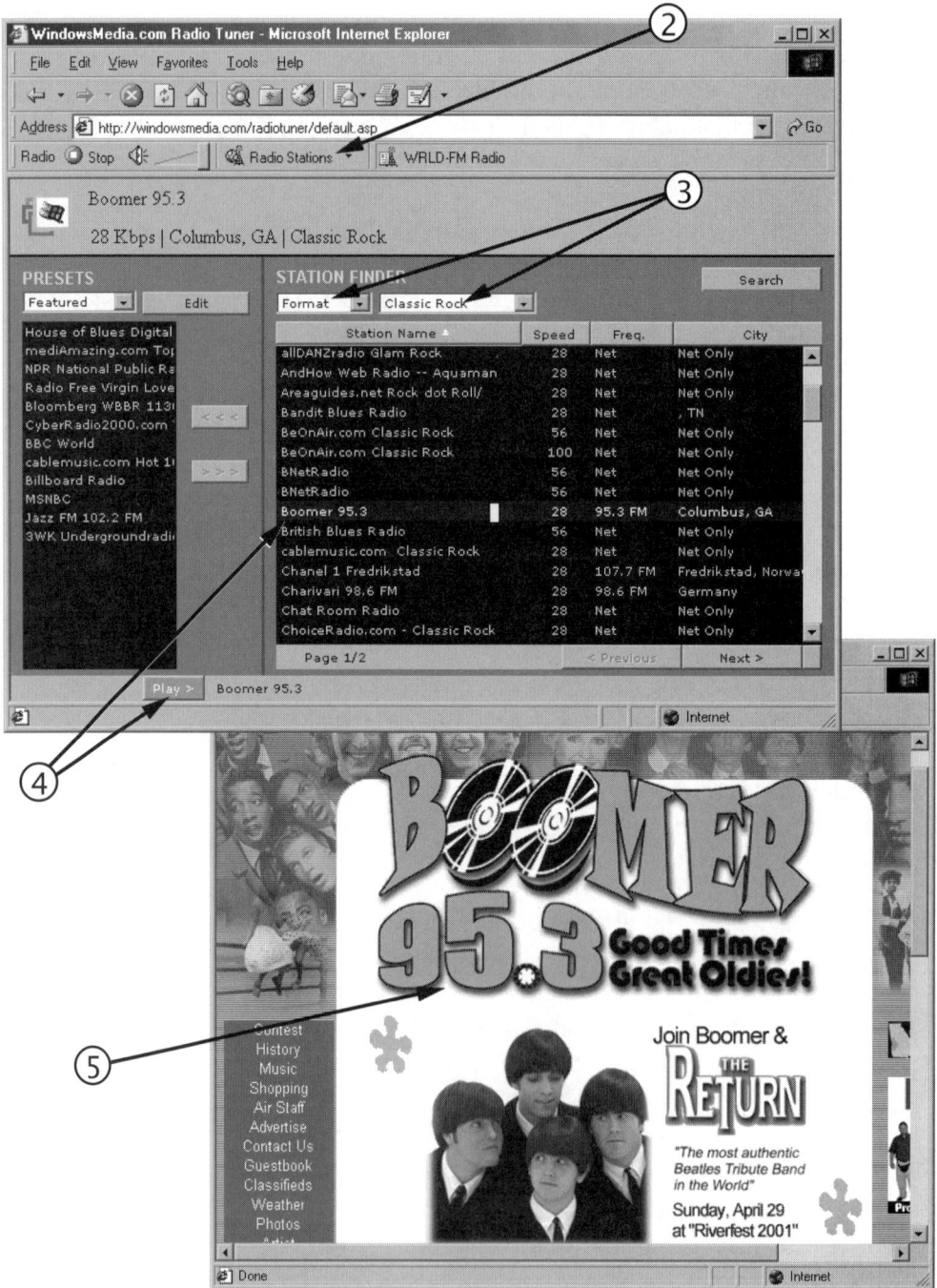

Figure 5.18 With Internet Radio, you can select your choice of music from thousands of stations from all over the world.

⑤ There will be a delay while Internet Explorer connects to the station and starts to load in its audio broadcast. It will normally also download the station's Web page, in a new window. If you don't want to read about the station, close down this window – you do not need to be at a station's site to listen to its broadcast.

The movies

Every self-respecting film nowadays has its own Web site. It will go online before the film is released and stay there for as long as it is being shown, offering trailers, behind-the-scenes stories and – if it wins any – details of its awards.

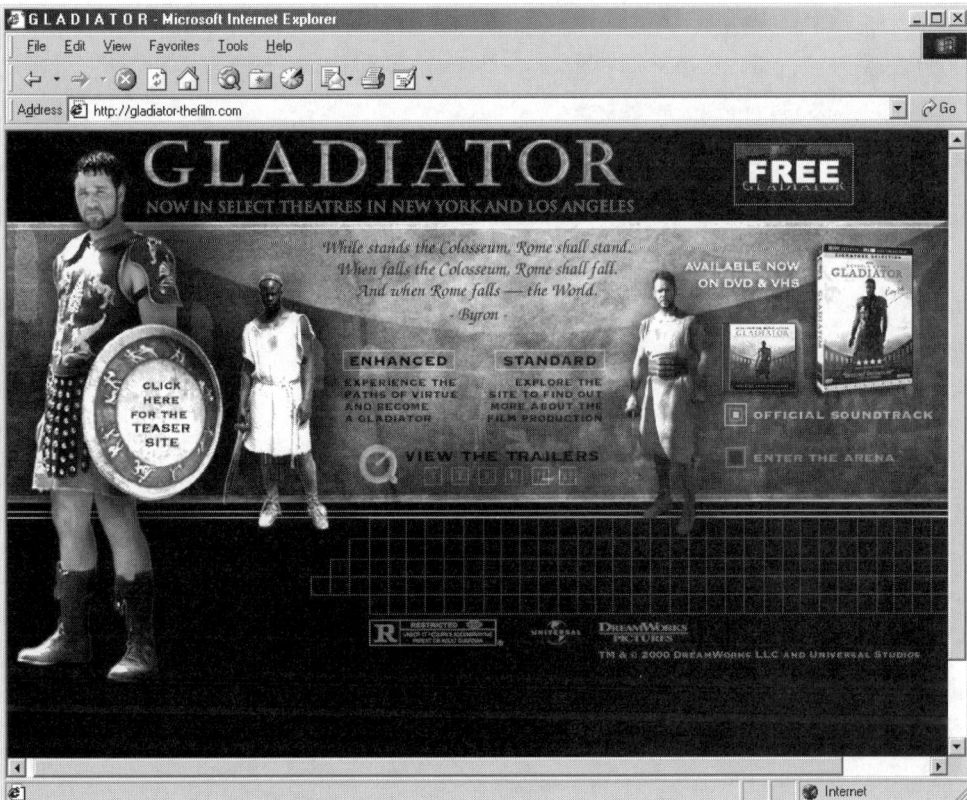

Figure 5.19 Web sites play an important part in promoting films. Whether you would want to download a trailer through a dial-up connection is another matter. Gladiator's low resolution trailer (gritty and jerky) was 9Mb, and it would be quicker to go to the cinema, queue for an hour and watch the film than to download the high-resolution one!

The IMDb

But if you really want to know about a movie, you should go to the International Movie Database. This has the credits, plot, trivia, goofs, stills and reviews from pretty well every movie ever made. Use it to get the lowdown on a film, to track an actor's career, or to answer 'Where did I see that face before?'

Try it: Buff up on a movie at the IMDb

① Go to the database at **uk.imdb.com** or **us.imdb.com**

② Select **Titles** as the search mode.

③ Enter the name to find and click (Go!).

④ Click the actors' links to find out what else they were in.

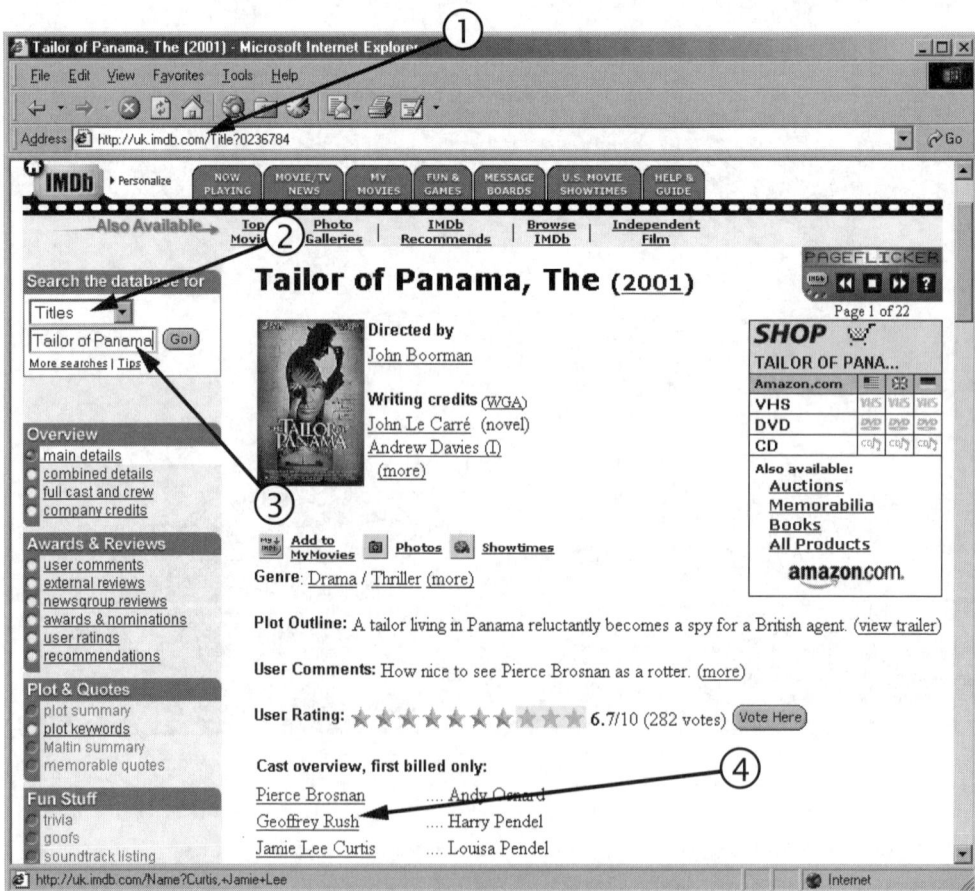

Figure 5.20 You too can become a movie buff, with the IMDb!

Film Finder

OK, so you've viewed the trailer, read the reviews and de-
cided you want to see the movie – so where's it on? The Film
Finder at Yell will tell you. You can use it to locate a cinema
that is showing a specific film, or to find out what's on in
your town.

Try it: Find a film

① Go to **uk.yell.com**, click **Film Finder** and pick a region.

② Tick the town(s), and select a specific film or leave that
set to **All**, then click Search .

③ Click on the cinema to get details of the showings.

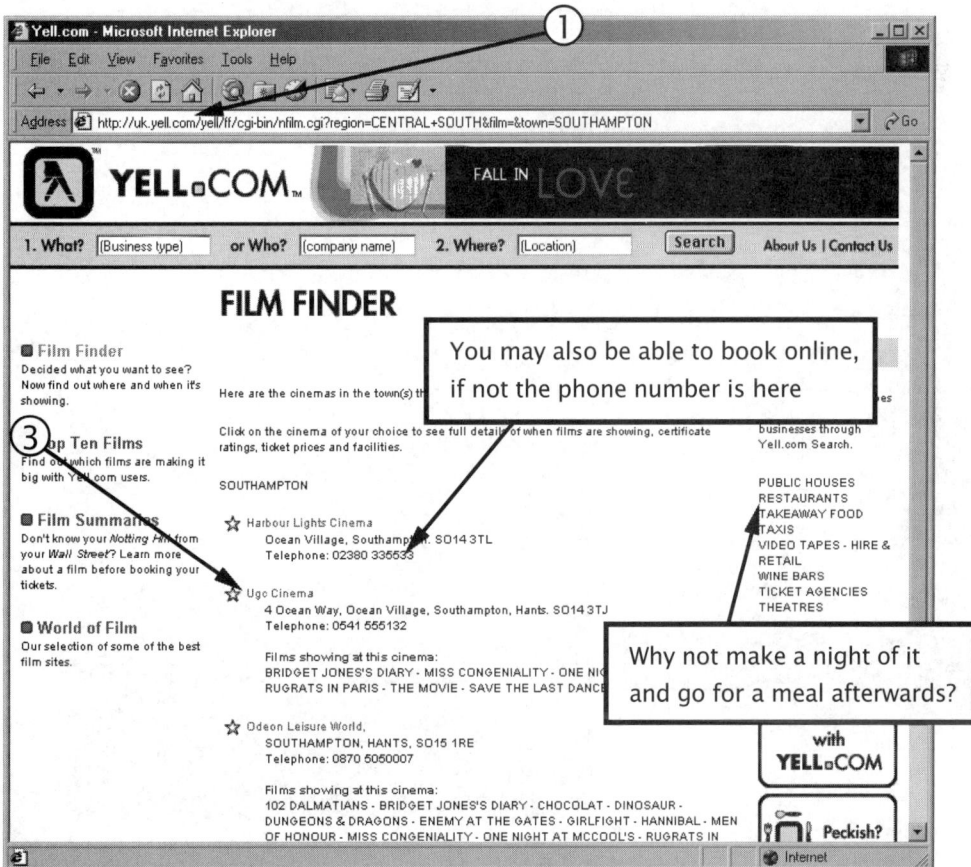

Figure 5.21 Film Finder is only one of the services offered by Yell (Electronic Yellow
Pages). You can also use it, like the printed version, to find firms and tradesmen.

Site seeing

Web cam =
camera attached
to the Web

One day you will be able to see the world, in high-resolution, full colour, real time without leaving your chair! One day, but not yet... There are *web cams* and virtual tours that will give you glimpses of Omsk, Tromso or the Bronx, and some are worth a visit. The picture quality is rarely brilliant – the pictures can be small and grainy – and it can take a while for the image to download, but a web cam gives you a window on to a place thousands of miles away. You can see things, as they are at that moment, on the other side of the world!

Try it: Go around the World in 80 clicks

① Go to **www.steveweb.com/80clicks/index.htm**

② Take the tour. Expect to wait a little for each new image, but be ready to move on to the next if it is too slow.

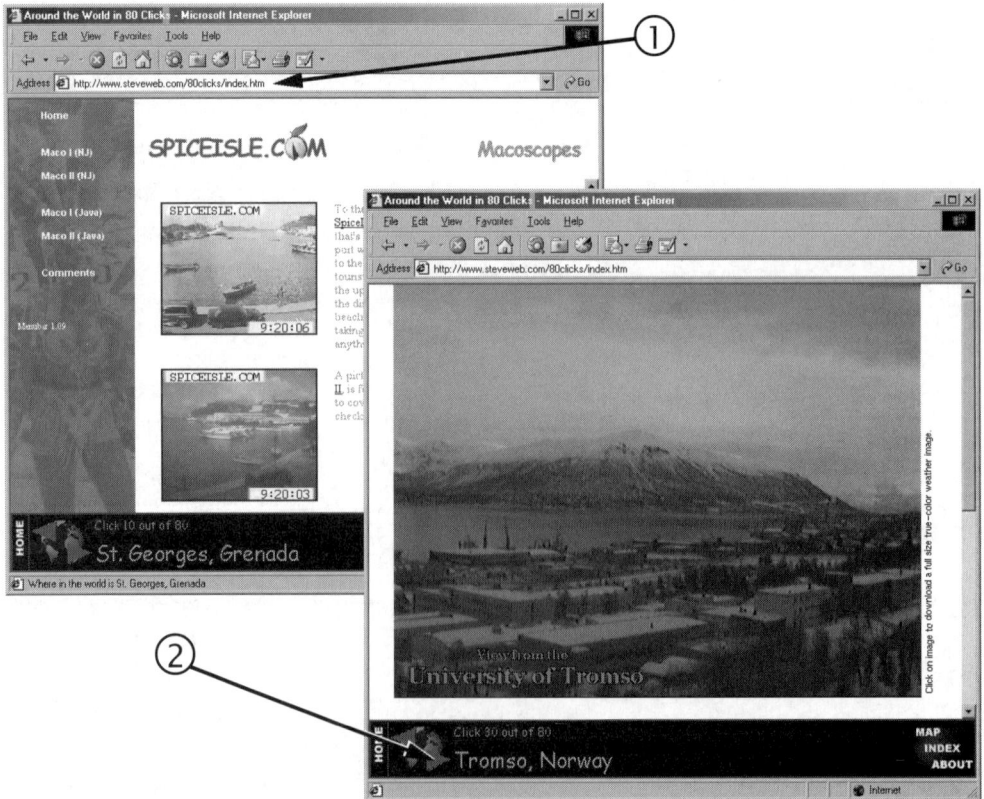

Figure 5.22 Two stops on the 80-click world tour!

If you want to find more web cams, there are links to lots of them at Yahoo! At the top menu, select *Internet*, then *Devices Connected to the Internet*.

The Web Museum

Many museums and art galleries have a Web site, but most of them use their sites merely to advertise their exhibitions and opening times (all very useful, as it can save you phoning in advance, or turning up to find they are closed!) – and perhaps to try to sell you something from the gift shop.

The Web Museum is something else altogether. It is an art gallery designed for the Web, an unfunded project started by Nicolas Pioch and grown with the help of volunteers, with the aim of making art more accessible to a wide audience.

The pictures are shown as thumbnails, grouped by theme and artist, and accompanied by thoughtful biographies and artisitic commentaries. These thumbnail images are all linked to much larger ones – sometimes full-screen. The quality is not as good as you would get in a good art book, but the images are readily available.

The museum is based in Paris, but there are *mirrors* of it all over the world. In the UK, the closest sites are at Southern Record and at Imperial College.

Mirror = copy of a set of files or of a whole Web site

Try it: Visit the Web Museum

① Go to the Web Museum at **www.southern.net**/wm or **sunsite.doc.ic.ac.uk/wm**

② Visit the special exhibition of *Cézanne* or the medieval art of the *Duc de Berry*.

Or

③ Go to the *Famous Paintings* collection and pick a theme, then an artist.

④ If you want to get a better view of a picture, click on its thumbnail.

⑤ If the picture is a big one, press **[F11]** or open the **View** menu and select **Full Screen** for a bigger viewing area.

⑥ If you really like a picture, right-click on it and select **Set as Wallpaper**, to put it on your desktop.

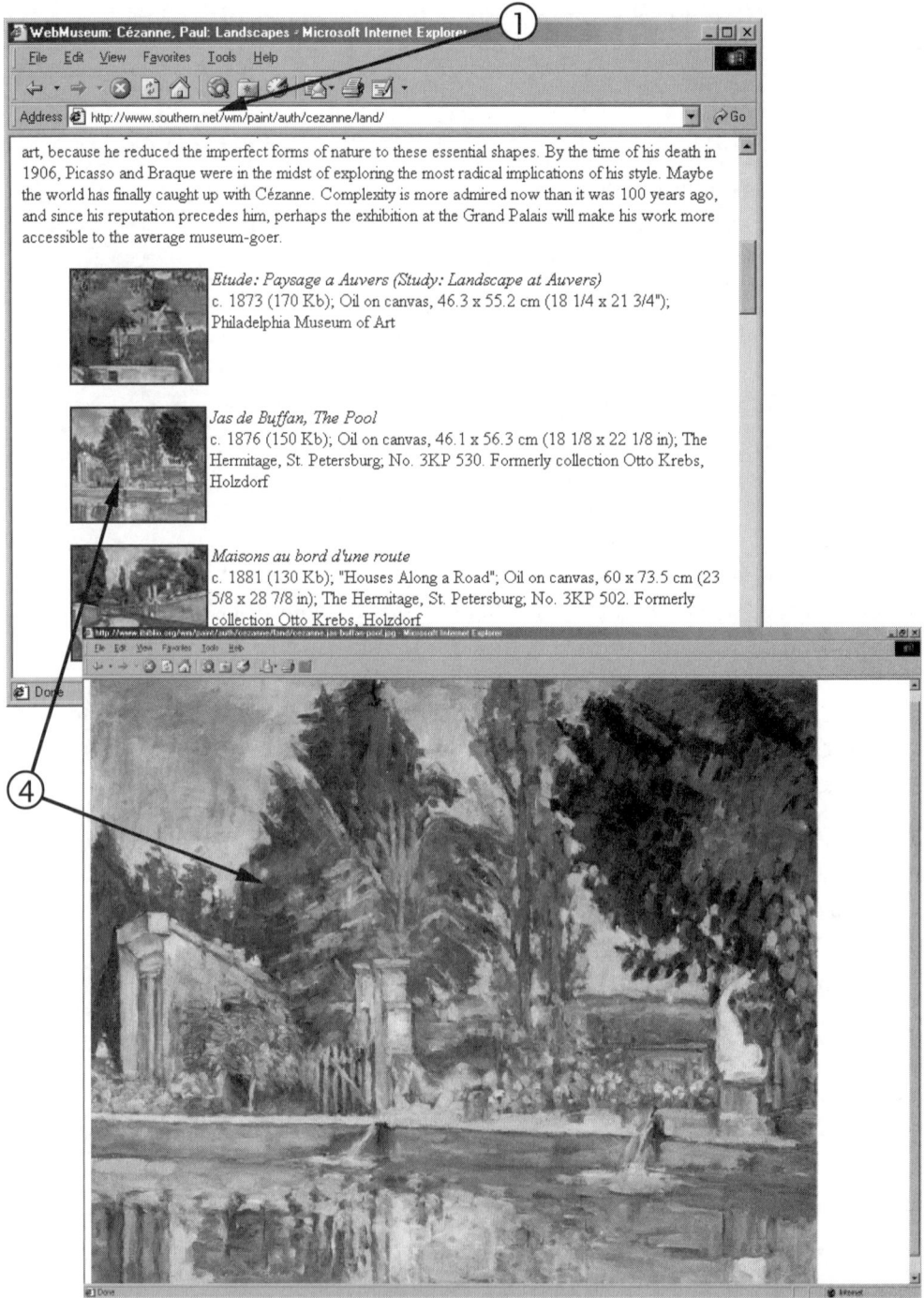

art, because he reduced the imperfect forms of nature to these essential shapes. By the time of his death in 1906, Picasso and Braque were in the midst of exploring the most radical implications of his style. Maybe the world has finally caught up with Cézanne. Complexity is more admired now than it was 100 years ago, and since his reputation precedes him, perhaps the exhibition at the Grand Palais will make his work more accessible to the average museum-goer.

Etude: Paysage a Auvers (Study: Landscape at Auvers)
c. 1873 (170 Kb); Oil on canvas, 46.3 x 55.2 cm (18 1/4 x 21 3/4");
Philadelphia Museum of Art

Jas de Buffan, The Pool
c. 1876 (150 Kb); Oil on canvas, 46.1 x 56.3 cm (18 1/8 x 22 1/8 in); The Hermitage, St. Petersburg; No. 3KP 530. Formerly collection Otto Krebs, Holzdorf

Maisons au bord d'une route
c. 1881 (130 Kb); "Houses Along a Road"; Oil on canvas, 60 x 73.5 cm (23 5/8 x 28 7/8 in); The Hermitage, St. Petersburg; No. 3KP 502. Formerly collection Otto Krebs, Holzdorf

Figure 5.23 Get some culture at the Web Museum!

Files from the Net

The Internet is a great source of files – games, utilities and application programs, updates and patches to fix bugs, academic papers, fonts, clipart and photos, audio and video clips and a whole lot more.

Software sites

If you are looking for programs of any sort, the best places to start looking are the software sites. Some are dedicated to particular operating systems or types of programs, while others aim to be the biggest, brightest or best. They are all generally well-organised, with good search facilities to help you track down software by type, operating system or name. Most of these sites have short reviews of the software on offer – very useful if you are not entirely sure what you want.

The software falls into three categories:

◆ **Freeware** is there for the taking. Any software arising from publicly-funded research in the US is normally made available to the public. Authors also give programs away from goodwill, or to promote themselves or their commercial products. Just because it is free does not mean it is no good. Internet Explorer is freeware!

◆ **Shareware** can be tried for free for a limited time, after which you should register and pay the fee. This is usually in the range of £10 to £30. Among the many excellent shareware programs are WinZip, the standard file compression utility, and Paint Shop Pro, one of the leading graphics packages.

◆ **Demos** will give you a taste of what the program can do, but prevent you from doing some key tasks.

Shareware.com

This excellent service is my normal first port of call when looking for software. There are over 250,000 programs and other files, but simple page design and well-organised storage ensure that it is quick and easy to use.

Try it: Download from shareware.com

Other shareware sites include **www.jumbo.com**, **www.tucows.com**, **www.zdnet.com/ downloads**

① Go to **shareware.cnet.com**.

② In the **Search** field, enter the name of a specific program or words to describe the type of software, e.g. 'graphics animation'.

③ Select the **platform** – *Windows*.

④ Click **Search**.

⑤ When you get the results, read the brief descriptions to identify the file you want.

⑥ Click on the filename. You will be taken to a new page to select a download site – pick one geographically close to you, as closer generally means faster downloading.

⑦ Select **Save to disk**, then choose a folder to save it in.

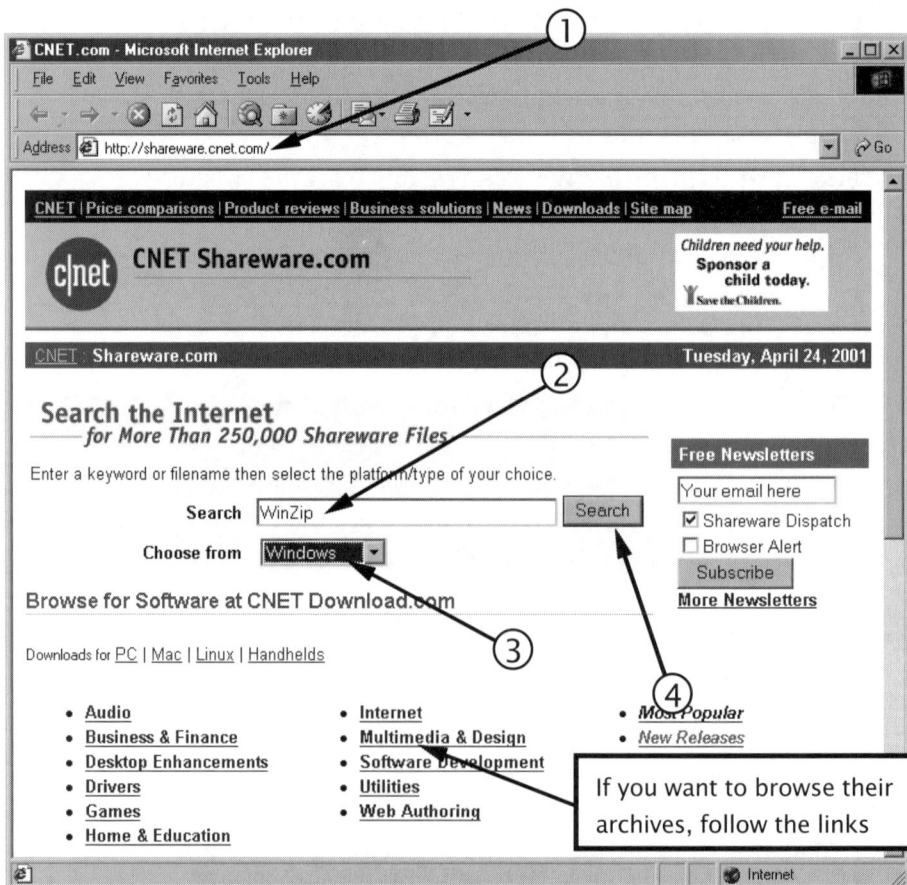

Figure 5.24 If you haven't got a copy of WinZip, get one at **shareware.com**.

Installing downloaded files

Downloaded software will come in one of three forms:

◆ *Ready-to-run programs* – just click and go! If you intend to keep the program, move it out of the temporary folder on your hard drive into safer storage.

◆ *Standard Zip files* – for which you need a copy of WinZip to unpack. These sometimes contain the program and associated files in ready-to-run form, but often have a set of installation files, and you must then run the *Setup* or *Install* file to get the actual program.

◆ *Self-extracting Zip files* – these have been created by WinZip, but have the unpacking routines built into them.

When you run a self-extracting Zip file, or unpack an ordinary Zip file, their constituent files will normally be unpacked into the same folder. If these are the program files, you may want to set up a new folder for them and move them into it. If they are installation files, you will be prompted to choose a folder for the program during installation. The installation files can then be deleted from your temporary folder.

Hardware and software companies

All firms in the computing industry run a Web site nowadays. Most use the Web for advertising – and selling – their products, and for providing technical support. Software firms use their sites for distributing updates and bug-fixes to their old software demos – and sometimes full versions – of their new software. Hardware firms use them to distribute manuals and drivers for their hardware.

Windows Update

Windows 98 and Me come with a built-in link – both in IE and on the Start menu – to Microsoft's 'Windows Update' site. This should be visited every couple of months to check for new 'patches' – program fragments to fix minor problems that have turned up on Windows or on applications. (No modern software is ever 100% free of errors. No matter how carefully it is tested, new errors will always be found once it gets put into use in the real world.) You may also find new add-ons, extras and new and improved versions of some Windows components.

Printer drivers

If you are trying to get an old printer to work on a new machine – or are having difficulty installing a new printer – you may well need a new driver. (Drivers convert the output from applications into the codes for the printer.) You will usually be able to find and download one at the manufacturer's site.

Epson, for example, has a Download Library where you will find not only the latest drivers for their current range, but also those for most of their older products. The Library is not well signposted. If you start at the main home page (**www.epson.com**), it takes a while to work through to the right part of their local site. UK users can go direct to it at: **www.epson.co.uk/support/download**

Files from Web pages

There are files for downloading all over the Web. You will find home movies and Hollywood movie trailers; music – the new MP3 format delivers high-quality sound in very compact files; art galleries and photographic libraries; and loads of resources for programmers and Web page developers. Look around and you will find some great collections of resources built by Internet content providers, businesses and dedicated individuals for their visitors, fellow enthusiasts, students or potential customers.

Viruses alert!

If you only download files from established Web sites, you shouldn't have any trouble with viruses, as these sites check files for viruses before accepting them. For safety, install anti-virus software on your PC and check your downloads.

6

The Interactive Web

IN THIS CHAPTER:

- Online shopping
- Online banking
- Chat and games rooms
- Internet communities

The Web is not just for visiting and viewing, it is also for using actively. You can now buy everything from baked beans to a house online, and manage your money and have a social life without moving from your desktop.

The Web is not merely a passive resource from which you can glean information, images or files. There are many sites that are designed to be used actively and interactively. You can shop, find a house (and fix up a mortgage for it), insure your car, play games, make new friends and so much more.

It is impossible to list all the services that are now available on the Web – there are just too many, with new ones appearing all the time. In the UK alone, thousands of firms large and small now provide information, offer services or sell their goods over the Internet.

This chapter just gives a taster. To find out more about what's available online – in the UK – head for these sites:

◆   the UK directory at **www.ukdirectory.co.uk**

◆   UK Plus at **www.ukplus.co.uk**

◆   UK Yahoo! at **www.yahoo.co.uk**

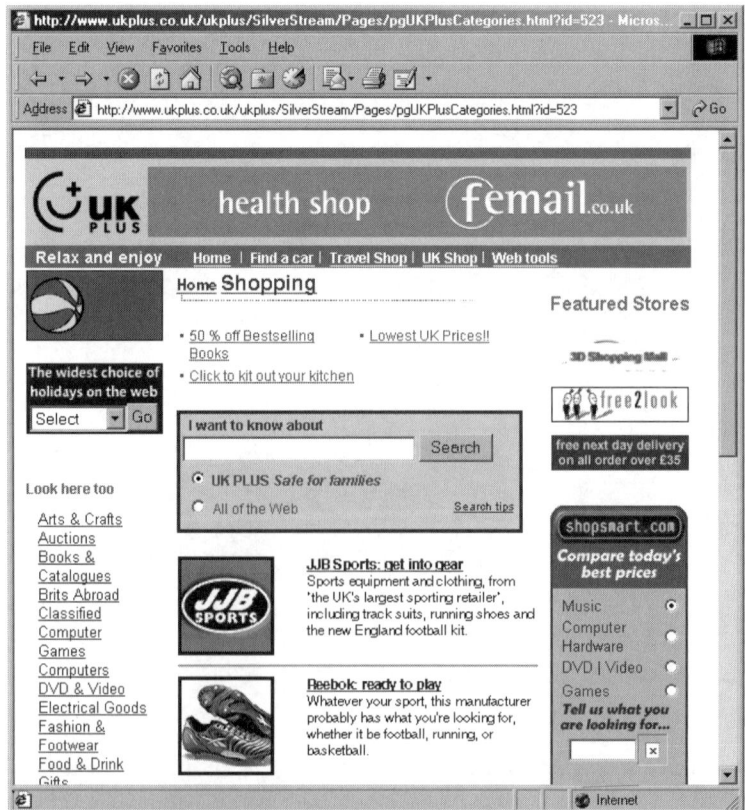

Figure 6.1 UK Plus is one of the best places to find Web retailers.

Online shopping

So what do they sell on the World Wide Web? You will find the kinds of goods that, five years ago, would have been sold by mail order or over the phone – the Web is a natural extension of these approaches.

The Web is a good place to sell anything which people buy on specification rather than by sitting on or trying on, e.g. computer hardware and software, books and CDs. It is also a logical place to sell those specialist goods that can be difficult to find in your local high street – a good range of organic foods, collectors' items, or almost anything handmade.

Buying online

Compared to a high street shop a Web retailer is likely to offer a wider choice of goods, and you can browse at your leisure for the best buy; but you can't try things for size or feel their quality, and returning faulty goods can be expensive in postage. In fact, Web retailing and mail order have a lot in common. There are the small, specialist suppliers who need to reach a wide audience to find enough customers to keep going, and the cut-price merchants who aim to pass on to their customers the savings they make through low overheads and bulk purchases.

Buying online works best where goods can be ordered on their descriptions or specifications

At BOL, they have in stock, or can quickly get, just about every book that's in print in the UK. Finding books is simpler here than on the shelves of a high street shop – though you can't browse them in the same way! The quick search will normally do the job, but there is also a full search where you can hunt by author, title, ISBN, publisher and other features.

Like most Internet stores, BOL uses the 'shopping basket' approach. After you have added all your items, you head for the checkout. There you'll register with the store, giving your credit card and contact details – you will normally only do this once. On future visits, only your shopper's name and password are needed.

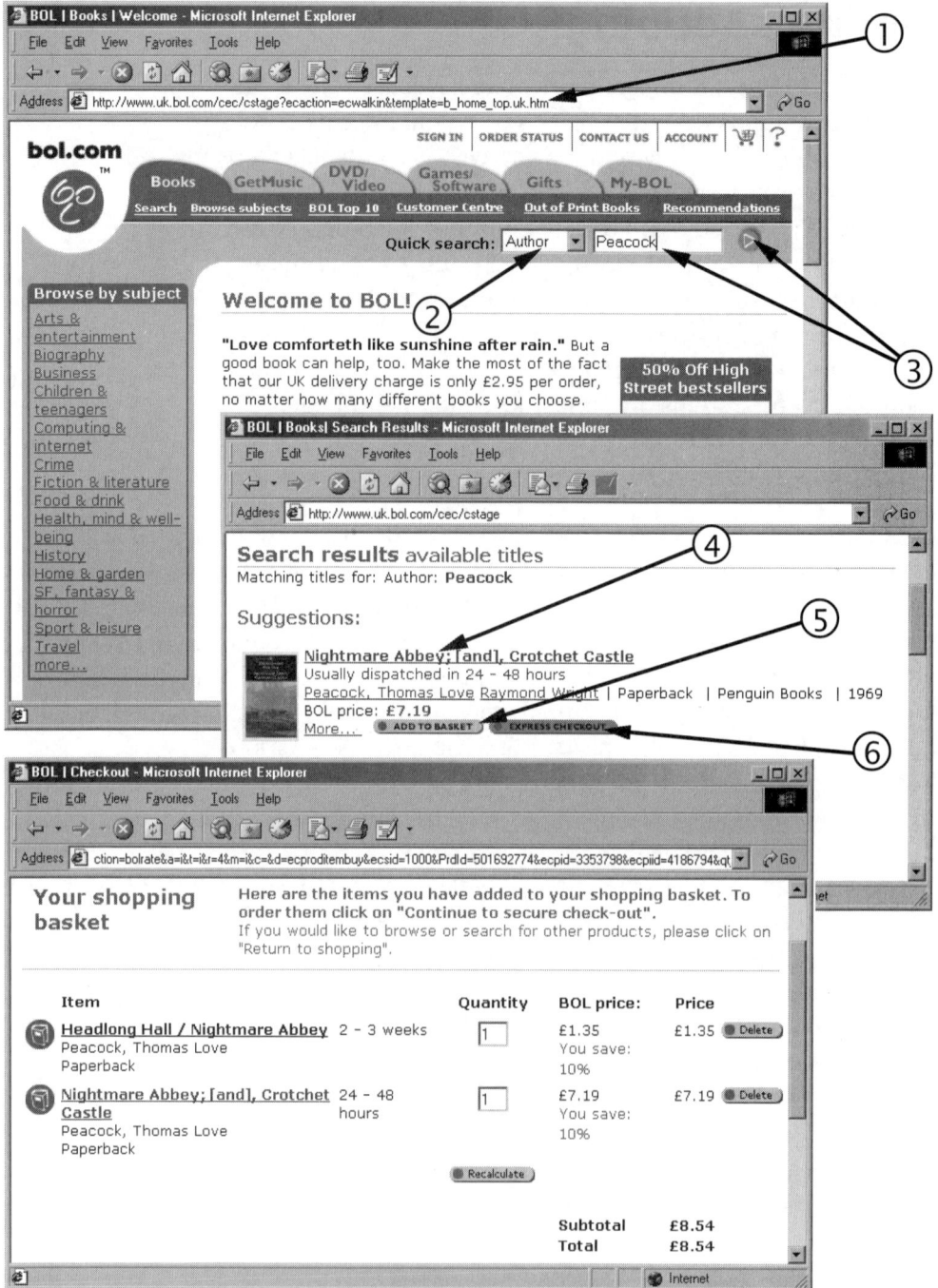

Figure 6.2 Buying a book at BOL – the other online bookshops such as **www.amazon.co.uk** and **www.whsmith.co.uk** offer very similar services.

Try it: Look for a book at BOL

① Go to BOL at **www.uk.bol.com**

② Select **Title** or **Author** in the first **Quick Search** slot.

③ Type the name and click ▶ .

④ If you want to know more about a book, click on its link.

⑤ To buy a book, click ● **ADD TO BASKET** if you want to go on and browse for more.

⑥ Or, click ● **EXPRESS CHECKOUT** to buy and exit.

Desk to door groceries

In the UK at present, the biggest online retailer is also the biggest supermarket – Tesco. Their success is well earned. Their site is simple to use, with some time-saving shortcuts if you are in a hurry, and they can deliver to anywhere within a few miles of most of their stores. There is a £5 charge, but it's worth it for the convenience if you don't have the time. energy or transport to visit the store.

Allow yourself half an hour for your first visit to Tesco online. Apart from registering, you'll also need to spend some time finding your way round. Subsequent shopping trips can be much faster as you can leap to your favourite products, or use a typed list for a very quick shop.

Smart shopping

We've already noted that one of the key advantages of Web retailing is lower prices. Several Web companies have built on this idea and will search for the best prices for you.

ShopSmart is currently the leader in this field. Their well-organised site offers an efficient search facility that will tell you where on the Web you can buy an item, and at what price. They also have some good gift ideas at Christmas!

Try it: Find a bargain at ShopSmart

① Go to ShopSmart at **uk.shopsmart.com**

② Select a category, then work through the following pages to identify the exact item.

③ Check the results for the best deal and click **Go to Shop** to find out more or to buy the item.

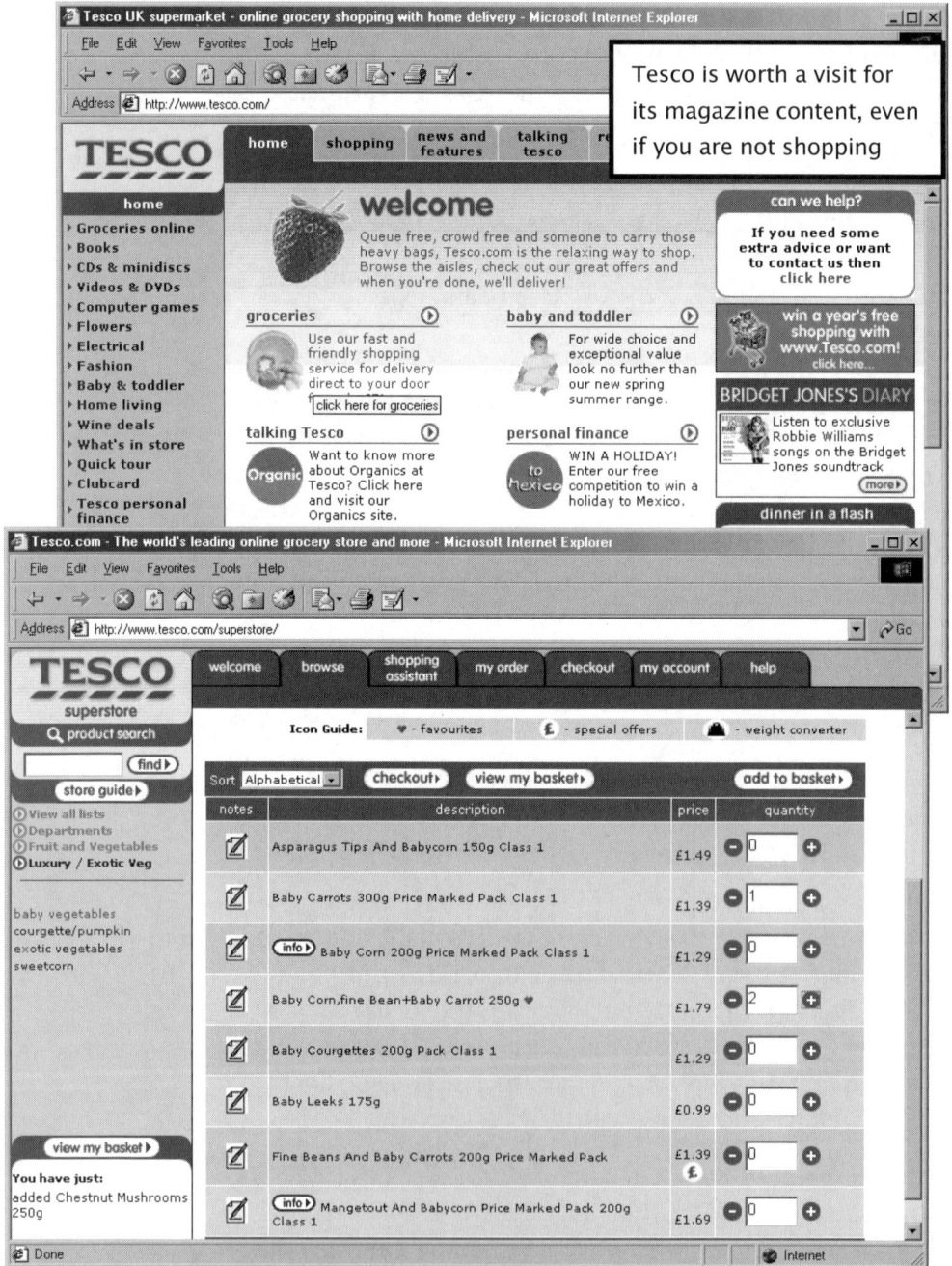

Figure 6.3 Shopping at Tesco. To reach this choice screen, I went to the Fruit and Vegetable department and selected Luxury/Exotic Veg. Most items can be reached with no more than two menu selections.

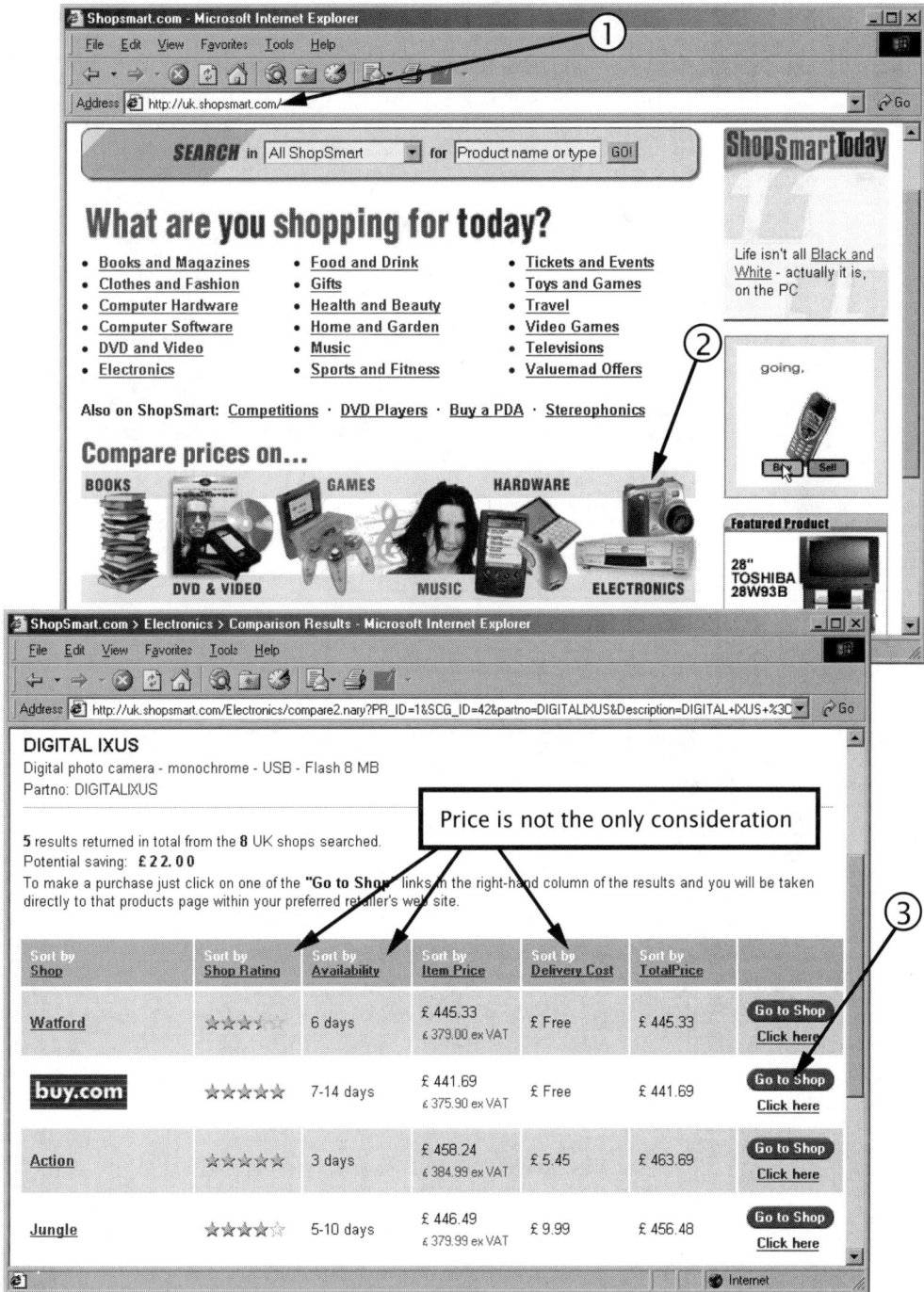

Figure 6.4 ShopSmart will point you towards the best bargains online.

Driving a bargain?

Next time that you are looking for a car, start online. You can buy online, or set up a deal which you then follow through with a local dealer – this is the approach taken at Broadspeed (see Figure 6.5), one of the leading Web-based car companies.

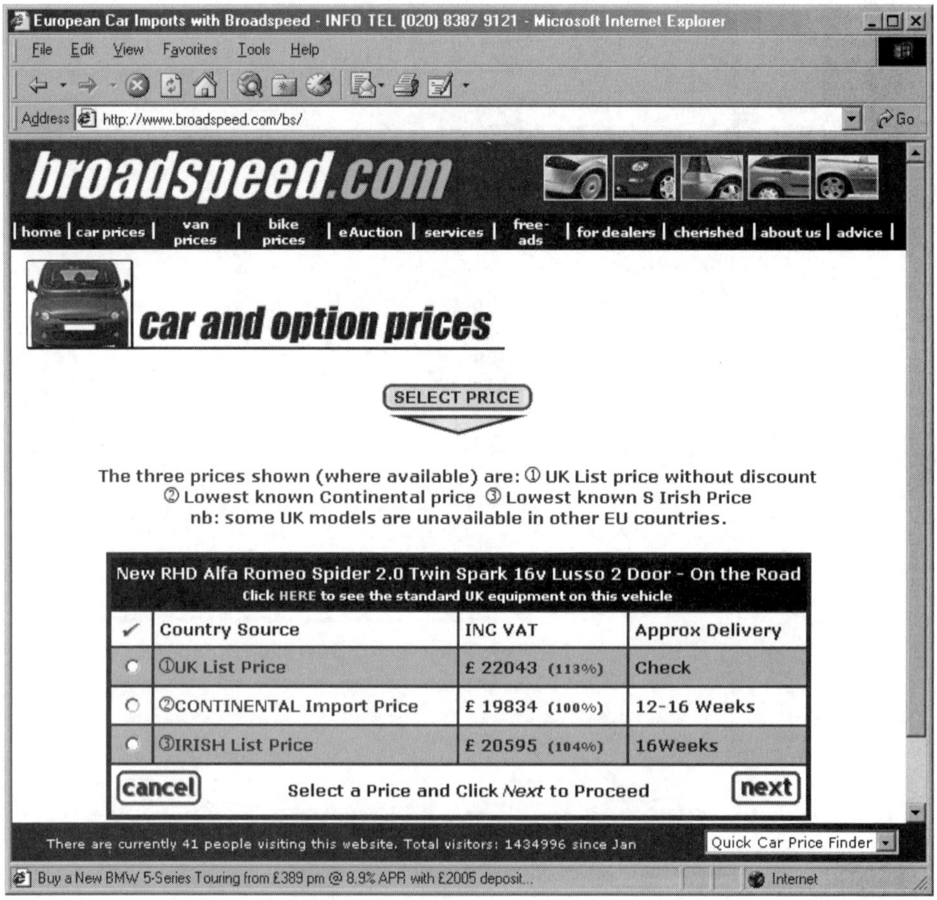

Figure 6.5 Importing your new car can be over 30% cheaper on some brands. The saving on the Spider isn't quite so dramatic, but I didn't want a Ford.

If you prefer to deal face-to-face, you can still use the Web to research the market. *Autotrader*, for example, has an excellent database of new and used cars, and efficient tools for querying it. Use it to work out which car is the best for you, and then locate a dealer or track down a used car.

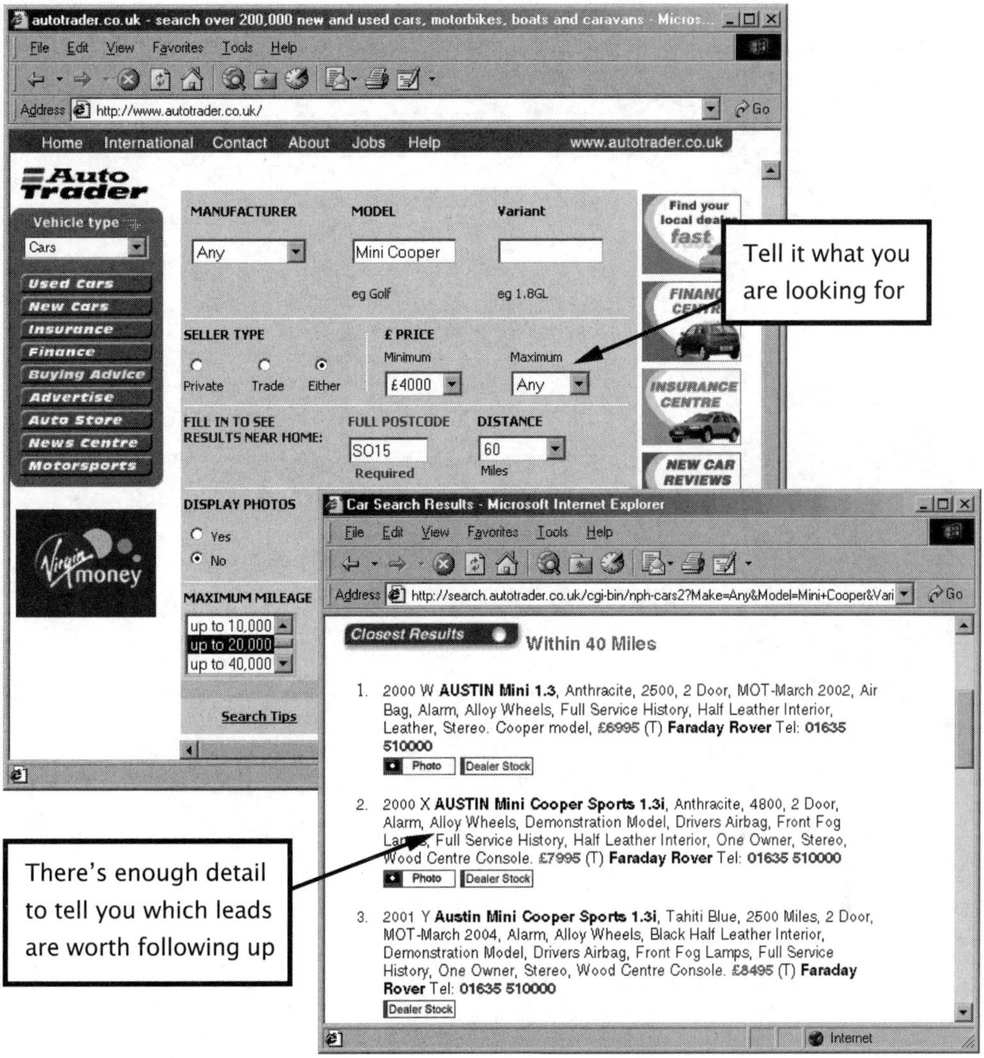

Figure 6.6 With my parking skills, I need something smaller than a Spider. Now who's got a Mini in reasonable nick round my way? *Autotrader* will find one for me.

Other car sites worth visiting include **www.allcarsites.co.uk** – a good starting point for the whole range of car-oriented sites – and **www.whatcar.co.uk**, the site of the magazine. Don't forget that most manufacturers will have their own sites, normally called www.*brandname*.com.

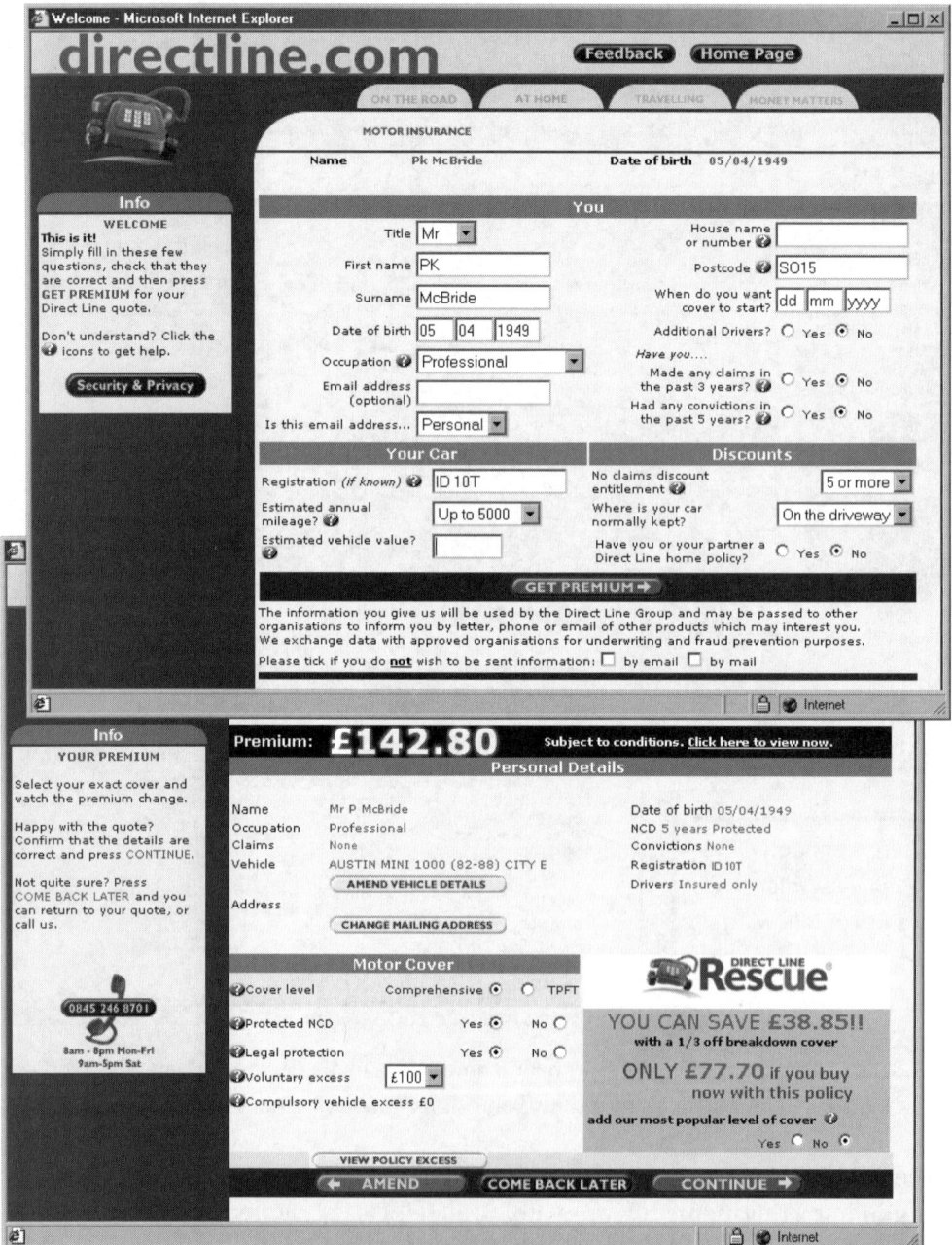

Figure 6.7 Having bought your new car online, you can go on to fix up its insurance. **Directline.com** will give you an instant quote. This works best for actual cars – it can find out all it needs to know from the registration number. The system can fall over if you try to get the cost for a make and model, as part of your pre-buying research.

Banks and finance

Does your bank offer an online banking facility? For keeping track of your money, paying bills and moving cash between accounts, online is as convenient as telephone banking and offers greater control. You can see what you are doing while you are online, and – if you have suitable software, such as Microsoft Money – you can download your account information for further work offline.

You can simply use online banking to manage your branch accounts, or you can take it further and open an Internet account – in addition to or instead of your existing ones. As Net accounts cost very little to run, they normally offer higher interest rates on deposits than branch accounts.

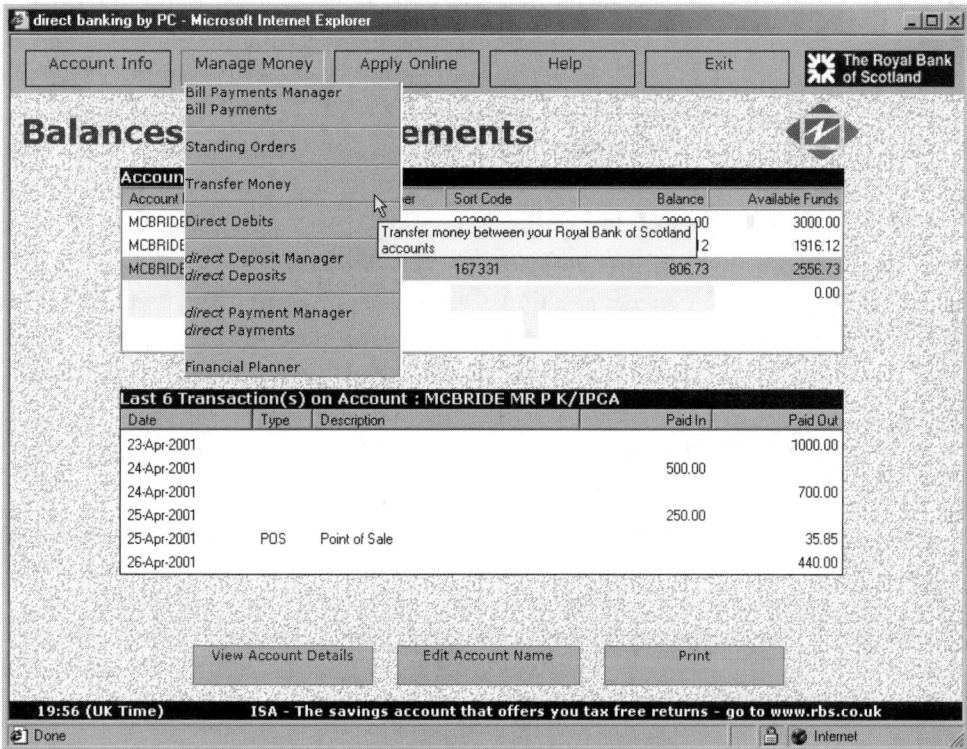

Figure 6.8 Online banking gives you control over your accounts – you can move money between them whenever and as often as you like, to maximise interest. (And, yes, I have faked this screenshot. After all, one advantage of online banking is its confidentiality!)

If you want a mortgage, pension, ISA or insurance, check out the Web. Most companies now run sites where you can, at the very least, read about their services. At the more interactive sites, you can get instant quotations or calculations based on your figures. While you may not want to rush into any long-term financial commitments, it's good to be able to get high-quality information online.

Is it safe?

The Internet has its fair share of crooks, but if you observe a few sensible precautions, you should be able to buy goods and services online as safely as you can by mail order or in the high street.

♦ It is cheaper to trade on the Internet than it is on the high street or by mail order, so you should expect to get a better deal, a faster service or a lower price. But if an offer sounds too good to be true, it probably is!

♦ Don't deal with people you don't know or with those that you can only contact over the Internet. If a firm is new to you, check that they exist by looking them up at Yell (**uk.yell.com**) or the Companies lists at Yahoo!

♦ You are as safe paying by credit card over the Internet as you are over the phone – which is not completely safe. Make sure that the SSL security checking is enabled on the Advanced Internet Options. This ensures that the transactions you have with the firm cannot be 'eaves-dropped' over the Internet.

Credit card fraud makes up less than 20% of Internet fraud – most victims paid by cheque, cash or money orders

♦ Security should not be a problem with established high street and telephone banks, which use secure systems and have reputations to protect. But online, offshore banks should be approached with great care – if at all.

Interacting with others

The Internet offers many ways to interact with other people, including e-mail, newsgroups, chat and games rooms, communities, 'net phones' and even live video links.

E-mail is covered in Chapter 7, **newsgroups** in Chapter 8

Chat rooms

A chat room is an open space where people can type messages to one another in real time. Some people find them a good place to while away the hours, but I'm afraid I'm not one of them. It is rare to find a chat room where an interesting conversation is going or can be started up and kept going. There are some practical problems:

◆ Most chat rooms will accommodate 20 or more people at a time. You cannot get this number of strangers chatting together – as a group – even in a face-to-face meeting. In practice, there will be several conversations going on at once, cutting across each other.

◆ The chat is typed and takes a few seconds to reach the screen. Between reading something and typing your response, several other messages – including some from other conversations – will have hit the screen.

◆ Too many chat users seem to be there for getting off or showing off. This is true even for those rooms that are supposed to be centred on a specific topic.

But these objections apply only to *public* rooms. There are also *private* rooms which you can enter only by invitation of the first one there. These can be a good way for scattered friends and family to gather. A private chat needs a bit of arranging – though less than the average family party! Someone will have to organise it, informing the others of the time and place through e-mail, and setting up the private room before the rest get there.

If you want to chat, try these places:

chat.yahoo.com
www.excite.com/communities
communities.msn.co.uk/people

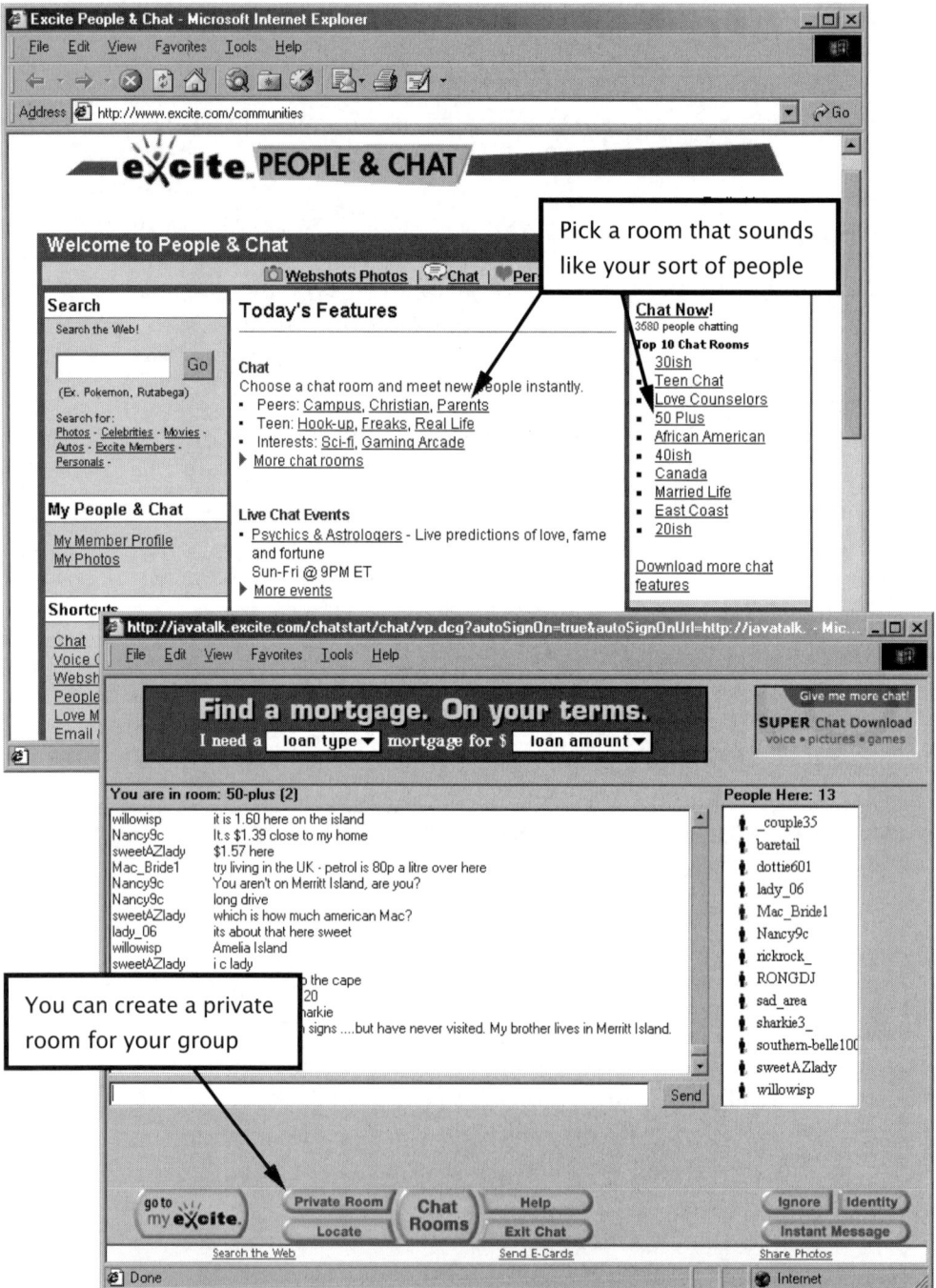

Figure 6.9 Chatting at Excite. The delays between typing and reading, and only being able to enter one short line at a time, make it hard to keep the chat flowing smoothly.

Games rooms

These are better places than chat rooms for having fun and making new friends. You can play your favourite card, board or table game, either as a serious competitor or using it as a vehicle for a gossip - just the same as in the real world.

To play games online, you will normally need some special software, and this can be in two forms.

♦ At MSN's GameZone (**zone.msn.com**), you have to download and install the software. This can take a little while - and several attempts - as there are several megabytes of files, but the games run well and look good.

♦ Yahoo! games use Java *applets*. These will normally download in a couple of minutes, though the game's appearance may not have quite the same gloss. In the **Security**

Applet = small program embedded in a Web page

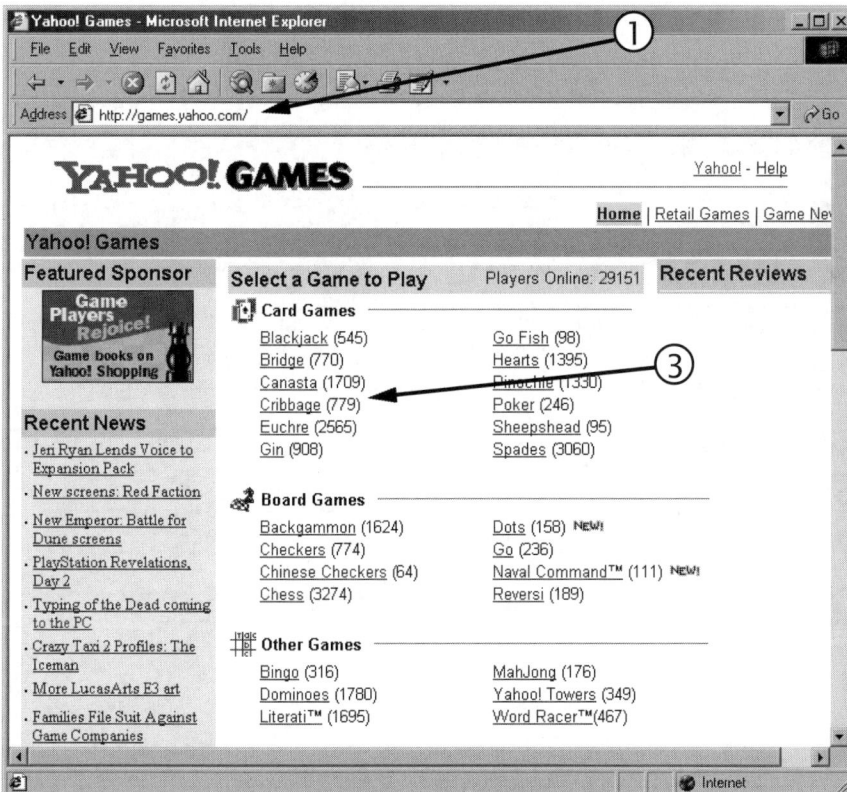

Figure 6.10 There is a good range of games to play at Yahoo! Games. Go and play - see the next page for instructions.

Settings dialog box, if you have the **Java permissions** set to *disable Java* (page 66), change it to *High Security* instead – this will allow games applets to run, but without putting your system at risk.

Try it: Have a game at Yahoo

① Go to Yahoo! games at **games.yahoo.com** (Figure 6.10)

② Register, if this is your first visit, or sign in.

③ Select a game (Figure 6.10). The first time you play, you will have to wait for the Java applet to download. When you return, the applet file should be still present in your Temporary Internet Files folder, and ready for use.

④ Pick a table, to watch or to join if there is a spare seat (Figure 6.11).

⑤ Have fun! If you don't know how to play the game, older hands will normally be happy to show you.

⑥ To chat while you are playing, type your words into the slot below the game board and press **[Enter]** (Figure 6.12).

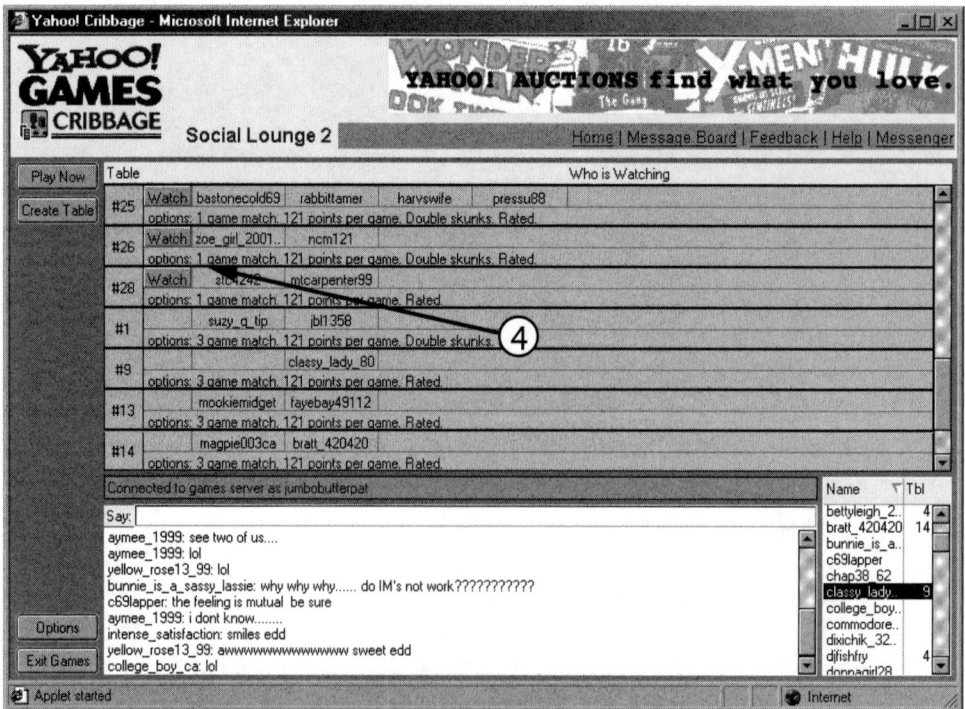

Figure 6.11 You might like to watch a few hands before you join in.

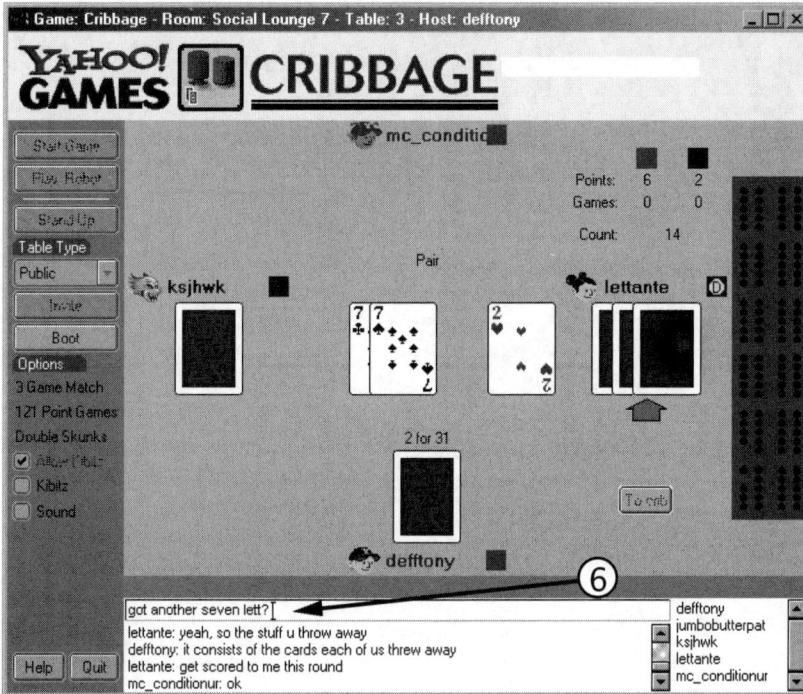

Figure 6.12 Cribbage was born in the taverns of the 17th century and is now being played in the virtual games rooms of cyberspace.

Communities

Internet communities take several forms but all share the same basic aims. They try to provide an environment where people can make and build friendships, share ideas and enthusiasms, and contribute to the growth of sites. (And, the more people that they can encourage to join and spend time there, the more they can charge advertisers, sponsors and linked e-retailers, to fund the community's staff and infrastructure.)

Some, like Hairnet, work largely through *forums*, where members can discuss topics by posting messages. These are very similar to newsgroups (see Chapter 8). The discussions here are not in real time – in fact, a conversation may run for weeks, with a couple of days or more between messages – but it tends to make for more thoughtful contributions.

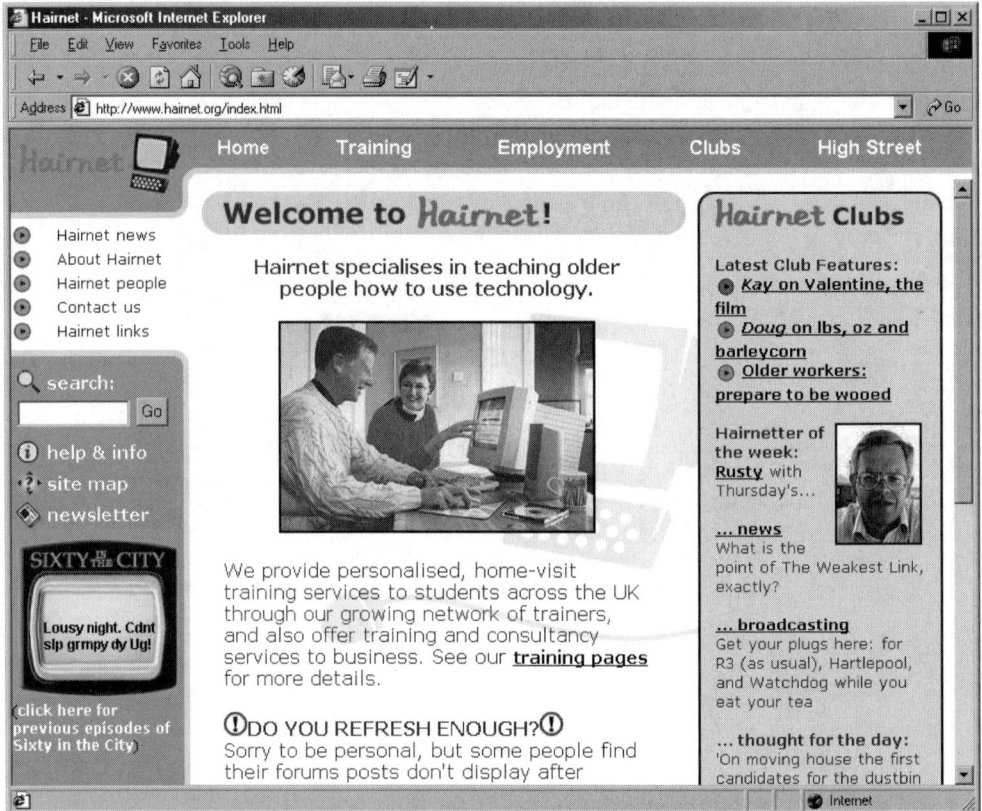

Figure 6.13 The Hairnet community, at **www.hairnet.org**, is built on a core of its past trainees, and aims to provide a place where they can continue to learn and to develop.

Others, such as Fortune City, are centred on the provision of free Web space. If you want to set up a Web site, but don't have an account with an ISP that offers Web space, FortuneCity and similar services are the solution. It's free; there are excellent Web site building tools (so that you can knock up a very creditable site in little time with no specialist knowledge); and you can also join in their community activities – get to know your neighbours, visit the forums, read and contribute to community newsletters.

If you want to know more, visit **www.fortunecity.com** or **www.geocities.com**.

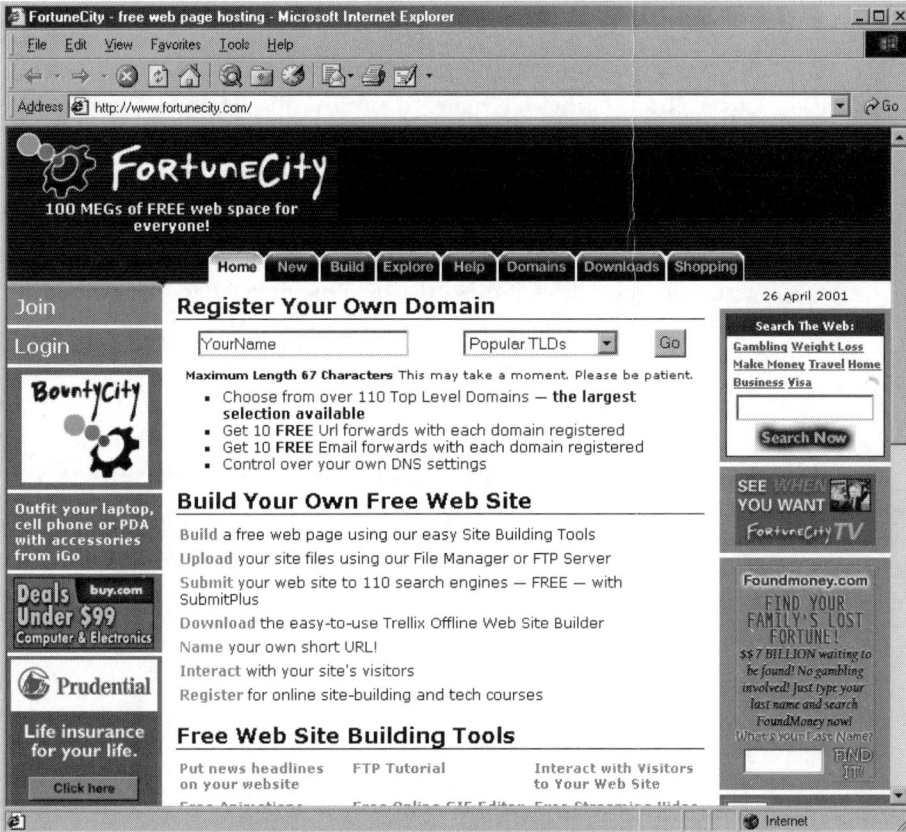

Figure 6.14 Fortune City is one of the leading 'Web space' communities.

Net phones and video links

'Net phones' allow you to talk over the Internet through a microphone and speakers on your PC. If you have a Web cam attached, you can also see and be seen while you talk. That's the theory. At present, the Internet's connections are really not good enough to carry the volume of information needed to run usable live video links. If you are connecting via a standard phone line, then data cannot travel at more than 5.6Kb a second – at best! In practice, data travels at half that speed or less. It is not enough to support continuous speech, let alone video. But keep an eye out. BT is starting to introduce newer, faster phone lines at reasonable prices, and the technology is still developing.

Your own Web site?

If your ISP offers Web space, have you thought about setting up a site? It doesn't have to be an 'all-about-me' site – and frankly, I don't think it should be unless you are a very interesting person – but it could act as a noticeboard for your club or society, or an advertisement for your business. It could be a photo album, where you post your holiday snaps for your family and friends to see. You don't have to go public and try to attract people. If you only tell the address of your site to those that you want to come, they are likely to be the only visitors.

Setting up a Web site is not difficult. Your ISP will almost certainly have a set of tools available to help you, and if not, it is not hard to construct a complete site from scratch. There are lots of books around, and plenty of advice to be found on the Web.

7

E-mail

IN THIS CHAPTER:

- Using Outlook Express
- E-mail addresses
- Sending and receiving messages
- Organising your mail
- Web mail

E-mail is one of the simplest Internet activities to use, but one that many people find the most useful. In this chapter we look at setting up your e-mail software, at sending and receiving e-mail, and dip into the conventions of electronic communications.

How does e-mail work?

It may help you to have an overview of the technology behind e-mail, so you can use it more efficiently and are less likely to get fazed when things don't quite go according to plan!

When you send an e-mail message, it does not go direct to your recipient, as a phone call does. Instead it will travel through perhaps a dozen or more computers before arriving at its destination – in the same way that *snail mail* passes through several post offices and depots. The message goes first to the mail server at your Internet service provider. This will work out which computer to send it to, to help it towards its destination. The server will normally hold the message briefly, while it assembles a handful of messages to send to the next place – again, in the same way that the Post Office sorts and bags its mail. Each mail server along the way will do the same thing, bundling the message with others heading in the same direction. This method gives more efficient Internet traffic and at the cost of very little delay – most messages will normally be delivered in less than an hour.

However, your recipients won't necessarily be reading the message within the hour. The delivery is to their mail boxes at their service providers. People only get their e-mail when they go online to collect it. (This is not true if they are on a network in an organisation, where the network management software will collect mail for everyone and distribute it.)

E-mail messages are sent as text files. An *unformatted* message will normally be very short, as it takes only one byte to represent a character – (plus about 10% more for error-checking). A 10-line message, for example, will make a file of around 1Kb, and that can be transmitted in about three seconds. Images, video clips and other files can be sent by mail (see page 221) but they must first be converted into text format. You don't need to worry about how this is done, as Outlook Express will do all the conversion automatically. What you do need to know is that conversion increases the size of files by around 50%, so even quite small images can significantly increase the time it takes to send or receive messages.

Snail mail = stamped stuff sent via the good old GPO

Messages can be in plain text or HTML-formatted – see page 210

The advantages of e-mail

◆ Delivery is fast, sometimes almost instantaneous and rarely taking more than a few hours.

◆ It's very cheap to use, costing only a few seconds of phone time, and possibly online charges, whether you are sending it overseas or down the road.

◆ You can send copies to a group of people at the same time and as easily as you can send to a single person. You only actually send one message – the mail server handles the copying and distribution.

◆ Incoming mail can be easily annotated and returned to its sender, or forwarded to other people.

◆ Images, documents and other files can be attached to messages, and detached and viewed at the other end.

And the disadvantages...

◆ E-mail does not always get through. The slightest error in the address will prevent a delivery, and even when you get it spot-on, there is always the chance of a failure in one of the links between you and your recipient. (It is a *very* small chance – e-mail is more reliable than snail mail.) Usually – though not always – you will get a notice back to let you know that your message has not been delivered.

◆ Delivery may be fast, but that doesn't mean a message will be read quickly. Not everyone checks their e-mail regularly – even some of us that work with computers normally only pick up the mail once a day.

◆ It is so easy and cheap to send out mass e-mailings, that junk e-mail is a real problem. No matter how careful you are about giving out your address, you will, inevitably, get on to some mailing lists. There are ways to reduce the level of the problem, but you won't stop it entirely.

Outlook Express

There are quite a few e-mail programs around, but Outlook Express is used far more than others. There are two reasons for its popularity: it's simple to use and efficient; and – the main reason – it is the software that comes with Windows, along with Internet Explorer, so it's probably in your machine already.

If you are one of those rare people with another e-mail program, don't stop reading. Almost all e-mail software works in virtually the same way as Outlook Express. Commands may be arranged on menus and toolbars in different orders, but they will still give you much the same range of facilities.

Screen layouts vary, but you will normally find three distinct areas, reflecting the way that mail is organised and handled.

- There will be a folder list, with folders for incoming, outgoing, recently deleted and copies of sent mail.
- Opening a folder will display, in another pane, a list of the messages within it, showing their headers – their key details, such as sender, subject and date.
- Clicking on a message opens it for reading. This will normally be in a preview pane in the main window, but may be in a new window. Messages are normally written in a separate composition window.

A few minutes is all it normally takes to find your way round an e-mail screen. The key things to remember are that the *Inbox* is where new messages arrive, that they will remain there until you delete them or move them to another folder; and that the *Outbox* is where your outgoing messages are stored if you write them when you are offline.

The Outlook Express screen

As well as the folder list, header area and message display area, Outlook Express has a number of other elements to the screen. They are all entirely optional and can be easily switched off if you decide that you do not want them.

Views bar   Toolbar

Folder bar   Headers

Outlook bar   Folder list   Preview pane header

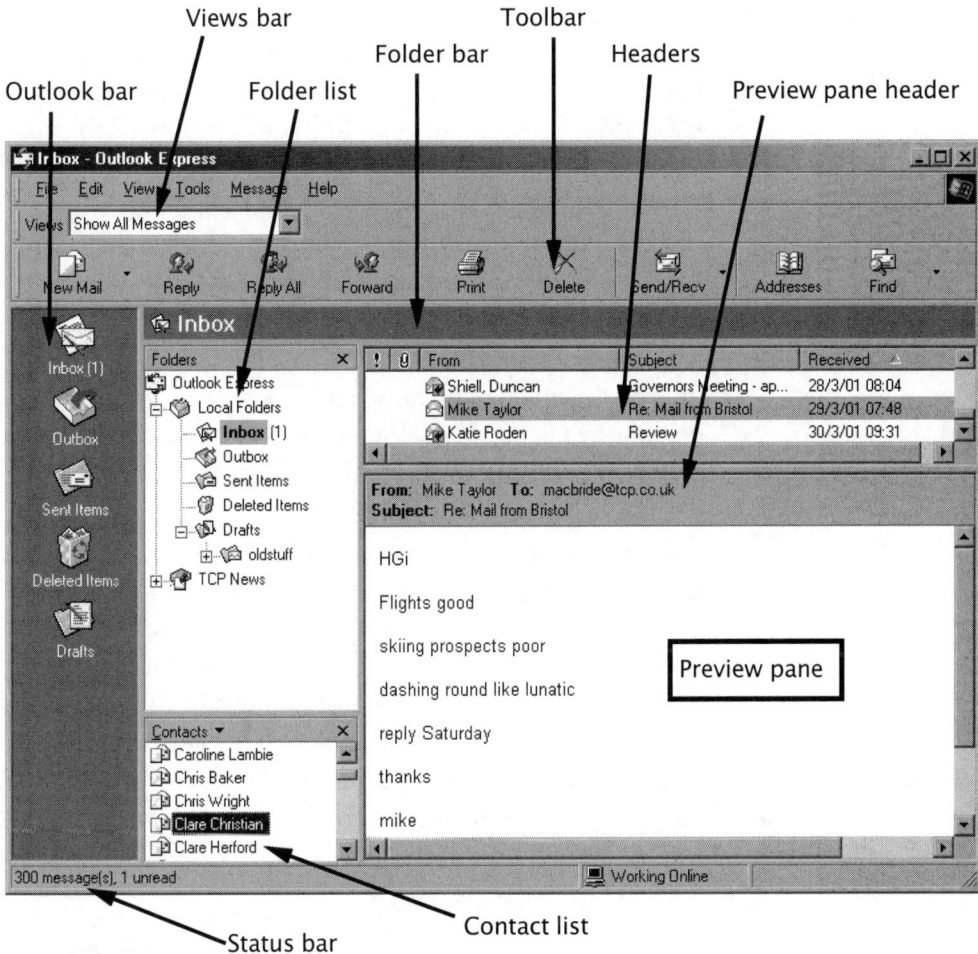

Figure 7.1 The Outlook Express screen, with all its elements turned on.

◆ The **Views bar** lets you switch between displaying all messages and those you have not yet read. The options are also available on the **View** menu.

◆ The **Folder bar** shows the name of the current folder.

◆ The **Outlook bar** is an alternative to the Folder list for moving between folders. This is something of a hangover from Outlook (Express's big brother), which has a calendar, contacts book and other features that can be reached through the Outlook bar. In Outlook Express, this bar is a waste of screen space.

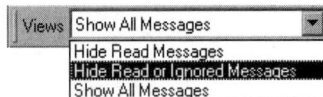

◆ The **Folder list** shows your e-mail and news folders. New e-mail folders can be created if needed (page 218) and newsgroups folders are created automatically when you subscribe to groups (page 238). The contents of the current folder are displayed in the Headers area.

◆ The **Headers area** is the only part of the display which is not optional, but even here you can control the layout and which items are displayed (page 184).

◆ The **Preview pane** displays the current message from the Headers area. If this pane is turned off, messages are displayed in a new window. The pane can sit below or beside the Headers – below is usually more convenient.

◆ The **Preview pane header** repeats the *From* and *Subject* details from the Headers area.

◆ The **Contact list** shows the people in your Address Book. You can start a message to someone by double-clicking on their entry in this list. As there are other – equally convenient – ways to start new messages, you may want to reduce screen clutter by not displaying this list.

◆ The **Status bar**, as always, helps to keep you informed of what's going on. If you are short of screen space, you could dispense with this.

Customising the display

The main display options are in the **Window Layout Properties** dialog box. Use this to turn screen elements on or off and to change the buttons on the toolbar.

Try it: Adjust the layout

① Open the **View** menu and select **Layout**...

② Click on the check boxes to turn an element on or off.

③ In the **Preview Pane** area, if the pane is on, select where you want it and whether or not to show the headers.

④ If you want to add buttons to, or remove them from the toolbar, click [Customize Toolbar...].

⑤ To add a button, select it from the *Available* list and click [Add ->].

⑥ To remove a button, select it from the *Current* list and
click `<- Remove`.

⑦ Click `Close`.

⑧ Click `OK`.

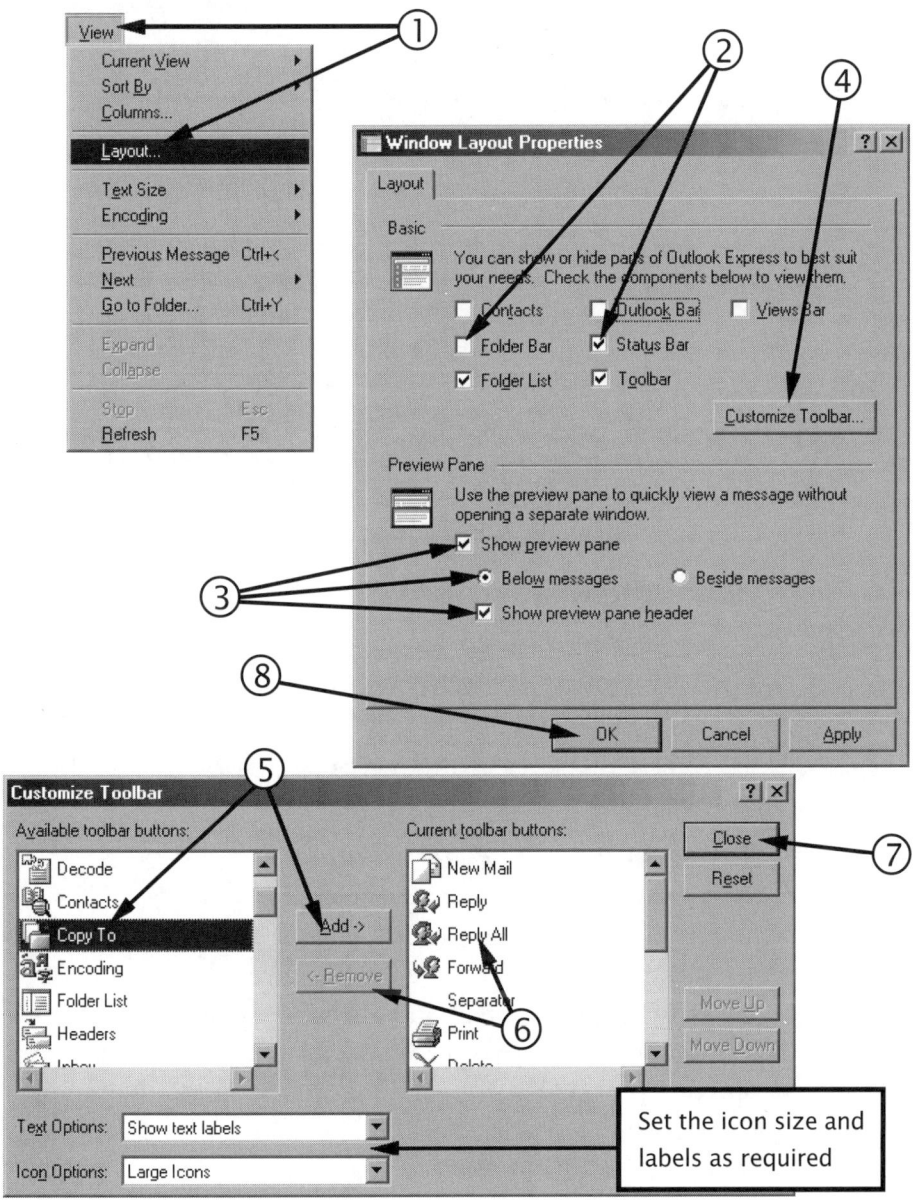

Figure 7.2 Customising the layout and the toolbar.

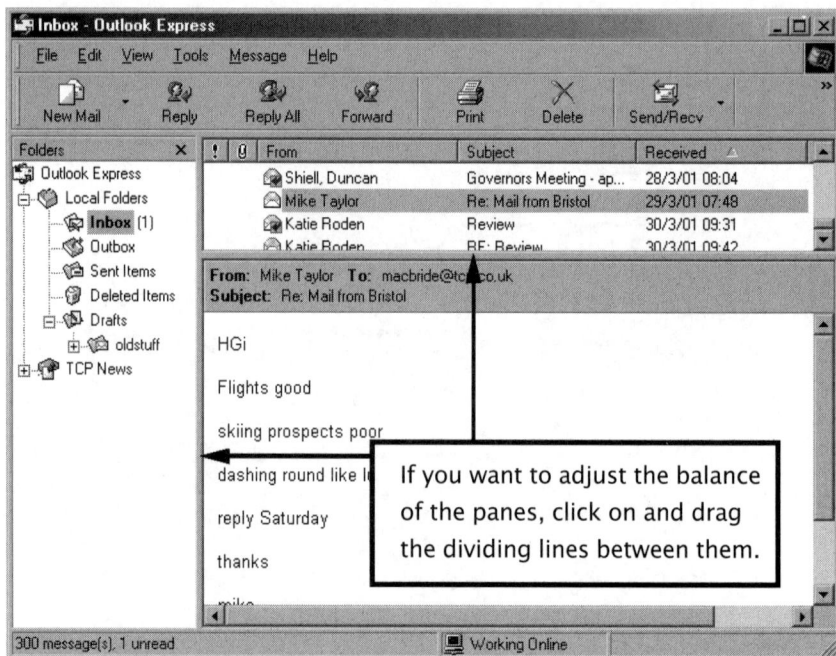

Figure 7.3 A simplified Outlook Express screen – if you do not use an element, turn it off and reduce the visual clutter.

Using the Headers area

The display of message headers is neither fixed nor static. You can change the layout, and the choice, of the columns, so that you can see the information that you need; and you can change the order of messages so that you can find (old) messages more easily.

Try it: Adjust the header columns

① Open the **View** menu and select **Columns**...

② In the **Columns** dialog box, tick the columns you want to include (click to remove the tick if you don't want them).

③ To change the position of a column, select it and click Move Up to move left or Move Down to move it to the right.

④ If you know how wide you want the column to be, enter the size in pixels.

⑤ Click OK .

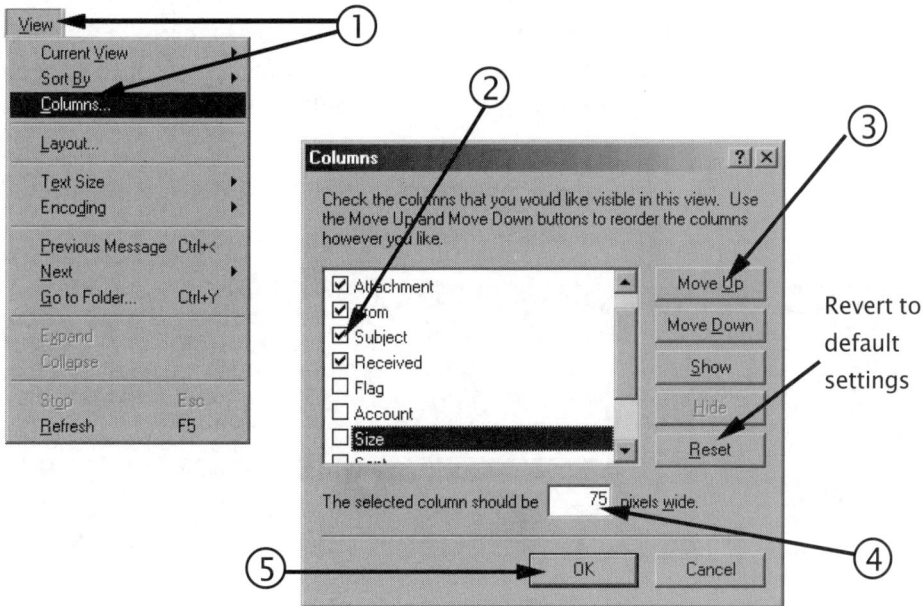

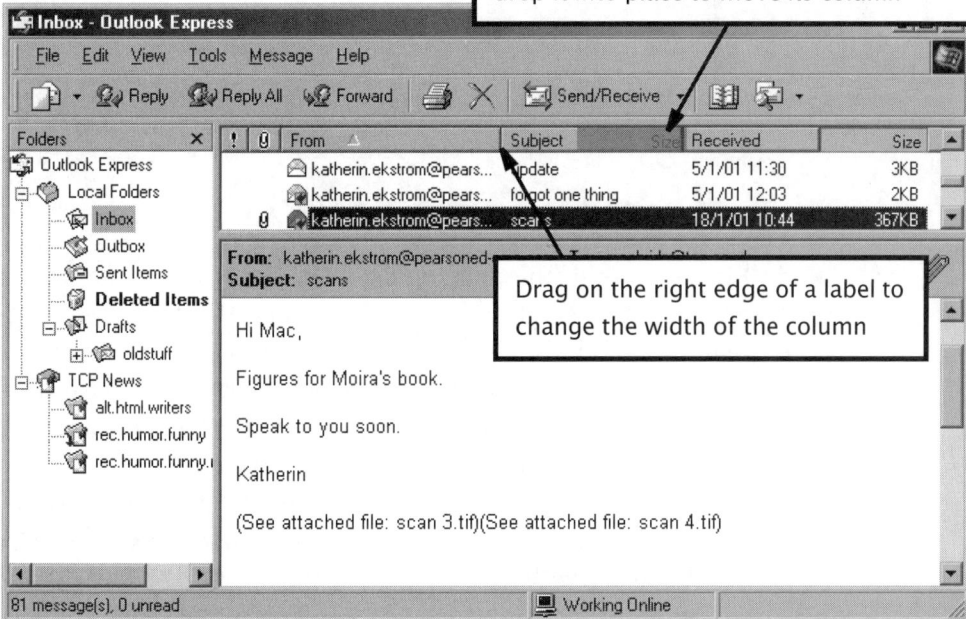

Figure 7.4 You can move and resize the columns by dragging their labels.

Try it: Sort the headers

① Click on the label to sort the messages into ascending order of that column – click again to sort into descending order. (An arrowhead will indicate the direction.)

Or

② Open the **View** menu, point to **Sort By** and select the column and the sort order.

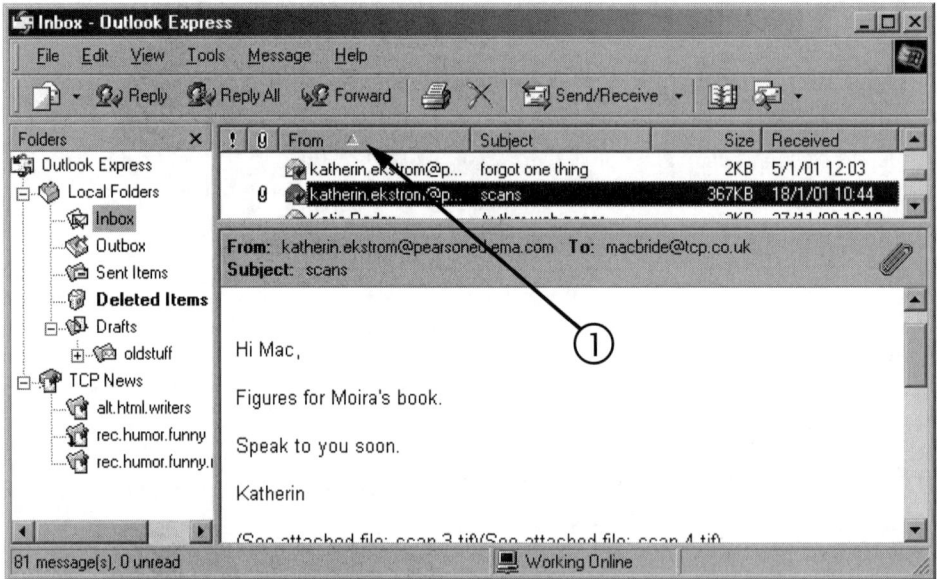

The menu commands

I have to admit that, having used Outlook Express for e-mail and news for the last four or five years, there are still commands that I have never used in earnest. I suspect that most of us will only use three of them regularly – for creating a message, replying to messages and for sending and receiving mail. There are others that you will need from time to time, and some that you may well never need. Some commands are purely, or mainly, for work with newsgroups, and we'll leave those until Chapter 8.

The File menu

New leads to a submenu from where you can:

◆ start a new mail (page 208) or news message (page 240),

◆ create a folder (page 218)

◆ or add a contact to your Address Book (page 206).

Open opens a new window to display the message currently selected in the Headers area.

Save As... opens the Save Message dialog box from where you can save a message either in mail (.eml) or text format.

Save Attachments... is one way to save files attached to messages. There is a simpler way (see page 223).

Save as Stationery... allows you to save the design (fonts, colours and background) of an HTML-formatted message, for later reuse (see page 211).

Folder leads to a submenu where you can:

◆ create a new folder (page 218),

◆ move, rename or delete an existing folder (of your own making only – Inbox, Outbox, Deleted and Sent items cannot be changed),

◆ compact the current or all folders. The messages in a folder are stored in a single file, not individually. When you delete a message, it is 'crossed off' within the file but is still physically present. Compacting cleans up the files, recovering the space that had been occupied by deleted messages.

Import is only of interest if you have previously been using a different e-mail program and want to import data from its Address Book or messages from its folders. You do not need this if you are upgrading from an earlier version of Outlook Express, as its data and messages are imported automatically during setup. If you should need to use it, the routine is virtually self-explanatory.

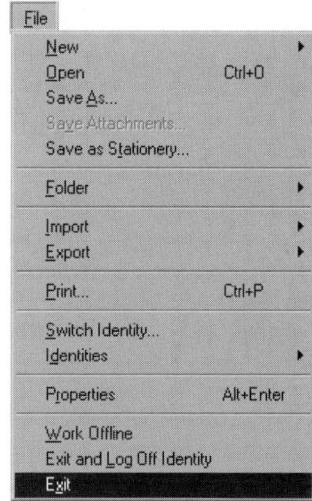

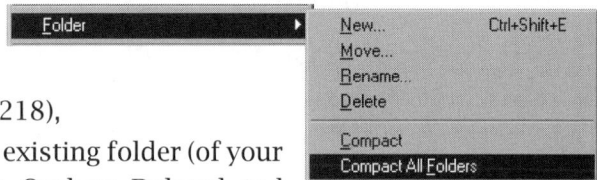

Export can be used to save your Address Book data as a comma-separated file (a standard format for transferring between different types of database). If you have people's snail mail addresses in there, then you might use this to create a data file for mail merging when you send off your Christmas cards (if you are very keen to be high-tech!). You can also export messages for use with Outlook, or Exchange – the mail software used in many larger organisations.

Print opens the **Print** dialog box, ready for sending the current message to the printer.

Switch identities and **Identities** are for people who share computers, allowing each person to have their own mail and contacts folders (see page 220).

Work Offline will stop Outlook Express from trying to connect and send mail when you have written a new message (if you have it set up for automatic sending – see page 198). It will generally work perfectly well offline, without using this command.

Exit and Log Off Identity only applies if more than one identity has been set up. When you next run Outlook Express, it will first ask which identity to use.

Exit closes the software.

The Edit menu

Clipboard = place in memory where data is stored for copying and pasting

Copy copies selected text from a message to the Clipboard. It can then be pasted into a new message, or into a word-processor or other external program.

Select All selects the entire text of the current message.

Find is mainly used for finding messages. You can search on the basis of the sender, subject, text within the message, date or other factors (page 219).

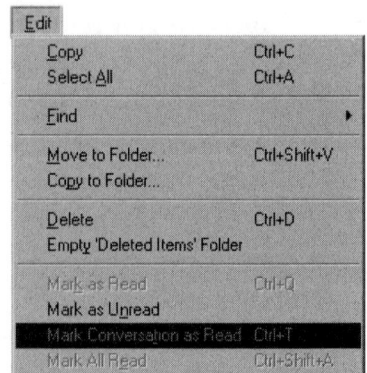

The **People Find** routines (page 203) can also be started from here.

Move to Folder... and **Copy to Folder**... can help you organise your messages (page 217).

Delete transfers a message to the Deleted Items folder, where it stays until the folder is emptied.

Empty 'Deleted Items' Folder does what it says! You can also set up Outlook Express to empty the folder on exit (page 200).

The **Mark** commands are intended for use with newsgroups, where you may be more selective about which ones you read.

The View menu

Current View leads to a submenu with options which determine the messages to display.

◆ **Show All Messages** is the default.

◆ **Hide Read Messages/Hide Read or Ignored Messages** are of more use with newsgroup articles than with mail. You will normally read e-mail messages as they come in, so that – if you have them in *Received* order – the unread ones are at the end. With newsgroups you are more likely to read scattered articles – and being able to hide the read ones is then useful.

◆ **Customize Current View**... and **Define Views**... are for the real enthusiasts. They allow you to set up tests to filter messages on the basis of their status, nature, size or other factors.

◆ **Group Messages by Conversation** is also mainly for newsgroups. It brings together messages with the same subject and tucks them into a folder within the headers. See Figure 7.5 on page 190.

Sort By sorts the headers into ascending or descending order by any of their columns.

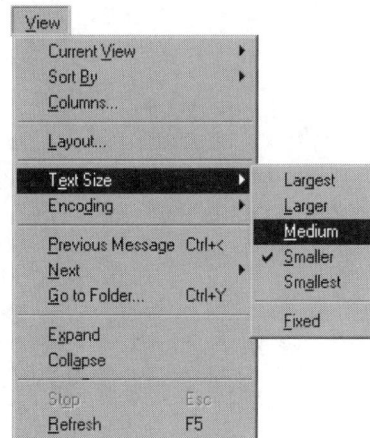

Conversation = set of messages with the same subject, more often found in newsgroups than in e-mail

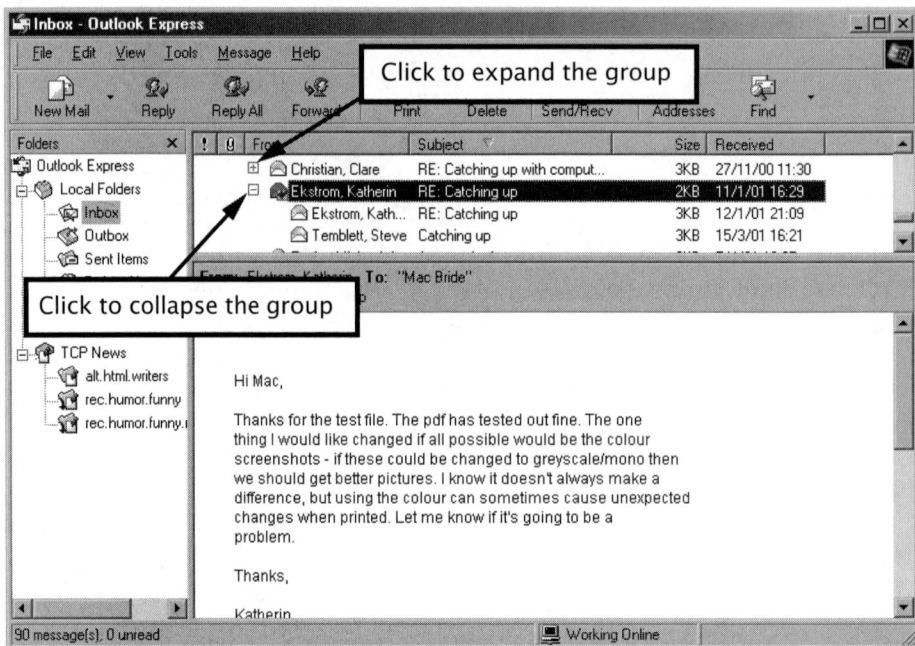

Figure 7.5 Grouping messages makes it easier to find them – especially if there are a lot in the folder. The groups can be expanded and collapsed as needed.

Columns… lets you control the choice and layout of columns (see page 184).

Layout… controls the screen display (see page 182).

Text size lets you set the size of the font to suit your eyes, on a scale from 14 point (largest) down to 8 point (smallest).

Encoding controls the character set used to display messages. The option is only really relevant for non-Western character sets. It should normally be set to **Western European (ISO)**.

Previous Message opens the message above the current one in the header list – whatever order they are arranged in.

Next leads to a submenu where you can choose what to move on to. You can go to the next:

◆ **Message** – the one below it in the headers list;

◆ **Unread message/conversation/folder** – which will jump down to the next unread message, or into the next conversation or folder with an unread message in it.

Go to Folder... serves no purpose if you include the Folder list in your screen display. This simply opens a dialog box showing the folders, where you can select one to go to.

Expand and **Collapse** are only available if **Group messages by conversation** is turned on. The commands display all the messages in the set or conceal all except the first.

Stop becomes active when someone sends you a Web page through the e-mail – interactive Web sites often keep in touch with their readers this way. Use this as in Internet Explorer.

Refresh redisplays an HTML-based message.

The Tools menu

Send and Receive leads to a submenu:

◆ **Send and Receive All** is the one you would normally use. It sends anything sitting in the Outbox and picks up any new mail.

◆ Use **Receive All** if there's something in your Outbox but you don't want to send it yet. You might, for instance, have ready a message with a big attachment, which you don't want to send until the evening cheap rate, but would like to check your mailbox before then.

◆ **Send All** sends outgoing mail but without picking up new mail. Use it when you are in a hurry to get a message off but don't have time to deal with incoming mail.

Synchronize All is used only with newsgroups (see page 243).

Address Book... opens your Address Book (see page 206)

Add Sender to Address Book adds the e-mail address of the sender of the current message to your Address Book.

Message Rules let you automate the handling of mail and news messages – mainly to filter out junk mail. The three submenu options, **Mail**..., **News**... and **Blocked Senders list**..., are all tabs within the same dialog box (see page 216).

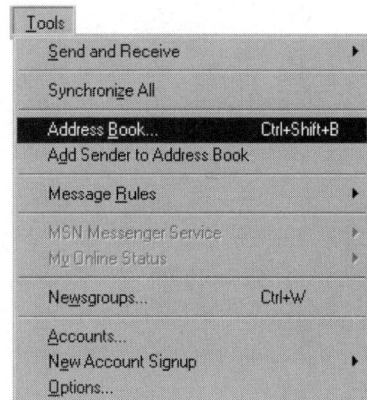

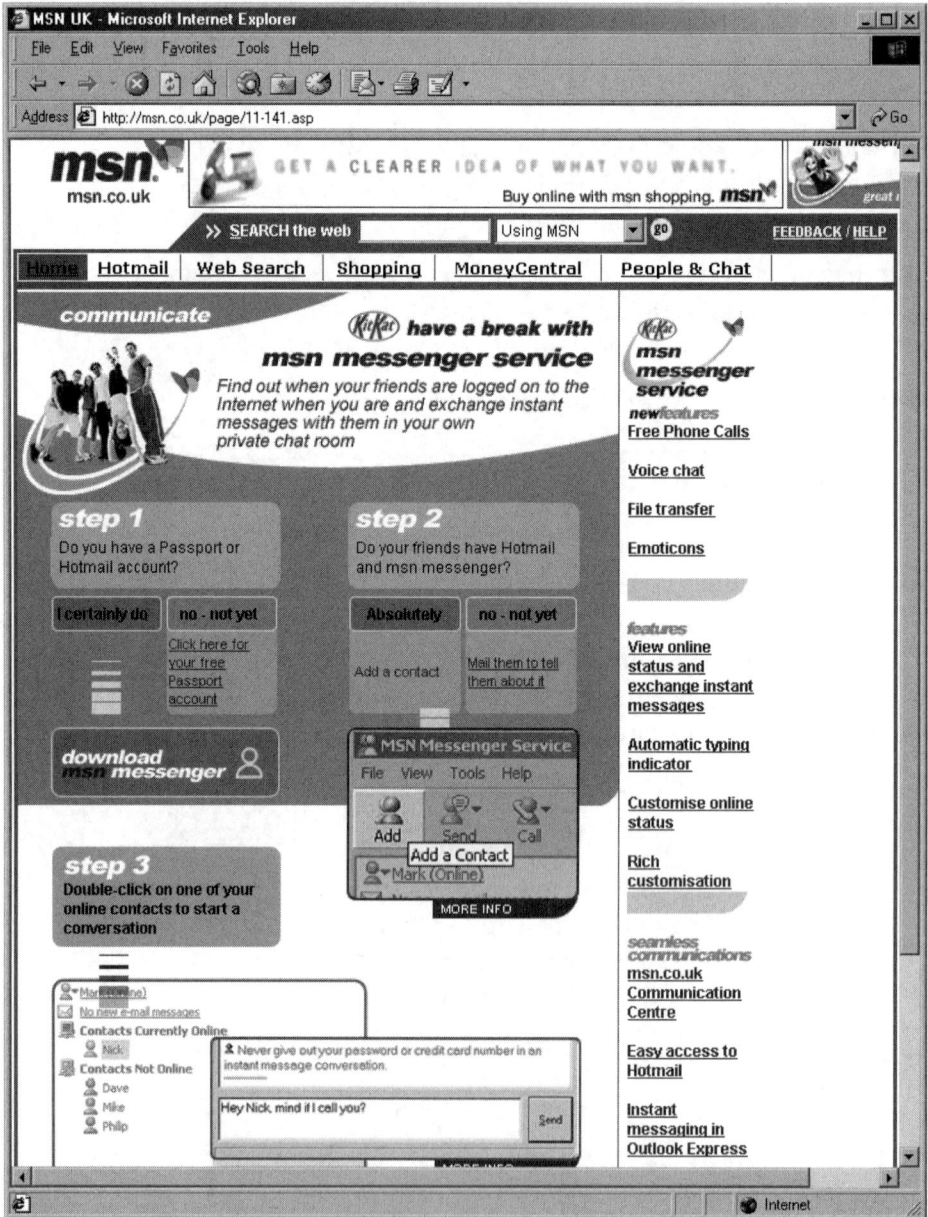

Figure 7.6 MSN Messenger Service is one way to keep in touch with people, but you have to be online a lot of the time or at the same time as your friends to be able to use it. The service will let you know when your Messenger contacts come online. You can then send them instant messages or talk to them – if you have a microphone, speakers and a suitable audio card in your machine. To find out more about it, go to **msn.co.uk** and look for a link to the Messenger service.

MSN Messenger Service and **My Online Status** are only available if you have signed up for this service and downloaded the software. See Figure 7.6 for a little more on this.

Newsgroups... is for selecting newsgroups (see page 238).

Accounts... can be used for setting up or removing accounts with mail or news services. As these are normally reached through your Internet Service Provider, it is usually simpler to set up or remove these services when – and if – you change providers.

New Account Signup can be used to get an account at Hotmail (see page 231).

Options... opens the Options dialog box, where you can specify how you want Outlook Express to work (see page 196).

The Message menu

New Message opens the New Message window for you to write an e-mail, using your default layout settings.

New Message Using leads to a submenu from which you can pick the 'Stationery' you want to use for that special mesage (see page 211).

Reply to Sender starts a new message to the sender of the current message (see page 213).

Reply to All sends a reply to all the people who had copies of the message (see page 213).

Message	
New Message	Ctrl+N
New Message Using	▶
Reply to Sender	Ctrl+R
Reply to All	Ctrl+Shft+R
Reply to Group	Ctrl+G
Forward	Ctrl+F
Forward As Attachment	
Create Rule From Message...	
Block Sender...	
Flag Message	
Watch Conversation	
Ignore Conversation	
Combine and Decode...	

Reply to Group is for use with newsgroups, and directs the message to the group, rather than the sender.

Forward copies the message into the New Message window, ready for you to send it on to another person.

Forward as Attachment is an alternative way to send on a message. You might use this if the original message was HTML-formatted (see page 210) but the person you are sending it to can only read plain text messages.

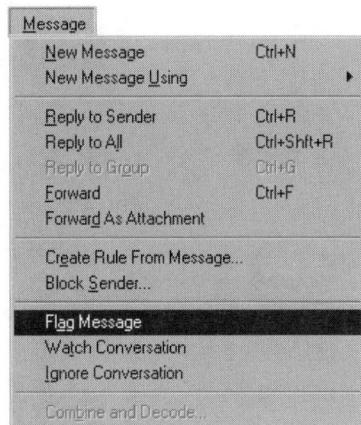

Create Rule from Message... and **Block Sender**... are two ways to filter junk mail (see page 216).

Flag Message puts a flag icon by the message in the headers list. You can then group by flags, or define a view that shows only flagged messages.

Watch Conversation and **Ignore Conversation** are other ways to flag messages, and are mainly used with newsgroups.

Combine and Decode... is a command that you are unlikely to need, but if you do, it's invaluable! Some e-mail systems set a limit to the size of files that can be attached to messages, so that big files have to be spread over several e-mails. Sticking the file back together again afterwards is a real pain. It requires very accurate work and a certain amount of technical knowledge. With **Combine and Decode**, all you need to do is select the messages and start this command.

The toolbar

New Mail

Click the button to start a new message in plain text or with the default formatting, or click the arrow to open a drop-down list and select your Stationery (see page 211).

Reply
The same as **Reply to Sender** on the **Message** menu.

Reply All
The same as **Reply to All** on the **Message** menu.

Forward
The same as **Forward** on the **Message** menu.

Print
The same as **Print** on the **File** menu.

Delete
Deletion is a two-stage process. Clicking this button transfers the selected message(s) to the Deleted Items folder. Messages are then deleted from there when you close Outlook

Express – if you have this option turned on (see page 200) – or when you delete them from the Deleted Items folder.

If you decide you need a message after all, it can be retrieved from here by opening the folder and dragging the message across the window to another folder (see Figure 7.7).

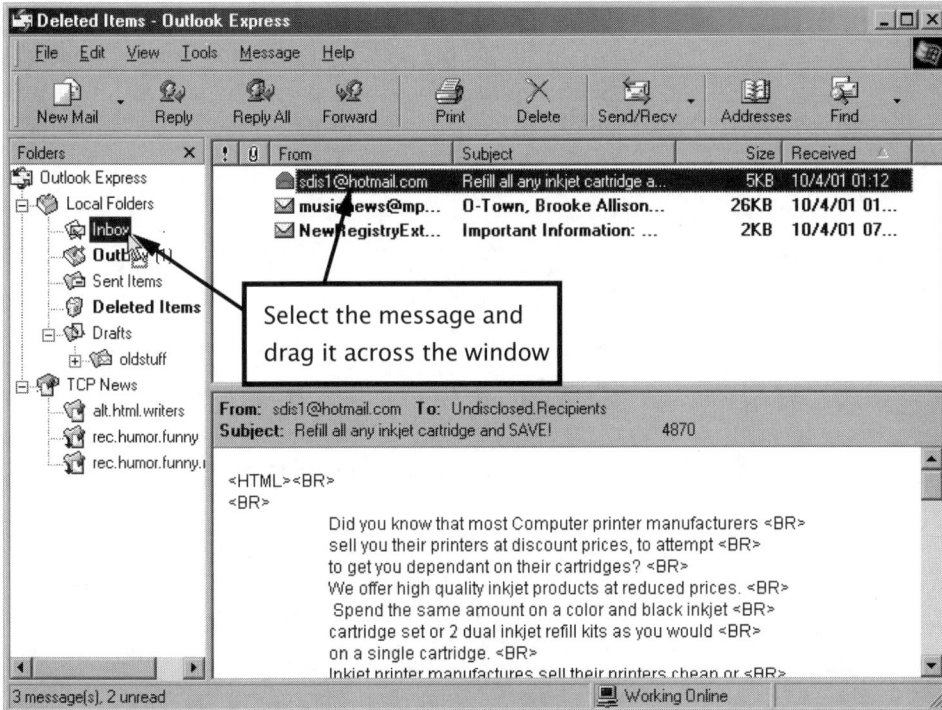

Figure 7.7 Messages can be recovered from the Deleted Items folder by dragging them back into the Inbox, or one of your storage folders.

Send/Receive
The same as **Send/Receive All** on the **Tools** menu.

Addresses
Opens your Address Book.

Find
The same as **Find** on the **Edit** menu (see page 188).

Setting the options

There are three things to bear in mind when setting options:

◆ The defaults work perfectly well, so if you are not sure what to choose, don't change a setting.

◆ If you make a poor choice for an option, at worst it will just be an irritant – none are potentially destructive.

◆ Options can be set and changed at any time. Some are worth experimenting with early on; others are best left at their defaults until you are an experienced e-mailer.

Try it: Explore the options

① Open the **Tools** menu and select **Options**...

② At the Options dialog box, click on the labels to work through the tabs.

③ Set options as required, using these notes for guidance.

④ Click [OK] to save your settings and close the box.

Or

⑤ Click [Cancel] to ignore your settings and close.

The Inbox is usually the best place to start

Mainly for those people who have an open line to the Internet through their organisation

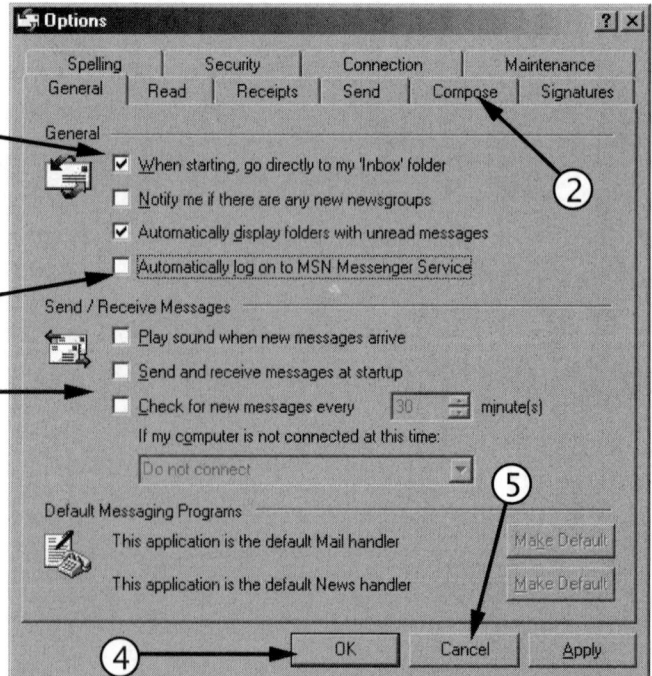

This is best set low, at the time it takes to read a short message

Leave these until you've been using newsgroups for a while

Set the fonts for reading comfort

Receipts are mainly for business use to acknowledge receipt of a message

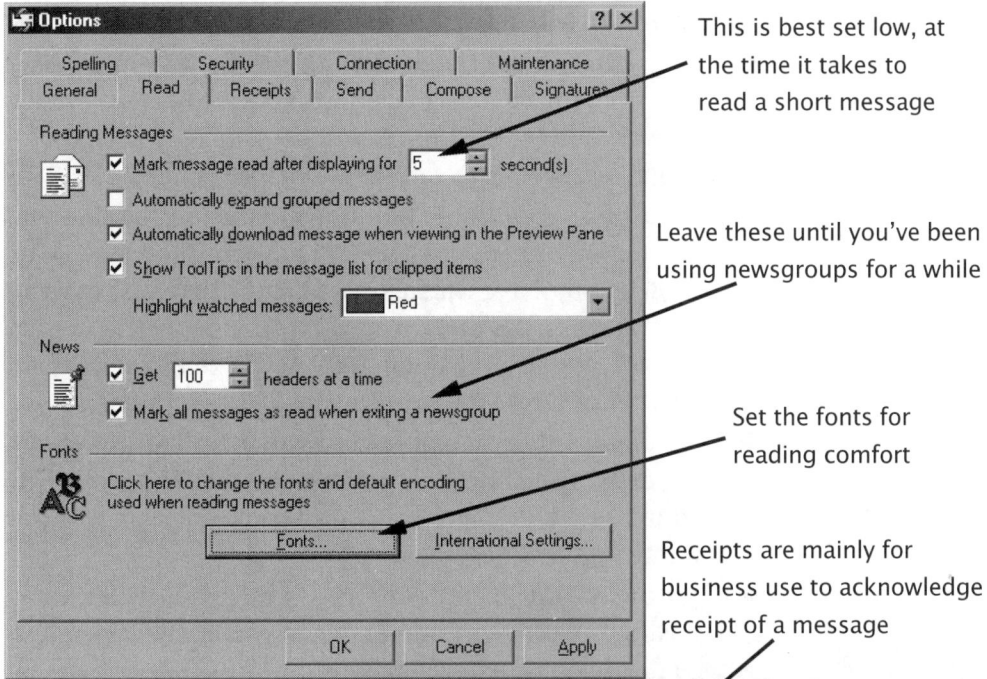

The Sending options are too important to cover in this space – see the next page.

Messages can be sent as Plain Text or HTML. Everyone can read Plain Text; anyone using Outlook Express or other modern software can read HTML. What do your contacts use?

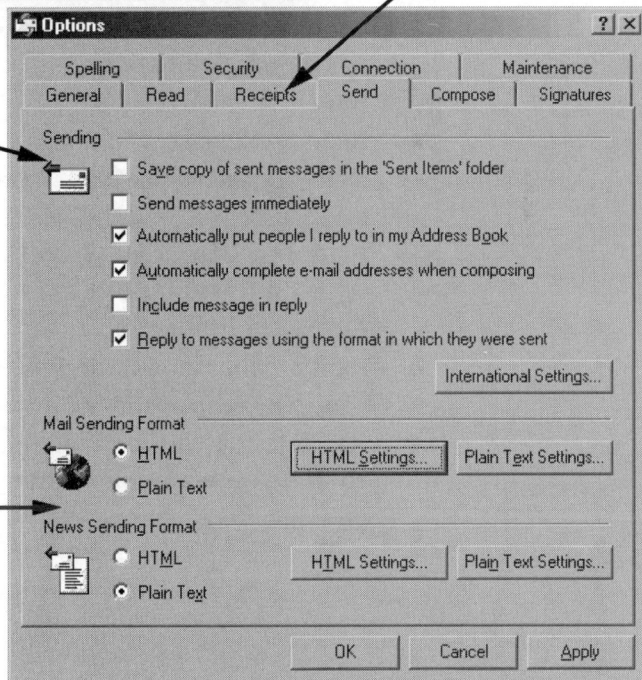

Figure 7.8 The Read and Send options should be set early on.

The Sending options

◆ **Save copy of sent messages in the 'Sent Items' folder** is mainly for business users who need to keep a record of everything they send. If you need to keep a copy of a single message, you can save it before you send it.

◆ **Send messages immediately** will start up the Connect routine (if you are not online) and send the message as soon as you have finished writing it. If you often write several messages at a time, you will find it better to turn this off, and use the **Send/Receive** button to send them all at once after you have finished writing them.

◆ **Automatically put people I reply to in my Address Book** is worth turning on, as it makes sure that you have their addresses. You can always go through and delete unwanted ones if necessary.

◆ **Automatically complete e-mail addresses when composing** is worth turning on. When you are writing a new e-mail, you can enter someone's address either by picking it from the Address Book or by typing it in. With this option on, you may only need to type two or three letters.

◆ **Include messages in reply** is best turned off, for home users. Business users may prefer to have a copy of the original message in the reply, so that it can be answered point by point. If you turn this on, use the **Settings** options on the **Compose** tab to define how the original is formatted in the reply.

◆ **Reply to messages using the format in which they were sent** will ensure that your replies are in Plain Text or HTML to match the format of the incoming messages – so that you won't be sending HTML to people who can only handle Plain Text.

A signature is a small text file that can be added to the end of your messages. It may just have your name, but could also include your snail mail address or other contact details, or a favourite quote or slogan. You can have several signatures and choose which to add when writing messages.

Sets the default formatting for HTML messages and the settings for Plain Text

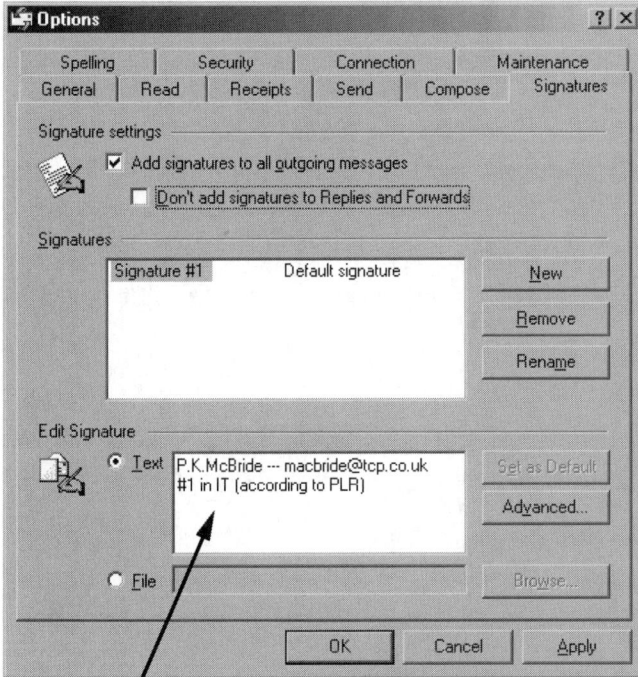

Create your signature here

The spell check is worth turning on, unless you are a good speller *and* an accurate typist, but do turn on all the **ignore** options

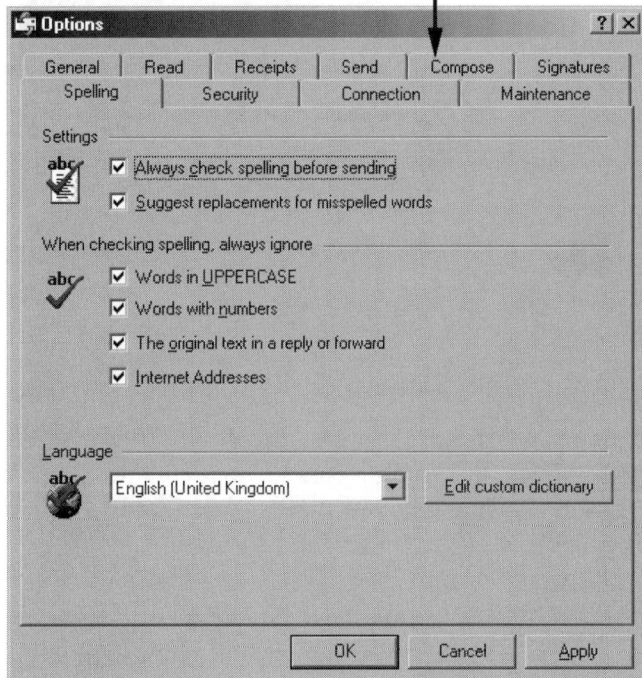

Figure 7.9 The Signature and Spelling tabs are worth a little attention.

If you don't turn these on, you'll have to clear out deleted messages by hand

Compacting ensures minimal use of disk space

How long will you want to keep (downloaded and read) messages from newsgroups?

If you have problems with your mail or news service, turn on the logs – they may help your ISP to solve them

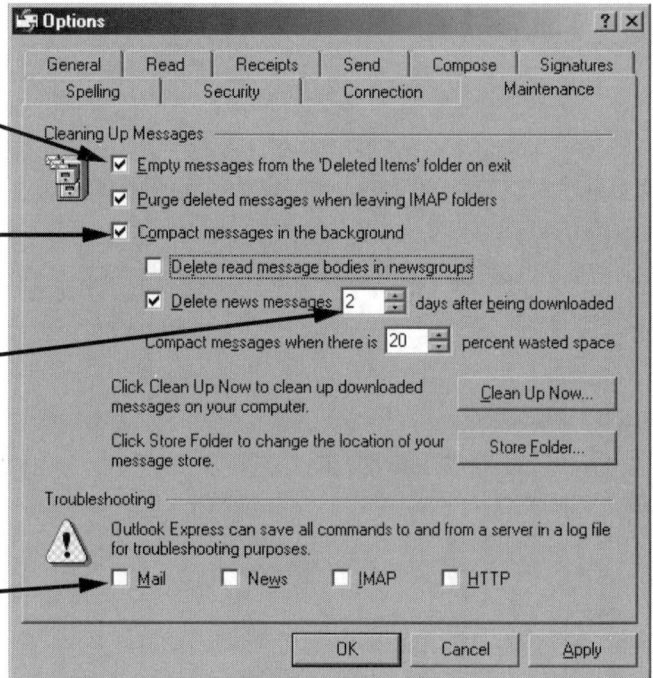

Options

| General | Read | Receipts | Send | Compose | Signatures |
| Spelling | Security | Connection | Maintenance |

Cleaning Up Messages

☑ Empty messages from the 'Deleted Items' folder on exit

☑ Purge deleted messages when leaving IMAP folders

☑ Compact messages in the background

☐ Delete read message bodies in newsgroups

☑ Delete news messages 2 days after being downloaded

Compact messages when there is 20 percent wasted space

Click Clean Up Now to clean up downloaded messages on your computer.   [Clean Up Now...]

Click Store Folder to change the location of your message store.   [Store Folder...]

Troubleshooting

⚠ Outlook Express can save all commands to and from a server in a log file for troubleshooting purposes.

☐ Mail   ☐ News   ☐ IMAP   ☐ HTTP

[OK]   [Cancel]   [Apply]

Figure 7.10 Deleting unwanted mail reduces clutter.

Incoming mail

Remember that, if you get online through an ISP, your e-mail does not get delivered directly to you. Instead, it goes into a mailbox at the provider and you must connect to get it.

Some services automatically delete mail from the mailbox once you have collected a copy; others give you the option of leaving it there or deleting it. Opt to have it deleted. There is little point in keeping it, and they may charge you for storage beyond a bare minimum. Checking and emptying your mailbox regularly will keep your service happy and your charges down.

New mail will normally be placed into an 'Inbox', where it will appear as a single line entry showing the sender, the date and whatever the sender wrote in their Subject line. After looking at the sender and the subject, you can decide whether you want to read it immediately, later or not at all. Select a message to read it.

Try it: Pick up your mail

① If you are not online already, get connected now.

② Click the **Send/Recv** button drop-down arrow (or open the **Tools** menu and point to **Send and Receive**) then select **Receive All**. Wait while the messages come in.

③ Click once on a message in the headers list to open it in the preview pane.

④ If a message is clearly junk mail, click ✕.

⑤ After reading, you have several options.

◆ **Reply** or **Reply to all** who had a copy.

◆ **Forward** it to someone else, perhaps after editing.

◆ **Save** the message as a message or as a plain text file.

◆ **Copy or cut** part of the message, pasting it into a word-processed file, using the standard cut-and-paste routines.

◆ **Move** the message to another folder, by dragging it from the message list into the target folder.

Replying will open the new message window (see page 208), and copy in the sender's address and the message. Forwarding will also open the new message window.

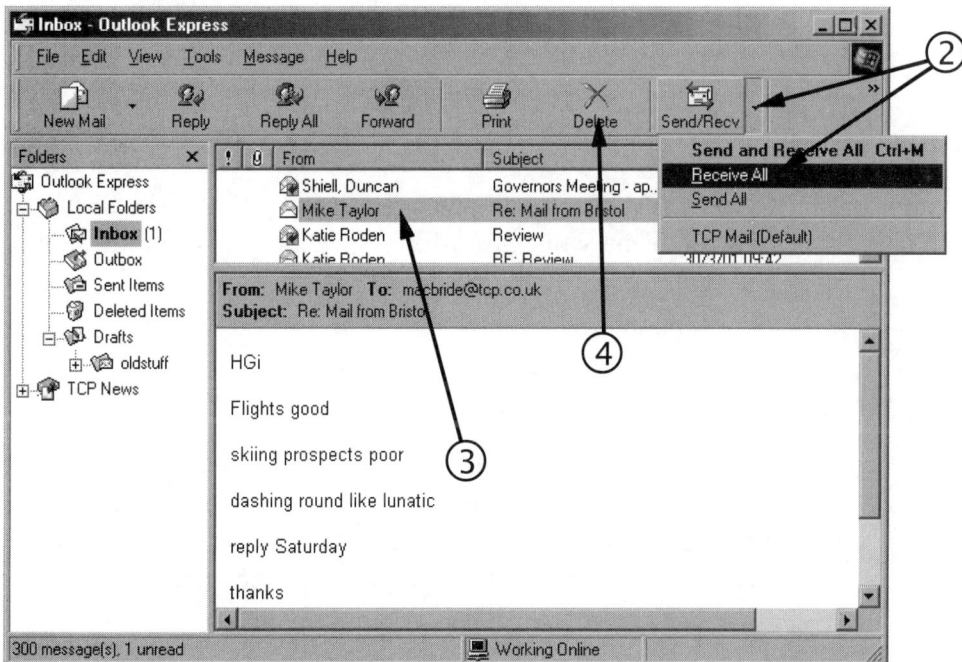

E-mail addresses

Before you can write to anyone, you must know their address. Now, while addresses follow simple rules and are fairly easy to remember, you cannot work them out for yourself and you must get them exactly right. The basic pattern is:

name@site.address

Notice the punctuation – an @ sign after the name, and dots between the constituent parts of the site address.

The **name** is usually based on the person's real name, though how it is formed varies. If the person works for an organisation, its IT service will probably have rules for creating names. Someone who gets online through an ISP, or has a *Web mail* account, will have more choice over their name, but even here there will be some constraints. For example, the name for 'Johnny B. Goode' might be 'jbgoode', 'johnnyg', 'John_Goode', 'johnny.b.goode', 'goode3' or other variations.

Web mail – see
page 225

Notice that both _ and . are used for punctuation, and that sometimes a number will be added, especially to common names. Some organisations ignore real names completely and allocate numbers or special user names.

The **site addresses** are often the same as those of the organisation to which the user belongs, though some service providers allocate a separate domain name to each of their members.

The following examples are of names that have been allocated to me while I have been trying out different service providers:

macbride@tcp.co.uk

macbride@macdesign2000.freeserve.co.uk

100407.2521@compuserve.com

Between them these cover many of the variations noted above. CompuServe now also allows people to have user names based on their real names, but you will find that some long-term CompuServe users have retained their number addresses.

Finding addresses

The simplest way to get someone's address is to ask them to send you an e-mail. When the message comes in it will have their address at the top, and you can be confident that it is exactly right.

Of course, you can only ask people for e-mail if you can contact them already, by phone or post. Let's see how you can find people.

If you are a member of AOL, MSN or other large online service, it is easy enough to find the e-mail address of any other member by using the service's internal directory – look for the link on the top page of the service's site.

If you want to find someone outside your own service, there are several people-finding directories on the Web – and it is often worth trying more than one. No single directory holds the names of everyone on the Internet. Each has its own database, built by drawing on the members' lists of e-mail service providers, with additional addresses that people have registered when visiting the directories.

Among the biggest people-finder sites are:

WhoWhere www.whowhere.com

Bigfoot www.bigfoot.com

InfoSpace www.infospaceuk.com

You can reach all of these through your browser and – in theory – through the *Find People* routine. In practice, the routine only worked reliably with Bigfoot when testing (Spring 2001), though the **Web site** button on the **Find People** dialog box connected to all of the sites.

The people-finder sites can all do approximate searches, to cope with variations in names. When looking for my old mate 'Clive Gladstone Postlethwaite', I don't know if he will be listed by this name or by his usual 'Clive Postlethwaite', or just by his initials and surname. A search for 'C Postlethwaite' should pick up all variations – and anyone else with the same surname and initial, but there shouldn't be too many of these. A brief e-mail asking 'are you the Clive Postlethwaite who shared a desk with me in Mr Whackham's class in Grimeforth

Juniors in 1956?', should be enough to confirm that you have found the right person. (And if you haven't, most people will take the trouble to send you a 'no, sorry' reply.) Tracking down your old mate 'John Smith' may not be quite as simple.

Try it: Find an old friend

① If you are not online already, get connected now.

② Click the **Find** button drop-down arrow (or open the **Edit** menu and point to **Find**) and select **People**...

③ Select *Bigfoot* from the **Look in:** list.

④ Type part or all of the name into the **Name** slot.

⑤ Click [Find Now] and wait a moment.

⑥ If the right (or a likely) person is in the list, select the entry and click [Add to Address Book].

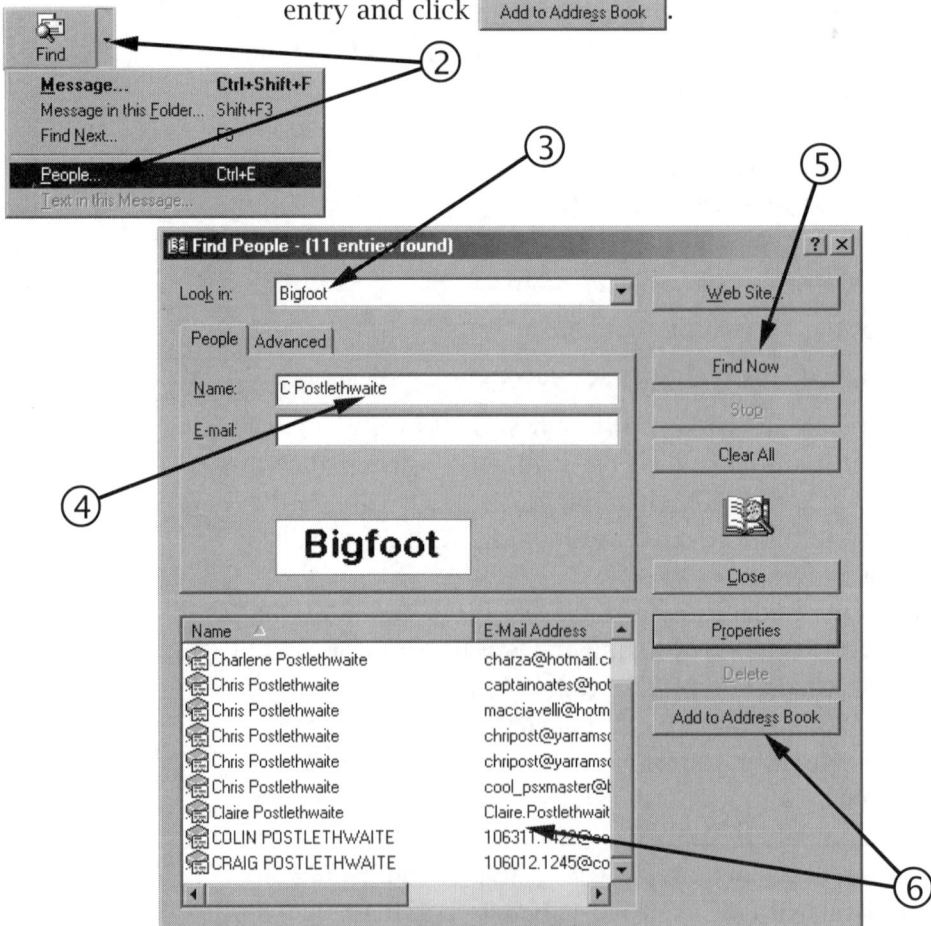

⑦ If Bigfoot doesn't deliver, select another site from the
    Look in: list and click [Web Site...], then search in the
    same way at the site.

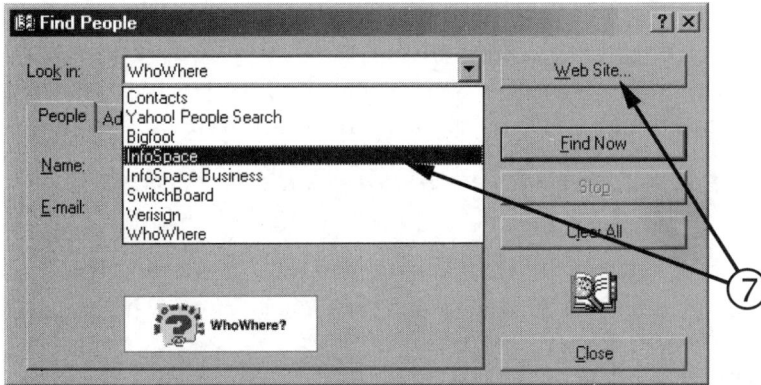

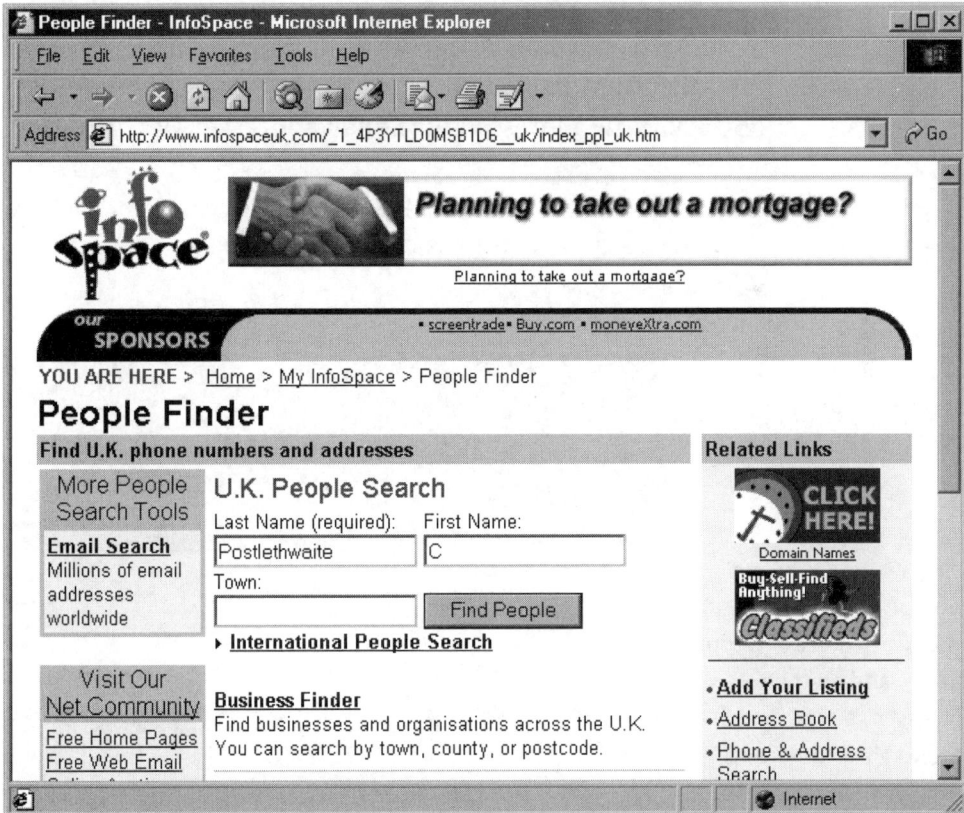

Figure 7.11 You may need to go to the Web site to run the search. At InfoSpace UK you
can search for a phone number, or click Email Search to track down an e-mail address.

Address Book

E-mail addresses are a pain to type. They are rarely easy to remember and if you get just one letter wrong, the message won't get through. The solution is to use your Address Book. Once an address is in here it can be recalled by picking it from the list, or by typing the first few letters of the name.

Try it: Add an address to your Address Book

① Open the **Tools** menu and select **Address Book**... or click the 🔖 button.

② When the Address Book opens, click the **New** button and select **New Contact**...

③ Type in the person's name, splitting it into **First**, **Middle** and **Last** – the separate parts can be used for sorting the list. You can miss out any you don't need, or even put the whole name into one slot.

④ Type the address in the **E-mail addresses** slot, then click [Add].

⑤ Switch to the **Home** or **Business** tab if you want to store the snail mail address or phone number.

⑥ Click [OK].

If you often send the same message to a set of people, you can add all their addresses to a group, then simply select the group name when you want to send a message

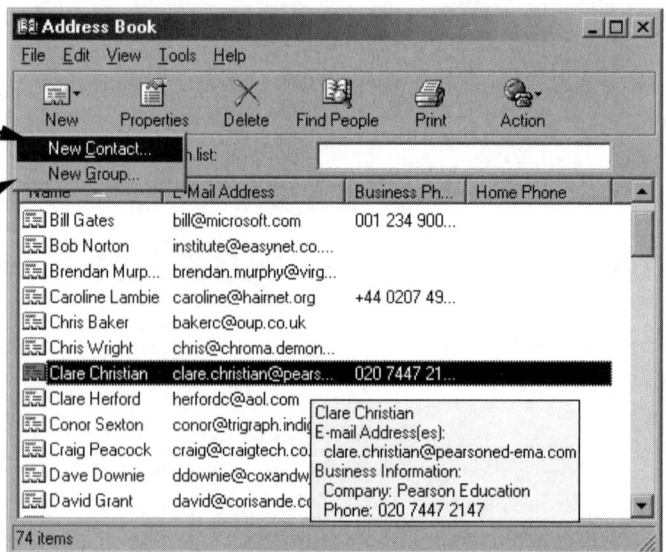

A **nickname** can be used to call up the address when writing a message (see page 209)

③

Jumbo F Butterpat Properties   ? X

| Name | Home | Business | Personal | Other | NetMeeting | Digital ID |

Enter name and e-mail information about this contact here.

First: Jumbo   Middle: F   Last: Butterpat

Title: [ ]   Display: Jumbo F Butterpat ▼   Nickname: JB

④

E-Mail Addresses: jumbobutterpat@hotmail.com   Add

✉ **jumbobutterpat@hotmail.com (Default E-Mail)**   Edit

Remove

Set as Default

☐ Send E-Mail using plain text only.

OK   Cancel

⑤

Jumbo F Butterpat Properties   ? X

| Name | Home | Business | Personal | Other | NetMeeting | Digital IDs |

Enter business-related information about this contact here.

Company: Green Gnome, The   Job Title: Landlord

Street Address: Bridge Street   Department: [ ]

Office: [ ]

City: Little Moaning   Phone: [ ]

State/Province: [ ]   Fax: [ ]

Zip Code: [ ]   Pager: [ ]

Country/Region: [ ]   IP Phone: [ ]

⑥

☑ Default   View Map

Web Page: http://   Go

OK   Cancel

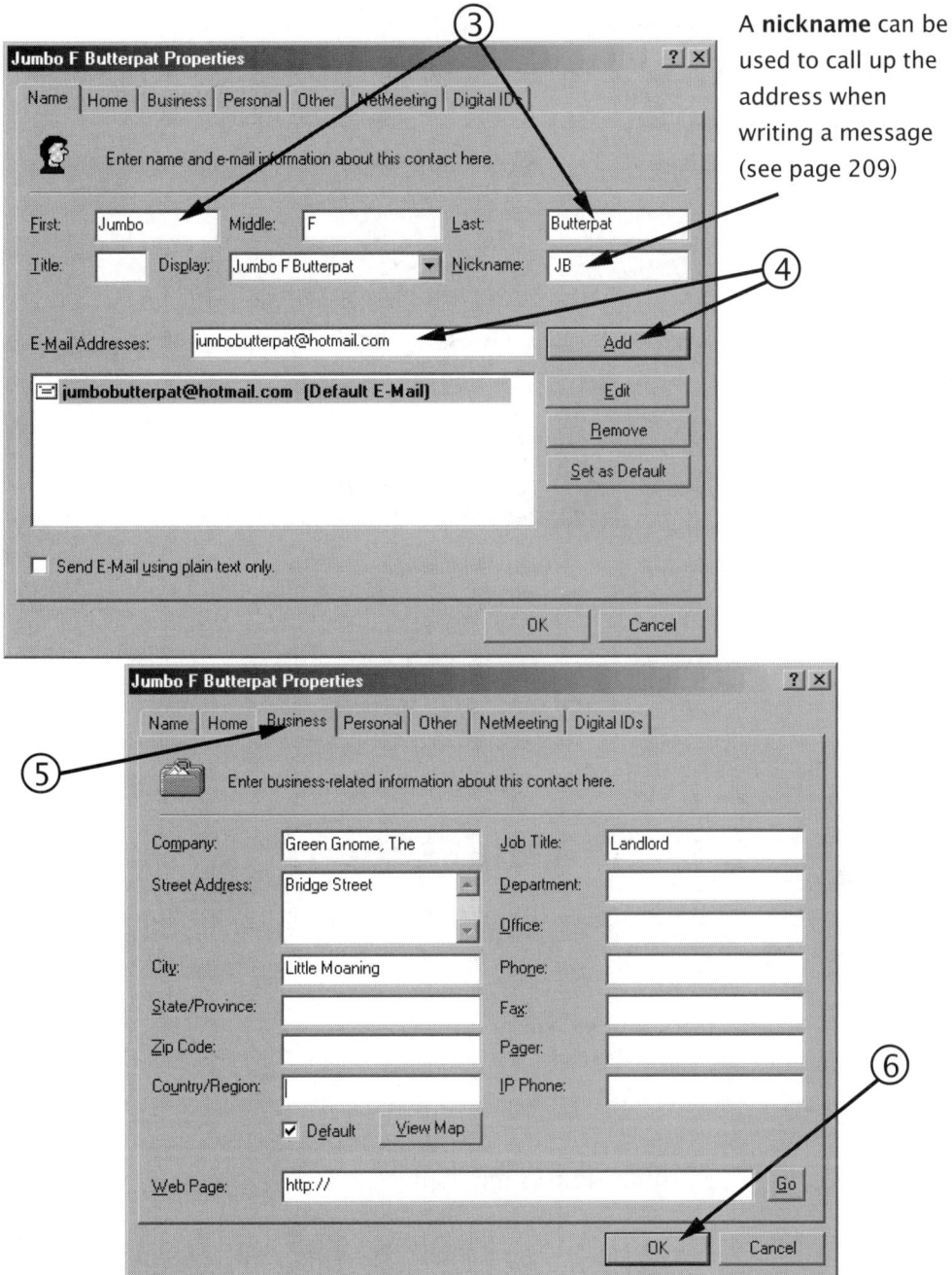

Figure 7.12 You can also store birthdays and family details on the **Personal** tab, any notes on the **Other** tab, and – if you and your contact use them – **NetMeeting** and **Digital ID** details.

If you want to add to or edit the contact's details, click **Properties**

Type the first few letters of the name to scroll to the right place in the list

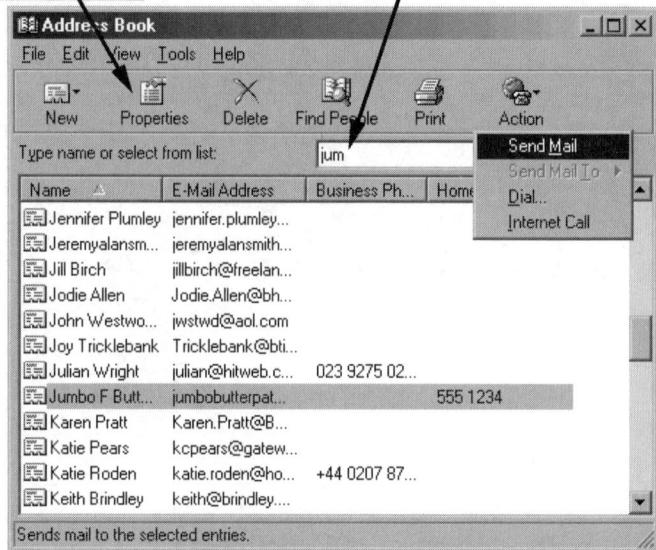

Figure 7.13 You can start to make contact with someone from the Address Book – select the name, then click **Action** and choose **Send Mail**, **Dial** or **Internet Call** from the drop-down list.

Sending messages

Messages are written in the **New Message** window. The main part of this is the writing area, which is used like a simple word-processor, but in the top part of the window there are several boxes which must be attended to.

You will find three boxes, headed **To:**, **Cc:** and **Subject:**.

◆ **To:** as you would expect, is the address of the recipient.

◆ **Cc:** is for the addresses of those people, if any, to whom you want to send copies.

You can also have **Bcc:** (**B**lind **c**arbon **c**opy) recipients if you select their names from your Address Book (see page 206). When people receive the e-mail, these names will not be listed, as the To and Cc recipients will be, at the top of the message.

♦ **Subject:** should have a few words outlining the nature of your message. This will let your recipients know what's coming and help them to organise their mail folders.

Try it: Start to write a new message

① Open the **File** menu, point to **New** and select **Mail Message** or click [icon].

② Click [icon To:] to open your Address Book.

③ Select a contact and click [To: ->], [Cc: ->] or [Bcc: ->], to copy the name into a recipient box.

④ Repeat Step 3 for multiple recipients.

⑤ Click [OK] to return to the New Message window.

⑥ Enter a **Subject** for the message.

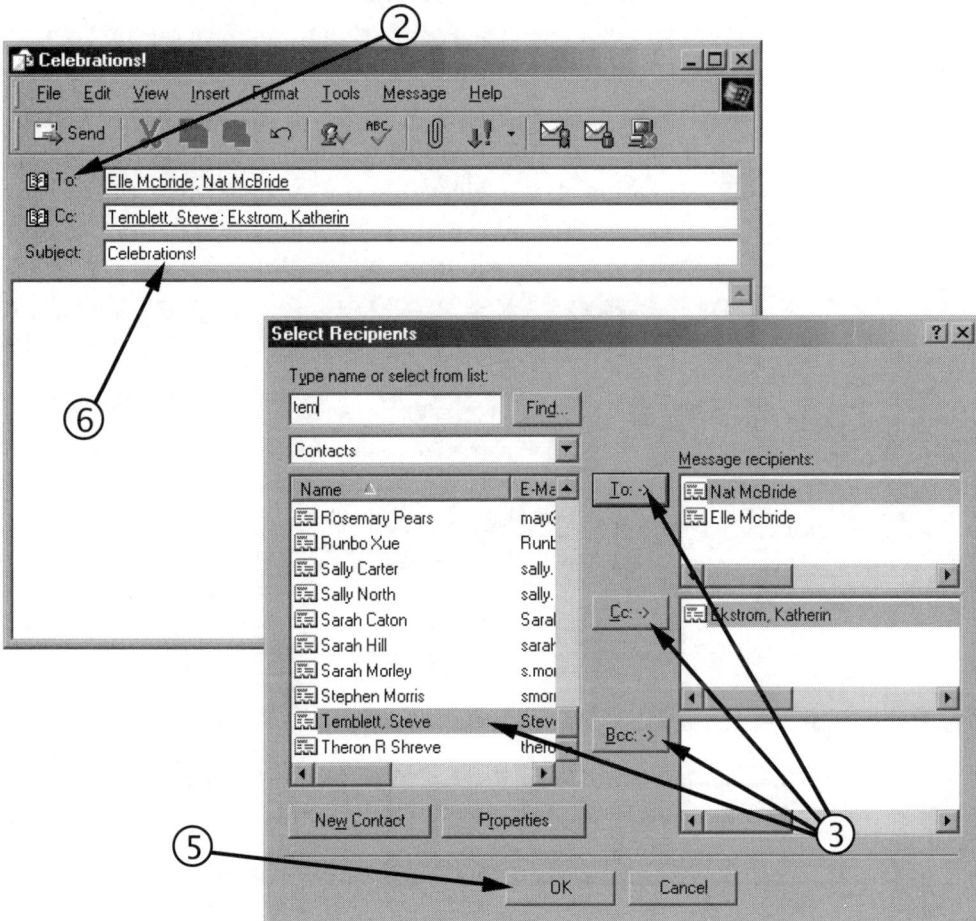

Formatted and plain text

Outlook Express, like most modern mail software, has the same sort of formatting capabilities that you would find in a word-processor. There are the normal range of fonts, size, style, colour and alignment options. You can write hyperlinks in your messages, so that your readers can go straight to a Web page – as long as their mail software can handle the link! You can also insert images, or text from other documents.

To send formatted messages, you must be using HTML – if it is set for this, the Formatting toolbar will be present. If you didn't set HTML as the default in the Options (page 198), you can switch to it while writing the message.

Try it: Format your message

① If you can't see the Formatting toolbar, open the **Format** menu and select **Rich Text (HTML)**.

② To change the paper colour, open the **Format** menu, point to **Background**, then **Color**, then pick a colour.

③ To format text, select it and use the toolbar buttons or open the **Format** menu, select **Font...** and define the font style, size and colour in the **Font** dialog box.

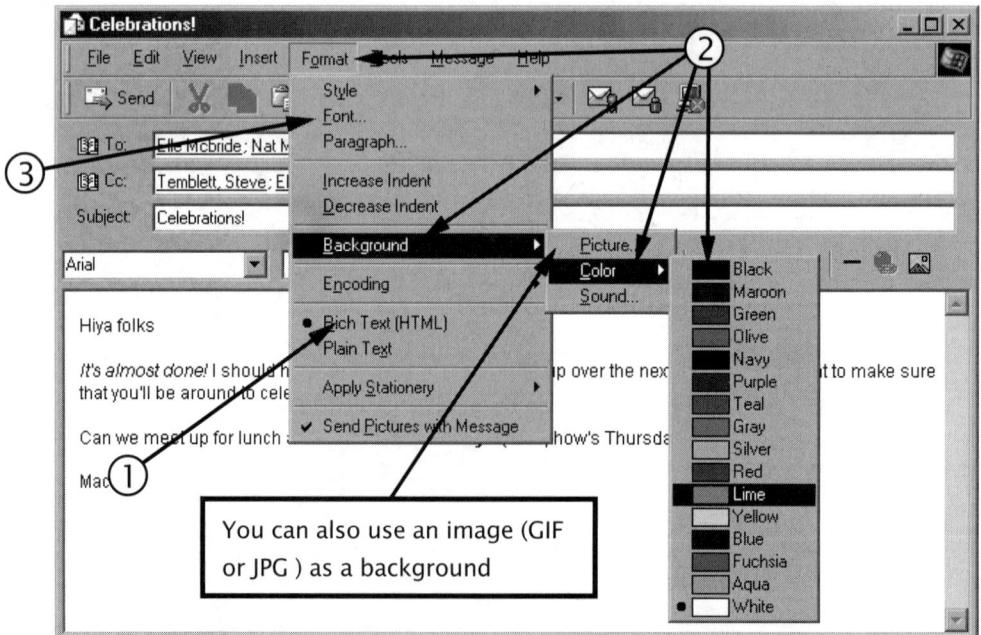

You can also use an image (GIF or JPG) as a background

Stationery

If you want a formatted message, but don't have time to set backgrounds and text formats, use the stationery.

Try it: Use the stationery

① Open the **Format** menu, point to **Apply Stationery** and pick one.

② Or, click on **More Stationery**..., then pick one from the **Select Stationery** dialog box.

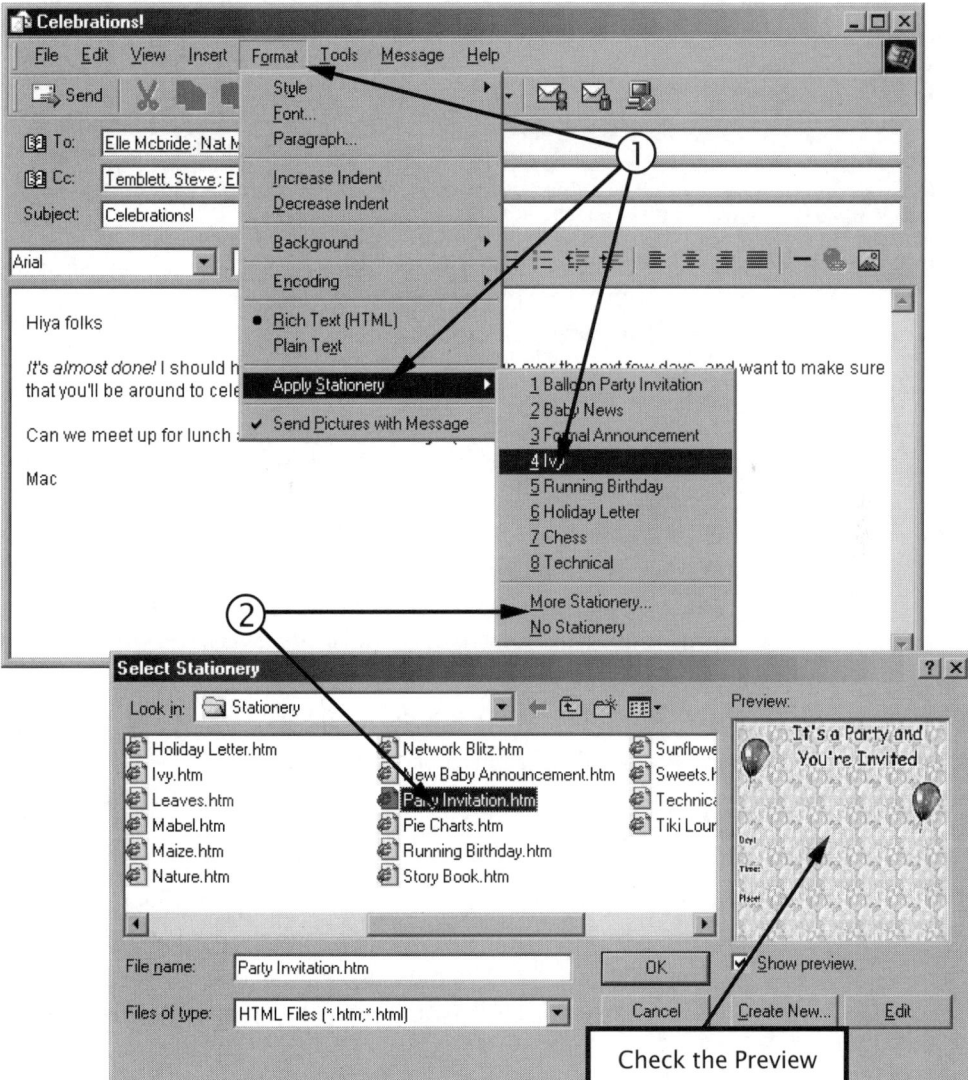

Check the Preview

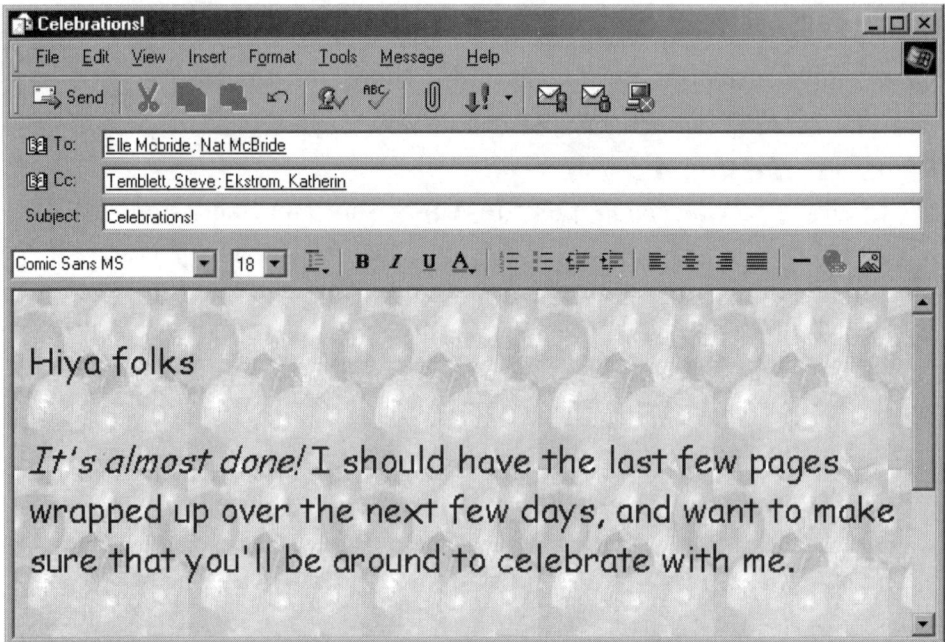

Figure 7.14 An HTML-formatted message ready to be sent.

Spell-checking

Even if you don't want the fancy formats – and if your recipients have old mail systems they will not be able to see the formatting – there's one word-processing feature that you may still find useful. Outlook has a spell-checker!

Even though e-mail is generally treated as a casual form of communication, spell-checking is still worthwhile – some mistypes can be causes of great confusion! If you haven't opted for automatic spell checking (see page 199), you can start the spell-checker by clicking ᴬᴮᶜ.

Sending mail

When you have finished, you can send the message immediately, if you are online already, or store it for sending later when you go online. The message will be held in your Outbox, and the software will prompt you to send it before closing down.

Try it: Send the message

① Click 🖳 Send . If you are online and you have turned on the **Send immediately** option (see page 198), the message will be sent now. If not...

② Click 📩 Send/Receive – if you aren't online, the Connect dialog box will appear, ready to connect to your ISP.

Receiving, replying, forwarding

When you use the Reply routine to reply to incoming mail, part of the work is done for you – the To: and Subject: slots will be already filled in when the New Message window opens. If you have turned on the **Include message in reply** option (see page 198), the original will have been copied in. This can be deleted or trimmed down to the relevant bits as needed.

Try it: Reply to a message

① Select the original message and click 🔁 Reply .

② Add your reply and – if it has been copied in – edit the original as required.

③ Click 🖳 Send . That's it!

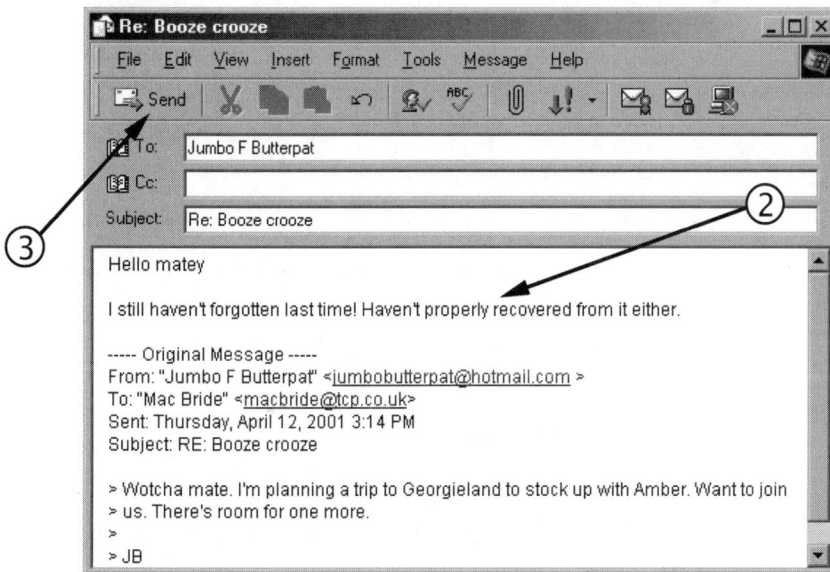

Figure 7.15 The To: and Subject: are written for you when replying.

Forwarding

If someone sends you a message of wider interest, or you find a good article in a newsgroup and want to share it with other people, you can do this easily by forwarding. The subject and message are copied into the New Message window, so all you have to do is add the address and any comments of your own.

Try it: Forward a message

① Select the message and click ⌐⌐⌐ Forward .

② Add the **To:** address and any comments, and trim out any unwanted material from the original.

③ Click ⌐⌐ Send .

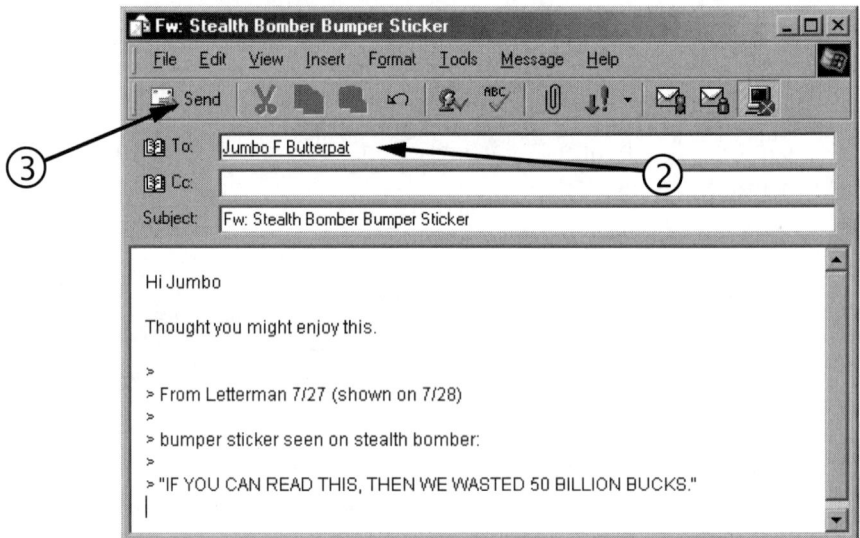

Figure 7.16 The Forward routine makes it easy to share messages with others.

E-mail etiquette

Where you are writing to people you know well, there are only a couple of rules of etiquette that you should observe – apart from those same niceties that apply to any form of mail.

◆ Try to keep your e-mail messages short and to the point. Most of us pay for phone time, and some of us pay for online time as we download the mail.

◆ Forwarding e-mail is easy to do, but other people's mail is their copyright, so don't forward without their permission.

◆ If you are writing to comparative strangers, follow the Newsgroup netiquette (see page 244).

◆ Smileys and abbreviations (see page 246) can add a touch of humour, while helping to keep messages short.

Information overload

E-mail is such a quick and easy way to communicate that it gets overused. Office workers today typically get five to ten times as many e-mails as they used to get memos, letters and phone calls – and they still get memos, letters and calls!

E-mails you can do without include:

◆ from friends, 'I saw this and thought of you' – and you wish they hadn't as you don't have the time to think about it (partly because you've got so many e-mails to deal with).

◆ from colleagues, 'I'm copying this to you to keep you in the loop on developments' – thanks but just tell me when I need to know!

◆ from hustlers, 'Make money fast!!' – you won't, but they might if they can find enough mugs.

The simplest way to deal with all of these is to select the messages by their subject/senders and delete them immediately. Whatever you do, don't reply – it only encourages them. This is particularly true in the case of *spam*. If you reply – to ask them to remove your name from their mailing list – it shows that the e-mail address is active, and they are likely to send even more.

Spam – junk mail from hustlers

If junk mail is a significant problem – particularly if a lot is coming from the same source – you might like to set up a message rule to deal with it. Let's see how.

Message rules

A message rule is an instruction to Outlook Express to look out for a certain type of message, and to deal with it automatically. Typically, the rule will pick up messages from a named sender and delete them immediately.

Try it: Create a message rule

① On the **Tools** menu, point to **Message Rules** and select **Mail**...

② If this is the first mail rule, you will be taken straight to the **New Mail Rule** dialog box. If not, click New... .

③ Select the **Condition** for the rule – how are messages to be selected?

④ Select the **Action** - what is to be done with the messages?

⑤ If the condition needs to be defined – which people? which words? how big? – click on the underlined value.

⑥ At the definition dialog box, enter the values that you want the system to check for.

⑦ Click OK .

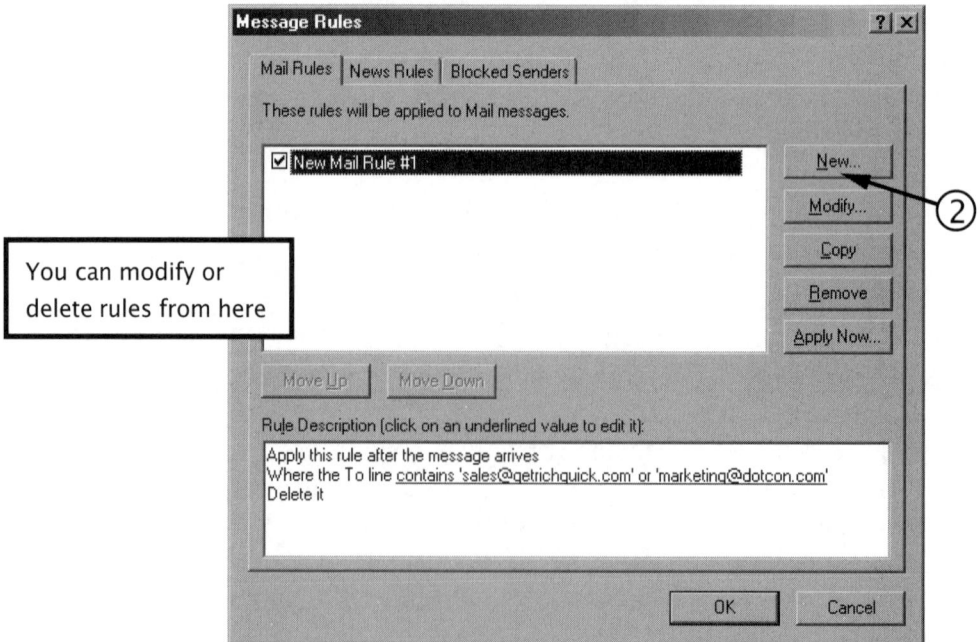

Figure 7.17 The Message Rules dialog box.

New Mail Rule ? ×

Select your Conditions and Actions first, then specify the values in the Description.

1. Select the Conditions for your rule:

③

- ☐ Where the From line contains people
- ☐ Where the Subject line contains specific words
- ☐ Where the message body contains specific words
- ☑ Where the To line contains people

2. Select the Actions for your rule:

④

- ☐ Move it to the specified folder
- ☐ Copy it to the specified folder
- ☑ Delete it
- ☐ Forward it to people

3. Rule Description (click on an underlined value to edit it):

Apply this rule after the message arrives
Where the To line contains people
Delete it

⑤

> If you expect to have several rules, give them meaningful names so that you can identify them later

4. Name of the rule:

New Mail Rule #1

OK   Cancel

Select People ×

Type one name at a time and click Add, or select people from the Address Book.

marketing@dotcon.com

Add

People:

Where the To line contains
'sales@getrichquick.com'

Address Book... ⑥

Remove

Options...

⑦

OK   Cancel

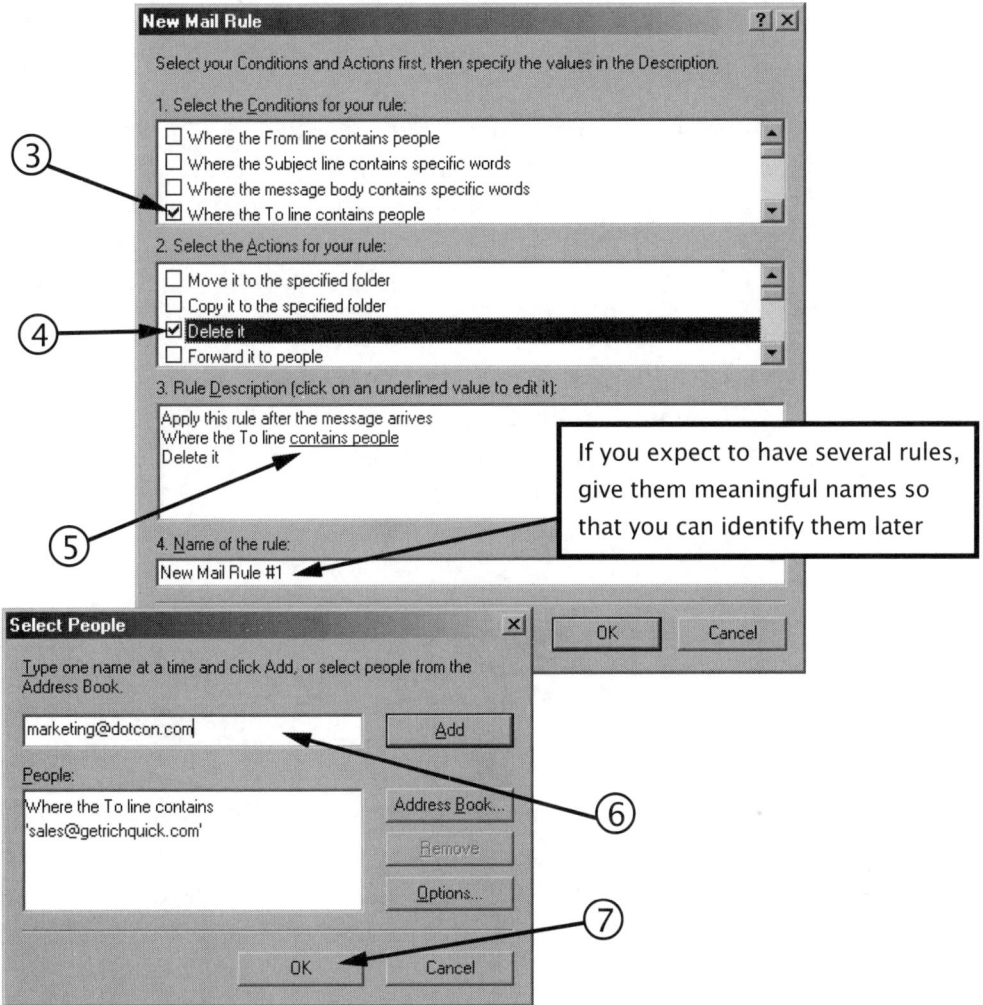

Figure 7.18 Message Rules can reduce the junk mail problem.

Organising old mail

E-mail can clog up your hard disk. This is only partly because you tend to get more than you want, but also because most of us tend to leave messages in the Inbox after reading. Think about what we do with letters and memos. After reading them, we normally either bin them immediately, or file them, or put them on one side until we have dealt with them and then bin or file them. Why don't we do the same with e-mail?

I think it's because old messages don't visibly clutter up your desk – but they are still clutter! Tidying up your Inbox takes little time, saves hard disk space and makes it easier to find those old messages that you did want to keep.

Create one or more folders for long-term storage using the **File > New Folder** command, then work through your old messages, deleting them or moving them to the appropriate folders.

Try it: Organise your old mail

① On the **File** menu, point to **New** and select **Folder**...
② Enter a meaningful name for the folder.
③ Pick the folder within which it is to go – select Inbox to put it at the top level.
④ Click OK.

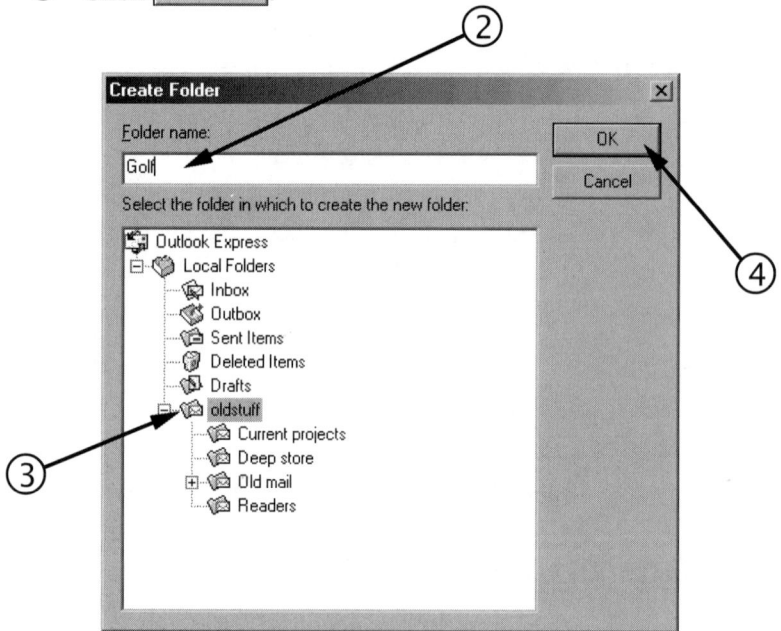

⑤ Open the Inbox.
⑥ To delete a message, select it and click ✕ or press the **[Delete]** key.
⑦ To move a message, select it, drag it across the window and drop it into the target folder.

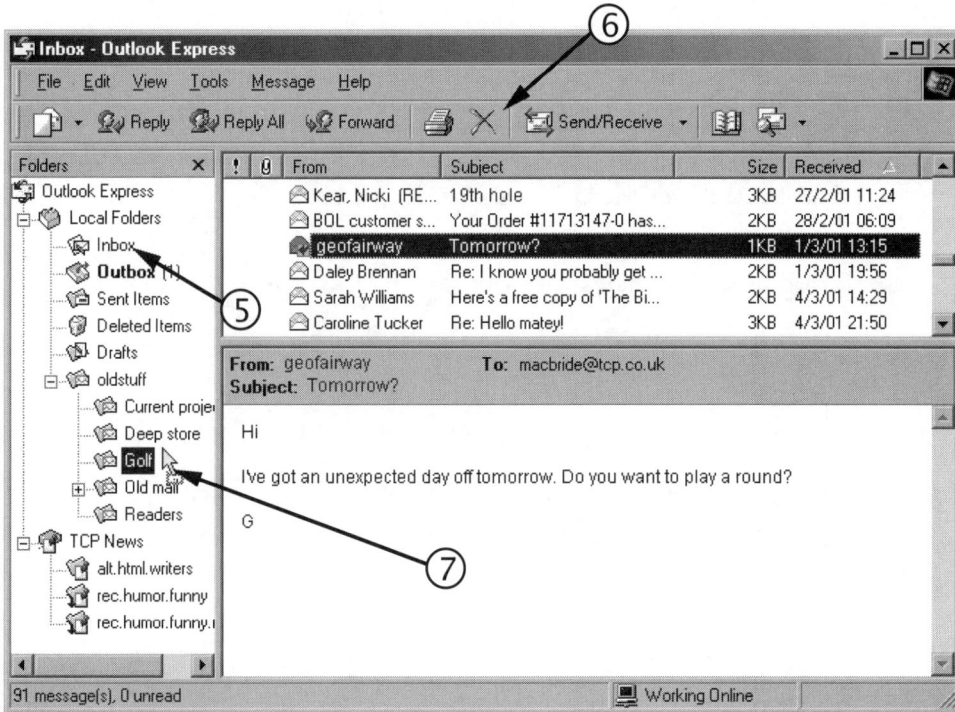

Figure 7.19 Organise your e-mail into folders.

Finding messages

Unless you are very organised (or keep very little old mail) there will be times when you can't lay your hands on a particular message. When this happens, try the Find routine, giving it whatever details you can remember.

Try it: Find an old message

① On the **Edit** menu, point to **Find** and select **Message**...

② Click [Browse..] and select the folder to search – if you want to search all the folders, select *Local Folders*.

③ Enter anything that will help to identify the message – who it was *From* or *To*, words in the *Subject* or *Message*, or the dates that it was *Received before* and/or after.

④ Click [Find Now] and wait a moment.

⑤ Double-click on a header line to open its message in a separate window.

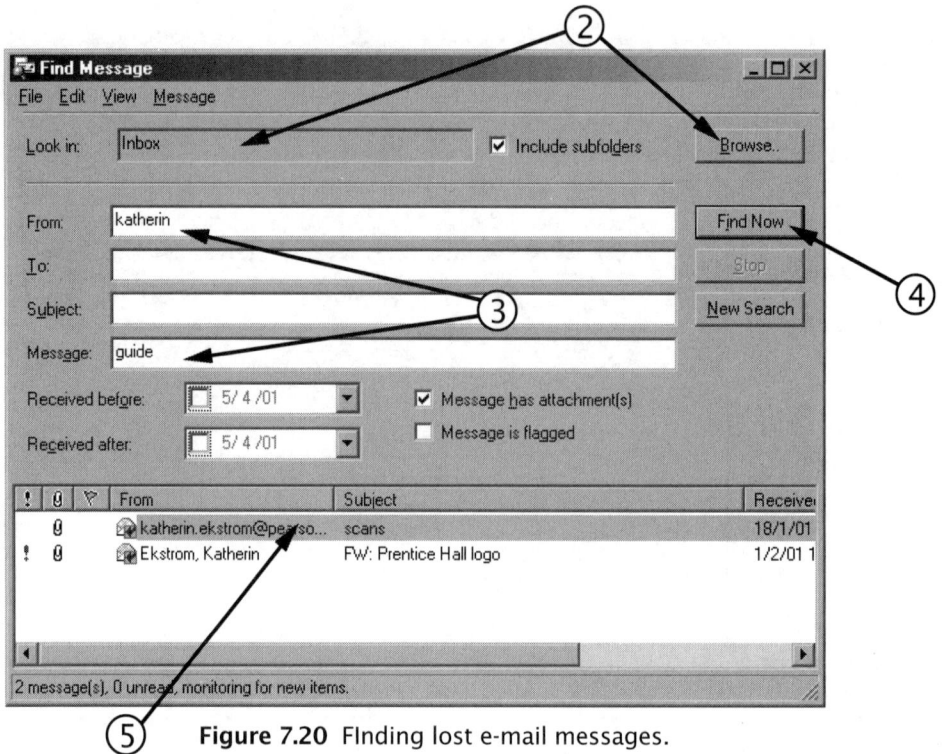

Figure 7.20 FInding lost e-mail messages.

Identities

If you share your computer and Internet access with other people, you can all have a distinct *identity*. Each identity has its own copy of Outlook Express with its own mail and news folders. These can be password-protected, if security is an issue.

◆ To set up a new identity, open the **File** menu, point to **Identities** and select **Add New Identity**. At the dialog box, enter a name and a password, if required.

◆ To remove or edit the properties of your own (and of any non-protected) identity, open the **File** menu, point to **Identities** and select **Manage Identities**.

In practice, separate identities are only really worth having if each person also has his/her own e-mail account. If you share an e-mail address, whoever logs on first will pick up the mail for everybody.

Attached files

Binary files (images, programs, documents and other non-text data) can be sent by mail, attached to messages. As the mail system was designed for transmitting plain text, binary files have to be converted to text for transfer, and back to binary on receipt. This is a technical, and sometimes quite tricky, operation if you have to do it 'by hand'. Fortunately Outlook Express, like most modern e-mail software, has built-in routines to handle these conversions. All you have to do is identify the file to attach, or select a folder to store an incoming attachment.

Binary = made up of 1s and 0s

You can use attachments to send documents, images – even videos – to people. It is generally very reliable, but there are a few snags you should be aware of. Most of these revolve around the size of binary files, which tend to be large – especially compared to simple text messages.

When a file is converted for transmission, it gets about 50% bigger, and it can take a while to send – or receive – messages with attachments. For example, the scan of the old photo shown below is around 1.4Mb, and as an attached file would be a little over 2Mb. E-mail is transmitted at around 3Kb per second, so it would take around 10 minutes to send (and receive) the message with this picture.

Figure 7.21 The meeting of old and new technology – a sepia print, scanned and ready for mailing.

If an e-mail transfer is interrupted part-way through – because of a faulty line, overcrowding at the service provider or whatever – it has to start again from scratch. Interruptions are more likely with larger files, simply because you have to be online longer.

When you pick up your mail, it is downloaded from your service provider in the order that it was received, and if there is a huge attachment to an early message, you will have to get that before you can pick up later ones. This can be a real pain, especially if you know that there is an urgent message somewhere down the line. Be kind – don't send people big binaries unless they really want them!

And finally, do note that not everyone has e-mail software that can handle attachments so check that your recipients can cope before relying on attachments for anything vital.

Try it: Attach a file to a message

① Start a new message as usual.

② Open the **Insert** menu and select **File Attachment**... or click 📎 .

③ The **Insert Attachment** dialog box is essentially the same as the **Open File** dialog box. Locate and select the file in the usual way. The file will be listed in a new **Attach** slot.

④ Click 📧 Send and wait – it takes a few moments for the system to convert the file.

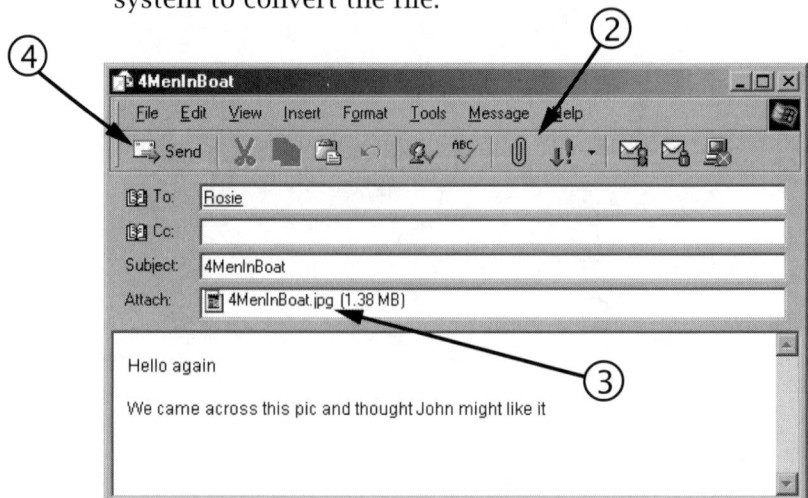

The **Insert** menu has a **Picture** option (when in HTML format) which is intended for pictures that are being included for decorative purposes. If you receive a message with an inserted picture, you can save its file by right-clicking on it and using the **Save Picture As**... command – it's exactly the same technique as you would use for capturing an image of a Web page.

Saving attachments

For the next '*Try it*', you need someone to send you a file! You'll know if a message has an attachment by the paperclip icon ₫ beside it in the header list, and larger clip icon in the right of the preview pane header.

Try it: Detach a file from a message

① Open the message.

② Click the paperclip and select **Save Attachments**...

③ Click Browse.. and locate the folder in which to store the file, then click Save .

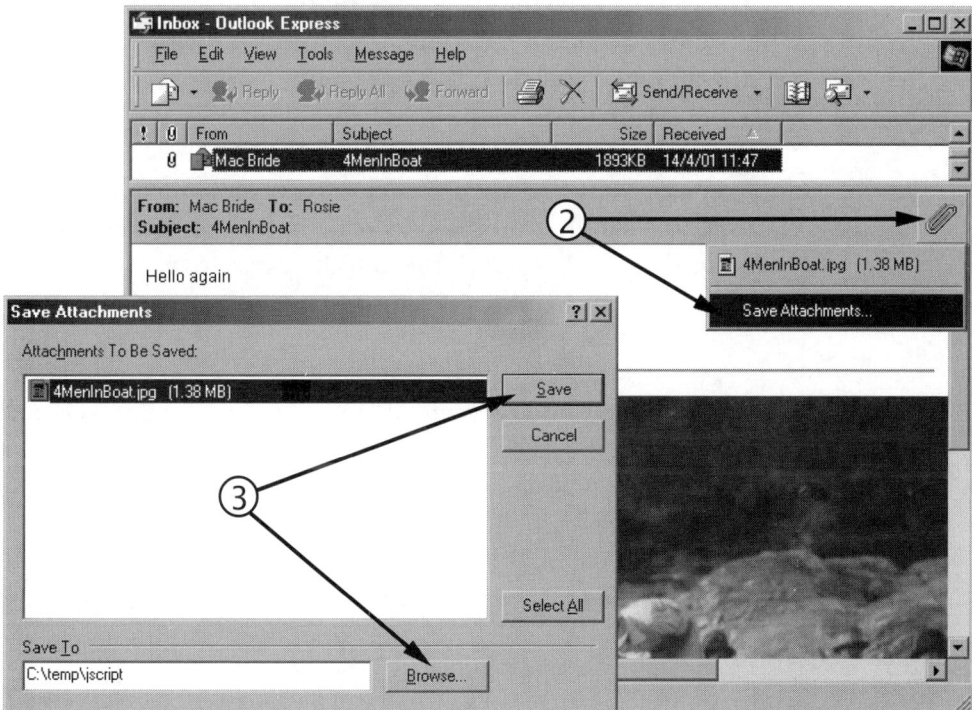

Opening attachments

If you want to view an attachment without saving it, click on its name in the 'paperclip' menu. The following dialog box will open.

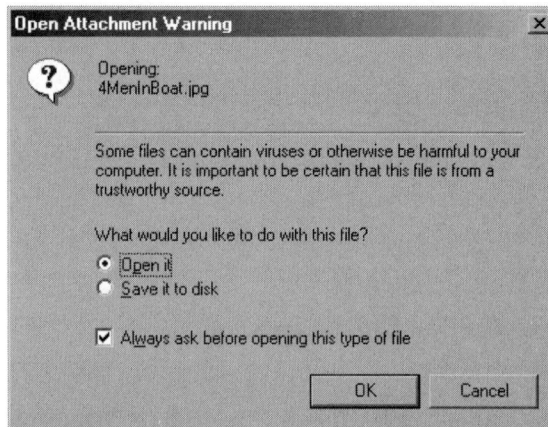

Take the warning seriously! In the last few years, some of the nastiest viruses have been spread through e-mail attachments. The victims get a message, apparently from an acquaintance, with an attachment that they are urged to look at. When the attachment is opened, the virus program is executed. Typically, it will go through the victims' address books, sending itself off to all their contacts. If that's all it does, then it is a nuisance – and an expensive one as it takes skilled personnel time to clean it out of the system – but some viruses will go on to destroy or corrupt files on the hard drive.

Any executable file (program) may be a virus. Common extensions for executable files include:

.exe .com .bat .vbx

Never open an executable file unless you had been expecting it and are absolutely certain that it is safe.

If a document can contain a macro, the macro could be a virus. Macros can be handled by many applications, including Word, Excel and PowerPoint.

Make sure that your applications are set for high security in respect of macros – in any Office application, go to the **Tools** menu, point to **Macros** and select **Security**...

Web mail

Go to almost any of the major directories and portals and you will be offered free Web mail. This is much the same as ordinary e-mail but with two big differences.

The first – and this is the most significant – is that you can handle your Web mail from anywhere as long as you can log on to the Internet somehow. This may be through a public terminal in a library or Internet cafe, from a friend's desktop, or through your (temporary) account at your place of work or study.

The second is that you can (normally) only use Web mail online. With ordinary e-mail, you only need to be online while you are sending and receiving messages – they can be read and written, moved and deleted offline. With Web mail, your messages are stored online and you must be online the whole time that you are dealing with your mail (though you can download messages for later reading, and upload messages written in a word-processor). As a result, dealing with the mail is slower – and more costly if you are paying for the online and telephone time.

If you are accessing your Hotmail account from home, you can send and receive messages through Outlook Express. This works almost the same as a normal e-mail account, with the most noticeable difference being that the text of messages is only downloaded when you select the headers, rather than the whole thing arriving in a single operation.

Hotmail is the biggest Web mail provider – and its offline read and write facility make it one of the best

A Web mail address is worth considering if:

◆ you are often away from home, either on holiday or staying with friends or family;
◆ you are likely to change your job or service provider and don't want the disruption of a change of address.

There are lots of Web mail providers including:

◆ **Hotmail** www.hotmail.com
◆ **MailCity** www.mailcity.com
◆ **Excite** mail.excite.co.uk *or* mail.excite.com
◆ **Yahoo!** mail.yahoo.co.uk *or* mail.yahoo.com

Try it: Set up a Hotmail account

① In *Outlook Express*, open the **Tools** menu, point to **New Account Signup** and click **Hotmail**.

② Or in *Internet Explorer*, go to **www.hotmail.com** and click **Sign up now!**

③ Enter your details into the **Setup Hotmail Account** wizard (or into the Sign-up Web page – they both collect the same information). You may wonder why they need to know so much about you, but if you don't tell them, you won't be able to get an account. (Of course, only you know which details are correct!)

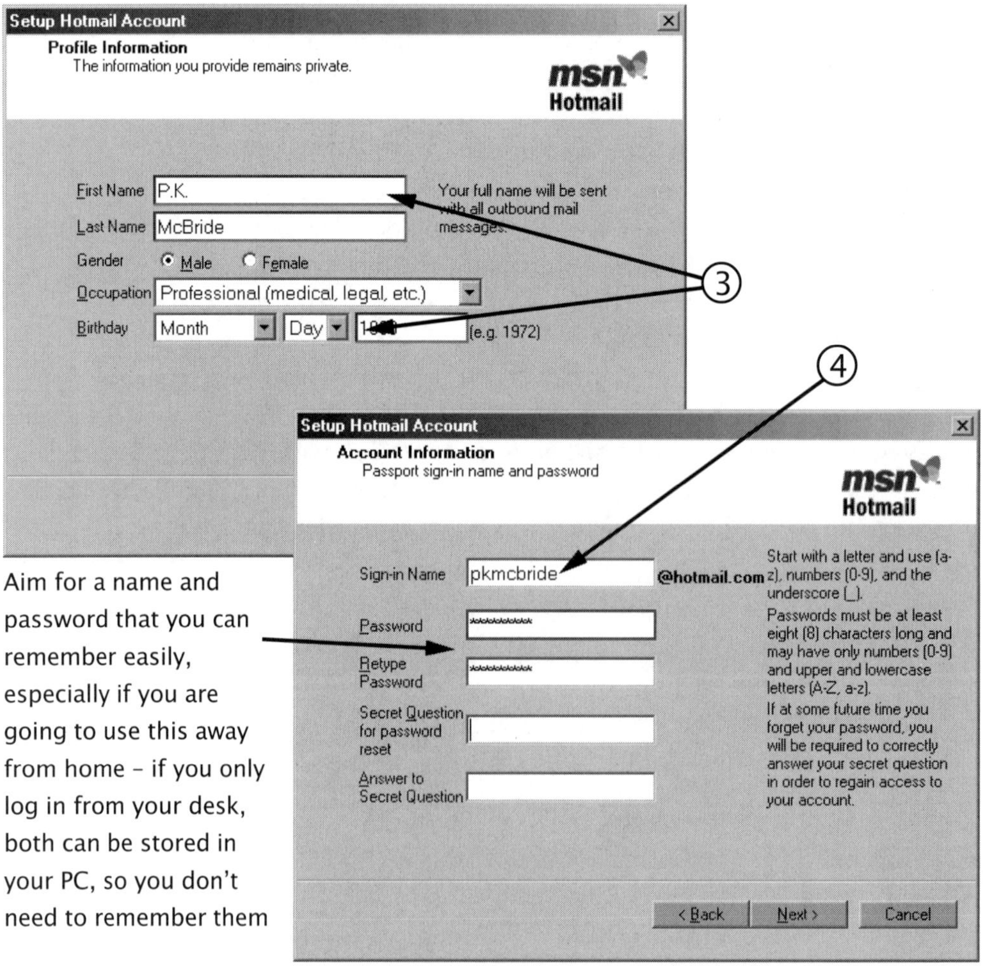

Aim for a name and password that you can remember easily, especially if you are going to use this away from home – if you only log in from your desk, both can be stored in your PC, so you don't need to remember them

Figure 7.22 Setting up a Hotmail account through the Wizard.

④ You will be asked to give a user name. Your first choice of name may already be in use, but there's no harm in trying. At the end of the sign-up, the membership lists will be checked and if your name is in use, you will be offered variations on it.

Configuring Hotmail

Once you're registered, you can start to configure your Hotmail account. WebCourier delivers newsletters directly to your mailbox. Tick any that sound interesting – you can easily unsubscribe later if you decide that you don't want to read them.

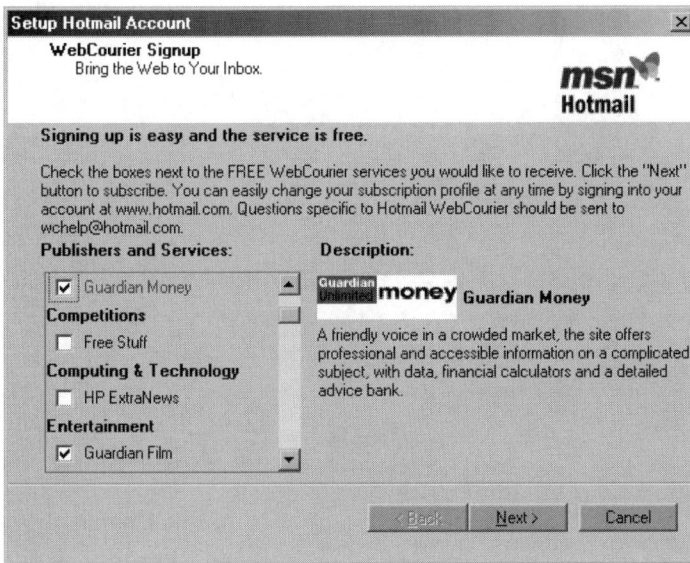

Figure 7.23 Like everything else at Hotmail, the Web Courier service is free – all it costs to give things a try is a little of your time!

You can use Inbox Protector to filter your mail. If you select the Typical setting, the only messages that will go into your Inbox are those from people that you have in your Hotmail Address Book, or who have Hotmail or MSN e-mail accounts (who are not allowed to send junk mail), or who are on your 'Safe List'. Those from anybody else will be directed to your Bulk Mail folder or the Trash Can, both of which are emptied automatically, at differing intervals.

This will filter out all junk mail, though it will also catch messages from new contacts. That's not a big problem if you opt to send potential junk to Bulk Mail. You can check this from time to time and if you find any messages that you want to read, you can add their senders to your Address Book or Safe List.

The simplest and safest options are to use Inbox Protector, on the Typical setting, with Bulk Mail as the 'discard folder' – messages will sit here for 30 days before they are deleted, but they are emptied from the Trash Can every few days.

Custom gives you a little more control over the filters – switch to this later if you find that the Typical setting is too intrusive

If people's names are in your Address Book or the Safe List, messages from them will get through. They do not need to be in both – an Address Book entry is more useful in most cases

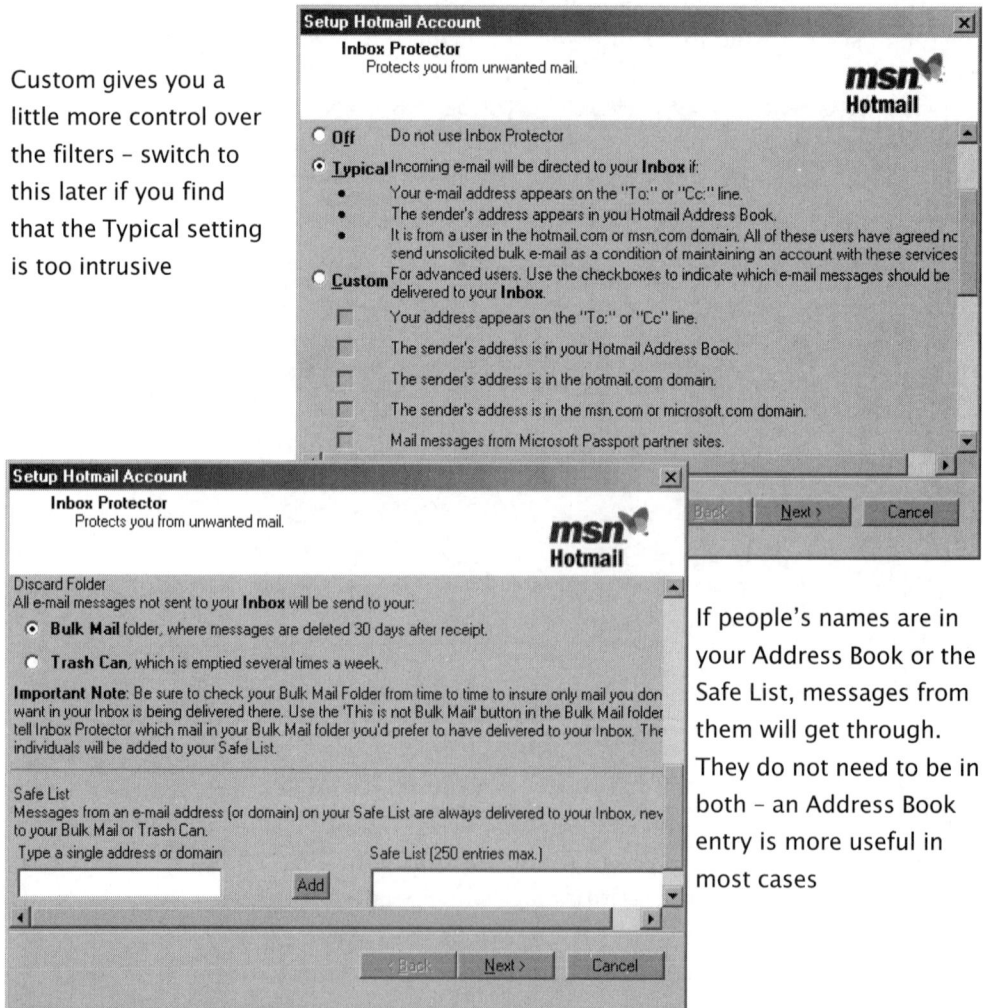

Figure 7.24 Inbox Protector helps to protect you from unwanted mail.

Using Hotmail through the Web

Hotmail offers all the core facilities of Outlook Express, and they are all used in much the same way.

◆ There is a similar set of folders, though no Outbox as messages are sent immediately after writing.

◆ Messages arrive in the Inbox and can be read by clicking on them.

◆ Messages can be written, in the Compose window, in plain or Rich Text (HTML), and can have files – from your PC or elsewhere on the Internet – attached to them.

◆ The Address Book can store lots of details about your contacts – though only the e-mail address is essential.

Try it: Explore Hotmail

① Got to Hotmail at **www.hotmail.com**

② Enter your **Sign-In Name** and **Password** and click Sign in .

The first time you sign in, you'll be asked if you want Windows to remember the password for you. Sounds good to me!

③ You will be taken to your Inbox. If nothing else, there should be a welcome message from Hotmail. Click on the link to read the message.

④ A tidy Inbox will load faster and be more efficient to use. After reading a message, either delete it or move it to another folder for long-term storage.

⑤ To write a message, click **Compose** .

⑥ At the Compose window, if you want to send a formatted message, tick the **Rich Text Format** box and wait a moment for the formatting toolbar to appear.

⑦ Fill in the **To:** and **Cc:** slots, either using names from your Hotmail Address Book or by typing them in.

⑧ Write and format your message as normal.

⑨ If you want to spell-check it, click Check Spelling .

⑩ When you are finished, click Send .

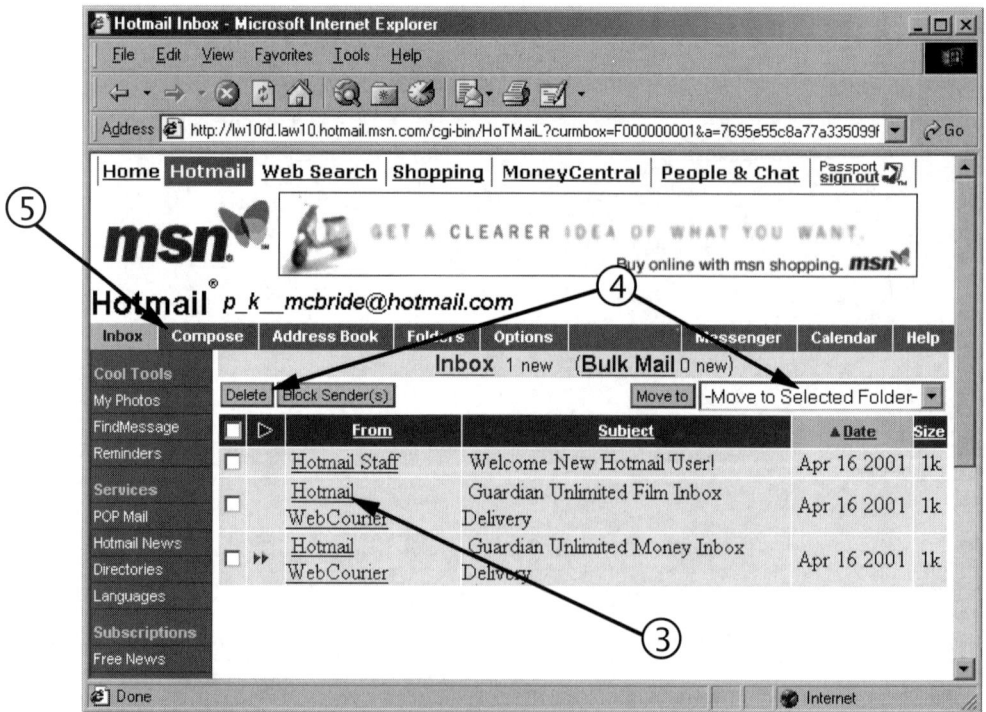

Figure 7.25 The Inbox at Hotmail.

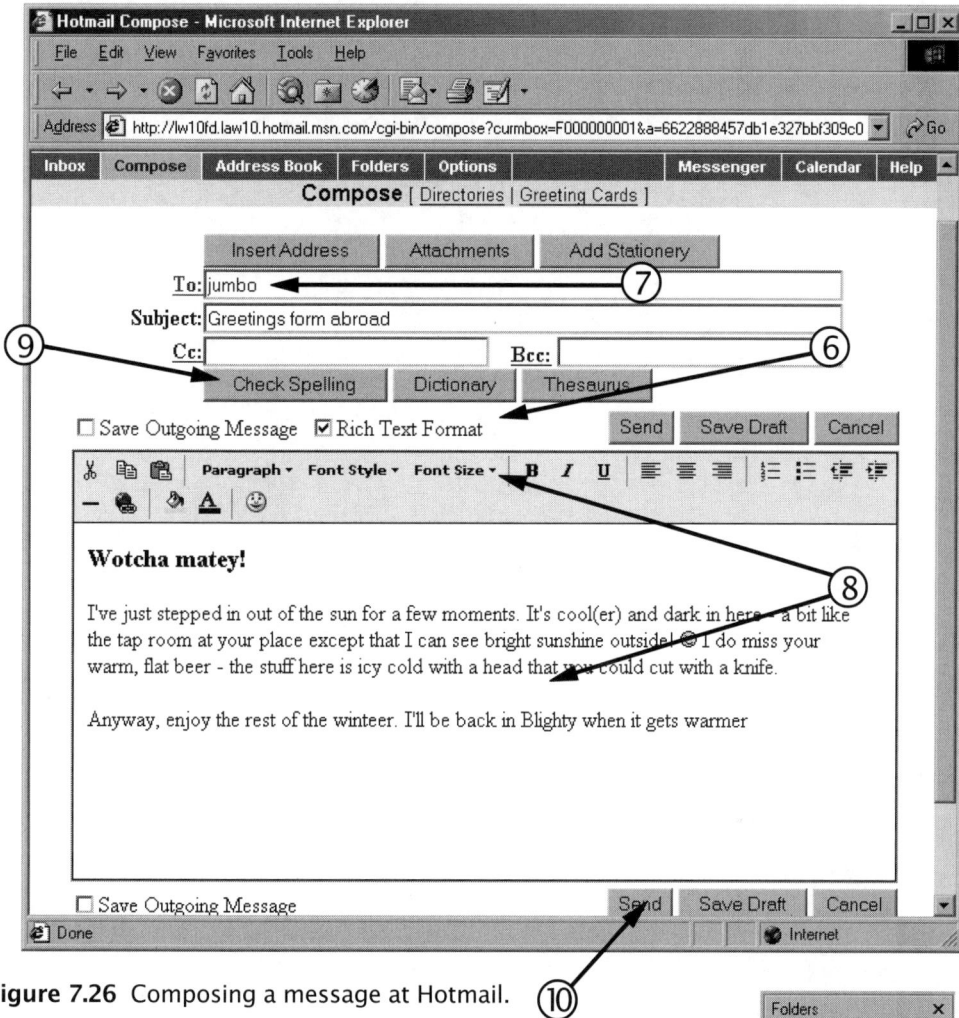

Figure 7.26 Composing a message at Hotmail.

Hotmail through Outlook Express

If you access Hotmail through your own PC, you can reach it through Outlook Express. Look in the Folder List and you will see that there is a Hotmail folder. When one of its folders is selected, if you start to write a new message, it will automatically have the Hotmail address. When you run the Send and Receive routine, it will handle the mail from both your Hotmail and your ISP accounts.

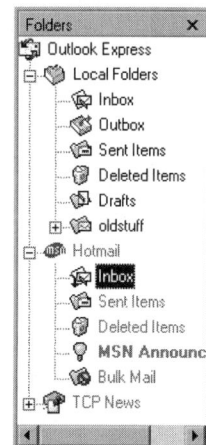

8

Newsgroups

IN THIS CHAPTER:

- Newsgroups and mailing lists
- Reading the news
- Newsgroup netiquette
- Files from newsgroups

People come together in newsgroups to share common interests and enthusiasms, to ask for and to give help, to debate – and to argue! There are thousands of them, each devoted to a different topic, from the seriously academic to the totally trivial.

Newsgroups and mailing lists

Newsgroups and mailing lists are two approaches to the same end – that of distributing a message from one person to all the others in the 'club'. The differences between them are largely in the ways that they are organised.

◆ With a mailing list, an individual copy of each message is sent to each subscriber, travelling through the e-mail system and arriving in the Inbox like any other message.

◆ With newsgroups, the articles are transferred in bulk between the sites that act as news servers. To read articles, you have to log on to your news server, download the headers and then download selected messages.

Both mailing lists and newsgroups can be accessed through Outlook Express or most other modern e-mail software – oddly enough, Outlook (Outlook Express's big brother) cannot handle newsgroups. Outlook Express is used for the examples in this chapter.

Newsgroups

There are over 30,000 newsgroups that can be accessed over the Internet, with new ones being started up every day. They are organised into about 20 major (and many more minor) divisions, subdivided by topic, and subdivided again where necessary.

Their names normally reflect this structure and describe the focus of their interest. For example, **rec.arts.animation** is found in the **arts** subdivision of the **rec** main division and is devoted to **animation** as an art form. (There are other animation groups elsewhere, with different focuses.) Sometimes, the dots are used for punctuation, and sometimes just for fun – there is, for instance one called **alt.buddha.short.fat.guy**!

With so many groups, it is not possible to cover them all here – that would take a whole book. The following brief survey should give some indication of the scope of newsgroups, and where to start looking for ones that might interest you.

alt

These are the alternative newsgroups, set up to cover topics that had not been included in the other main divisions. This set is enormous both in number and in range, so if you can't find a newsgroup anywhere else, try **alt**. Hobbies, obsessions and fan clubs form a substantial part of the alt groups, though there are also groups for specialist software, professional interests and discussions.

Dipping into those starting with 'a' we find:

alt.aldus.freehand

which contains discussions, tips, problems and solutions for users of the Aldus design/drawing package, while

alt.alien.visitors

is for people who have met them or are looking for them and are struggling against the government conspiracy to suppress the facts. Join it and find out the truth – but watch your phone bills mount as a hundreds of articles pour in every day!

alt.animation.warner-bros

is for the animation fans.

alt.architecture.int-design
alt.aromatherapy

are adjacent in the listings, but neatly show the diversity of interests.

biz

These are business-oriented groups. Here you will find announcements of new products, offers of services, job opportunities and discussions of market-related issues.

comp

This is a very large set of newsgroups (there are over 1000) which gives a good example of the subdivided structure. It covers many aspects of computing, including programming languages, applications, hardware and standards among its 70 first level divisions.

One of these, **comp.sys**, then splits over 40 ways, devoted to different hardware and operating systems. If we focus on the **comp.sys.ibm** groups, we find five subsets – including one for PCs, **comp.sys.ibm.pc**, which then divides into:

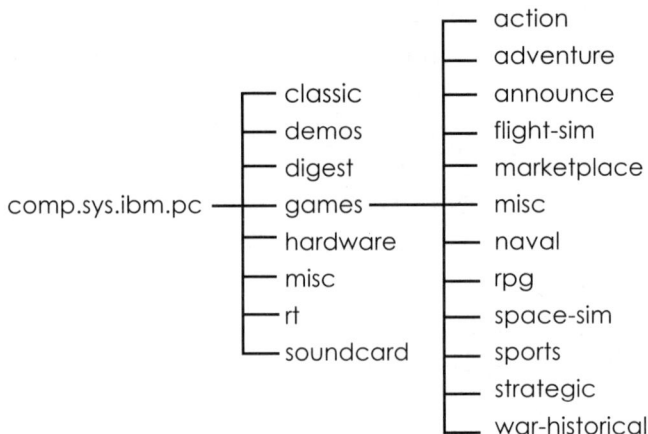

```
                                          ┌── action
                                          ├── adventure
                          ┌── classic      ├── announce
                          ├── demos        ├── flight-sim
                          ├── digest       ├── marketplace
comp.sys.ibm.pc ─────────┼── games ──────┼── misc
                          ├── hardware     ├── naval
                          ├── misc         ├── rpg
                          ├── rt           ├── space-sim
                          └── soundcard    ├── sports
                                          ├── strategic
                                          └── war-historical
```

info

This is a fairly small but very mixed set of newsgroups, with discussions ranging from the politics of firearms control to the management of Sun computer systems, but with a core focusing on NSF, the US National Science Foundation network whose hardware forms the backbone of the Internet in the USA.

misc

Short, of course, for miscellaneous, and mainly to be missed. Books, health, education, kids, 'for sale' and job opportunities (all US-based) make up the bulk of these.

news

Some of these are about *news*, in the sense of current affairs, but many are actually about *newsgroups*. Amongst these, are several specially for new users. **news.announce.newusers** and **news.newusers** are two good sources of advice, while **news.answers** may solve your problems. If it doesn't, ask in **news.newusers.questions**.

rec

This is a large set covering the whole range of recreational activities from arts through games to sports, with virtually everything in between. These three alone should give you an idea of the diversity:

    rec.arts.sf.tv.quantum-leap
    rec.games.xtank.programmer
    rec.gardens.orchids

sci and *bionet*

In these academic and professional scientific groups you will find some of the most illuminating discussions on the Net.

soc

These groups are mainly for discussions of different cultures, religions and social issues.

Other newsgroups

There are also sets of newsgroups for most countries. Join the **uk.local** group for your area to find out what's going on nearby, one of the many **uk.rec** or **uk.sport** groups to find fellow enthusiasts, or **uk.jobs.offered** (or **uk.jobs.fortyplus**) if you are looking for a career change.

Mailing lists

Mailing lists fall into two broad, but overlapping, categories: some act as site newsletters, others are true discussion groups. In all cases, you can only read the articles if you have joined the list. They are then sent sent directly to you, through the normal e-mail system, from the list's moderator – not personally, it is all automated!

Most portals and directories, and many commercial sites run mailing lists. Most of these are simply newsletters to keep you informed of what's new at their sites, though some encourage members to submit contributions. Subscribing to these is simple – if the site runs a list, there will be a clearly labelled link or button somewhere.

Subscribing to a discussion group's mailing list is a little trickier. For a start, you have to know the list exists! There are useful links at Yahoo! (**www.yahoo.co.uk/Computers_ and_Internet/Internet/Mailing_Lists**) and a few specialist sites, including ListQuest (**www.listquest.com**) where you can search for lists on chosen topics. The alternative is to just keep an eye out for them. If there is a mailing list on the topic that particularly interests you, you will probably find a reference to it in Web pages or newsgroup articles on that topic.

The method for subscribing to lists varies, but normally involves mailing a request to the list server on the moderator's server. This will be addressed to listserv@*name_of_server* or majordomo@*name_of_ server* and carry the line:

> SUBSCRIBE *list_name*

Subscribing to newsgroups

This is not like subscribing to a mailing list. Subscribing to a newsgroup brings it into your news folder for easy access and makes it available for synchronising (see page 243). The process is managed through the Newsgroup Subscriptions dialog box.

When you first use this routine, be prepared for a wait as Outlook Express must download the list of newsgroups held on your Internet service provider's news server. The lists vary. Not all providers accept and distribute all newsgroups – some are specific to individual providers or to local areas, others will only be handled if a user requests subscription. Nevertheless, most lists are enormous – typically over 200Kb – and take time to download.

The Newsgroup Subscription dialog box has three tabs:

◆ **All** lists all the newsgroups held on the server – browse through it sometime, just to see the range and variety.

◆ The **Subscribed** tab lists those to which you are currently subscribed – these will also be in the Folders list.

◆ **New** shows any newsgroups which have been added since you last contacted the server.

On any panel, you can subscribe to a group by selecting it and clicking **Subscribe**. When you close the dialog box, the group will be present in your Folders list. If, after sampling a group, you decide that it is not for you, you can unsubscribe by simply deleting it from that list.

Of course, before you can subscribe, you have to find the newsgroup. That is not as difficult as it might appear when you first see that 30,000-strong list! At the top of the dialog box is a slot marked *Display newsgroups which contain.* Type a word in here, wait a moment, and the list will reset to display only those containing the search word.

Try it: Subscribe to a newsgroup

① On the **Tools** menu, select **Newsgroups**... or click 🔳.

② Enter one or more words to describe what interests you in the **Display newsgroups which contain** slot.

③ Scroll through the list and select a newsgroup.

④ Click Subscribe .

⑤ Repeat Steps ② – ④ to add any other groups then click OK .

You can sort out your subscriptions offline – you don't need to go online until you want to read the news

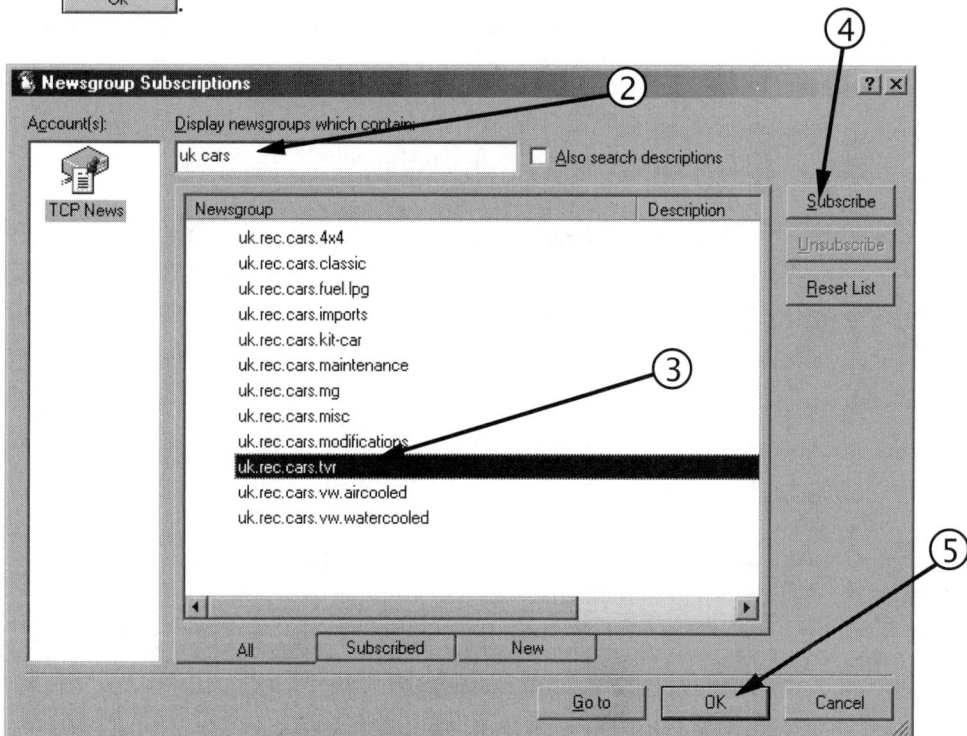

Go to see

Note that Go to button at the bottom of the dialog box. Click this if you want to dip into a group, to see what's there, but without adding it to your list of subscribed groups, or if you want to catch up with the news in your favourite groups while working on someone else's machine. When you **Go to** a newsgroup, you can read its articles during that session, but the link will be discarded when you close down Outlook.

Reading the news

A newsgroup may generate anything from 2 to 200 articles every day. Even if you are fascinated by the topic of the newsgroup, you are unlikely to want to read every article, and that is where the subject line helps. Unlike e-mail, where the headers and body text of new messages are downloaded together, with newsgroups, only the headers are normally downloaded at first. The body text doesn't follow until you select a message from the header lines – one reason why a clear subject is essential in newsgroup articles.

Try it: Read the news

① Go online, if you are not already connected.

Either

② On the **Tools** menu, select **Synchronize Newsgroup**.

③ At the **Synchronize Newsgroups** dialog box, tick the **Get the following items:** checkbox, select *All messages*, or *New messages only* or *Headers only* and click [OK].

Or

◆ Click on the newsgroup to download the headers.

④ Scan through the subjects in the header lines to find out what the articles are about.

Thread = a whole set of linked articles

⑤ Click ⊞ to expand *threads* so that you can see the follow-up articles.

⑥ Click on an article to read it in the preview pane.

Having read an article, you can respond in two ways – send an e-mail to the author only, or post a follow-up article to the group. In general, if the original article was a request for information, reply to the author, as this is not likely to be of general interest. If you want to follow up on an article with your own contribution to the discussion, you would normally

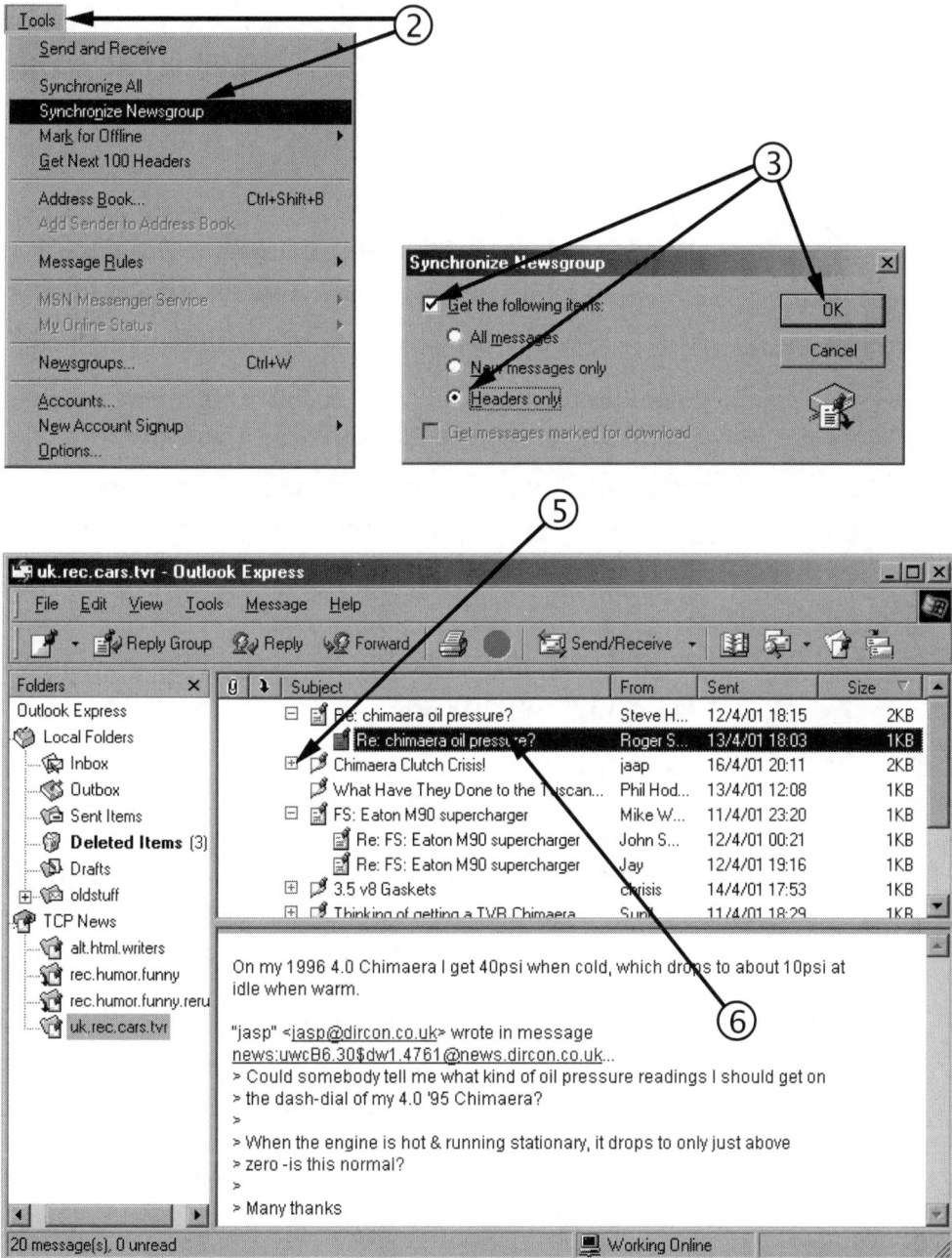

Figure 8.1 Reading the news in Outlook Express. Newsgroups can be an excellent source of specialist help – and an opportunity to share your own specialist knowledge with others.

quote the relevant lines from the original article or give a brief summary of the key points that you want to pick up.

Outlook Express has three reply and forward buttons:

◆ **Reply Group** posts your article to the group, adding it to the thread – the Subject will be created for you by putting **Re:** before the original subject.

◆ **Reply** posts an e-mail message to the author. This may be an appropriate way to respond to a request for specific information that is not likely to be of wide interest – e.g. answers to homework questions!

◆ **Forward** prepares to send a copy as an e-mail message to whoever you then specify in the **To:** or **Cc:** boxes.

There is also a **Reply to All** option on the **Message** menu. This posts a reply to the group and sends a copy as an e-mail to the article's author.

When you reply to the group, your message will be attached to the original message – and any reply to your reply will be attached to that – so one article may generate a *thread* – a whole set of linked articles.

Posting

If you want to put out your own request for information, or to start a new discussion, then you *post* your article to the group.

Don't rush into posting articles. There are few things old members find more irritating than a 'newbie' asking obvious questions or rehearsing ancient arguments.

◆ Take time to read enough to pick up the true flavour of the group and to find out what topics have been discussed recently.

◆ Take time also to track down the group's Frequently Asked Questions list – this is posted regularly in most groups.

◆ Most groups also maintain a collection or a digest of old articles. Check their dates to find the most recent and scan them to see what has been covered before you post.

Reading without posting is known as *lurking*. It's OK to lurk. Some groups, especially the smaller and more intense discussion groups dislike lurkers – they see it almost as a form of eavesdropping – but even here it is better to lurk until you have got into the swing of things.

When you want to contribute, select the newsgroup in the Folder list and click the **New Post** button. When the **New Message** window opens, the newsgroup name will be in place for you. Remember to write a clear subject line.

Managing subscriptions

If you only subscribe to one or two newsgroups, and they are ones that do not have huge numbers of articles, then little management is needed. It will be enough to click on the group when you want to get the latest headers, then click to read a few selected articles when you are online.

If you make more use of newsgroups than this – and some people do find them an excellent resource and a good way to meet and interact with fellow enthusiasts – then you might want to make more use of the synchronisation facilities.

You can set up your subscribed newsgroups so that with one click of a button the system will go off and download all their messages, or just the new ones, or the headers.

With busy newsgroups, where only a few of the messages are likely to be of interest, you can get the headers, skim through these, marking those you want to read, then download the marked messages. If you are paying for phone time, this is the most efficient way to read the news.

Try it: Get synchronised

① Click on the top level news folder – it will probably be named after your ISP.

② Select a newsgroup and drop down the **Settings** list.

③ Select what you want to be downloaded when you use the Synchronization routine.

④ Repeat ② and ③ for all your newsgroups.

⑤ Open the **Tools** menu and select **Synchronize All**.

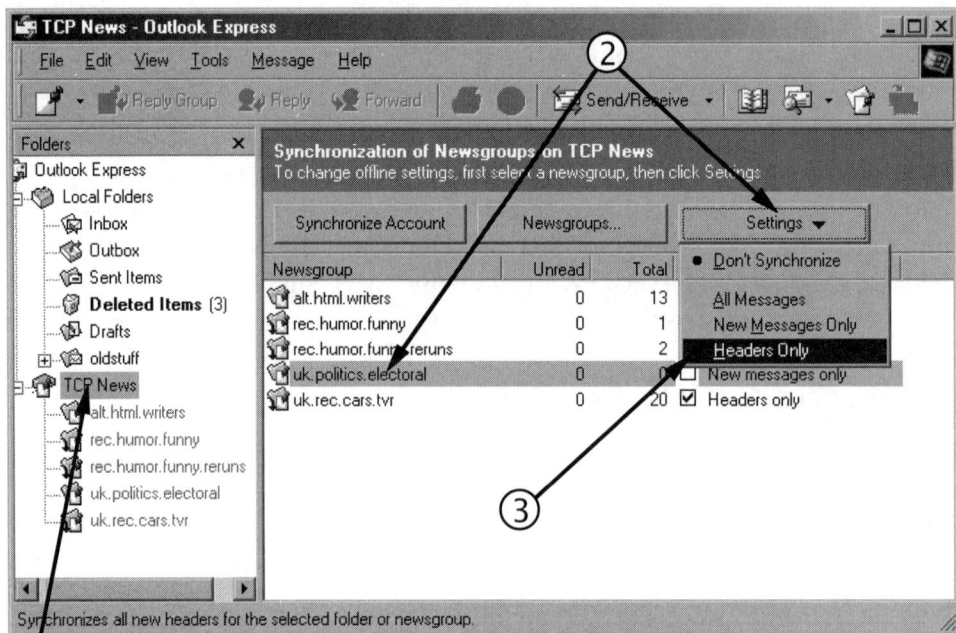

Figure 8.2 Setting up synchronisation.

Newsgroup netiquette

Like much of the rest of the Internet, the newsgroup system relies on cooperation, voluntary labour, some sponsorship and a set of agreed rules – its *netiquette*. Take the trouble to learn the rules and use them.

Using netiquette is not just about being a good news user – it is also a matter of self-preservation. The thing to remember is that, with a popular group, any article you write is going to be downloaded by several thousand people, and many of these will be paying phone and online charges for receiving your article. If you waste their time and money, they will not be happy and may well respond with *flames*. Follow the rules and make life easier for others and for yourself.

Flames = angry mail

◆ **Do** KISS – Keep It Short and Simple. Keep it short to save phone time; keep it simple because the Internet is an international community and not all users speak English as their first language – and even those that do are of varying abilities and ages.

- **Do** top and tail thoughtfully. Write a clear and descriptive subject line, and don't overdo your signature.

- **Do** be relevant. Every newsgroup has its own focus; if what you want to say is not within its focus, find one where it does fit. Straying off-topic will get you flamed.

- **Do** read any follow-ups to an article – the subject line will have **Re:** at the start – before writing yours. Someone else may already have made the same points.

- **Do** summarise, or crop the copy of the original article when following up.

- **Don't** overreact. Ignore bad spelling and poor grammar – this is a multilingual community; if you spot crass mistakes, drop the writer an e-mail, don't humiliate him or her in public; if you are angered by an offensive article, wait until you are calm, and write a reasoned rebuttal.

- **Don't** try subtle jokes or irony. This sort of humour does not travel well. If there is any chance of a humorous comment being misunderstood, add a smiley (see page 246).

- **Don't** advertise, except in newsgroups that are for this purpose – 'for sales', business announcements, etc.

- **Don't** send an article more than once. There is little point in repeating one across a set of related newsgroups as many of them cross-post to each other automatically.

- **Don't** post reviews of books or films that reveal the plot, or jokes that might offend tender sensibilities, without first encoding the article with *rot13*.

rot13

This is a simple letter-substitution code, where each letter is swapped with the one at the equivalent place in the other half of the alphabet – A to M move 13 places on, N to Z, 13 places back. Outlook Express has an **Unscramble** tool on the **Message** menu. Unfortunately there is no **Scramble** tool, so if you want to send a risqué joke to *rec.humor.funny*, you will have to encode it yourself by hand. Here's the pattern:

```
A B C D E F G H I J K L M N O P Q R S T U V W X Y Z
N O P Q R S T U V W X Y Z A B C D E F G H I J K L M
```

Smileys and other conventions

Being good news users (and perhaps indifferent typists?), we try to keep our articles short – abbreviations help here. But as we keep them short, and as we may not know our potential readers very well, if at all, there is a chance of our attempts at humour being misunderstood. Smileys were developed to help overcome this.

Smileys

Smileys are also called *emoticons*

Smileys are little pictures, made up of typed characters, which are intended to replace the facial expressions that we use to convey the emotions or hidden meanings behind what we say.

The basic smiley of **:-)** is the one you will see most often, though there are many other weird and wonderful smileys around. In this brief collection, the top four are in common use and the others are ones that amused me :-)

:-)	The basic smiley, saying 'Don't take this seriously'
'-)	Wink – 'Only joking!'
:-(	Frowning or sad
:-o	Wow!
:-|	Grim
:-C	'I do not believe it!'
%-)	User has been staring at a screen for hours

Abbreviations

These are mainly used in real-time conferences and chat lines, though some crop up quite regularly in newsgroup articles.

BTW	By The Way
BWQ	Buzz Word Quotient
DL	DownLoad
FYI	For Your Information
GIGO	Garbage In Garbage Out
IMO	In My Opinion
IMHO	In My Humble Opinion (typically used ironically)
POV	Point Of View

RTFM	Read The F***ing Manual
TIA	Thanks In Advance
TTFN	Ta Ta For Now
UL	UpLoad
WRT	With Reference To
<g>	Grin

If you want to track down more abbreviations or the acronyms used elsewhere in the computing world, an excellent list called Babel is maintained by Irving and Richard Kind at Columbia University in the States. You can read it at this URL:

http://www.cis.columbia.edu/glossary.html

Emphasis

Articles for newsgroups should be written in plain text – no formatting – for the benefit of readers working on older or simpler systems. This means that you cannot underline or embolden words. If you want to make a word stand out, enclose it in *asterisks* or _underscores_, or use CAPITALS. But *don't* write whole articles in capitals. This is known as 'SHOUTING' and is much frowned upon!

Files from newsgroups

There are a lot of files circulating round the Internet through the newsgroups. Some groups exist largely to share binary files – there are, for instance around 300 newsgroups for different sorts of pictures (and all but a dozen or so are soft or hard porn!), over two dozen that circulate sound files and ten dedicated to MIDI music. Binary files will also turn up regularly in many other groups, particularly those on topics like music (demos and recordings) and computer programming (program samples and utility files).

In most cases, detaching a file from a newsgroup article is no different from detaching it from an e-mail message – use the **File > Save attachments**... command or click the paperclip icon. Sometimes it is not so easy...

Try it: Save a file from a newsgroup message

① Go to a newsgroup where messages are likely to have attached files – try **alt.binaries.clip-art**

② Select a message with an attachment. (You can tell by the size – plain messages are rarely more than 2 or 3Kb.)

③ If you can see the image, right-click on it and select **Save Picture As**... and complete the **Save** dialog box as usual.

◆ GIF and JPG files can be saved this way. For other types of files:

④ Open the **File** menu or click the paperclip icon in the right corner of the preview pane header.

⑤ Select **Save Attachment**... .

⑥ Click [Browse..] and select the folder to save the file in.

⑦ Click [Save].

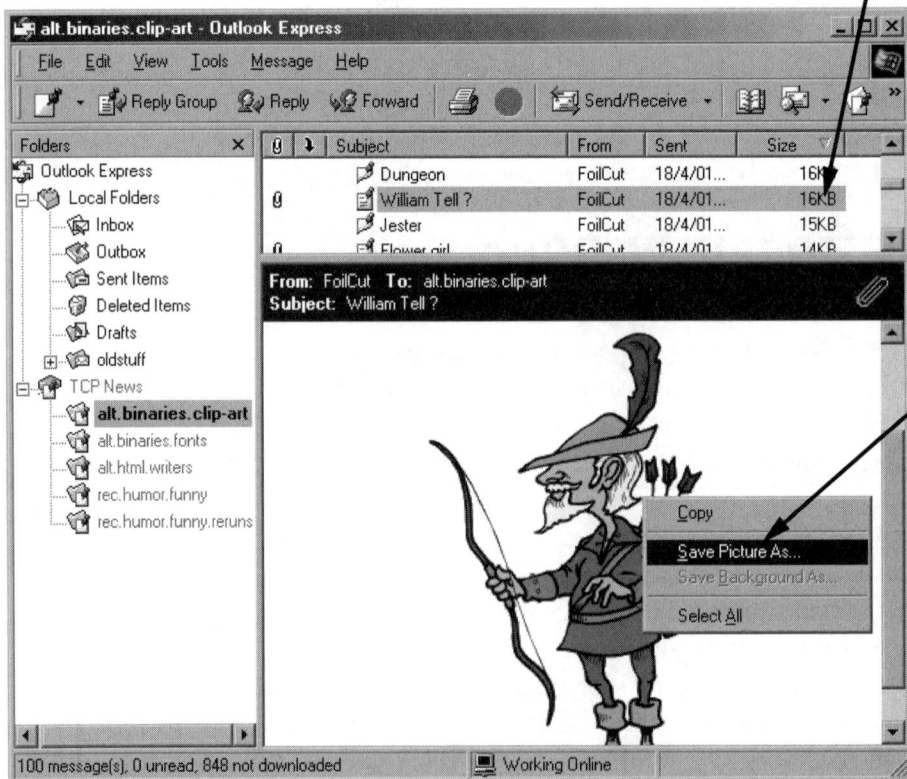

Figure 8.3 If you can see a picture, saving it is simple.

The attachment icon only appears when the message is downloaded – until then, Outlook Express doesn't know that the file is there.

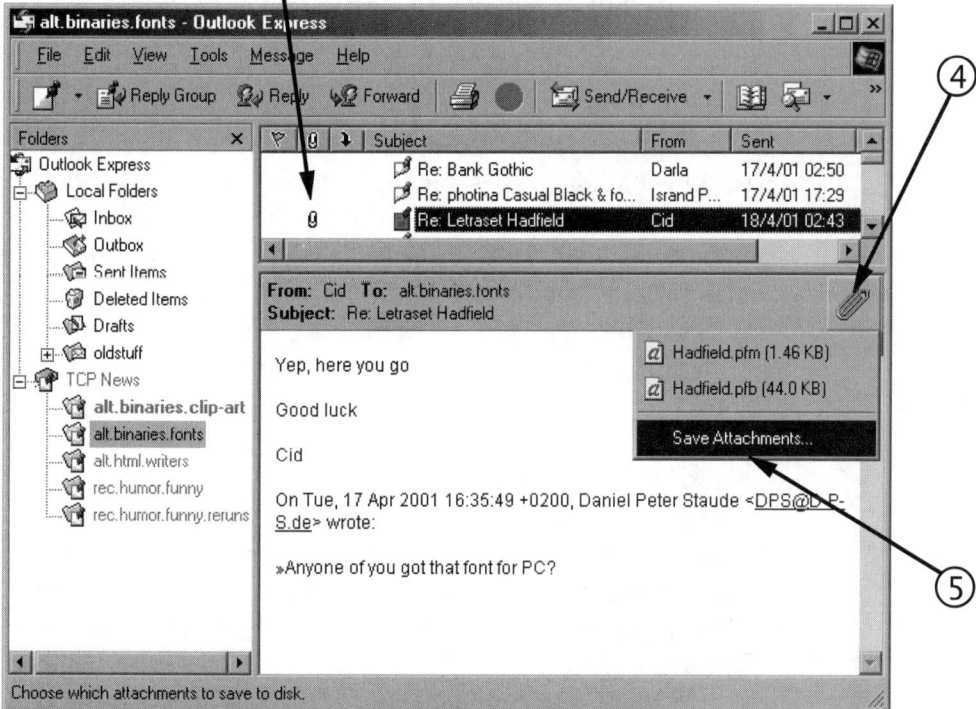

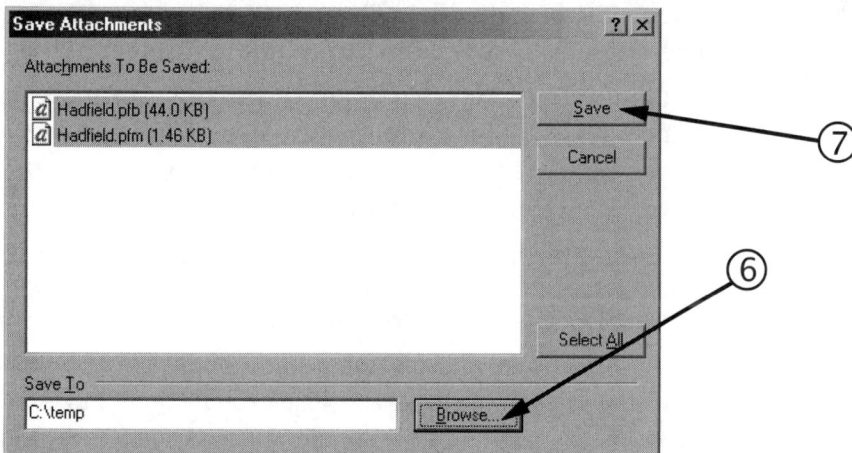

alt.binaries.fonts - Outlook Express

File   Edit   View   Tools   Message   Help

▪ ▾ 🖋 Reply Group 🗩 Reply 🗩 Forward   🖨 ●   🖃 Send/Receive ▾   📖 🖼 ▾   »

Folders   ×

Outlook Express
Local Folders
   Inbox
   Outbox
   Sent Items
   Deleted Items
   Drafts
   oldstuff
TCP News
   alt.binaries.clip-art
   alt.binaries.fonts
   alt.html.writers
   rec.humor.funny
   rec.humor.funny.reruns

▽	🔗	⬇	Subject	From	Sent
			Re: Bank Gothic	Darla	17/4/01 02:50
	🔗		Re: photina Casual Black & fo...	Isrand P...	17/4/01 17:29
			Re: Letraset Hadfield	Cid	18/4/01 02:43

From: Cid To: alt.binaries.fonts
Subject: Re: Letraset Hadfield

Yep, here you go

Good luck

Cid

On Tue, 17 Apr 2001 16:35:49 +0200, Daniel Peter Staude <DPS@D-P-S.de> wrote:

»Anyone of you got that font for PC?

Hadfield.pfm (1.46 KB)
Hadfield.pfb (44.0 KB)

Save Attachments...

Choose which attachments to save to disk.

④

⑤

Save Attachments   ? ✕

Attachments To Be Saved:

Hadfield.pfb (44.0 KB)
Hadfield.pfm (1.46 KB)

Save

Cancel

Select All

Save To
C:\temp   Browse...

⑦

⑥

Figure 8.4 Saving an attached file. If the preview pane header is not displayed, use **View > Layout**... and turn it on at the Properties dialog box.

Combine and Decode

E-mail messages and newsgroup articles are restricted by some systems to a maximum of around 1000 lines (64Kb) and a program or image file could well convert to far more than that. These can still be sent, but only after they have been chopped up into chunks. It's easy enough to recognise these part files as their subject lines will have 'Part 2 of 6' (or whatever numbers) at the end. The trouble is that you have to collect all the pieces and stitch them back together before they can be converted back into their original form.

Outlook Express has a neat **Combine and Decode** command which will do this. All you have to do is select the articles, shuffle them into the right order and set the routine off.

Joining files by hand is a pain and full of potential for errors. Each message must be saved as a text file. You then open the first of the set in a word-processor and go to the end of the coded part. This will be marked clearly. Trim off everything from there to the end of the message. Now open the second part in a second word-processor window and copy the coded part from there, pasting onto the end of the first. This must be repeated for all parts and the resulting file saved as text.

The new file can then be run through a decoder, but the question is, which decoder? There are three main methods of converting files between binary and ASCII formats:

◆ **uuencoding** is very common in the Unix world, which includes the newsgroups and much of the e-mail system. Uuencoded attachments can be recognised by their top line which starts 'BEGIN...'

◆ The **MIME** (Multi-purpose Internet Mail Extension) format is favoured by Microsoft. These attachments are identified by 'MIME...' in their top line.

◆ The **BinHex** format originated among Mac users, but is now also used elsewhere. These are labelled 'BinHex'.

To convert these back to binary you need the appropriate decoder. *Stuffit Expander* can handle uuencoded and BinHex files – and many other formats. For MIME files you will need *munpack* to convert them back to binary. Both can be downloaded from any good shareware site.

Stuffit Expander

This can handle a wide range of file formats. It is one of the few programs that can decode and decompress **BinHex** files and **.SIT** files (produced by Stuffit compressor), but can also cope with ZIP, ARC and uuencoded files. You can get a free copy from **www.alladinsys.com**.

To decode a uuencoded or BinHex file:

① Join the chunks together and save the file as text, as explained above. The filename can be anything, as Stuffit Expander will be looking at its contents, not its name.

② Run Windows Explorer and locate the file's folder.

③ Run Stuffit and arrange the windows so that you can see both.

④ Drag the file across and drop it into Stuffit. It will find the encoded part of the message, decode it and store the new file in the same folder.

Munpack

Munpack is a DOS program and needs a bit more work, though not much. For simplicity, save the message in the same folder as munpack. Run the MS-DOS prompt and switch to that folder, then use the command line:

```
munpack filename
```

where *filename* is the name of the message file. The decoded file will be saved with its original name in the munpack folder.

Munpack is freely available on the Net. You can pick up a copy at any good shareware site.

Appendix

Using Windows

IN THIS CHAPTER:

- Windows, Desktop
- Icons and toolbar buttons
- Mouse click/double-click, right-click
- Menus, smart, shortcut

This appendix is for readers who are new to Windows. It aims to cover enough of the techniques and concepts for you to be able to work safely and confidently with your browser and e-mail software.

The Windows environment

A brief history

Up until around 15 years ago, the only way to tell a computer to do something was to type out the instructions on its keyboard – and before that you had to set switches, but we won't go back that far! There are still some computer systems that rely on typed instructions, and they are fine for experts – as long as you know what commands and options are available, they can be typed in quickly and the computer can act on them immediately. The catch is that you have to be an expert to use the systems efficiently.

The development of GUIs has changed the face of computing. A GUI (pronounced 'gooey' and meaning Graphical User Interface) displays for its user, *icons* that represent files and programs, presents menus of commands and sets of options, allowing its user to run operations by simply pointing and clicking at things on screen. You do not need to be an expert to use a GUI computer. All you need is to be able to work out what a command does or what an icon represents – and most of them are pretty obvious.

Icon – small picture, usually with a label

Windows is a GUI. It wasn't the first, but it has become the standard. The first version that was released, Windows 2.0 (1.0 never made it to the streets), appeared in 1988 and was virtually unusable. The problem was that while the graphical display made life so much easier for the user, it also made far more work for the computer. The microprocessors in PCs in 1988 simply weren't up to the job of running a GUI. It was only with the next version – along with faster processors – that Windows became viable. Since then, it has gone through several major and minor revisions. These have improved its ease of use and extended its facilities, and have taken advantage of the ever-increasing power of microprocessors and the steadily falling costs of memory and hard disk space. At the time of writing, the current version of Windows is *Me* (Millenium Edition), which is only marginally different from Windows 98, itself a minor upgrade from Windows 95.

Why 'Windows'?

It's called Windows because programs are displayed on screen in windows – distinct, framed areas.

Key points to note about windows

♦ When you start a program, its window opens. Closing a window automatically shuts down the program.

♦ They can be expanded to fill the screen, adjusted to any size within the screen, or shrunk to buttons on the *Taskbar*.

♦ Windows can overlap or be laid out however you like.

Taskbar – the strip containing icons and buttons along the bottom of the screen

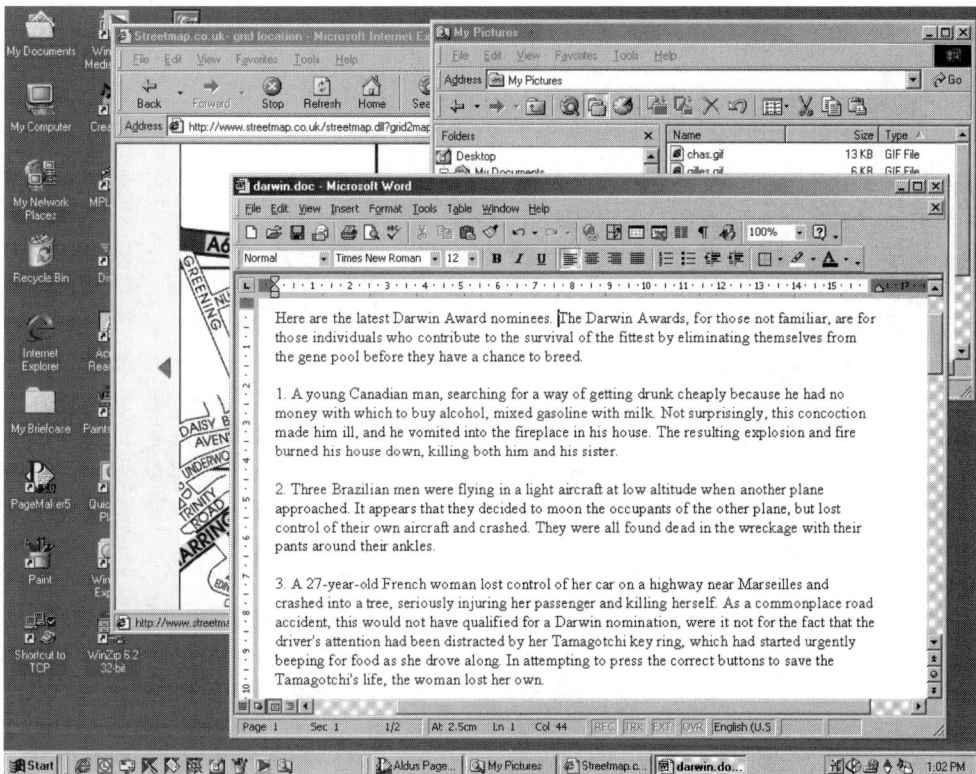

Figure 1 Windows at work! There are four programs running in this screenshot – three are visible in the overlapping windows, one has been shrunk out of the way and is present only as a button on the Taskbar. Notice the similarities in the window 'frames' of the three programs.

◆ You can have any number of windows open – i.e. programs running – at the same time. A typical modern computer can run dozens (probably hundreds – I've never tried to find the maximum) without strain, but the practical limit is around eight or ten. Once you get above that, you tend to lose track of where you are.

Essential jargon

The Desktop

This is the screen. The idea is that you should think of the screen as if it were a physical desktop and lay out your documents and tools on it to suit the way that you work.

At the start of a session, the desktop is empty except for some icons – how many, and how they are arranged will vary.

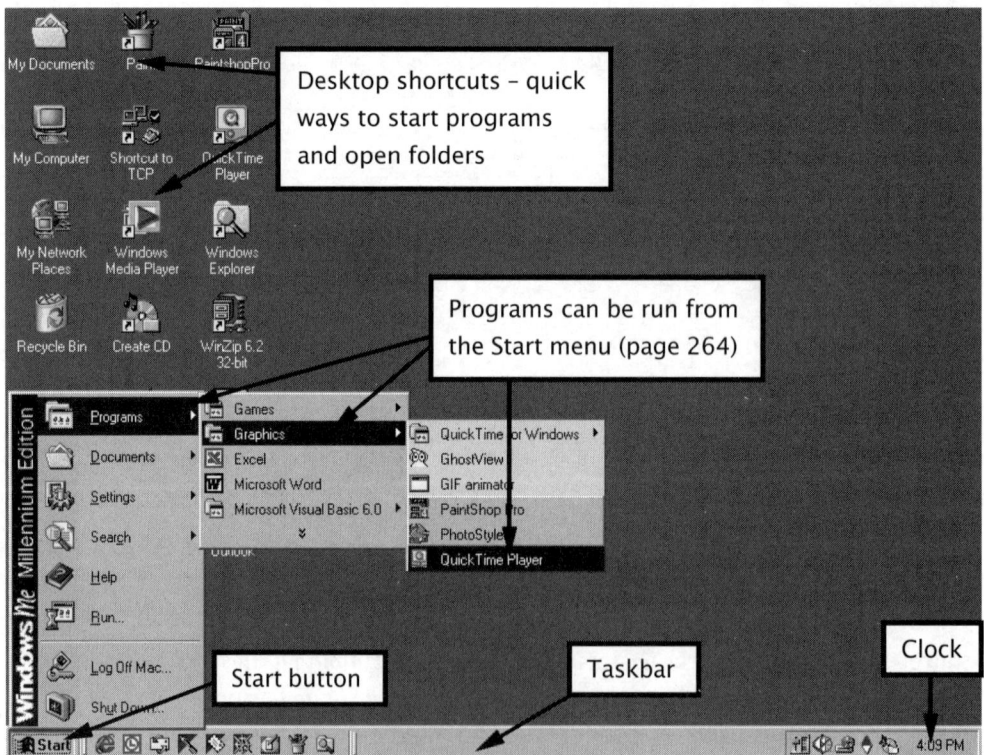

Figure 2   The Desktop at the start of a session (Windows Me).

These are desktop shortcuts, which you can use to start the programs or open the *folders*.

Folder – a division of a disk (see page 258)

The Taskbar and Start menu

At the bottom of the screen is the Taskbar. At the left is the Start button which leads to the Start menu (see page 264). Next to that are icons for some commonly-used programs. Over on the right is the Taskbar tray which contains the clock, the volume control and perhaps some other icons for programs that control parts of the PC – you should see a modem icon here when you are online. The main area holds buttons for programs when they are running.

Hardware and software

A computer system has two aspects: hardware and software.

Peripheral – piece of hardware that can be connected to a PC

♦ **Hardware** refers to all the physical components – the PC's main box, the monitor, keyboard and mouse, plus the printer, scanner and any other *peripheral*.

♦ **Software** refers to programs and associated files that enable the hardware to function.

Program

A program is a set of instructions to a computer. They can be divided into two types.

♦ Operating system programs handle the interaction between the components of the system. They perform low-level chores such as producing the screen display, organising the storage of data on disks, picking up your keystrokes and mouse movements and interpreting them for the PC. You don't have anything to do with these programs directly, though you can customise some of them through the *Control Panel*.

Control Panel – folder of utility programs that allow you to tailor aspects of the Windows system

♦ Application programs are the ones that you use for processing data, viewing files, entertainment or other activities. Word, Internet Explorer, My Computer and Minesweeper are all application programs.

'Application programs' is a mouthful. Most people simply refer to them as 'applications' or as 'programs'.

Document

A document is a body of text and/or other data that can be displayed or processed by an application program, such as a letter in Word, a Web page in Internet Explorer or a spreadsheet in Excel. It can be saved on a disk as a *file*.

File

A body of data stored on a disk. Some files are documents; others are programs or sets of data used by programs. A file is identified by a two-part name.

◆ The main part is given by you (or whoever created the file) and will normally be something meaningful, like 'newsletter jan 99' or 'xmaslist'.

◆ This is followed by an extension, normally of three letters, which identifies the nature of the file. For example, Word files have the extension 'doc'; Web pages written in HTML are marked by 'htm' or 'html' at the end; programs have 'exe' (short for executable); image files may have 'bmp', 'gif', 'jpg', 'wmf' or any one of several dozen extensions, depending on which of the many graphics programs they were created in.

Folder

There's lots more about folders and managing files in *Catching up with computers*

A typical modern hard drive is 10 Gigabytes (or larger), and will store an incredible amount of data. That's enough to hold the files for several million letters, or around 1000 full-length novels, or over 100 illustrated books like this! If you want to be able to find anything in that much space, it must be organised, and this is done with folders.

A folder is an elastic-sided division of a disk. Like a hanging file in a filing cabinet, a folder takes up virtually no space when it's empty, but can expand to hold whatever you want to put in it. You can create folders whenever and wherever – including inside existing folders – you need them. Ideally you should have one for each area of your work, and each folder should contain no more than a few dozen files.

Window components

Most program windows have these components. Some may not be present, especially in games and similar software.

◆ **Title bar** – normally showing the name of the program and of the current document.

◆ **Menu bar** – the program's commands are grouped by function on to menus that drop down from here.

◆ **Toolbar** – containing buttons that call up the most commonly-used commands.

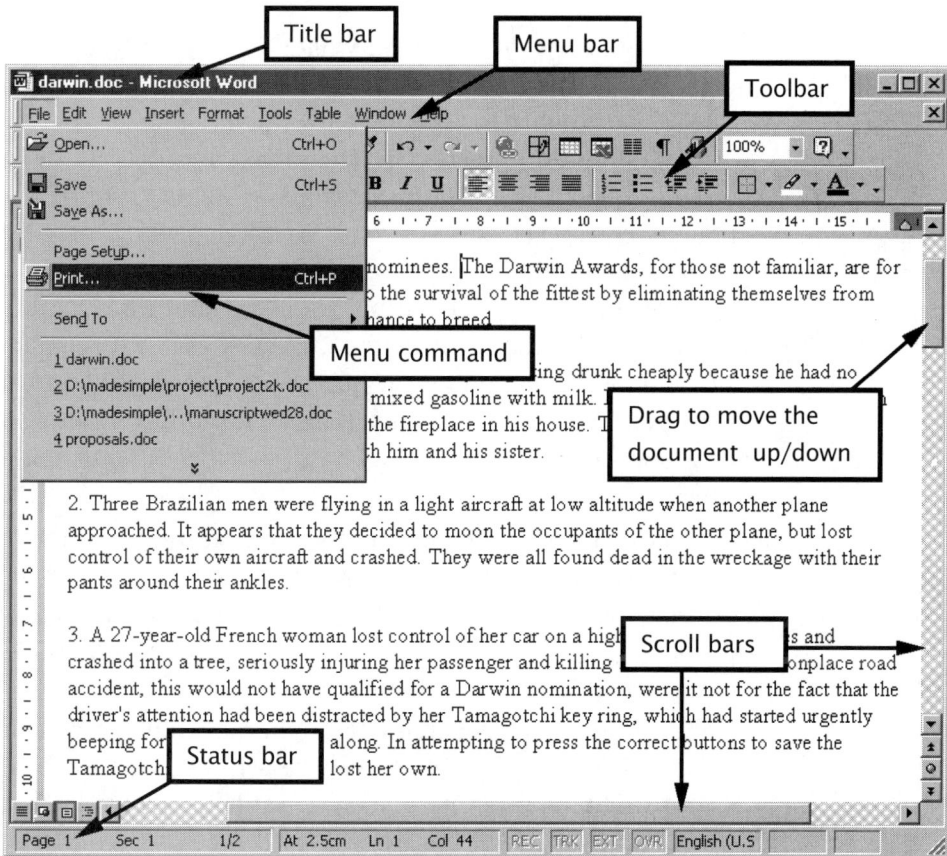

Figure 3 A typical window – this one is from Word 2000.

- **Status bar** - showing information about the current state of the program and/or document.
- **Scroll bars** - these appear if the document is too wide or too long to fit in the window. Click the arrowheads or on the bars, or drag the sliders to scroll the document.

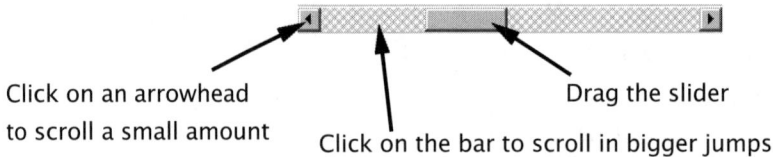

Click on an arrowhead
to scroll a small amount

Click on the bar to scroll in bigger jumps

Drag the slider

The mouse

When an object is selected it is highlighted. The object can be an icon, a menu item, a block of text or any other identifiable screen component

Before we go any further with what's on screen, let's turn our attention to the mouse. You need to be able to control this before you can do much else. The mouse is used for selecting, activating buttons, resizing and moving objects, and otherwise interacting with the screen.

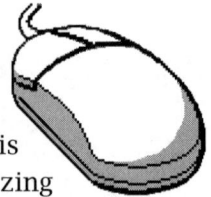

Just to make life interesting, the ways that you use the mouse to select things or activate choices vary between applications and depending on how the PC is set up! Sometimes you point to select and click to go; other times you click to select and double-click to go. Whatever, you should know how to do these things:

- **Point** - move the mouse on its mat until the cursor is in the right place. If you need to go beyond the edge of the mat, pick the mouse up and place it back into the centre of the mat then carry on moving from there. Sometimes simply pointing at an object will select it.
- **Click** - press down on the left mouse button and release it immediately. In most cases, you select objects by clicking on them. If pointing at an object has selected it, then clicking on it will start it working (if it was an icon or menu command).

- **Double-click** – click the left button twice in quick succession. (You can set how quick on the Mouse utility in the Control Panel.) If you have to click on an object to select it, then you have to double-click to activate it.
- **Right-click** – click the right mouse button once. In many Windows applications, if you right-click on an object, you will open up a menu of commands that can be used on that object.
- **Drag** – hold down the left mouse button and move the mouse. This is mainly used to move objects across the screen. If you drag on the boundary of an object, e.g. a window frame, you can move the boundary to make the object bigger or smaller.

Menus

A menu is a list of commands and options. All menus have the same features and are used in the same way. There are five types of menu items:

- *Commands* – on Explorer's **View** menu shown overleaf, **Line Up Icons** will tidy up the display if you have been moving or deleting files.
- *Submenu headings* have ▶ on the right. Simply pointing to the heading will open the submenu.
- *Toggle switches* turn options on or off. A ✓ to the left shows that it is on. On the **View** menu, you can control the display of the four **Toolbars**.
- *Sets of options*, of which only one can be selected at a time. The set will be marked by a line above and below, and the currently-selected item will have a ● to its left. In the **View** menu, you can choose to list files either as **Large Icons**, **Small Icons**, **List**, **Details** or **Thumbnails**.
- Items ending with … lead to a dialog box in which you can set options, e.g. clicking **Customize**… (on the **Toolbars** submenu) opens the **Customize** dialog box where you can tailor the appearance of your toolbars.

Menus arise from four different sources.

This leads to a submenu ▶

Click on the menu
name to open it

Toggle switch –
this one is on ✓

The selected option
of a set has ●

... after the item name shows
that it leads to a dialog box

My Documents

File   Edit   View   Favorites   Tools   Help

Toolbars   ▶
✓ Status Bar
Explorer Bar   ▶

● Large Icons
Small Icons
List
Details
Thumbnails

Arrange Icons   ▶
Line Up Icons

Customize This Folder...

Go To   ▶
Refresh

✓ Standard Buttons
✓ Address Bar
Links
Radio

Customize...

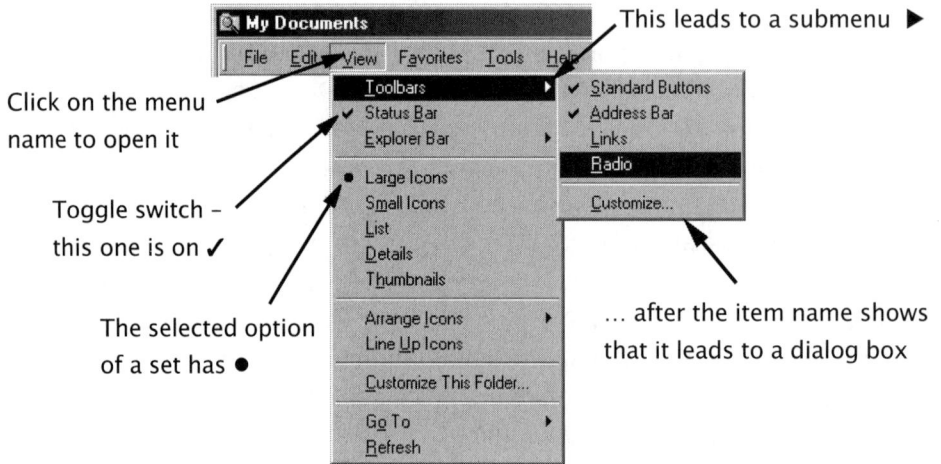

Figure 4   All menus have the same basic features.

The Menu bar

Every application window has a Menu bar which gives access
to the full range of commands available in the program. The
bar will have a set of header names, each of which leads to a
menu of more-or-less related commands. The grouping isn't
perfect as it is not always possible to fit everything neatly
into a limited number of sets, but you only have to hunt
through the menus a few times before you get the hang of
where everything is.

Menus from the toolbars

Mail

Read Mail
New Message...
Send a Link...
Send Page...
Read News

Some toolbar buttons have drop-down menus
with a set of related commands or options –
a down arrow to the right of the icon shows
that there's a menu.

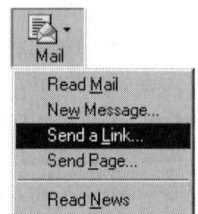

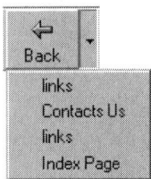

Back

links
Contacts Us
links
Index Page

Sometimes the drop-down arrow will be clearly separate
from the main button. With these, click the button itself to
get the most commonly-used command, or click the arrow to
open the related – and less-used – commands. For example,
the **Back** button in IE takes you back to the previous page; its
drop-down arrow lists the last few pages visited.

Shortcut menus

If you right-click on any object on the Desktop, or on pretty well any object – even a block of selected text – in a modern Windows application, a *shortcut*, or *context* menu will appear. This contains the commands that are available for use with that object at that time. It's a neat idea – use it. If you are going to do something with a screen object, it is normally quicker to right-click and select from the shortcut menu than to hunt around for the command in the main menu system.

The contents of a shortcut menu depend upon the nature of the object that you click on and its context. In Figure 5, I've right-clicked on a JPG image file in Windows Explorer. Whatever the type of file, the shortcut menu here will always offer **Open**, **Send To**, **Cut**, **Copy**, **Create Shortcut**, **Delete**, **Rename** and **Properties** as these are the core file-management commands. With images or other document files, you will also expect to get **Print** and some **Open With** options – my system has three applications that can handle JPG files.

Figure 5 Right-clicking on an object usually opens a menu of relevant commands.

The **Add to Zip** command is present as I have WinZip, the file-compression utility, installed on my PC.

The Start menu

Last, but by no means least, is the **Start** menu. Open this by clicking the [Start] button or pressing [⊞] on the keyboard.

The Start menu has six main options:

◆ **Programs** opens a menu of all the programs installed on your PC. Some will be there directly as menu items, others will be in submenus.

◆ **Documents** lists up to 15 of those that you have used most recently. Opening a document automatically opens the application in which is can be viewed or edited.

◆ **Settings** leads to utilities for configuring your system. Most of these are to be found in the **Control Panel** folder.

◆ **Search** (Windows Me) or **Find** (Windows 95/98) takes you to routines for finding files on your system, or Web pages or people on the Internet.

◆ **Help** opens the Windows Help system – take *the Tour* or browse through the *Contents* sometime.

◆ **Shut Down** is what you should click at the end of a working session. Don't just turn off – you may lose data from any open documents. Even if nothing is lost, Windows will assume that something has gone wrong and will run its fault-finding routine when you next start up.

◆ **Log off** is only present on networked PCs.

At the top of the menu, you may also have **Windows Update** (which links to Microsoft's Web site); and if Microsoft Office is installed you may have **New** and **Open Office Document**.

Try it: Start a program from the Start menu
① Click the **Start** button to open the Start menu.
② Point to **Programs** – its menu will open.
③ If you are working in Windows Me and the item you want has been tucked away, click the [≫] to open the menu fully.

Accessories   Communications

Accessories	Communications
Adobe	Entertainment
Games	System Tools
Graphics	Address Book
Internet Tools	Calculator
Iomega ZipCD	Character map
Microsoft Office	MS-DOS Prompt
Microsoft Works	NOTEPAD
Online Services	Paint
StartUp	Synchronize
System stuff	Windows Explorer
WinZip	Windows Movie Maker
Excel	WORDPAD
Internet Explorer	
Microsoft Outlook	
Microsoft Word	
Microsoft Works	
Outlook Express	
Windows Media Player	
Microsoft Access	
Microsoft Office Tools	
Microsoft Web Publishing	
Microsoft Visual Basic 6.0	
Microsoft Developer Network	

System Tools:
- Disk Cleanup
- Disk Defragmenter
- DriveSpace
- Maintenance Wizard
- SCANDISK
- Scheduled Tasks
- System Information
- System Restore
- Windows Update

④

⑤

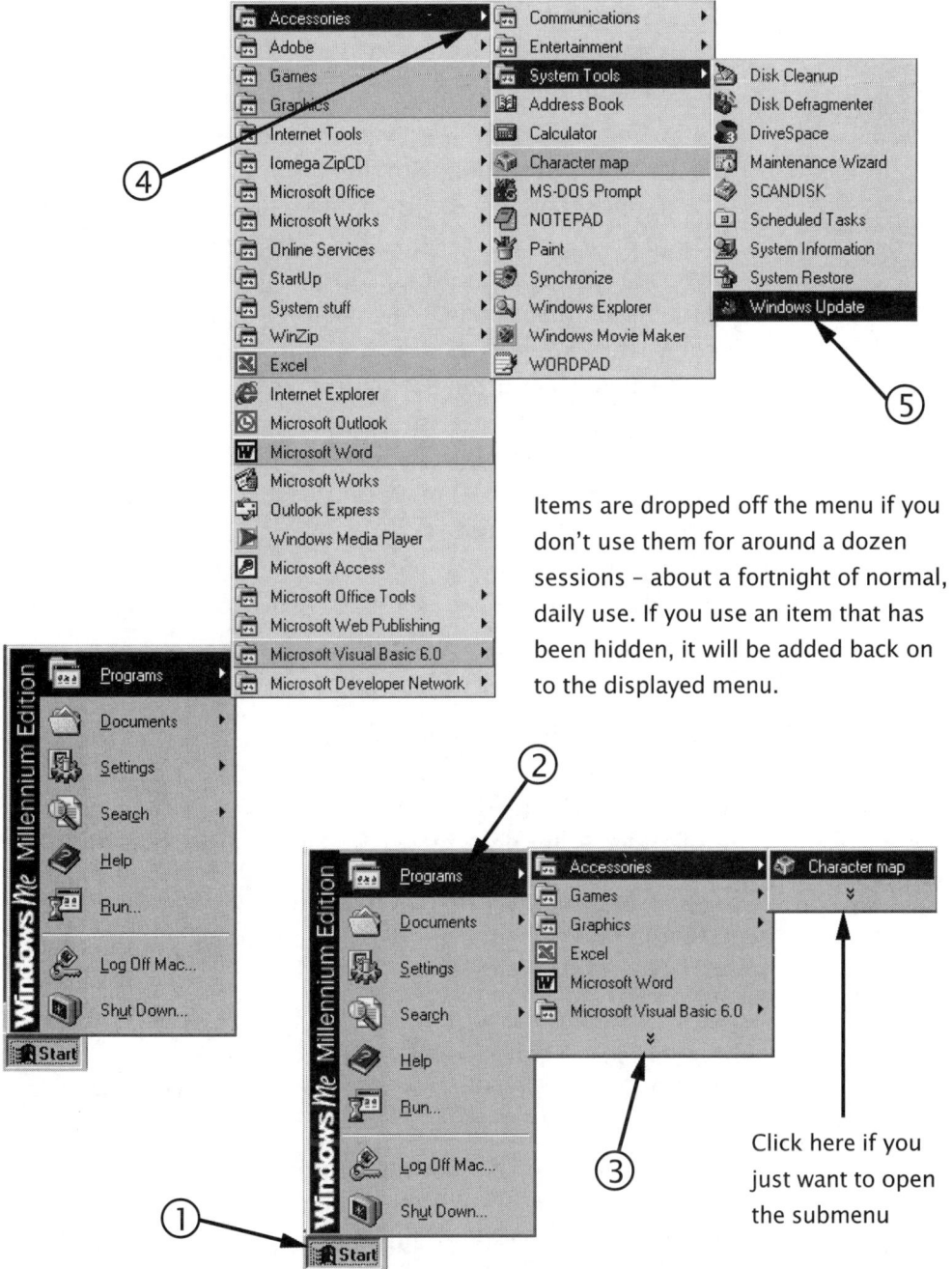

Items are dropped off the menu if you don't use them for around a dozen sessions – about a fortnight of normal, daily use. If you use an item that has been hidden, it will be added back on to the displayed menu.

Windows Me Millennium Edition

- Programs
- Documents
- Settings
- Search
- Help
- Run...
- Log Off Mac...
- Shut Down...

Start

②

Windows Me Millennium Edition

- Programs
- Documents
- Settings
- Search
- Help
- Run...
- Log Off Mac...
- Shut Down...

Start

Accessories	Character map
Games	
Graphics	
Excel	
Microsoft Word	
Microsoft Visual Basic 6.0	

①

③

Click here if you just want to open the submenu

Figure 6   Below: a windows Me Start menu when first opened.
Above: The same Start menu, fully extended.

④ If you cannot see the name of the program that you want, point to the submenu on which it is located.

⑤ Click on the program.

In Windows Me, the latest version, the **Start** menu is a *smart* menu – one that responds to the way you use it. If you do not use an option for a while, the system hides it out of the way. After a dozen or so sessions, the **Programs** part of the Start menu shrinks until it only normally displays those submenus and options that you use regularly. If you need to get to the others, they are still there – just wait a few seconds or click on the arrow bar at the bottom to open the menu out fully.

When you install new software, new entries will be added to your Start menu. Over time the menu system can get very cluttered, but the smart menu approach will ensure that those programs that you use regularly are easy to find.

◆ If yours is a Windows 95 or 98 PC, try to keep the menus tidy – learn to use the **Taskbar and Start menu** settings.

Menus and the keyboard

When you are typing in any program, you may find it simpler to access the menus from the keyboard rather than by using the mouse. The technique is based on the [**Alt**] key and the underlined letter that you will find in (almost) all menu items.

Try it: Select from the menus with the keyboard

① Run My Computer by clicking (or double-clicking) on its icon on the Desktop.

② We want an item on the **Tools** menu. Hold down [**Alt**] and press [**T**]. You can release [**Alt**] now.

③ At the open menu, press [**O**] to select **Folder Options**....

Or

Once one menu has opened, you can move across to any other by pressing the Left/Right arrow keys

◆ Press the down arrow key until **Folder Options** is highlighted then press [**Enter**].

④ The **Folder Options** dialog box will open. Have a look around – it's probably best not to change any settings at . this point – then click the **OK** button to close it.

Figure 7 Selecting from a menu – experiment using the mouse and the keyboard.

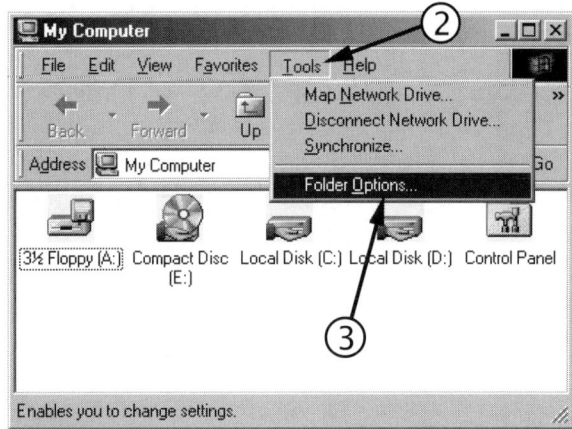

Click the label at the top to open its tab

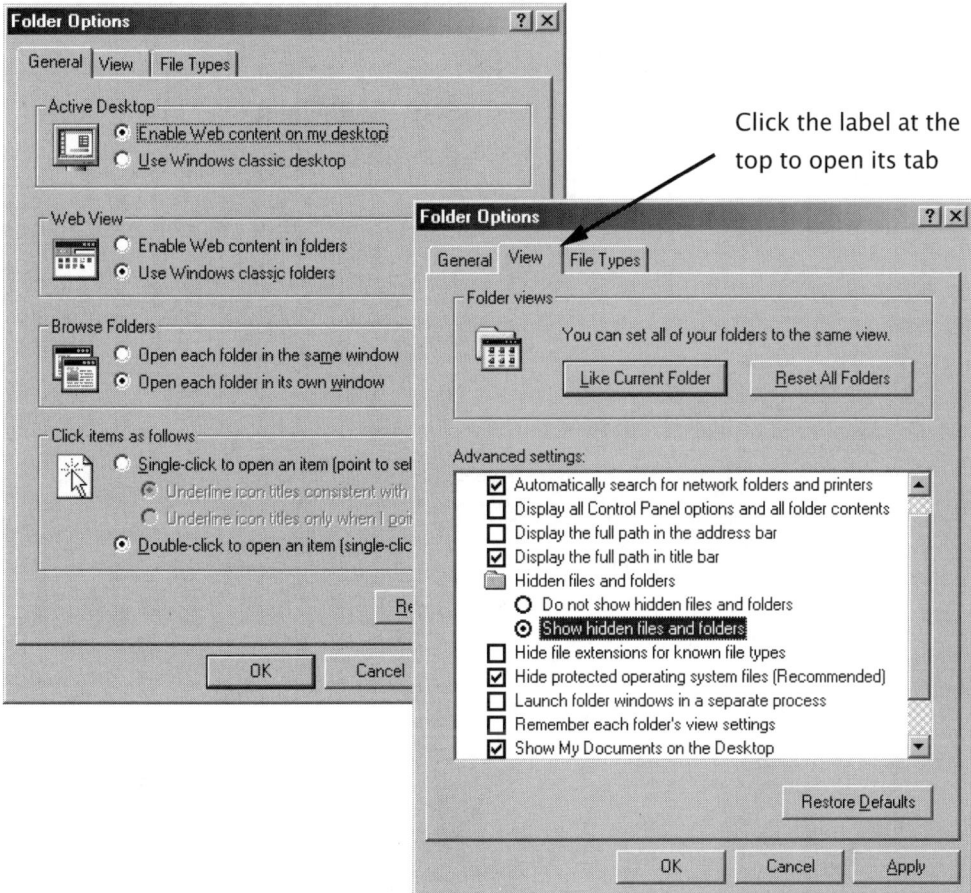

Figure 8 Two of the tabs on the **Folders Options** dialog box – notice the checkboxes and radio buttons (see below) for setting options.

Making choices

In any Windows application, in any situation where you are being asked to supply several bits of information or make several choices – e.g. when saving a file or defining the layout of a page – it will normally be done through a dialog box. In a dialog box, options are selected and information given through some or all of these features.

Text boxes

These are used to collect information from you. A typical use is the **Filename** text box that you see when you start to save or open a file.

① If the box is active – ready for you to type into it – it will have the insertion point (a flashing line) in it.

◆ If you cannot see the insertion point, click in the text box with the mouse.

② Type the filename, or other details, as required, using the backspace key [←] to erase any mistakes.

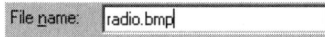

| File name: | radio.bmp |

Checkboxes

These are on/off switches. The option is turned on when the box is ticked, or 'checked' as they say in the USA, hence the term 'checkbox'.

◆ Click in the box (or on its label) to set the tick, or to remove it.

Click the box
or its label

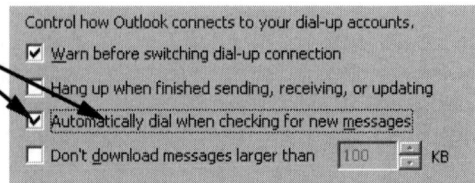

Press **[Alt]** and the
underlined letter to
turn options on or off

Control how Outlook connects to your dial-up accounts.

☑ Warn before switching dial-up connection

☐ Hang up when finished sending, receiving, or updating

☑ Automatically dial when checking for new messages

☐ Don't download messages larger than ☐ 100 ☐ KB

Radio buttons

These are used where you have a set of options, only one of which can be active at a time.

◆ Click on the button (or its label) to set an option.

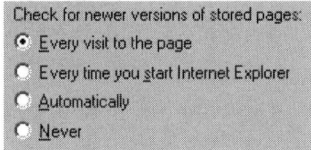

Check for newer versions of stored pages:
- ● Every visit to the page
- ○ Every time you start Internet Explorer
- ○ Automatically
- ○ Never

Most radio buttons will have a default setting – if in doubt, always leave options at their defaults!

Drop-down lists and combo boxes

Where there are more half a dozen choices, radio buttons are replaced with lists. These normally display five or six options, and will have a scroll bar if more are available.

◆ To select from a list, scroll through, if necessary, and click on the option, or use the arrow keys to move down to the option, then press [Enter].

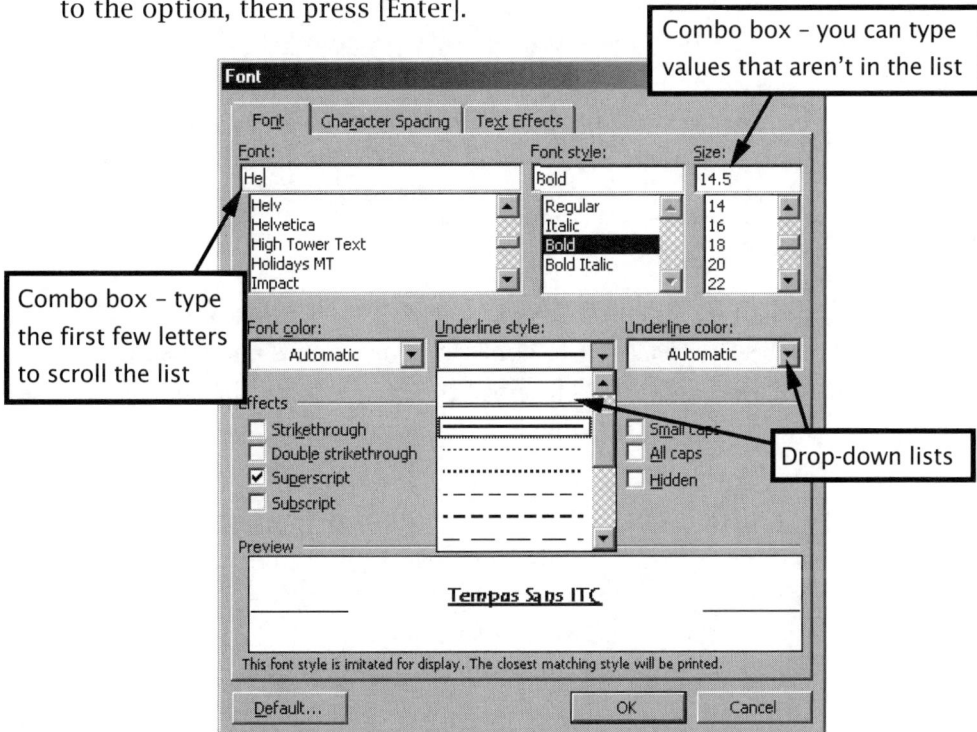

Combo box – you can type values that aren't in the list

Combo box – type the first few letters to scroll the list

Drop-down lists

Figure 9 Lists are used where there are lots of alternative settings, as here in the **Font** dialog box from Word.

There are two main varieties of lists.

◆ A drop-down list looks like a text box with a down arrow button on its right. Click on the arrow to open the list.

◆ A combo box has a text box with an open list underneath. The text box serves two purposes. You can use it to type in values that aren't available in the list, such as a non-standard font size; or you can type the first few letters of the option, and the list will scroll to those that start with those letters.

Number values

Number values can be set in two ways.

◆ Where precise values are wanted, you will see a text box with tiny up/down arrows to the right. Type a value here, or use the arrows to change the value – click to change in steps of one, or hold down the mouse button to set the numbers moving more rapidly in the direction of the arrow.

◆ Where approximate values are wanted, you will find sliders. Drag the marker, or click on the bar beside it.

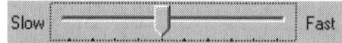

Buttons

Every dialog box has at least two buttons on it:

◆ OK to confirm your choices and close the box,

◆ Cancel to close the box, leaving the settings as they were previously.

Buttons may also be used where there is a single choice or action, and to lead to subsidiary dialog boxes. For example:

◆ Apply tells the system to apply the new selections, but without closing the dialog box – this is often found on boxes with several tabs.

◆ Settings... or any other button with ... after the name will open a dialog box to set more options. When you close the subsidiary dialog box, you will be returned to the one containing the button.

Internet Options ? X

General | Security | Content | Connections | Programs | Advanced |

Home page
You can change which page to use for your home page.

Address: http://homepages.tcp.co.uk/~macbride/

[Use Current] [Use Default] [Use Blank]

> As these three are alternatives, radio buttons would have done the job

Temporary Internet files
Pages you view on the Internet are stored in a special folder for quick viewing later.

[Delete Files...] [Settings...]

> These all lead to dialog boxes

History
The History folder contains links to pages you've visited, for quick access to recently viewed pages.

Days to keep pages in history: 7 ▼   [Clear History]

[Colors...] [Fonts...] [Languages...] [Accessibility...]

[OK] [Cancel] [Apply]

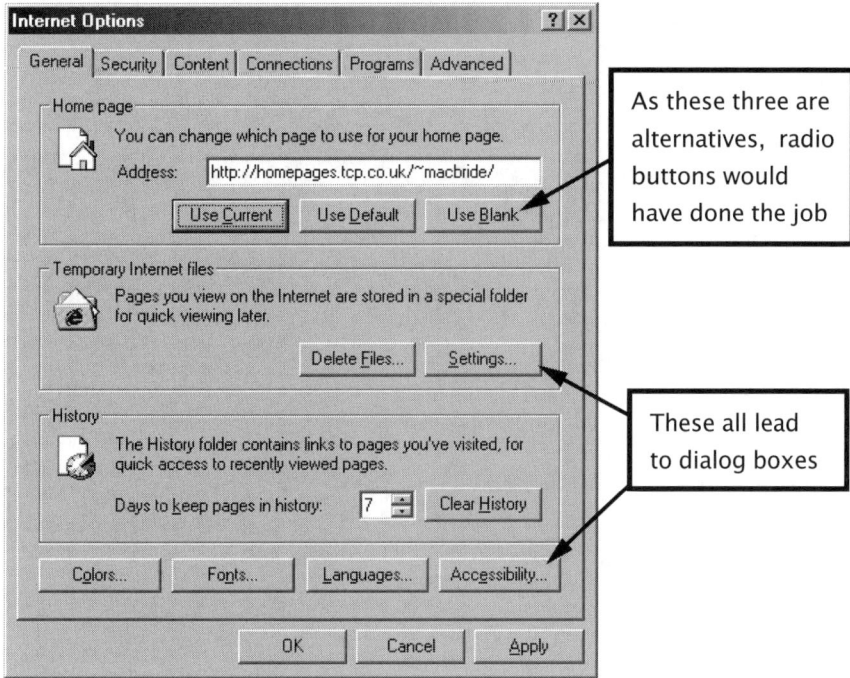

Figure 10   Buttons are often used to activate single choices or actions.

Try it!

Windows claims to be – and very largely is – an intuitive system. In general, things do what you would expect and the 'obvious' approach is usually the right one. The best way to learn how to use your software is to experiment. There's rarely much to be lost by trying things – click that button, use that menu command, set that option!

Remember that short of taking a hammer to your PC, it is very unlikely that anything that you do will cause a major problem. The worst that is likely to happen is that you may sometimes have to turn it off and start again, and this may mean that you lose a little bit of work.

Index

Don't stop!!

Hairnet

If you've found this book enjoyable and useful, why stop learning just because you've got to the end of it? Hairnet has a network of licensed Trainers who can provide personalised one-to-one tuition, in your own home or office, on your own computer.

Hairnet has been running since 1997 and boasts a successful course completion rate of 99.9%.

♦ Award-winning teaching method and materials
♦ Lessons tailored to your own needs at times to suit your schedule
♦ Learn at your own pace
♦ Friendly, professional, older tutors

Hairnet trainers are specially trained to teach newcomers to computing and the Internet. If you'd like to find out how to make your computer work for you, if you'd like someone to explain what you might enjoy and appreciate using a computer or the Internet for, then the Hairnet training service would suit you very well.

Hairnet:

♦ Was awarded Millennium Product status in 1999 by the Design Council for 'excellence and innovation in training'
♦ Is an accredited training provider to the Department of Education
♦ Is an accredited training provider to Lantra (training for the land based sector)
♦ Is in endorsed by the Department of Trade and Industry
♦ Was invited to 10 Downing Street to discuss its pioneering training work with older learners

Find out more

For more information, or to be put in touch with your local Hairnet Trainer, please contact us:

Hairnet UK Ltd
Tel: 0870 241 5091
Web site: www.hairnet.org
E-mail: info@hairnet.org

Free lessons for readers of this book!

Ask your Hairnet trainer about the *Catching up with the Internet* promotional offer – you can get six training sessions for the price of five if you bring this book with you to the first lesson.